Democratizing Communication?
Comparative Perspectives On Information And Power

The Hampton Communication Series

International Communication

Richard Vincent, supervisory editor

Good-Bye, Gweilo: Public Opinion and the 1997 Problem in Hong Kong
L. Erwin Atwood and Ann Marie Major

Democratizing Communication?: Comparative Perspectives on Information and
Power
Mashoed Bailie and Dwayne Winseck, eds.

forthcoming

Towards Equity in Global Communication: MacBride Report Update
Richard Vincent, Kaarle Nordenstreng, and Michael Traber, eds.

Democratizing Communication?
Comparative Perspectives On Information And Power

edited by

Mashoed Bailie
Eastern Mediterranean University

Dwayne Winseck
University of Leicester

HAMPTON PRESS INC.
CRESSKILL, NEW JERSEY

Library of Congress Cataloging-in-Publication Data

Democratizing communication? : comparative perspectives on information and
    power / edited by Mashoed Bailie, Dwayne Winseck.
        p. cm. -- (The Hampton Press communication series)
    Includes bibliographical references and indexes.
    ISBN 1-57273-064-1 (cl). -- ISBN 1-57273-065-X (pb)
        1. Communication policy. 2. Democracy. 3. Communication-
    -International cooperation. I. Bailie, Mashoed. II. Winseck,
    Dwayne, Roy, 1964-   III. Series.
    P95.8.D44 1997   97-1993
                                                                CIP

Hampton Press, Inc.
23 Broadway
Cresskill, NJ 07626

Contents

Foreword

Dan Schiller

How are the world's systems of communication faring in the present period of multifaceted social transformation? Has the durable impress left on them by dominative social relations begun to fade? Are communication practices and institutions contributing to vindicative social action? Or, do communication systems work predominantly to succor the scourges of exploitation and inequality? What, in short, is the nature of communication as a contemporary social force? *Democratizing Communication?*, edited by Mashoed Bailie and Dwayne Winseck, is preoccupied with nothing less than these grave and momentous issues.

Democratization is hardly a new theme for critical communication study, but one, rather, that has exercised an abiding influence, often as a conscious and sometimes as an urgent intellectual priority. But if critical communication study has evinced an unusually robust and enduring democratic temper, then this commitment itself has taken a succession of distinct shapes. Theory, that is, has encountered an intrinsic need to respond to the sometimes dizzying swings of the 20th century—what Hobsbawm pithily labels an "age of extremes."

Consider, for example, the conceptual synthesis that is usually consigned to the "prehistory" of communication study in the United States: "propaganda analysis." The democratic inspiration behind propaganda analysis cannot be disentangled from the politically polarized context of the 1930s. Powerful institutions—principally corporations, trade associations, and, though it was less marked at the time, philanthropic foundations—were working overtime to bend the media to self-interested purposes, by means of unprecedented, systematic, and pervasive public relations campaigns. Even if all those engaged in such efforts did not possess the ferocious reactionary instincts of *Chicago Tribune* owner Colonel Robert McCormick, the majority of newspaper publishers were implacably hostile in their own right to the ameliorative program of the New Deal.

Concentration of ownership, moreover, constituted a growing threat to any species of democratic communication. Chains controlled an increasing proportion of newspapers; a pair of network owners dominated radio; and a handful of major Hollywood studios ran the U.S. movie industry. A single, vertically integrated company virtually monopolized telephone service provision. As if all this were not enough, Father Coughlin (the "Radio Priest") and a host of lesser figures were demonstrating (this long before today's talk radio) how broadcasting could be used to spread demagoguery far beyond any mere political fringe. Did these developments portend a slide into authoritarian capitalism, replete with the qualitatively more explicit, rigid, and encompassing controls that were being imposed in Germany—a state whose Nazi dictatorship seemed to many, in this generation, to be suitably emblematized by its ministry of "propaganda and public enlightenment"?

Opinion polls showed, during the late 1930s, that the majority of the U.S. population believed the press to be in the pocket of big business. Equally skeptical, some scholars likewise found good reason to view the agencies of "mass persuasion"—notably including film and radio as well as the press—as profoundly implicated in the threat to the commonweal. In laying bare the structure of organized capitalism in the United States, analysts such as N. B. Danielian, Alfred Lee, Robert Lynd, and James Rorty believed it was incumbent on them to look long and hard at the nation's communication and entertainment media—whose antidemocratic and often downright predatory tendencies they now began systematically to adduce. The "propaganda analysis" that became a leading feature of this engagement, remains a needful, indeed an all-too-necessary, tradition of inquiry. And, thankfully, it has survived. Today it is evident in its most unyielding form, perhaps, in a series of trenchant studies of the contemporary news system authored by Edward Herman and others.

Whereas this early generation of critical communication study spoke of mass persuasion and propaganda, a later synthesis, developed during the late 1960s and 1970s, originated in a need to grapple afresh with changed contemporary circumstances. If, during the interwar period, critical research had been inspired by anti-fascism, now anti-imperialism set the dominant tone. In turn, what had been a predominantly Euro-American interpretive axis was radically extended, to engage with a newly superordinate global reality of the early postwar epoch. On one side might be seen a succession of struggles for national liberation, as peoples in Africa and Asia sought, with striking success, to free themselves from the policies and prerogatives of now-weakened overlords: Britain, France, Japan, and a few lesser imperialist powers. On the other side was an aspirant mode of informal imperialism, whose historical source and center clearly lay in the United States. This emergent form of transnational domination trumpeted the idea of freedom for all peoples, but concealed under this notional idea a pair of countermanding imperatives: first, to forestall the dozens of new nations from adopting a socialist direction; and second, to reintegrate the new states within a system of global capitalism presided over not by the displaced imperial powers, but by U.S. elites. It should be recalled that, in both regards, the existence of the Soviet Union still significantly constrained U.S. strategy.

Works by Herbert I. Schiller, Dallas Smythe, Thomas Guback, Armand Mattelart, Tapio Varis, and many others assayed to detail state and corporate contributions to the emergence of a transnational culture industry. In consequence, a lengthening series of workaday structures within international communications soon could be seen as abridging and obstructing democratic national reconstruction across much of the so-called Third World. A common logic, guiding everything from spectrum and satellite orbit allocation decisions to news depictions to television program flows was preempting any hope of autonomous cultural development. As mass communication fused with global capitalist ambition, Third World societies were being purposefully reintegrated within an informal, but no less palpable, "American empire." The latter's chief directors and beneficiaries were, of course, the transnational corporations which, remember, throughout the first postwar decade were still based overwhelmingly in the United States.

Some 60 years have passed since the formulation of propaganda analysis, and we are more than a generation removed from the latter synthesis around cultural imperialism. Yet, have the power relations that prompted propaganda analysis been obviated? Have the transnational inequality and exploitation against which critics of cultural imperialism struggled been positively transcended? Hardly; and thus the thematic concern for democratization again ascends. Where, however, lies a valid measure of the distance that has intervened between our own time and the perspectives and insights of these two earlier syntheses? May it be sought in the demise of the Soviet Union and the apparent embrace of the market by China? Or, in the continuing transnationalization of capital and the re-emergence of competition between U.S., Japanese, and European business interests? Or again, in the formidable growth of national bourgeoisies, and of associated social strata possessed of significant discretionary income, throughout a series of poor world states from Korea to Mexico to India? Or, once more, in the apparent growing dissidence and unruliness of popular elements, even—as Chomsky has asserted —within the United States? Or, tacking to the other side of the question, do the principal changes for which account must be made spring from the communication sector itself? We speak today of "information" and "information technology," for example, and with this change has come a need to address questions of [un]employment and division of labor; and of policies systematically supportive of information privatization and commoditization.

Although the pivots of a full-fledged new conceptual synthesis are by no means yet fully apparent, in *Democratizing Communication?* all of these vital issues are emphasized. The editors' enterprise thus permits us to think afresh—and, notably, in reference to an unusually inclusive roster of national settings—about what such a synthesis will have to encompass and entail. *Democratizing Communication?* makes it plain, therefore, that critical communication study is readying itself to engage what is incontestably a new epoch. What more important challenge is there?

About The Authors

Mashoed Bailie focuses on the link between education theory and critical communication theory within the context of media production in higher education. Bailie has published articles on the possibilities of a democratic and liberatory form of media education, children and their understanding of media, and representations of the Middle East during the Gulf War. He is assistant professor in the Department of Communication and Media Studies at the Eastern Mediterranean University, in the Turkish Republic of Northern Cyprus.

Aggrey Brown is professor of communication at the University of the West Indies, Kingston, Jamaica. Brown is a member of the International Council of the International Association of Mass Communication Research and Director of the Caribbean media research center, CARIMAC, also located at the University of the West Indies. His research and publications focus on media technologies and communication policies in the Caribbean region.

Andrew Calabrese is associate professor of communication at the University of Colorado-Boulder. His work applies critical theory to the understanding of telecommunications and telecommunications policy in the United States and Europe. Calabrese's work appears in *Gazette, Telecommunications* Policy, and several edited volumes.

Howard Frederick is author of *Global Communication and International Relations* (Wadsworth, 1993) and numerous other articles on the relationship between computer networking, social organizations, and peace. Frederick is an active member of the Association for Progressive Communications and is associate professor, Division of Mass Communication, Emerson College, Boston, MA.

Cees Hamelink is the former President of the IAMCR and is professor of International Communication, University of Amsterdam, the Netherlands. Hamelink's work focuses on the international political economy of communication, the New International Information Order, and new technologies. In addition to extensive journal articles, Hamelink has authored the books Finance and Information Ablex, (1983), *Cultural Autonomy and Global Communication* (1983), *Trends in World Communication* (1994), and *The Politics of World Communication* (1994).

Jun Hao Hong is currently an assistant professor, Department of Communication, State University of New York-Buffalo. His research on Chinese media has appeared in *Gazette, Media Development, Media Information Australia,* among others.

Jyostna Kapur is a doctoral student in the Department of Radio-TV-Film, Northwestern University, Evanston, IL. Kapur is interested in the problems of democratizing communications and alternative media.

Wolfgang Kleinwaechter is President of the Law Section of the IAMCR and Director of the NETCOM Institute in Leipzig, Germany. Kleinwaechter's research interests include international communication law, media reform in Central and Eastern Europe, and the New World Information and Communication Order (NWICO).

Rick Maxwell teaches international political economy of media and culture at the Department of Radio-TV-Film, Northwestern University, Evanston, IL. Maxwell is the author of *The Spectacle of Democracy: Spanish Television, Nationalism and Political Transition* (University of Minnesota, 1995).

Robert McChesney's research focuses on the history and political economy of U.S. broadcasting. He has numerous articles in academic journals, including the *Journal of Communication,* several book chapters, and a co-edited book. He is also the author of *Telecommunications, Mass Media, and Democracy: The Battle for the Control of US Broadcasting, 1928-35* (Oxford University Press, 1993). McChesney is associate professor of communications, School of Journalism and Mass Communication, University of Wisconsin-Madison.

Ole-Ronkei, Morumpei is a recent graduate from the Department of Journalism and Communication at the University of Oregon. His research focuses on the relationship between media, the church, and politics in Africa, generally, and, Kenya, particularly. Ole-Ronkei currently teaches at Daystar University, Nairobi, Kenya.

Vincent Mosco is professor of communication at Carleton University, Ottawa, Canada. He has published extensively in the areas of new communication technologies, political economy, and communication policy. Mosco has several edited books with Janet Wasko. His own publications include *Push-Button Fantasies* (Ablex, 1982), *The Pay-Per Society* (Garamond, 1989), and *The Political Economy of Communication: Rethinking and Renewal* (Sage, 1996).

Manjunath Pendakur is professor and director of the Program on Communication and Development Studies (School of Speech) at Northwestern University in Evanston, IL. He is also the chairperson of the Department of the Radio-TV-Film. Pendakur has written numerous articles on the media in major international journals and has authored *Canadian Dreams and American Control: The Political Economy of the Canadian Film Industry* (Wayne State University Press, 1990); and co-edited with Janet Wasko and Vincent Mosco *Illuminating the Blind Spots: Essays Honoring Dallas Smythe* (Ablex, 1993). His forthcoming books include *Indian Cinema: Industry, Ideology and Consciousness.*

Wendy Redal is a doctoral student in the Department of Communication at the University of Colorado at Boulder. Redal's interests center around U.S. communication policy, the role of the United States in shaping communication policy internationally and the possibilities for the development of an expanded concept of the public interest -both domestically and internationally.

Andrew Reddick is an Ottawa-based communications consultant. He currently works as a research consultant for the Public Interest Advocacy Centre, Ottawa, Canada. Andrew has an M.A. in Communications from Carleton University, Ottawa and is currently working on his Ph.D. Andrew has previously worked as a senior executive in the film, video, and television industry and has been a communications policy advisor for the federal departments of Communication and Industry. He was a member of the Advisory Panel for the British Columbia government's study on the Socio-Economic Impacts of a British Columbia Information Highway.

Vanda Rideout is a doctoral student in the Department of Sociology and Anthropology, Carleton University, Ottawa, Canada. Her major interests are in the political economy of communications and communication policy. Vanda applies these interests regularly as a consultant to labor unions, government, and industry.

Richard Vincent is associate professor in the Department of Communication, University of Hawaii-Honolulu. His research interests are primarily in the area of the New World Information and Communication Order (NWICO). In addition to many published articles, Vincent is co-author with Johann Galtung of *Global Glasnost: Towards a New World Information and Communication Order?* (Hampton Press, 1992) and the forthcoming book, *USA Glasnost: Missing Political Themes in US Media Discourse* (Hampton Press 1996). He is past chair of the international communication advocacy group, the MacBride Round Table.

Dwayne Winseck's research focuses on national and international media and communication policy, with a recent emphasis on NAFTA and GATT. Winseck has published articles on these topics in *Gazette,* the *Canadian Journal of Communication,* and in several edited volumes. His book, *Telecoms, People, and Media Reconvergence: A History and Political Economy of Canadian Telecoms (1846-1996),* will be published in 1997 by Hampton Press. He is lecturer at the Centre for Mass Communication Research, University of Leicester, England.

Sunny Yoon is lecturer in the Department of Political Science at Sonyang University, Seoul, Korea. Yoon has written several book chapters for edited collections and presented papers at international conferences on computerization and telecommunications in Korea.

Introduction

Critical Communication Studies and Theories of Communication and Democracy

Mashoed Bailie
Dwayne Winseck

Recent technological, economic and political upheavals are transforming our means of communication. In response, policymakers, citizens, and those within the communication industries throughout the world are struggling with issues of regulatory reform, privatization, economic development, and the democratization of communication, among other objectives. From a cross-national comparative perspective, this book engages the discourses of communication, power, and democracy implicated in these developments. From the vantage point of 19 scholars, from 10 different countries, we explore these contemporary universal developments as they take form within specific national, regional, and international contexts.

The theoretical perspectives developed by the authors in this book explore and analyze the social, political, and economic determinants of communication. Each contribution is linked to the critical theoretical concern with understanding the relationship between global developments, local permutations, and the central role of human beings in actively shaping the world. Particular attention is given to the historical contexts within which the changes in media and communication are occurring, and to the potential of people to participate in the transformation of their social and communicative environments. Throughout the book, several key theoretical concepts are employed by the authors: social structure, historical context, social and historical change, determination, power, and agency. These theoretical concepts support a broad array of critical theories, including political economy, historical inquiry, critical education theory, cultural analysis, and discourse analysis.

More importantly, the approaches developed by the authors provide a number of helpful analytical frameworks for seeing, understanding, evaluating, and acting on what may well be one of the most important historical periods since the Enlightenment. These are not grandiose statements made lightly, but judicious appraisals of the changes in the field of communication and the radical political, economic, and theological restructuring of the globe. The integration of British telecommunications firms with those from Canada, the linking of private sector broadcasters in the United States with their public sector counter-parts in Europe, the merger of European private communication firms with state-controlled broadcasters in Africa, and the commercialization of military broadcast units in parts of Asia attest to the vast development in the field of communication. The reader need not be reminded too much about the withering of the Soviet Union and the consequent proliferation of states in Eastern Europe and Central Asia, the election of Nelson Mandela in South Africa, and the explosion of nation-states in Yugoslavia, Yemen, and Rwanda to grasp the larger geopolitical and historical context within which the developments in communication are taking place. We can note that in a very short period of time the number of countries has expanded from about 180 to over 200. Communication is such an exciting and unique field of inquiry because of its ability to focus theory, the transformation of communication, and the transmutation of society into a reasonably coherent area of study.

These bold statements are premised on the following observations. First, the collection of articles shares the assumption that from the pedagogical relations developed in media education to the sophisticated global electronic networks of commerce, communication is now central to social understanding, critique, and the way people and institutions act in the world. Although critical pedagogy highlights the relationships between teaching and learning practices in the classroom, the authors also realize that the everyday processes of learning and citizenship are being transformed by the instrumental application of new technologies in the home, school, business, and state organizations. Fundamental new ways of knowing the world are promoted through the industrialization of communication policies and human relations on a global basis.

The centrality of communication is most pronounced in the industrial and modernization policies of countries throughout the world. Although policymakers, industrialists, and futurists amplify the discourses of communication, culture, and democracy, it is also true that these same spokespersons are simultaneously engaged in the construction of industrial policies based on communication technologies for the conquest of internal and global markets (Mattelart & Mattelart, 1992). In this discourse, market reforms are equal to or cause democratic reforms. As Vincent Mosco and Andrew Reddick indicate in their chapter, however, public policy issues cannot be reduced to questions of market reforms and technique. They suggest that a political economy of communication perspective is increasingly relevant to public policy as information technologies and services become key sites of state-sponsored industrial policy. Such a perspective helps us understand the social implications of technological change, the factors behind these changes, and what they mean in terms of communication, distributive justice, and people's ability to participate in the range of institutions and issues shaping the social landscape.

Many of the authors, especially Aggrey Brown, Jun Hao Hong, Richard Maxwell, Manjunath Pendakur and Jyotsna Kapur, Dwayne Winseck (chapter 5) and Sunny Yoon, consider the various ways in which the communication sectors of societies around the world have been harnessed to the imperatives of market reform and expansion, global competitiveness, and technological innovation. In each of their respective approaches to the structural reorganization of the communication industry and policies in the Caribbean, the People's Republic of China, Spain, India, Canada, and South Korea, this group of authors illuminates the tensions between industrial strategies and democratic spheres of communication. By uncovering these contradictions, these authors explore how instrumental conceptions of communication, divorced from concepts of citizenship, power and democracy, frustrate the social, political, and humanistic potentials of the new technologies. Yet, more than just counterposing technological potentials to the socioeconomic and political relations shaping communication technologies, some of the authors—Hamelink, Winseck and Yoon, for instance—point out that the general public often has an ambivalent view of new communication technologies. Although this observation no doubt requires further investigation and qualification, it is true that the public's less than full embrace of the new information machines has led states and industries to adopt measures—used in schools, the mass media and other public spaces—to sell the virtues of the new technics (Mumford, 1934/1963). As Mashoed Bailie's chapter, in particular points out, such initiatives are particularly prominent in university media education programs and serve to severe technologies from human purposes in that and other contexts.

The chapters by McChesney, Vanda Rideout and Vincent Mosco, and Mosco and Reddick are crucial to understanding the tenuous relationship between communication policy, the creation of electronic public space, and other important public policy goals for the emerging broadband networks in the United States. The jointly authored articles of Mosco, Reddick, and Rideout suggest that although the economic dimensions of national communication systems are no doubt enormous, crucial questions remain about what sectors of society will benefit most, how the costs of accessing the networks will be allocated, the possibility of noninstrumental uses of technology, and the ability to enlarge traditional regulatory concerns with universal service, nondiscriminatory access, and public sector use of communication facilities. Such questions, they indicate, will be shaped by the interplay of key participants in the communication regulatory process, the incisive role of the state in mediating the public and private sectors of society, and how policymakers and social analysts think about communication, society, and technology. Continuing this discussion, Robert McChesney draws on his historical research into the evolution of the institutional structure of broadcasting in the United States to suggest that the extension of corporate concentration and commercialization threaten the democratic objectives associated with the emerging national information infrastructure in the United States. He goes on to suggest that communication scholars should take communication policy debates seriously, while promoting alternative possibilities for the democratic organization and uses of the new technologies.

Furthermore, as McChesney, Rideout and Mosco's chapters point out, and Andrew Calabrese and Wendy Redal, Cees Hamelink, Richard Vincent and Dwayne Winseck's (chapter 15) chapters illustrate, policy directions originating in the United States have an uncanny way of proliferating around the world. These chapters trace the formation, dissemination, and global adoption of communication policies, regulatory procedures and methodologies, and normative principles. A further contribution is their analysis of challenges to traditional institutions involved in international communication policy, such as the United Nations Education, Scientific and Cultural Organization (UNESCO) and the International Telecommunication Union (ITU), and the establishment of new sites for the development of international communication policy, such as the General Agreement on Trades and Tariffs (GATT) and the World Trade Organization (WTO).

Yet, as a note of caution, it is imperative that this process not be seen as uniform and inexorable. Although we acknowledge that the tripartite forces of technological convergence, regulatory change, and economic restructuring appear to hold a monopoly over the global imagination, the authors in this collection ably demonstrate the proliferation of social forces challenging any hegemonic view of global communication. As the chapters by Hamelink, Vincent, and Winseck on UNESCO, the New World Information and Communication Order (NWICO), and the new contexts of international communication policy aptly illustrate, attempts to establish a monopoly over the communication industries, the normative principles governing the international flow of images, data, and voices, and the relationship between communication and society have never been without challenges. As these chapters illustrate, many of the world's countries have made sophisticated linkages between communication and international economics, national sovereignty, and cultural identity, on the one hand, and the concentrated control over the means of communication by a small number of countries in North America and Europe, on the other. Indeed, these critical connections allowed NWICO efforts, like communication policy in the United States, to diffuse to large geographical areas and to international agencies, such as the ITU, the World Bank, and INTELSAT, and even the creation of new ones, such as the International Program for Development Communication (IPDC), or to precipitate the exit of major geopolitical actors, such as the United States, Britain, and Singapore, from UNESCO. Eventually, the juxtapositioning of these world historical ideas in international communication during the 1970s and 1980s came to be encased in the radical opposition between those supporting the United States' initiated free flow of communication doctrine and those supporting the NWICO goals of communication equity and a right to communicate.

If we can make one broad, sweeping statement about the international relations of communication during the 1970s and 1980s, it is that the actors of civil society were not key participants (Roach, 1990). At best, they stood in the shadows of representative democracy; at worst, citizens were oblivious or seriously misinformed about the nature of NWICO. It is fair to say that the primary actors were states, supranational agencies, and capital. This created a situation in which there was a lot of thunder, but little public discourse.

The critical perspectives developed in this book aim to contribute a remedy to this situation. The authors emphasize the social relations of communication by focusing on the major communicative actors of modernity— state, capital, and civil society—and extending the analytical lens to incorporate supranational agencies, such as the ITU, UNESCO, and the World Bank; the transnational enterprises that straddle the globe through private and public networks, the church, and ethnic identity as resurgent axis of popular cohesion; the education system and its ambivalent status in the production of future labor power as well as critical thought, labor unions, information pirates, and other constituents of high modernity.

The authors identify and explore several key factors in the proliferation of actors in civil society. The disintegration of the Soviet Union, the fundamental economic reforms in the People's Republic of China, and the radical democratic implications of the new South African government are some of the key historical events framing the investigations by several contributing authors. For example, Wolfgang Kleinwaechter considers the conflicting tensions within efforts to restructure media systems in the Eastern European countries of the former Soviet Union. Howard Frederick focuses on how the uses of computer networking by nongovernmental organizations (NGOs) have strengthened their position in international relations while increasing their opportunities to influence the outcomes of major political events. Hong provides an overview of the implications of economic reform in the People's Republic of China for the domestic media system. In his chapter, Hong demonstrates how the state-directed project of economic reform has transformed the media into multipurpose tools of socioeconomic development, on the one hand, and social control on the other. In addition, Hong's chapter reminds us that the dominant perspective in international communication that emerged during the 1960s and 1970s, the so-called modernization paradigm, is still alive and kicking as it influences the use of media for national development in the People's Republic of China. As such, this case study offers readers a valuable opportunity to compare the modernization perspective with other approaches to international communication elsewhere in the book.

The chapters in this section provide a framework for considering the rising salience of ethnicity as a focal point of cultural identity, the increasing centrality of the church and religion as a site of popular cohesion, and the role of communication as the medium in which the often conflicting discourses of modernity, ethnicity, religion, economic forces, and democracy are played out. The chapter by Morompi Ole-Ronkei on private sector broadcasting, the church, and state in Kenya rounds out this section by focusing on the church's use of the mass media to affect Kenyan politics.

The convergence of communication theory with theology, philosophy, and critical theory as a major mode of reflection continues the historical centrality of communication to modernity (i.e., notions of the free press, communication, and institutional autonomy, and communication as an expression and validation of the self in social interaction; Habermas, 1989). All are concerned with the ability of human beings to shape their social environment through public discourse, reflective thought, cohesive social action, and the application of technology to democratic ends.

Reflecting these developments, Bailie integrates critical communication and critical pedagogical theories as a way for suggesting how communication educators can go beyond merely providing skills training for entry-level employment in media markets. Rather, Bailie argues, educators can engage students dialogically in the resources of citizenship and concepts of self located in history. From Bailie's perspective, critical communication education provides students of media with a sense of agency and a capacity for actively shaping of the world in which they live. Illustrating the practical importance of the global circulation of ideas, Bailie draws on the work of Brazilian education theorist, Paulo Freire, among others, to demonstrate the necessity of education as praxis. For Bailie, the classroom and other social environments represent opportunities to engage citizenship and modernity and not the evasion of politics, power, and class, so often suggested by those who focus on the radical indeterminacy, uniqueness, and pleasure of personal experiences.

Thus, we can see this collection of chapters as accomplishing four main tasks. First, the chapters provide theoretical frameworks for grasping the essence of the momentous changes in communication and world history now in progress. Second, they expand the range of concerns central to communication studies by complementing the study of state-capital-technological relations with an increased emphasis on the actors of civil society. Third, the critical perspectives developed in these chapters demonstrate the continued viability of a modernist frame of reference. These chapters suggest that critical theories originating in Enlightenment thought are essential intellectual vehicles for understanding, evaluating, and acting in the world.

Finally, although all the analysts recognize that the potentials of communication technologies are very real, the emphasis on communicative actors and the critical analyses presented in this book suggest that technological possibilities are structured by social, economic, and political determinants. Although the perspectives presented here acknowledge the important role played by the new technologies in expanding the range of consumer goods and their potential of allowing people to become producers of information, rather than merely consumers, the notion that technologies are the primary agents of change eliminates history and the social relations of technology. Instead, by locating technologies in their social, cultural, and historical contexts, each author reveals that technology, rather than being a neutral instrument to be used for good or ill, is shaped, influenced, and constrained by the imperatives constructed into and around them. This is realized as soon as we ask, "Where do technologies come from?" As Herbert Schiller (1986) noted:

> Satellites, computers, and cable make possible a qualitatively new level of information availability. . . . Viewed exclusively as a technological capability, it is hardly unrealistic to regard the present situation as one of potential unprecedented abundance and richness of information. It seems all the more shocking therefore, to acknowledge at the same time, the deepening division of the society into informationally-privileged and informationally-impoverished sectors. What accounts for this? (p. 102)

Communication is not just an important resource and commodity, but also a crucial factor in the shaping of perceptions and a constitutive force of society and culture. By providing the means through which we share interpretations and understandings with one another and our respective experiences, communication is culture. Information and communication are also crucial aspects of the political process and citizenship. Library expansion at the turn of the century in the United States provided substance to the concept of citizenship by opening access to the resources needed to fulfill that role in society. Expanded access to communication was also part and parcel of the expansion of citizenship rights through the 19th and 20th centuries, such as the decoupling of citizenship rights from property ownership, the creation of universal suffrage for women and blacks, social security, and the right to public information through the creation of the national government document depository system (in 1902). It was on this basis that people could have access to the flow of information and communication and participate in the democratic process.

In the 1990s, what do technological, political, and economical restructuring hold in store for the historical synthesis of communication, citizenship, and democracy? Will information superhighways expand the envelope of citizenship and communication rights, maintain the status quo, in which the public interest is defined in and through paternalistic forms of state regulation or market transactions, or will the linkages between these concepts be fragmented and individually eroded? From Kenya to Korea, to Canada and the United States, the authors in this book explore these important questions as they think through the linkages between global and local communicative contexts around the world.

REFERENCES

Habermas, J. (1989). *Jurgen Habermas on politics and society*. Boston: Beacon.

Mattelart, A., & Mattelart, M. (1992). *Rethinking media theory: Signposts and new directions* (J. A. Cohen & M. Urquidi, trans.). Minnesota: University of Minnesota.

Mumford, L. (1963). *Technics and civilization*. New York: Free Press. (original work published 1934)

Roach, C. (1990). The movement for a New World Information and Communication Order: A second wave. *Media, Culture and Society, 12*, 283-307.

Schiller, H. (1986). *Information and the crisis economy*. New York: Oxford University Press.

Section I

Theories of Communication and Theories of Democracy

Chapter 1

Political Economy, Communication, and Policy*

Vincent Mosco
Andrew Reddick

This chapter provides an overview of the political economy approach to communication and policy studies. This approach has informed a large body of research on national and international communication policy. It is also the theoretical starting point explicitly or implicitly contained in other chapters of this book.

The chapter is divided into two sections, the first of which defines political economy and charts its use in communication research. The second provides guidance for rethinking and renewing the philosophical roots and substantive terrain of the approach and suggests how this might be used to understand communication policy. The time is ripe for such a rethinking because transformations in the world political economy and in intellectual life have raised fundamental challenges to this approach. The former include the near death of communism, the continued stagnation in capitalist societies, the

*Vincent Mosco acknowledges the assistance of a grant from the Canadian Social Sciences and Humanities Research Council for ongoing research in the political economy of communication.

breakup of what unity once existed in the Third World, and the rise of social movements, particularly feminism and environmentalism, that cut across traditional political economic categories such as social class. Among the numerous intellectual challenges to political economy, two stand out for their significance in policymaking in communication. On the one hand, cultural studies challenges the institutional ground of political economy and raises questions about analyzing the role of the state and other social actors in the policy process. On the other hand, an approach variously called policy science, public choice theory, rational expectations, and "positive" political economy applies neoclassical economic theory to social behavior, thereby reducing the policy process to a pluralist marketplace whereby the state mediates between competing social claims.

The first part begins by defining the political economy approach, identifies its fundamental characteristics, and maps major schools of thought. From here, it proceeds to examine how communication scholars have drawn on the theoretical framework to carry out research on communication policy. This section highlights divisions that distinguish research approaches in North America, Europe, and the Third World. The second section begins the process of rethinking the political economy of communication by proposing the means to address its epistemological and ontological foundations. Specifically, it calls for an epistemology founded on a realist, nonessentialist, inclusive, and critical approach to knowledge and an ontology that foregrounds social change, social process, and social relations over the traditional tendency in political economy to start from structures and institutions. Putting this agenda into practice, the chapter identifies three processes that constitute the central entry points for political economy research—commodification, spatialization, and structuration—and suggests how they can be used to comprehend policymaking and communication.

WHAT IS POLITICAL ECONOMY?

Two definitions of political economy capture the wide range of specific and general approaches to the discipline that social theory presents. In the narrow sense, political economy is the study of the social relations, particularly the power relations, that mutually constitute the production, distribution, and consumption of resources, including communication resources. This formulation has a certain heuristic value because it calls attention to the institutional circuit of communications products that link, for example, a chain of primary producers to wholesalers, retailers, and consumers, whose purchases, rentals, and attention are fed back into new processes of production. However, there is sufficient ambiguity about what constitutes a producer, distributor, or consumer, so that one needs to be cautious in using it. A more general and ambitious definition of political economy is the study of control and survival in social life. Control refers to the internal organization of group members and the process of adapting to change. Survival means how they produce what is needed for social reproduction and continuity. In this reading, control processes are broadly political in that they constitute the social organization of relationships within a community, and survival processes are fundamentally economic because they concern processes of production and reproduction. The strength of this definition is that it gives political economy the breadth to encompass at least all human activity and, arguably, all organic processes, a tendency reflected in environmental, ecological, and biodiversity studies (Benton, 1989).[1] Its principal drawback is that it can lead one to overlook what distinguishes human political economy from general processes of survival and control.

Another way to describe political economy is to broaden its meaning beyond what is typically considered in definitions, by focusing on a set of central qualities that characterize the approach. Drawing particularly on the work of Golding and Murdock (1991), this section focuses on four ideas—social transformation, social totality, moral philosophy, and praxis—that different schools of political economic thought tend to share.

Political economy has consistently placed in the foreground the goal of understanding social change and historical transformation. For classical political economists such as Smith, Ricardo, and Mill, this meant comprehending the great capitalist revolution, the vast social upheaval that would transform societies based primarily on agricultural labor into commercial, manufacturing, and, eventually, industrial societies. For Marx, it meant examining the dynamic forces within capitalism and between it and other forms of political economic organization, in order to understand the processes of social change that would, ultimately, transform capitalism into socialism. Orthodox economics, which began to coalesce against political economy in the late 19th century, tended to set aside this concern for the dynamics of history and social change in order to turn political economy into the science of economics, whose lawlike statements were best constructed to fit static rather than dynamic social conditions. Contemporary political economists, occupying various heterodox positions distinct from what has become economic orthodoxy, continue to take up the concept of social transformation. However, humbled by a century that has eroded the ideology of progress they tend to focus attention more modestly around the axes formed by various "post" formulations, particularly postfordism, postindustrialism, and postmodernism.

Political economy is also characterized by an interest in examining the social whole or the totality of social relations that constitute the economic, political, social, and cultural fields. Academic orthodoxy tends to compartmentalize these into distinct disciplines, each with its own rules of entry, border controls, and systems of overall surveillance. Currently

[1]This definition grows out of a suggestion that Dallas Smythe offered in a series of discussions in December 1991.

fashionable poststructuralist thought, although laudable in its attack on this and other orthodoxies, also tends to deny the existence of social, or even of discursive, totalities that argue for principles of order across the range of discrete social practices. From Adam Smith, to Karl Marx, to contemporary institutional, conservative, and neomarxian theorists, political economy has consistently aimed to build on the unity of the political and the economic— accounting for their mutual constitution and relationships to wider social and symbolic spheres of activity.

Political economy is also noted for its commitment to moral philosophy, understood as both an interest in the values that help to constitute social behavior and, normatively, in those moral principles that ought to guide efforts to change it. For Adam Smith, as evidenced in his *Theory of Moral Sentiments* (1759/1976), a book he favored more than the popular *Wealth of Nations* (1776/1937), this meant understanding values such as acquisitiveness and individual freedom that were contributing to the rise of commercial capitalism. Whereas for Marx (1973, 1976), moral philosophy meant the ongoing struggle between the drive to realize self- and social value in human labor and the drive to reduce labor to a marketable commodity. Contemporary political economy leans to moral philosophical standpoints that foreground the extension of democracy beyond the political realm, in which it is variously legitimated in formal, legal instruments to encompass the economic, social, and cultural domains that tend to be shaped by the requirements of capital.

Following from this view, social praxis, or the fundamental unity of theory and practice, also occupies a central place in political economy. Specifically, against orthodox positions, which separate, at least formally, the sphere of research from social intervention, political economists, in a tradition tracing its roots to preclassical practices of providing advice and counsel to power, have consistently viewed intellectual life as a form of social transformation and social intervention as a form of knowledge. Although they differ fundamentally on what should characterize intervention—from Malthus (1798/1966) who supported rigid methods of population control, to Marx who called on labor to realize itself in revolution—political economists are united in the view that the division between research and action is artificial and must be overturned.

The political economy approach is also distinguished by the many schools of thought that guarantee significant variety of viewpoints and vigorous internal debate. Arguably the most important divide emerged in responses to the classical political economy of Smith and his followers. One set aimed to build on the classical emphasis on the individual as the primary unit of analysis and the market as the principal structure. The unity of the two concepts lay in the ability of markets to register the demands of the individual. Over time, this response progressively eliminated the classical concerns for history, social totality, moral philosophy, and praxis. As a result, political economy was transformed into a science of economics founded on an empirical investigation of marketplace behavior and the representations of these observations in the language of mathematics. This approach is broadly understood as neoclassical economics (Jevons, 1965; Marshall, 1890/1961).

A second set of responses opposed this tendency by retaining the classical concern for history, the social whole, moral philosophy, and praxis, even if that meant giving up the goal of creating a positive science. This set constitutes the wide variety of approaches to political economy. A first wave was led by conservative neo-Burkeans, who replaced marketplace individualism with the collective authority of tradition (Carlyle, 1984); by Utopian Socialists, who accepted the classical faith in social intervention and urged putting community ahead of the market (Owen, 1851); and by Marxian thought, which placed labor at the center of political economy. According to the latter, the labor process, among other things, integrated people's ability to think abstractly with the ability to transform the material world to serve human needs. This linking of conception with praxis through labor was the characteristic of human beings, which in Marx's famous phrase separated the architect from the bee.

Subsequent formulations built on these perspectives, leaving a wide range of contemporary formulations. For example, Orthodox economists occupying the center and center-right of the intellectual spectrum seek to extend the categories of neoclassical economics to all social behavior with the aim of expanding individual freedom. This perspective thrives in the work of people such as George J. Stigler (1988), James M. Buchanan (Brennan & Buchanan, 1985), and Ronald Coase (1991; Coase & Barrett, 1968), recent recipients of the Nobel prize in economics. Another approach—institutional political economy—occupies a slightly left of center view. An example of this approach is found in the work of Galbraith (1985), who, drawing principally on Veblen (1899/1934, 1932), argues that institutional and technological constraints shape markets to the advantage of those corporations and governments with the power to control them. Neomarxian approaches, including the French Regulation School (Lipietz, 1988), world systems theory (Wallerstein, 1979), and others engaged in the debate over Fordism (Foster, 1988), continue to place economics and international trade relations at the center of analysis. Finally, social movements have spawned their own schools of political economy, principally feminist political economy, which addresses the persistence of patriarchy in policymaking and institutions, and environmental political economy, which concentrates on the links between social behavior and the wider organic environment (Benton, 1989).

THE POLITICAL ECONOMY OF COMMUNICATION

Communication studies has drawn on various schools of political economic analysis. This section concentrates on research situated in institutional and neomarxian approaches because these have largely informed research in communication policy. Although both neoclassical economists and conservative political economists have theorized the communication industries, policy has largely been seen as subordinate or driven by market forces and economic contingencies.

At this stage in its development, it is useful to map the political economy of communication from the perspective of regional emphases. Although there are important exceptions and cross-currents, North American, European, and Third World approaches differ enough to receive distinctive treatment. Moreover, the political economy approach to communication is not sufficiently developed theoretically to be explained in a single analytical map.

North American research has been extensively influenced by the contributions of two founding figures: Dallas Smythe and Herbert Schiller. Smythe taught the first course in the political economy of communication at the University of Illinois and is the first of four generations of scholars linked together in this research tradition.[2] Schiller, who worked for a time with Smythe at Illinois, has similarly influenced several generations of subsequent political economists. Their approach to communication studies draws on both institutional and Marxian traditions. However, they have been less interested than, for example, European scholars, in providing a theoretical account of communication. Rather, their work and, through their influence, a great deal of the research in this region, has been driven more explicitly by a sense of injustice that the communication industry has become an integral part of a wider corporate order that is both exploitative and undemocratic. Although they have been concerned with the impact within their respective national bases, both have led a research program that charts the growth in power and influence of transnational media companies throughout the world (Schiller, 1989, 1969/1992; Smythe, 1977, 1981). Partly owing to their influence, North American research has produced a large literature on industry and class specific manifestations of transnational corporate and state power, distinguished by its concern to participate in ongoing struggles to change the dominant media and to create alternatives (Douglas, 1986; Mosco & Wasko, 1983; Wasko & Mosco, 1992). A major objective of this work is to advance public interest concerns before government regulatory and policy organs. This includes support for those movements that have taken an active role before international fora, such as the United Nations, in defense of a new international economic, information, and communication order (Roach, 1993).

European research is less clearly linked to specific founding figures and, although it is also connected to movements for social change, particularly the defense of public service media systems, the leading work in this region has

---

[2]Smythe's student Thomas Guback works at the University of Illinois in the political economy of film. Janet Wasko, a student of Guback, also works in this area at the University of Oregon, whereas a student of hers, Jack Banks, does research on the political economy of music at the University of Hartford.

been more concerned with integrating communication research within various neomarxian theoretical traditions. Of the two principal directions this research has taken, one, most prominent in the work of Garnham (1990) and Golding and Murdock (1991; see also Murdock & Golding, 1979), has emphasized class power. Building on the Frankfurt School tradition, as well as that of Raymond Williams, the class power perspective documents the integration of communication institutions, mainly business and state policy authorities, within the wider capitalist economy, and the resistance of subaltern classes and movements to neoconservative state practices promoting liberalization, commercialization, and privatization of the communication industries. A second stream of research foregrounds class struggle and is most prominent in the work of Armand Mattelart (Mattelart & Mattelart, 1986/1992; Mattelart & Siegelaub, 1983). Mattelart has drawn from a range of traditions including dependency theory, western Marxism, and the worldwide experience of national liberation movements to understand communication as one among the principal sources of resistance to power.

Third World research on the political economy of communication has covered a wide area of interests, although a major stream has grown in response to the modernization or developmentalist paradigm that originated in Western, particularly U.S., attempts to incorporate communication into an explanatory paradigm congenial to mainstream intellectual and political interests. The thesis held that the media were resources that, along with urbanization, education, and other social forces, would mutually stimulate progressive economic, social, and cultural modernization. As a result, media growth was viewed as an index of development. Drawing on, variously, dependency, world systems, and other streams of international neomarxian political economy, Third World political economists challenged the fundamental premises of the model, particularly its technological determinism and the omission of practically any interest in the power relations that shape the terms of relationships between First and Third World nations and the multilayered class relations between and within them (Boafo, 1991; Cardoso & Faletto, 1979; Roncagliolo, 1986; Tang & Chan, 1990). The failure of development schemes incorporating media investment sent modernization theorists in search of revised models that have tended to incorporate telecommunication and new computer technologies into the mix (Jussawalla, 1986). Political economists have responded principally by addressing the power of these new technologies to integrate a global division of labor. A first wave of research saw the division largely in territorial terms: Unskilled labor concentrated in the poorest nations; semiskilled and more complex assembly labor in semiperipheral societies; and research, development, and strategic planning limited to First World corporate headquarters, to which the bulk of profit would flow. More recent research acknowledges that class divisions cut across territorial lines and maintains that what is central to the evolving international division of labor is the growth in flexibility for firms that control the range of technologies that overcome traditional time and space constraints (Harvey, 1989; Morris-Suzuki, 1986).

RETHINKING POLITICAL ECONOMY

Although most assessments of political economy, including its application to communication research, acknowledge its contribution to intellectual life and political struggles, these also raise concerns about the need to rethink and renew the discipline in light of recent upheavals. This section responds to this general ferment by suggesting starting points for rethinking political economy that can guide research in communication, including the relationship to policy.

The philosophical foundations of a political economy approach to communication provide an important starting point. Drawing on recent critical literature that reflects on the state of the field, it is first useful to advance basic epistemological and ontological principles (Gandy, 1992; Golding & Murdock, 1991). An *epistemology* is a theory of a theory, or an approach to understanding a field of knowledge. The political economy of communication needs to be grounded in a realist, inclusive, constitutive, and critical epistemology. It is realist in that it recognizes the reality of both concepts and social practices, thereby eschewing idiographic and nomothetic approaches, currently fashionable in poststructural thought, which argue respectively for the reality of discourse only or reject the reality premises of both concepts and practices. Following from this, the approach is inclusive in that it rejects essentialism, which would reduce all social practices to a single political economic explanation, in favor of an approach that views concepts as entry points into a social field (Resnick & Wolff, 1987). The choice of certain concepts and theories over others means that priority is given to these over others as useful means of explanation. They are not assertions of the one best, or only, way to understand social practices. Additionally, the epistemology is constitutive in that it recognizes the limits of causal determination, including the assumption that units of social analysis interact as fully formed wholes and in a linear fashion. Rather, it approaches the social as a set of mutually constitutive processes, acting on one another—an ongoing dynamic interaction—in various stages of formation and with a direction and impact that can only be comprehended in specific research. Finally, the approach is critical in that knowledge, the mutual constitution of theory and practice, is viewed as the product of an ongoing set of comparisons to other bodies of knowledge and to a set of normative considerations that guide social praxis. For example, the political economy used in the earlier overview is critical in that it suggests a need to situate the knowledge acquired in research against alternative bodies of knowledge in, for example, neoclassical economics, pluralist political science, and cultural studies. Furthermore, it requires the measurement of political economic knowledge against the values of social democracy, including public participation and equality, that guide praxis.

Connected to this epistemological approach is an ontology that foregrounds social change, social process, and social relations against the tendency in social research, particularly in political economy, to concentrate on structures and institutions. This means that research starts from the view that social change is ubiquitous, that structures and institutions are in a process of constant change, and that it is therefore more useful to develop entry points that characterize processes rather than to name institutions. Guided by this principle, it is useful to develop a substantive map of political economy with three entry processes, starting with *commodification*, the process of transforming use to exchange value. From this, it moves on to *spatialization*, the transformation of the temporal dimension of space, or the process of institutional extension, and finally to *structuration*, the mutually constitutive relationship between social structure and human agency. Foregrounding social change with these processes does not replace structures and institutions, something that would substitute one form of essentialism for another. Rather, these are entry points for a substantive theory of political economy, one preferred choice among a range of possible means of understanding society. The next section takes up these entry points, using them to suggest the boundaries of a political economic analysis and, more specifically, to understand the contribution of communication research to communication policy.

Commodification has long been understood as the process of taking goods and services that are valued for their use, such as food to satisfy hunger, and transforming them into commodities that are valued for what they can bring in the marketplace. The process of commodification holds a dual significance for communication research. First, communication practices and technologies contribute to the general commodification process throughout society. For example, the introduction of computer communication gives companies greater control over the entire circuit of production, distribution, and exchange, permitting retailers to monitor sales and inventory levels with ever-improving precision, thereby enabling them to produce and ship only what they know is likely to sell quickly, and reducing inventory requirements and unnecessary merchandise. Second, commodification helps us understand specific communication institutions and practices. For example, the general, worldwide expansion of commodification in the 1980s, responding in part to global declines in economic growth, led to the increased commercialization of programming, the privatization of public service media and telecommunications institutions, and the liberalization of communication markets.

Political economy policy research on the process of commodification has focused on class power, media elites, ownership patterns, and the audience commodity. Moreover, it has examined how the interests of dominant class interests are met for capital accumulation and social control. Clement (1975) and Bagdikian (1988), in research on Canada and the United States, have shown how implicit and explicit state approval has permitted the development of industry concentration, monopoly formation, and powerful interconnected elites in print, broadcasting, telecommunications, and the cable industry. Similarly, other research has documented how dominant media corporations and their government allies developed and protected mass markets in broadcasting media in a process that commodified public space and the audience. This work shows that in some constituencies the alliance with government was useful when corporate media power was challenged by educational, labor, and other nonprofit efforts attempting to meet noncommercial, social needs. In other instances, for example, Canada and Europe, different forms of state policy led to the creation of mixed public and private systems that attempted some balance between commodified and decommodified national media systems (Mander, 1978; Raboy, 1990; Smythe, 1981; Vipond, 1989). International research (MacDonald, 1990) has documented and analyzed the major international print and media concentration and ownership patterns.

Current research on communication policy that pushes the margins of political economy also grows out of earlier books of wider scope, such as those of Harold Innis (1972) and Raymond Williams (1974). Innis's broad focus on the role of the state and the increasing importance of communication in social control, the nature of the commodity, and commodity exchange continues to offer lessons for the analysis of privatization, internationalization, reregulation, and commodification. Williams's discussions on the historical and institutional development of media systems within a dynamic political, economic, and sociocultural totality contributed useful insights about the tensions in policymaking and the public good versus commodity value of the media content, audience, and overall infrastructures.

More recent political economy of communication research has been notable for its emphasis on describing and examining the significance of those structural forms responsible for the production, distribution, and exchange of communication commodities and for the regulation of the communication marketplace. This research has focused on the processes by which policy, directly or indirectly, has contributed to the extension of commodification within existing or new, developing markets and deeper social and cultural relations and activities. These discussions view the expansion of capitalism through the global extension of markets, the privatization of public space, and the growth of exchange value in interpersonal life (Ewen, 1976; H. Schiller, 1981, 1989; Webster & Robins, 1986).

Recent political economic research in policy has examined the process of expansion of commodification to areas that, for a range of social, political, and economic reasons, were only lightly affected, if at all, by the process. These include numerous information and cultural areas that have been taken up prominently in communications studies (Garnham, 1990; Schiller, 1989), geography (Harvey, 1989), urban studies (Davis, 1990), and cultural studies (Davis, 1986). This work describes how the process of commodification, as part of policy shifts, has been extended to institutional areas such as public education, government information, media, culture, and telecommunications that were certainly created out of a range of contested forces and motives, but that nevertheless preserved principles of universal access, irrespective of one's position in the marketplace.

Policy research also concentrates on the process by which changes in the process of commodification have been pursued in policymaking and regulation in the established broadcast, cable, and telecommunications industries. The struggle for competition and reregulation of domestic business and services has been led by large business users and new providers. These groups are organized into large cross-cutting national and international associations (Coulter, 1992; Mosco, 1990b; Rideout, 1993; Winseck, 1993). This research emphasizes the growing complexity of communications relations and underlies the increasing importance of an enhanced policy role in these changed relations. The privatization, reregulation model, which promotes the deepening and extension of commodity forms (entertainment, information and services) in national and international markets, has also led to an increased focus by political economy on the international policy dimension. Expansionist strategies at this level are being pursued in bilateral arrangements with developing and developed countries and multilaterally through trade initiatives such as the European Community agreements and the North American Free Trade Agreement (NAFTA). Communication policy changes are a part of the wider changes taking place across most major industrial sectors. This economic and political restructuring is part of the internationalization process that permits cross-national alliances and mergers, as well as national media policy reorganization to accommodate the interests of dominant multinational corporations (Dyson, 1990; Hills, 1991; Mosco, 1989; 1990a; Negrine, 1990). One of the important contributions of the political economy perspective has been to document the process by which the state and corporate power extend commodification. What this perspective needs to address more substantially is how or by what process political and economic power interacts in a hegemonic way to frame the agenda, prescribe the policy alternatives, and gain general social acceptance and institutional standing, even in the face of contradictions that give rise to opposition by social interests both during and after policy change.

A current challenge in understanding policy and the process of commodification is to better define and examine the notion of "public" and how this opposes the essentialism of a market agenda. On the one hand, the public sphere is set forward as a set of principles, including democracy, equality, participation, and citizenship, that points to an alternative to the set of practices bound up with commodification (Garnham, 1986; Murdock, 1990; Sparks & Dahlgren, 1991). This, however, can be a difficult concept to apply in a substantive way because the public sphere umbrella covers a wide range of definitions and positionings, whereby, for example, the state can be seen as an ally or foe of the public interest (Schiller, 1989). Moreover, the concept of public interest is generally applied in a legalistic manner to the regulation of the communication industries. This is problematic because it causes the concept of the public interest to lose its concrete reference to the subjects it purports to represent. As a result, the viability of the public interest concept appears particularly weak when set against the seemingly clearer tests of the marketplace and processes of commodification. As Anthony Smith (1989) argues, under these conditions the public good is increasingly defined in economic terms. It becomes mainly concerned with broadening consumer choice in a competitive market, as opposed to the notion of interests that transcend commercial gain and consumerism (Melody, 1990).

Although not abandoning these locational or philosophical approaches to the public interest, we suggest that some of the limitations of this concept can be overcome by defining the *public* as a set of social processes in the political economic matrix of society. These processes carry out democracy, namely, advancing equality and the fullest possible participation in the range of economic, political, social, and cultural decision making. The value of this approach is that the contestation for social equality and participation as opposed to commodification, or citizen versus consumer, is not restricted to a particular structure or location. In the case of policy, seen as a process, this central tension can more accurately be described in a number of terrains involving the market, the state, or social movements (Murdock, 1993).

The second substantive entry point is *spatialization*, or the process of overcoming the constraints of space and time in social life. Marx (1973) comes close to our interest here when, in the *Grundrisse*, he noted that capitalism "annihilates space with time." By this he meant that capital makes use of the means of transportation and communication to diminish the time it takes to move goods, people, and messages over space. Harold Innis (1972) developed this theme in analyses that established the connections among forms of media, time and space, and structures of power. Recent theorists modify Marx's view by suggesting that rather than annihilate space, capital transforms it (Lash & Urry, 1987; Webster & Robins, 1986). They remind us that people, products, and messages have to be somewhere, and it is this somewhere that is undergoing significant transformation. This is occurring both within national social and economic relations and globally through the internationalization of production and expanding industrialization. State policy changes at a broad level play a central role in these transformations. Communication policy is of particular interest because communications is one of the key infrastructural underpins of all social and economic activity and is a central component in the process of spatialization.

Spatialization is similar to concepts offered by geographers and sociologists to address structural changes brought about by the shifting uses of space and time. Giddens (1990) refers to the centrality of *time-space distanciation* in order to examine the decline of time-space dependency and the ways through which time and space become resources for those who can make use of them. Harvey (1989) identifies *time-space compression* to suggest how the effective map of the world is shrinking, again for those who can take advantage of it. Castells (1989) calls our attention to the declining importance of physical space, the space of places, and the rising significance of the *space of flows* to suggest that the world map is being redrawn according to boundaries established by flows of people, goods, and services. This creates what Massey (1992) calls a transformed "power-geometry."

Communication is central to spatialization because communication and information processes and technologies promote flexibility and control throughout business, particularly within the communication and information businesses themselves. Spatialization encompasses the much-abused term *globalization*, which perhaps best refers to the worldwide restructuring of industries and firms. Restructuring at the industry level is exemplified by the development of integrated markets based on digital technologies and, at the firm level, by the growth of the flexible or "virtual" company, which makes use of communication and information systems to continuously change structure, product line, marketing, and relationships to other companies, suppliers, its work force, and customers.

The political economy of communication addresses this process principally in terms of the institutional extension of corporate power in the communication industry. This is manifested in the sheer growth in size of media firms, measured by assets, revenues, profit, employees, or share value. Political economy has specifically examined growth in relation to different forms of corporate concentration in the communication industries (Herman & Chomsky, 1988). These forms are horizontal concentration, vertical integration, backward vertical integration (down the production process), and joint ventures, strategic alliances, and other short-term, project-specific "teaming arrangements."

In addition to the reactive policy role by the state to these changes in corporate and industry structure, political economy has paid, and needs to increase, attention to the political or constitutive role of communication policy. Spatialization is not only driven by changing economic practices or the use of technology, but also by political actors. This involves the logic of concentrating power in order to gain some measure of control over decision making by those who, directly or indirectly, hold substantial sway over policymaking—internationally, regionally, nationally, and locally. This process of mutual constitution in policymaking also involves those who offer alternative or opposing objectives, such as government bureaucracies, trade unions, special interests and social movements, among others.

In the extensive literature on the regulation of communication industries, there is a consistent view that communication policy is driven by government reaction to market behaviors. This conception of regulation has led to considerable debate over a polarized choice between regulation and deregulation. However, the broader political economy view takes the entire social field, including the pattern of industry activity, as a form of regulation.

Rather than a narrow choice between market regulation (decision making) or state regulation, greater understanding can be achieved by concentrating and assessing the merits of a mix of different forms of regulation that foreground the market, the state, or interests that lie outside both for different groups in society.

As a starting point for a broader perspective, following the work of Murdock (1990), one can identify four dimensions of changed state constitutive activity. *Commercialization* establishes state functions, such as providing post- and telecommunications services, principally along business or revenue-generating lines. *Privatization* takes this a step further by turning these units into private businesses. *Liberalization* gives the state's approval to opening markets to competition. Finally, *internationalization* links the state to other states to shift economic and political authority to regional (EC, NAFTA) and international (GATT) commercial systems.

Commercialization takes place when the state replaces forms of regulation based on public interest, public service, and related standards, such as universality, with forms of regulation by markets. In practice this has meant greater emphasis on market position and profitability, such as audience size, advertising revenue, and exportable products in broadcasting, and investments in new telecommunications services to increase revenues from the more affluent, principally business, customers and lucrative international market places. Supporters of these policies (Noam, 1987) argue that public service goals are enhanced, whereas opponents maintain that commercially based decision making inevitably means one class of users benefits over others (Castells, 1989).

In the privatization process, the state sells off a public enterprise such as a broadcaster or telecommunications company. This process often stems from an ideological commitment to private control over any economic activity. The enterprise and market may, however, still be subject to some regulatory measures dealing with issues such as ownership requirements and types or areas of market participation. However, many have noticed that this involves a considerable narrowing of the public policy agenda, at the expense of social and cultural and longer term national policy objectives (Negrine & Papathanassopoulos, 1990; Noam, 1991).

State communication policies of liberalization expand the number of participants or competitors in the market. Over the past 20 years, states have changed the communication industry in most parts of the world by introducing private competitors over a range of broadcasting and, increasingly, telecommunications services. Although some prices may drop and new services created (Owen & Wildman, 1992), market regulation does not ensure that more than a narrowly privileged customer segment realizes the full range of potential benefits (Mosco, 1989).

Finally, states are also creating their own wide range of teaming arrangements or strategic alliances that integrate them in different degrees of internationalization. These include regional trade alliances, such as the North

American Free Trade Agreement, trade plus (such as financial, political and social links) arrangements like the EC, as well as institutional planning organizations, such as GATT. This has been particularly important in the communication arena because the transnationalization of communication networks requires some degree of intrastate coordination.

Commercialization, liberalization, privatization, and internationalization are among the more significant examples of the state's constitutive role. More importantly, they suggest the value of a political economy approach that starts from the mutual constitution of the industry and the state in the creation of forms of regulation. These reflect the needs and interests of capital and the nature of opposition at a particular historical period. Both industry and state are central to a political economy analysis for creating the form of regulation that governs the industry and the social field, including oppositional forces with a relationship to the industry.

The third entry point is *structuration*, a process given recent prominence in Giddens's (1984) work. Structuration describes the mutually constitutive interaction between social structures and human agency, with the former providing the very "medium" for this interaction. This amounts to a contemporary rendering of Marx's notion that people make history, but not under conditions of their own making. The term responds to concerns with functionalist, institutional, and structuralist approaches, arising out of their tendency to present structures as fully formed, determining entities. Specifically, it helps to balance a tendency in political economic analysis to concentrate on structures, typically business and governmental institutions, by incorporating the ideas of agency, social process, and social practice. Concretely, this means broadening the conception of class from its structural or categorical sense, which defines it in terms of what some have and others do not, to incorporate both a relational and constitutional sense of the term. A relational view of class foregrounds the connections, for example, between capital and labor, and the ways in which labor constitutes itself within the relationship and as an independent force in its own right. This takes nothing away from the value of seeing class, in part, as a zero-sum game that pits haves against have nots. The political economy of communication has addressed class in these terms by producing research that documents persistent inequities in communication systems, particularly access to the means of communication and to the reproduction of these inequities in social institutions (Golding & Murdock, 1991; Schiller, 1989).

Rethinking the political economy approach means expanding on this conception with, first, a relational view of class that defines it according to those practices and processes that link class categories. In this view, the working class is not defined simply by a lack of access to the means of communication, but by its relationships of harmony, dependency, and conflict that mutually constitute the capitalist class. Moreover, a constitutional conception of class views the working class as producer of its own, however tenuous, volatile, and conflicted, identity in relation to capital and independently of it. There is a pressing need to address the ways oppositional and alternative class-based movements, ranging from revolutionary struggles in Latin America, Asia, Africa and Eastern Europe, have used the mass media for social and political change to the uses of alternative media in the West by trade unions to provide an alternative to capitalist "common sense." The point is not to engage in romantic celebration, but, at the very least, to demonstrate how classes constitute themselves, how they make history, in the face of well-researched analysis of the conditions that constrain this history-making activity.

Rethinking political economy also means balancing another tendency in political economy: When it has given attention to agency, process, and social practice, it tends to focus on social class. There are good reasons for this emphasis. Class structuration is a central entry point for comprehending social life, and numerous studies have documented the persistence of class divisions in the political economy of communication. There are a number of studies that concentrate on the process by which class rule takes place in policymaking and regulation (Mosco, 1982; D. Schiller, 1981). These studies contribute to understanding the structure and process of elite rule. However, less attention has been paid to the consequences of this rule for the remainder of the class structure, by, for example, addressing the relationship of social class to communication access throughout the class structure. This is particularly relevant in the recent policy environment whereby state privatization, commercialization, and liberalization of communication systems have permitted market power to determine access to services. Additionally, the endorsement of user pay practices, such as by program or channel in cable, contribute to the formation of communication hierarchies, increasingly based on the ability to pay.

Other social class work includes studies on media elite class composition and its control over the media. For example, Clement's (1975) analysis included an assessment of media elites in Canada. More recent work pays greater attention to media outside of North America (Tunstall & Palmer, 1991) and to the growing networks of class rule that link mass media to new communication and information technologies (Mattelart, 1991). There are also studies that examine the dense web of connections between media entrepreneurs and the rest of the elite class, through the range of connections on corporate boards, business associations, civic organizations, and private clubs (Dreier, 1982; Herman & Chomsky, 1988; H. Schiller, 1981).

There are other dimensions to structuration that complement and conflict with class structuration, including gender, race, and those broadly defined social movements, which, along with class, constitute much of the social relations of communication. Unlike other approaches, political economy has not been entirely silent on the issue of gender, although it typically addresses the subject as a dimension of social class relations. Additionally, although communication studies has addressed the question of imperialism extensively, principally by examining the role of the media and information technology in its constitution, it has done so primarily to advance a sense of the world as class divided or, although less frequently, as gender divided, rather than to understand it as race divided. But one does not have to focus on South Africa to recognize that racial divisions are a principal constituent of the manifold hierarchies of the contemporary global political economy, and that race, as both category and social relationship, contributes fundamentally to one's access to national and global resources, including communications media and information technology (Ahmad, 1992; Sivanandan, 1990).

From this use of structuration theory, one might think about society as the ensemble of structuring actions initiated by agents that shape and are shaped by class, gender, race, and social movement relations. According to this view, society exists, if not as a seamless, sutured whole, at least as a field on which various processes mutually constitute identifiable social relationships. It thereby rejects the poststructuralist view that the social field is a continuum of subjectivities produced by purely nominal processes of categorization. Accordingly, class, race, gender, and social movements are real as both social relationships and instruments of analysis.

Social movements are particularly important for policy analysis because they influence the development of the means and content of communication. Analyses organized around social movements hold out the advantage of transcending traditional social categories by concentrating on social agency and social action. United by a specific interest, people from a range of identities oppose dominant power relations in policymaking. The success of social movements typically depends on their ability to transcend particular social categories by uniting diverse interests around a specific interest or cause. For example, the most significant international effort to oppose dominant forms of communication policymaking was the New World Communication and Information Order (Traber & Nordenstreng, 1992). Numerous social movements have taken on national and local policymaking processes, including efforts to democratize decisions about licensing, spectrum allocation, industry structure, and media content. Contemporary interest in the development of interactive cable and telecommunications networks and services, particularly the ferment over the state policies of several countries on the development of information superhighways, has breathed new life into the public interest movement (Coalition for Public Information, 1994; Electronic Frontier Foundation, 1994).

One of the major activities in structuration is the process of constructing hegemony, defined as what comes to be incorporated and contested as the taken-for-granted, common-sense, natural way of thinking about the world, including everything from cosmology through ethics to everyday social practices. Hegemony is a lived network of meanings and values, which, as they are experienced in practice, appear as mutually confirming and natural. Although political economy addresses agents as social rather than individual actors, one of the most significant features that needs to be addressed through the theory of hegemony is the process of individuation. This concept, taken chiefly from Poulantzas (1978), refers to the practice of redefining social actors, particularly capital and labor, as subjects whose values are articulated through notions of individual rights, individual expression, the individual right and responsibility to vote, and individual freedom of consumption. These actions are grounded in the philosophy of liberalism and instituted through legal systems and the exercise of class rule. Yet, despite these systemic characteristics, they isolate individuals from one another, from their social identities, and from those with the power to carry out individuation. Given this, one of the central tensions in contemporary political economy is between the social and individuating dimensions of structuration. In terms of the policymaking process, two major tasks for political economy are to recognize these tensions while identifying the sources of instability in the dominant hegemony and to assess the range of forms taken by oppositional and alternative hegemonies. Out of the tensions and clashes within various structuration processes, the media come to be organized in its full mainstream, oppositional, and alternative forms (Williams, 1974).

CONCLUSION

In exploring its mutual constitution with other disciplines, such as cultural studies and policy studies, political economy has taken on a philosophical approach that is open to subjectivity, more broadly inclusive, recognizes a more constitutive role of the state, and extends analysis over the entire social totality, with an eye to social transformation. Nevertheless, political economy rejects the tendencies to obscurantism, essentialism, and pluralism also found in these disciplines. Political economy insists on a realist epistemology that maintains the value of historical research, of thinking in terms of concrete social totalities, moral commitment, and overcoming the distinction between social research and social practice. Political economy also insists on the power of capital and the processes of commodification, spatialization, and structuration as the entry points for social analysis.

REFERENCES

Ahmad, A. (1992). *In theory: Classes, nations, literatures.* London: Verso.

Bagdikian, B.H. (1988). *The media monopoly* (2nd ed.). Boston: Beacon Press.

Benton, T. (1989). Marxism and natural limits: An ecological critique and reconstruction. *New Left Review, 178*, 51-86.

Boafo, S.T.K. (1991). Communication technology and dependent development in sub Saharan Africa. In G. Sussman & J.A. Lent (Eds.), *Transnational communications: Wiring the Third World* (pp. 103-124). Newbury Park, CA: Sage.

Brennan, G., & Buchanan, J.M. (1985). *The reason of rules: Constitutional political economy.* New York: Cambridge University Press.

Cardoso, F.H., & Faletto, E. (1979). *Dependency and development in Latin America.* Berkeley: University of California Press.

Carlyle, T. (1984). *A Carlyle reader* (G.B. Tennyson, Ed.). New York: Cambridge University Press.

Castells, M. (1989). *The informational city: Information technology, economic restructuring, and the urban-regional process.* Oxford: Basil Blackwell.

Clement, W. (1975). *The Canadian corporate elite: An analysis of economic power.* Toronto: McClelland and Stewart.

Coalition for Public Information. (1994). *Principles for information policy.* Ottawa: Author.

Coase, R.H., & Barrett, E. W. (1968). *Educational TV: Who should pay?* Washington, DC: American Enterprise Institute for Public Policy.

Coase, R.H. (1991). *The nature of the firm: Origins, evolution, and development* (O.E. Williamson & S.G. Winter, Eds.). New York: Oxford University Press.

Coulter, B. G. (1992). *A new social contract for Canadian telecommunication policy.* Unpublished doctoral dissertation, Carleton University, Department of Sociology and Anthropology, Ottawa, Canada.

Davis, M. (1990). *City of quartz.* New York: Verso.

Davis, S.G. (1986). *Parades and power: Street theatre in nineteenth-century Philadelphia.* Philadelphia: Temple University Press.

Douglas, S. (1986). *Labor's new voice: Unions and the mass media.* Norwood, NJ: Ablex.

Dreier, P. (1982). The position of the press in the US power structure. *Social Problems, 29*(3), 293-310.

Dyson, K. (1990). Luxembourg: Changing autonomy of an international broadcasting power. In K. Dyson & P. Humphreys (Eds.), *The political economy of communications: International and European dimensions* (pp. 125-147). London: Routledge.

Electronic Frontier Foundation. (1994). *The open platform.* Washington, DC: Author.

Ewen, S. (1976). *Captains of consciousness.* New York: McGraw Hill.

Foster, J.B. (1988). The fetish of Fordism. *Monthly Review, 39,* 14-20.

Galbraith, J.K. (1985). *The new industrial state* (4th ed.). Boston: Houghton Mifflin.

Gandy, O.H., Jr. (1992, Summer). The political economy approach: A critical challenge. *Journal of Media Economics,* pp. 23-42.

Garnham, N. (1986). The media and the public sphere. In P. Golding, G.Murdock & P. Schlesinger (Eds.), *Communicating politics: Mass communication and the political process* (pp. 37-52). Leicester: Leicester University Press.

Garnham, N. (1990). *Capitalism and communication.* London: Sage.

Giddens, A. (1984). *The constitution of society: Outline of a theory of structuration.* Berkeley: University of California Press.

Giddens, A. (1990). *The consequences of modernity.* Stanford: Stanford University Press.

Golding, P., & Murdock, G. (1991). Culture, communication, and political economy. In J. Curran & M. Gurevitch (Eds.), *Mass media and society* (pp. 15-32). London: Edward Arnold.

Harvey, D. (1989). *The condition of postmodernity.* Oxford: Basil Blackwell.

Herman, E.S., & Chomsky, N. (1988). *Manufacturing consent: The political economy of the mass media.* New York: Pantheon.

Hills, J., with Papathanassopoulos, S. (1991). *The democracy gap: The politics of information and communication technologies in the United States and Europe.* New York: Greenwood.

Innis, H. (1972). *Empire and communications.* Toronto: University of Toronto.

Jevons, W.S. (1965). *The theory of political economy.* New York: A.M. Kelley.

Jussawalla, M. (1986). *The passing of remoteness: the information revolution in the Asia-Pacific.* Singapore: Institute of Southeast Asian Studies.

Lash, S., & Urry, J. (1987). *The end of organized capitalism.* Madison: University of Wisconsin.

Lipietz, A. (1988). Reflections on a tale: The Marxist foundations of the concepts of regulation and accumulation. *Studies in Political Economy, 26,* 7-36.

MacDonald, G. (1990). *The emergence of global multi-media conglomerates.* (Working Paper No. 70, Multinational Enterprises Program). Geneva: International Labor Office.

Malthus, T.R. (1966). *Essay on population.* New York: Macmillan. (Original work published 1798)

Mander, J. (1978). *Four arguments for the elimination of television.* New York: Morrow.

Marshall, A. (1961). *Principles of economics.* London: Macmillan. (Original work published 1890)

Marx, K. (1973). *The Grundrisse: Foundations of the critique of political economy* (M. Nicolaus, Trans.). Harmondsworth: Penguin.

Marx, K. (1976). *Capital: A critique of political economy* (Vol. 1, B. Fowkes, Trans.). London: Penguin.

Massey, D. (1992). Politics and space/time. *New Left Review, 196,* 65-84.

Mattelart, A. (1991). *Advertising international: The privatization of public space* (M. Chanan, Trans.). London: Comedia and Routledge.

Mattelart, A., & Mattelart, M. (1992). *Rethinking media theory: Signposts and new directions* (J. A. Cohen & M. Urquidi, Trans.). Minneapolis: University of Minnesota. (Original work published 1986)

Mattelart, A., & Siegelaub, S. (1983). *Communication and class struggle. Vol. 2: Liberation, socialism.* New York: International General.

Melody, W. (1990). The information in I.T.: Where lies the public interest. *Intermedia, 18*(3), 10-18.

Morris-Suzuki, T. (1986). The challenge of computers. *New Left Review, 160,* 81-91.

Mosco, V. (1982). *Pushbutton fantasies: Critical perspectives on videotex and information technology.* Norwood, NJ: Ablex.

Mosco, V. (1989). *The pay-per society: Computers and communication in the information Age.* Toronto: Garamond; Norwood, NJ: Ablex.

Mosco, V. (1990a). The mythology of telecommunications deregulation. *Journal of Communication, 40*(1), 36-49.

Mosco, V. (1990b). Toward a transnational world information order. *Canadian Journal of Communication, 15*(2), 46-63.

Mosco, V. & Wasko, J. (Eds.). (1983). *The critical communications review. Vol.1: Labor, the working class, and the media.* Norwood, NJ: Ablex.

Murdock, G. (1990). Redrawing the map of the communication industries. In M. Ferguson (Ed.), *Public communication: The new imperatives* (pp. 1-15). Beverly Hills: Sage.

Murdock, G. (1993). Communication and the constitution of modernity. *Media, Culture & Society, 15*(4), 521-539.

Murdock, G., & Golding, P. (1979). Capitalism, communication, and class relations. In J. Curran, M. Gurevitch, & J. Woolacott (Eds.), *Mass communication and society* (pp. 12-43). Beverly Hills: Sage.

Negrine, R (1990). British television in the age of change. In K. Dyson & P. Humphreys (Eds.), *The political economy of communications: International and European Dimensions* (pp. 148-170). London: Routledge.

Negrine, R., & Papathanassopoulos, S. (1990). *The internalization of television.* London: Pinter.

Noam, E.M. (1987). The public telecommunications network: A concept in transition. *Journal of Communication, 37*(1), 30-48.

Noam, E.M. (1991). *Television in Europe.* New York: Oxford University.

Owen, R. (1851). *Labor: Its history and prospects.* New York. n. p.

Owen, B.M., & Wildman, S.S. (1992). *Video economics.* Cambridge, MA: Harvard University Press.

Poulantzas, N. (1978). *State, power, and socialism.* London: New Left Books.

Raboy, M. (1990). *Missed opportunities.* Montreal: McGill-Queens.

Resnick, S.A., & Wolff, R.D. (1987). *Knowledge and class: A Marxian critique of political economy.* Chicago: University of Chicago.

Rideout, V. (1993). Telecommunication policy for whom?: An analysis of recent CRTC decisions. *Alternate Routes, 10,* 27-56.

Roach, C. (Ed.). (1993). *Communication and culture in war and peace.* Newbury Park, CA: Sage.

Roncagliolo, R. (1986). Transnational communication and culture. In R. Atwood & E. G. McAnany (Eds.), *Communication and Latin American society* (pp. 79-88). Madison: University of Wisconsin.

Schiller, D. (1981). *Objectivity and the news.* Philadelphia: University of Pennsylvania Press.

Schiller, H.I. (1981). *Who knows: Information in the age of the Fortune 500.* Norwood, NJ: Ablex.

Schiller, H. I. (1989). *Culture, Inc.* New York: Oxford University Press.

Schiller, H. I. (1992). *Mass communication and American empire.* Boston: Beacon Press. (Original work published 1969)

Sivanandan, A. (1990). *Communities of resistance: Writings on black struggles for socialism.* London: Verso.

Smith, A. (1937). *An inquiry into the nature and causes of the wealth of nations.* New York: Modern Library. (Original work published 1776)

Smith, A. (1976). *The theory of moral sentiments.* Indianapolis: Liberty Classics. (Original work published 1759)

Smith, A. (1989). The public interest. *Intermedia, 17*(2), 10-24.

Smythe, D.W. (1977). Communications: Blindspot of Western Marxism. *Canadian journal of political and social theory, I*(3), 1-27.

Smythe, D.W. (1981). *Dependency road: Communication, capitalism, consciousness and Canada.* Norwood, NJ: Ablex.

Sparks, C., & Dahlgren, P. (Eds.). (1991). *Communication and citizenship: Journalism and the public sphere in the new media age.* London: Routledge.

Stigler, G. J. (Ed.). (1988). *Chicago studies in political economy.* Chicago: University of Chicago.

Tang,W.H., & Chan, J.M. (1990). The political economy of international news coverage: A study of dependent communication development. *Asian Journal of Communication, 1*(1), 53-80.

Traber, M., & Nordenstreng, K. (Eds.). (1992). *Few voices, many worlds: Towards a media reform movement.* London: World Association for Christian Communication.

Tunstall, J., & Palmer, M. (1991). *Media moguls.* London: Routledge.

Veblen, T. (1932). *The theory of the business enterprise.* New York: Scribner's.

Veblen, T. (1934). *The theory of the leisure class.* New York: Modern Library. (Original work published 1899)

Vipond, M. (1989). *The mass media in Canada.* Toronto: James Lorimer and Company.

Wallerstein, I. (1979). *The capitalist world economy.* New York: Cambridge University.

Wasko, J., & Mosco, V. (Eds.). (1992). *Democratic communication in the information age.* Toronto: Garamond.

Webster, F., & Robins, K. (1986). *Information technology: A Luddite analysis.* Norwood, NJ: Ablex.

Williams, R. (1974). *Television, technology and cultural form.* London: Fontana.

Winseck, D. (1993). *A study of regulatory change and the deregulatory process in Canadian telecommunications with particular emphasis on telecommunications labor unions.* Unpublished doctoral dissertation, University of Oregon, School of Journalism and Communication, Eugene, OR.

Chapter 2

Critical Communication Pedagogy: Teaching and Learning for Democratic Life

Mashoed Bailie

Critical communication scholarship is rooted in the assumption that social institutions and human relations are relations of history, power, and struggle. As such, institutions and social relations tend to reflect the outcomes of historical struggles. At the level of institutional structures, these outcomes are often described in terms of continued concentration of ownership and/or control of communication technologies. At the level of agency, questions concerning the relations between the necessary conditions for democracy(freedom of speech, access to the means of communication, mechanisms for effective participation in the political process, and emancipation from oppression and unjust social relations) are weighed against actual life conditions. A goal of critical communication studies is for more democratic, emancipatory forms of citizenship: forms that promote and provide room for the diverse voices and stories of multiple communities of persons. To this end, critical communication studies are intricately linked to a project that promotes a critical imagination: the ability to think beyond present social, political, and economic conditions and to participate in the construction of alternative futures.

In this chapter, the broad goals of critical communication theory are problematized in relation to the existing institutional arrangements of communication studies in higher education in the United States: specifically, the undergraduate arrangements of skills-oriented programs that perpetuate a reproduction model of education that situates students as potential labor, communication industries as prospective employers, and educators as skills trainers—intermediaries—between workers and employers. Often, this "skills orientation" devalues participatory and dialogical classroom practices in favor of didactic pedagogical methods and what Freire (1981) has called a "banking" model of education.

The discussion concerning information and power, in relation to communication technologies and the potential for the promotion of more democratic social and political economic institutions and practices, is situated within the reality of television production practices in institutions of higher learning. The questions raised here focus on what it means for citizens to be educated in an increasingly concentrated "community" of corporate and governmental agencies. Although the discussion certainly pertains to communication studies in general (and broadly to education as an instrument of democracy), the locus of this chapter is on television production in particular. The intention here is to deliberately rend television production practices from their normative moorings within particular corporate histories that tend to justify the instrumental and often undemocratic uses of communication technologies.

The history of communication technologies, and their corresponding cultural goods, is a history of power: a history of political, economic, and social struggle over who controls the innovation, production, distribution, and delivery of the products of human labor. Although "television" often debates (and mainstream media education takes this up as a normative issue) what can and cannot be shown on television (censorship issues, freedom of the press, etc.), what is always lacking in this intracommunicational debate is precisely what critical communication scholars relentlessly strive to uncover: the ownership, the control, the production, the distribution, and the consumption contexts of technological and cultural commodities. It is exactly these areas of technological configuration, as they collectively provide ritualistic meaning to lived experiences, that students of television production in institutions of higher learning are asked to normalize and habituate themselves to. Indeed, not only are students of television production generally habituated to the processes of global capital in the form of multinational corporate control over communication technologies and products, they are simultaneously encouraged to reproduce the human relations of power that these same industries inculcate in practice.

Critical communication scholarship takes seriously the development of democratic institutions and social practices that increase the value of democracy for global human life. The information produced and provided by critical communication scholarship in the various fields of critical political economy of communication and critical cultural studies provides powerful and necessary correctives to our understanding of the relationship between technology, communication, and political, economic, and social life. Yet, having said this, it is lamentable to note an inadequate reformation of television production theory and practice in higher education: a reinvention that might counteract the decidedly undemocratic and oppressive tendencies inherent in mainstream media production courses. It is disingenuous to conscientiously participate in the production of knowledge appropriate for the development of a just and democratic society while simultaneously neglecting the very reproduction of unjust and undemocratic practices within the institutional theater of higher learning. University television production courses most often take place in a climate of "hire" education: one that unproblematically conditions students to the norms of media institutions and practices while leaving unquestioned the repressive and unrepresentative views of human possibilities advanced by concentrated power.

CRITICAL COMMUNICATION PEDAGOGY
IN A CLIMATE OF "HIRE" EDUCATION

"Hire" education as a climate surrounding television production courses within academe is a specific system of educational rituals, attitudes, relationships, and practices, with a predilection for situating students as potential labor, mainstream media industries as prospective employers, and faculty as mediators between the needs of communication corporations and student potentialities. Within this framework, communication education is reduced to "skills training," and the outcomes are measured in terms of securing entry-level, low-paying jobs in media markets. It is an onerous task indeed to separate out the various institutionalized taken-for-granted and unquestioned associations within the teaching and learning site that normalize corporate communication practices and routinize television production teaching and learning: rationalizing pedagogy within the logic of the marketplace. Furthermore, this is not a question that can be answered directly. Television production courses within "hire" learning makes sense precisely because they appeal to power: The curriculum is reasonable because it is rational, and it is rational because it satisfies the needs of a particularly dominant view of the world wherein human agents are viewed not as creative subjects that might understand and change the world, but as objects that might reproduce the needs of industries. Students are never seen as potential inscribers of their own unique visions, but as those who are inscribed on with the visions of others: encouraged to live out their lives envisioning and bringing to fruition the dominant imaginings of concentrated power.

When looked at from the vantage point of critical communication scholarship's mission to advance understandings that might potentially transform the world—that promulgate humane institutional arrangements and practices—mainstream television production courses are indeed fraudulent representations of, and missed opportunities for, pedagogical possibilities. It becomes quite clear, as we uncover the strategy of capital as a system of thought that links democracy to the global marketplace, that conflicting perspectives will be met with confrontation. On Garnham's (1990) account: "It is in the interest of the controllers of multinational capital to keep nation-states and their citizens in a state of disunity and dysfunctional ignorance unified only by market structures" (p. 113).

Garnham's perception can be located in the television production site—both in pedagogical practices and technological engagements. Briefly, mainstream television production education as currently contrived is inadequate to the task of promoting the transformation that critical communication scholarship strives toward. The product of critical communication scholarship is insufficient to the development of critical citizenship because it fails to problematize the teaching and learning environment in which knowledge is engaged. The result of this undertheorizing of pedagogy results in the reproduction of relations of power that promote, rather than challenge and transform, the unjust and undemocratic hierarchies of power in society. Knowledge simply cannot be "transmitted" unproblematically. This maxim should not be overlooked: "critical" knowledge remains critical only insofar as the conditions of its practice are critical. Education for critical citizenship then requires a rethinking of the grounds upon which our various knowledges are engaged.

Television production practices in higher education require scrutiny precisely because they offer students the possibility of combining critical communication theory and media production practice. However, the problem is not merely how one might "inject" critical communication theory into television production courses in order to promote praxis: substantively, it concerns the ways in which we understand our responsibilities as pedagogues and how we develop the possibility for the exercise of critical citizenship at the teaching and learning site. The following discussion concerns the development of precisely these conditions that might enhance the potential for a critical communication pedagogy. First, I review the challenge that critical education theory has provided within the broad field of education theory over the last few decades. Second, the dominant trends of television production theory are examined. Finally, the possibilities for developing a critical communication pedagogy for television production courses are discussed.

CRITICAL EDUCATION THEORY

There has been considerable effort within the field of critical education theory to challenge dominant mainstream teaching and learning practices as currently constituted in the United States. Much of this work is pertinent to a critical communication pedagogy as it anticipates in essence and in substance the intentions of critical communication scholarship generally. Critical pedagogy proffers a discourse on schooling that privileges the development of the necessary conditions, both ideological and material, for the development of a democratic public sphere (Apple, 1981; Giroux, 1983; Gouldner, 1979). Underlying this perspective are a number of critical assumptions concerning the nature of schooling. First, that it is necessary to develop a discourse that uncovers the dialectic relations between social classes and their maintenance of, or resistance to, social limitations. Second, that schools are perceived of as sites of social contradiction (see Giroux, 1983).

Mainstream education theory and practice as currently constituted has come under increased scrutiny during the last two decades (Apple, 1990; Aronowitz & Giroux, 1985; Bowles & Gintis, 1976; Freire, 1981; Giroux, 1981), although much of this research has yet to be taken up within the field of critical communication studies. Essentially, critical pedagogy challenges educators to take the political nature of education seriously: to appreciate that education does more than merely represent political and cultural relations in society—that it also reproduces the conditions for these relations and practices. Thus, education is not politically, economically, or socially neutral. On the contrary, all education can be located as a "technology of power."[1] When understood in this light, the role of the educator becomes one of advocate, implicit or explicit, for the continued reproduction of the status quo or, contrarily, for change. Giroux (1983) also warns against the functionalist approaches of traditional mainstream education that celebrate individualism and emphasize skills training over preparation of students to take an active role in shaping the societies in which they live. The traditional "transmission" approach to teaching and learning fails in this regard; the development of a critical citizenry requires students to actively engage in, participate in, and transform their knowledge base in critical pedagogical and dialogical practices (Trent, 1990).

Critical education theory begins with the assumption that educational practices are never value neutral; that implicit in theories of education are "particular version[s] of what knowledge is of most worth . . . what direction we should desire, what it means to know something . . . how we might construct representations of ourselves, others and our physical and social environment" (Giroux, 1988, p. 12).

For example, although it may appear to be self-evident that educators encourage students to become successful and responsible citizens, this assumption carries with it unspoken views of what kind of world one wants to live in, what it means to be responsible, and how one should measure success.

---

[1]Pedagogical practice refers to forms of cultural production that are inextricably historical and political. Pedagogy is, in part, a technology of power, language, and practice that produces and legitimates forms of moral and political regulation that construct and offer human beings particular views of themselves and the world.

Such notions are embedded in ideologies that promote normative interpretations of the social and its relationship to the personal. These normative assumptions about the social world help reproduce the economic and political structures and relations in society. In turn, these relations conceal interpretations of what democracy might mean and the role that a truly critical citizenry might play within it. Understanding the relationship between pedagogy and the promotion of democracy is vital for critical communication scholars especially because our field generally fails to ask substantive questions concerning the practices of teaching and learning. Paulo Friere (1981), the Brazilian educator and theorist, has consistently argued for the political nature of, and the active participation of students in, their education for life:

> There is no such thing as a neutral educational process. Education either functions as an instrument which is used to facilitate the integration of the younger generation into the logic of the present system and bring about conformity to it, or it becomes the "practice of freedom" — the means by which men and women deal critically with reality and discover how to participate in the transformation of their world. (p. 15)

Critical education then embraces a concept of education that challenges students to take their responsibility as moral citizens seriously: to participate in the development of conditions and critiques that promote social transformation while uncovering, resisting, and challenging the supposed "naturalness" or "neutralness" of the way things are. Education for democracy must provide the conditions for critical reflection, social critique, and the possibility for change.

Ira Shor (1988), while attempting to develop a critical approach to teaching and learning, offers an historical backdrop to the conservative emphasis on vocational training in education. His analysis argues that the historical emphasis on liberal arts in U.S. education was compromised in the 1970s when the Nixon Administration spent "tens of millions of dollars" to "vocationalize school systems from the top to bottom" (p. 104). Shor argues that the conservative governmental and corporate attack on liberal arts education was a reaction to the mass movements of the 1960s that raised serious questions concerning the nature of society as a whole. According to Shor's analysis, the political economy of the 1970s—a reactionary government and corporate response to the student movements of the 1960s and a deepening economic recession—gave rise to "a curricular model that blamed underemployment on the victim for lacking job skills and literacy skills, and turned finally to an aggressive careerism that was opposed to the people's historical aspirations about school" (p. 105).

The trend to link education with the global marketplace has increased over the last decade as students come to classes determined to understand "knowledge" in instrumental terms that situate them as objects to be molded rather than as subjects who might contribute meaningfully to the social debate. This tendency to locate schools as training grounds for skills that promise to make one "employable" contradict the more powerful potential inherent in the pedagogical space: As Gramsci (1971) argued: "But democracy by definition, cannot mean merely that an unskilled worker become skilled. It must mean that every citizen can govern and that society places [citizens] even if only abstractly, in a general condition to achieve this" (p. 40).

Critical pedagogy understands citizenship in this active sense, situating itself in opposition to the dominant mainstream or vocational paradigm that adheres to a form of instrumental rationality. Instrumental is used here in Giroux's sense to mean that the languages and practices of education theory have tended to benefit "certain groups of elites who become the managers of society," or the way in which these discourses "[narrow] the scope of education so severely that schools become mere factories to train the work force" (Giroux, 1992, p. 114). Rather than understanding education as merely functioning to provide occupational skills or unproblematically reproducing contemporary social relations, critical pedagogy encourages students "to take risks and struggle with ongoing relations of power . . . to envisage a world which is 'not yet' in order to . . . improve the grounds upon which life is lived" (Simon, 1989, p. 375). Importantly, with this approach to education, students have the opportunity to critically examine the role that society in its various guises has played in their own self-formation and to explore and uncover the predominant social function of schooling and knowledge as it reproduces sometimes unequal social relations and practices.

Critical education theory is an avenue for the linkage of critical communication theory and media production practices in the lives of students as they engage in school life as social and political beings. By drawing on central concerns raised by critical education theory around notions of citizenship, participatory democracy, and school life, a bridge can be built between critical communication theory and media production teaching and learning. Television production courses are precisely located in the instrumental logic described previously: They are legitimized by their perceived and often very real relationship to corporate communication institutions. Indeed, television production courses are most often justified on the grounds that they provide students with the necessary skills for employment. The dominant approaches toward television production in higher education are presented next followed by a discussion concerning the possibilities for, and the potentials of, a critical communication pedagogy for television production education.

MAINSTREAM TELEVISION PRODUCTION COURSES

Television production courses in higher education are explicitly concerned with the "disciplines" and "techniques" associated with the production of visual and audio messages for audiences of consumers.[2] Furthermore, and as discussed shortly, such courses model student performances on perceived industry norms. Essentially, television production courses provide students with the opportunity to drill and become proficient in the processes of producing programming for broadcast television. In order to accomplish this task, students take up various "roles" in the production process from director to actor (Zettl, 1992). The positions that students assume provide boundaries within which performances take place; in other words, student impersonations correspond to hierarchies within the broadcast television workplace. Television production requires not only a specialized personnel, but also a "language" for students that consists of technical and implicitly aesthetic commands that reflect the director's desired aims. Beyond commands, it is necessary to know the names for, and the functioning of, the technical equipment: to be able to distinguish between various types of microphones, lights, cables, adapters, splitters, converters, and so on. Students also have to understand the technical processes such as white balancing a camera, setting the iris, or checking vectorscopes and wave-form monitors. Furthermore, they have to appreciate the principles of light control: how to set lighting, how to eliminate or create shadow, or how to block cameras for shooting.

Nothing discussed thus far indicates what the content of the program might be, what form it may take, nor the relationships that will develop among and between the students and the teacher. Indeed, there are no "natural" outcomes in this regard, for theory is not something that the equipment dictates. Rather, theory is what students and teachers bring with them to the process of television production—a life-long experience of using the technologies and consuming the products of television. What generally passes for "television production theory" is presented as nothing other than how to "use" the equipment to produce standards that allow the technology to function at its full capacity.

This "neutral" perspective presented by mainstream television production theory rests on an unproblematic association between education and the business of media industries. However, when looked at carefully, it becomes apparent that "neutral" means nothing other than the reproduction of the status quo. Television production courses (limited to "news" "weather" "advertising" and "documentary" genres as they often are)[3] teach students skills and habituate them to relationships that are deemed necessary by the managers of the electronic media for entry-level, low-paying jobs in the industry. These courses also enforce the "professional" rules of conduct that students might expect to meet in the "real world" and "on the job."

---

[2]Indeed, the title of these texts (e.g., Burrows, Wood, & Gross, 1989) speaks directly to this pervasive form of reasoning.

[3]Communication studies students who major in television production most often find themselves placed in introductory courses that feed into mainstream news programs, in which "professional" deadlines, formats, and production relations force particular ways of understanding media in society.

There should be little doubt concerning the interrelatedness between mainstream television production workshops and professional electronic media corporations: The relationship is based on an unproblematized notion of the role of media education in democratic society. For example, Stephens (1981) has argued that "journalism departments are not English literature departments. They are by definition training people to practice a profession" (p. 49). The source of this "definition" is never mentioned, but clearly the point here is that "journalism department" means "skills training"—something quite different from preparing student citizens to take up active and critical roles in society. When television production courses are seen, by definition, as a "skills training ground" for corporate interests, it should not seem strange that they will be measured according to industry standards. Funkhouser and Savage (1987) provide us with this next step as they bemoan: "Unfortunately, there is evidence which indicates many broadcast managers may be dissatisfied with the job-related attitudes and behaviour of these young people" (p. 23). Pedagogy, as they understand it, amounts to preparing students for the needs of mainstream media industries. Thus, students are, within this context, encouraged to submit and to conform, to reproduce rather than to challenge and transform.

Although television production courses potentially provide a space for the coming together of a critically oriented theory of communication and democracy in practice, mainstream television production "theory" suggests an uncritical acceptance of the "professionalism" that makes student voices invisible and, thus, true dialogue impossible.

Dominant mainstream television production courses, rather than preparing students for positions as critical citizens and transformers of their worlds, prepare students for jobs. Before students begin to question, struggle, or express their own unique visions of the world, they are trained to conform and adapt. Mainstream communication research supports this pedagogical ideology by seeking out the "objective" and "real" needs of potential employers and transmitting them to students and teachers as a form of "objective' knowledge (see e.g., Hudson, 1987; Roosenraad & Wares, 1983).

MAINSTREAM PRODUCTION "THEORY"

Television production courses are situated at an intersection between two powerful cultural agencies: the university and the electronic media. Far from being "neutral" transmitters of knowledge, television production courses are informed by actively constructed knowledge that rests on fixed assumptions about the social world and human agency. Indeed, mainstream communication research solicits, and attempts to transmit to students, this ideologically laden knowledge provided by media institutions. Although television production courses are presented as "neutral" or "natural" teaching and learning sites, the knowledge-informing production practice is highly ideological. The underlying aggressiveness of mainstream broadcast teaching and learning practices moves beyond the "necessity" to conform to industry norms and to struggle and compete with other students for limited positions within the industry to reflect, only too well, the "realities" of market-driven, profit-oriented institutions:

> Fired from an agency? By students? That's a possibility that advertising students in our beginning creative class take seriously. They have the power to fire. Or they might be fired. The option of firing is one more step toward realism that we've successfully introduced into creative assignments. (Whitlow, 1983, p. 19)

It is clear from this quotation that these practices are unconscionable celebrations of an instrumental view of human life. Here, the educational process, along with any possibility for social transformation, is reduced to the objectification of market relations and practices. Students are reduced to "workers," whereas human relations are concentrated into instrumental routines. Meanwhile, the potentially liberating opportunities that might inhere in a dialogical pedagogy that favored critical self-reflectivity and the possibility for social and personal transformation is silenced while the status quo is unapologetically reproduced. In effect, this dominant form of teaching and learning in television production legitimates and privileges a particular form of knowing the world that takes shape and becomes real in practice. Of all possible worlds, students are inculcated into relations and practices that reproduce the conditions of domination and control under which they will later be expected to live and work. It is a self-legitimating, self-fulfilling prophesy that re-enforces an inflexible conception of the world: It is a world that must be accommodated, not transformed. Schiller (1973) has similarly argued, although in another context: "It can be demonstrated that the content and form of messages, far from being value-free, are deliberately designed to promote dominant institutional outlooks and behaviour" (p. 80).

It is important to understand that what gets taught in communication studies departments—specifically, television production courses—is evidence of particular ways of understanding the relationship among technology, human agency, and democratic life. Teaching practices are woven with research agendas in that what is taken as valuable, meaningful, or necessary research shapes the kinds of knowledge produced by academics. Smith (1983), for example, reports on a symposium held by industry managers and academics from the field of communication studies. Melvin Goldberg, Vice President of Technological research for ABC Television calls on academics to focus on audience behaviors because "we need to know who is watching what and why they are watching." Goldberg argues for "studies on social values, attitudes, lifestyles" and explains the necessity of linking this knowledge production to the "effect" it will have on "commercial sales" (cited in Smith, 1983, p. 186). Robert Maxwell, Vice President of Research for Home Box Office (HBO), called for the development of "more precise and sophisticated audience measurement tools," and Marshall Ottenfeld of the Masius Advertising Agency demanded that "media research mature. Advertisers, like broadcasters, need more valid and reliable counts of media vehicle audiences" (cited in Smith, 1983, p. 187).

What becomes apparent from the preceding is an acquiescence of pedagogy to economic relations and a form of technological determinism. The real dichotomy is not between skills building and active critical citizenship, for clearly there is a need for both. Rather, it is between the fortification of what is and the possibilities for change. The issue here is whether we resist or facilitate human and societal transformation. There is no question that students require skills. If their intended goal is to work in the media industries, they will require considerable skill in the uses of technologies of communication—that is not at issue. What is at issue is the context within which students learn and teachers teach. At risk is the reduction of human relationships to the economic and technical.

If ideology is a socially constructed way of understanding the world, all teaching is ideological. The question facing pedagogues is what visions of the world find spaces for articulation, which social, cultural, ethnic, and gender utterances find space to breath. Mainstream pedagogical theory supports these normative values of the dominant media, and although this knowledge is not unproblematically transmitted to students, it does serve to "mobilize support for the special interests that dominate" media institutions and practices (Chomsky, 1988, p. xi). Tied to the cultural and political economy, this perspective curtails students' capacities to take risks and struggle with the dominant television form because the context within which they are asked to perform and succeed is normalized within the values provided by contemporary media institutions. Success means the ability to reproduce oneself in terms of mainstream media norms. Failure is anything "short' of that goal.

Television production research and practice is supported by a multitude of technical and/or aesthetic texts designed to indoctrinate students with industry attitudes and perspectives although purporting to provide "neutral" or "value-free" information to students concerning such concepts as camera use, lighting techniques, or sound and editing styles. Such texts come replete with narrative and pictorial examples of the dominant mainstream media and their technologies that reinforce the values embedded in their orientation.

TELEVISION PRODUCTION TEXTS AND TEACHER KNOWLEDGE: DRAWING THE BOUNDARIES

It is difficult to open an introduction to television production text without being overwhelmed by the technological. This is, of course, understandable: The text is demonstrating the technologies involved in producing television programs.

The term itself—*television*—is imbued with history and expectation. Our students have grown up with television: They have known it, befriended it, at an early and uncritical age. They have accepted its production values; its narrative structures; its violence, sexism, racism; its entertainment value; its news, commentaries, talk shows, sporting events, and its underlying commercial character. Thus, in coming to the television production site, students often are in awe of, as well as have an expectation of learning to reproduce, mainstream television productions. The following critique of TV production texts refuses the normative grounds upon which such texts are situated. The texts are not critiqued on the basis of how well they perform the function of acclimatizing students to the values inherent in mainstream media practices as discussed previously. Rather, they are discussed within a concept of pedagogical practice: How are they implicated in a refusal to dialogical and dialectical praxis? By contextualizing the television production text in a concept of critical teaching and learning practices, we can uncover the didactic and anti-liberatory tendencies inherent in their suggested uses.

Television production texts providing students with an "introduction to television production" are abundant (see e.g., Aldridge & Liggett, 1990; Armer, 1990; Burrows et al., 1989; Compesi & Sherriffs, 1990; Fielding, 1990; Richards, 1992; Whittaker, 1989, 1993; Zettl, 1990, 1992). These textbooks vary considerably, no doubt, as they compete for "audiences" in their style, formatting, shape, color, and layout, although their content is essentially similar. They represent themselves as "objective" transmitters of technological knowledge necessary to communicate through the electronic media. Indeed, their very abundance speaks to the power behind them: the publishing industry. The original audience for these texts is hardly the students: It is the academics who teach television production courses who have to be "sold" on the "image" the text is attempting to sell. Thus, the final form that these texts take may be as much the constraints placed on writers by publishers as it is the writers themselves.

None of the texts surveyed provided substantial critiques of the media. To the contrary, there is an explicit celebration of mainstream media structures, relations, and practices. The texts challenge students to struggle and compete to secure entry-level jobs and reproduce the status quo. Whittaker (1993) argues that students have to "face the realities of an extremely competitive profession" and to think of their educational experience in production as evidence to a potential employer of "proof of performance," as a way for an employer to "identify good prospects from a torrent of applicants," and as serving the interests of employers by "reducing expensive on-the-job training" (p. v). This orientation to television production encourages students to accept unproblematically the logic of the dominant ideology and separates the "real world" of practical application from the "unreal world' of media theory and critique.

Giroux (1992) raises questions pertinent to this discussion concerning the ways in which technologies of communication, and the logic that drives them, reproduce unequal and unjust social relations: "How are communicational devices able to re-inscribe the human subject into prevailing social relations so that these relations are seen as conventional and uncontested?" (p. xxi). The acceptance of the "naturalness" of television that students bring with them to TV production courses, the instrumental logic embedded in mainstream production teaching and learning practices, and the apparently taken-for-granted common sense of the dominant industries emerging from the textbooks collectively act as impediments to a critique of the objectives of television production courses.

Burrows et al., (1989) assure students that it is possible to separate the acquisition of "skills" from the ideology embedded in production practices. They argue that although "this text may appear to be concerned primarily with developing proficiency," the primary purpose is to "simply be that of creating an understanding of the video production process—regardless of one's ultimate vocational objectives" (p. 1). Even if these authors were not merely paying lip service to the concept of intellectual critique, on what grounds might they hope to achieve the goal? The text is quite clearly a manifesto on mainstream broadcasting practices. Clearly, television production texts are situated within institutional settings that impose relations and practices that are necessarily partisan—essentially toward dominant industries and capitalist formations. However, and the authors surely know this too, these texts are course specific: They inform and do not dictate classroom practices. Thus, television production courses in which the text is used normalize the information within the vocational paradigm. However, the authors' claim to objectivity and "neutrality" is soon lost (it lasts merely one paragraph). The student is soon informed that "successful television" depends on "techniques" and "disciplines." These, in turn, comprise "proper voice," "proper interaction," "responsibility," and "self-control" (p. 2).

Fielding (1990) similarly makes claims that it cannot engage substantively (at all, actually). The book begins: "Throughout this book, emphasis is placed on the use of TV production tools and processes as a means to an end, not as an end in themselves" (p. ix). The "end" to which Fielding suggests television production technology is merely the "means" is explained some 280 pages later: "Your goal should be honesty and a commitment to use television for the good of the society and the world in which we live" (p. 279). How? What is "good" for society, what is "good" for the world? How should we understand "honesty"? When television production courses "succeed" in giving students the ability to fire each other in order to come closer to a "real-world" experience, how should students understand Fielding's call? The claim to objectivity is clearly erroneous. The text is blatantly technocratic, undemocratic, and tends to unproblematically reproduce the status quo. The concept of "audience" is extremely limited and unengaged. Students are told that if audiences do not like what they see on television they can "change the channel or put in a different tape" (p. 6). What this means for students who also happen to be "audiences" is not clear, but certainly this perspective encourages a view of "audiences" as things that have to be manipulated rather than respected, especially when applied in conjunction with the previously discussed philosophy of a mainstream television production course.

Zettl (1992) is comfortable separating communication theory of any sort from television production theory and practice. The text is clearly technologically driven: Its only reason for existing, the author explains, is that technology is there; therefore, we should learn how to use it—clearly an ahistorical approach to the whole question of technology, society, and power. Zettl claims that his text "reflects" the rapid development of television production tools and techniques. Indeed it does. He also claims that his text is a "guide, not a credo." But how can he assure the many student readers of this freedom of interpretation in university TV production courses? He cannot, of course. Indeed, the whole curriculum process down to multiple choice exams and graded critiques of student productions ensures that this "guide" becomes "gospel." Again, we find on the final page of the 607-page text a call to the wise: "You are now in command of one of the most powerful means of communication and persuasion. Use it wisely and responsibly. Treat your audience with respect and compassion" (p. 607). Zettl then defends the "helpless" audience: "Because they cannot communicate back to you very readily, they must—and do—trust your professional skills and judgement. Do not betray that trust" (p. 607). However, Zettl may merely be suggesting that students entering into the "business" try not to bite the hand that feeds them: "As frustrating as the ratings system is, you should nevertheless realize that, in broadcast television, you are working with a mass medium that, by definition, bases its existence on large audiences" (p. 490).

How are students to make sense out of the relationship between not betraying an audience's trust and a system that develops sophisticated surveillance mechanisms in order to monitor, motivate, and modify their behavior? What is "betrayal" in this context? Questions such as these are understandably lost to the author, whose task is to competently and accessibly explain complex and intricate technological knowledge. But if not they, who? And if not now, when? Finally, what hope is there for students to engage with the world in order to change it when, as Zettl explained, the mass media "by definition" must attract and sell large audiences of consumers?

Compesi and Sherriffs (1990) provide a similar technological service to mainstream broadcast practices and relations. The text begins with a day-in-the-life of an Evening Magazine news crew as it scours a big city in search of stories to tell, not an example of video use in campus life and students exploring the radical potential of video cameras, nor a pedagogical tale of teacher and student interaction and how their relationships were enhanced during a video production course over a semester. Not a word is given on how students developed a deeper understanding of video and its potential uses and misuses by engaging with television production courses in higher education. In other words, the examples were not drawn from pedagogical practice. Rather, a lesson is provided on how video is used in the "real" world and, by implication, how students should "think" about the technology and its legitimate uses.

What becomes apparent is that these texts project the student into a pseudo-work environment, in which they perform and experience themselves in roles other than what they really are: student citizens. Clearly, texts do not determine outcomes. The texts discussed in this chapter have been engaged in light of a particular and dominant form of pedagogical practice conducted in universities and expressed through mainstream academic journals. What is apparent, however, is just how easily these texts perform a supporting function for mainstream production teaching practices.

Television production courses in institutions of higher learning are reduced from their various potentials for providing students with opportunities to seriously challenge the grounds upon which the industry itself reproduces. What is never mentioned, or rarely in an critical sense, is that "television" is not primarily about producing information or entertainment or informed citizens. Rather, and to the contrary, "television" is about producing audiences that can be sold to advertisers: Human creativity and imagination is expropriated in the process of learning how to "do" television "professionally." Given the powerful influences exerted on the pedagogical television production site, the knowledge that students and teachers bring with them to the teaching and learning process, and the role that television production texts play in supporting and reproducing the status quo, how do critical communication scholars infuse the television production area of communication studies with knowledge that promotes radical alternative relations and practices? It is to this issue that this discussion now turns.

CRITICAL COMMUNICATION PEDAGOGY: RESISTING ROUTINE

According to some media analysts (Bazalgette, 1986; Burns, 1991; Cook, 1975; Denski, 1991; Lusted, 1986; Swanson, 1985), attempts at combining critical communication studies and media production practices are generally improvisations on the part of individual instructors as they struggle with the contradictions inherent in the tensions between critique and reproduction of dominant media relations and practices. This contradictory dual role often played by critical scholars/TV production instructors represents a dialectic that can alert students and teachers to the inherent contradiction between the promise of democracy, equality, and justice on the one hand and a social political and economic system based on the unequal distribution of power and privilege on the other. This contradictory role stands as a central problem for critical communication scholars: It is precisely this unproblematized pedagogic moment that serves to reproduce the very instrumental relations that represent the heart of the critical communication project. It is only by translating the assumptions of critical communication studies into ongoing pedagogic praxis that critical scholars might bridge the gap between critical communication studies and TV production courses in higher education.

Freire (1981) argues that not only do institutional knowledges and practices impinge upon students in educational settings, but that students themselves have developed a "fear of freedom" that inhibits their ability to critically challenge received institutional wisdom. Freire suggests that teacher-intellectuals might encourage students toward *conscientization*—a way of being in the world wherein the student is able to "perceive social, political and economic contradictions, and to take action against the oppressive elements of reality" (p. 19). To facilitate conscientization of student citizens, a critical communication pedagogy for television production must encourage a dialogical critique of cultural industries, their technologies and their practices, and provide a space for students to articulate their developing awareness in television production practices. This means not only that students must be unimpeded by the common forms that mainstream media take, but also that they work within an atmosphere that encourages difference, one that privileges the unfamiliar and the exotic. From this perspective, television and video industries are spheres of social struggle over meaning, and students are perceived as potential co-constructors of new ways of seeing and school production courses as sites in which students use television production technology to critique dominant and alternative communicative strategies while learning to acquire their own unique voices. Students explore the ways in which the business of television operates within and reproduces the hegemony of political, economic, and social relations and control.

The argument is not that a transformation in teaching and learning practices in television production courses can change the world. Universities are situated within the political, economic, and cultural reality, not outside of it. Conscientization is a process whereby students come to understand the ways in which knowledge is produced and struggled over: It provides them with the opportunity to explore the possibilities for social transformation, recognize the part they play in resisting or representing dominant interests, and promote the possibility for student activism in the sense that students might claim the right to develop alternative and unique cultural practices and products.

Freire's argument is paralleled with that of the research conducted by critical communication theorists. These theorists suggest that the democratic transformation of society is partially dependent on our coming to terms with the mediated construction of social reality and the constraints within which struggle takes place. Golding and Murdock (1991), for instance, argue that:

> People depend in large measure on the cultural industries for their images, symbols, and vocabulary with which they interpret and respond to their social environment. It is vital . . . that we understand these industries in a comprehensive and theoretically adequate way which enables the analysis of communications to take place at the heart of social and cultural research. (p. 30)

In this instance, the "analysis" of communication takes the form of praxis: It is the conscious realization of the potential of communication technologies in democratic life. Here students' work is informed by a critical awareness of the structural constraints within which they act. Furthermore, students are enabled to link their awareness of the limited ways in which human life is represented in mass-mediated images to their own explorations of the multiple possibilities for presentations of, for instance, gender, race, and class and the unique opportunities for various publics to represent themselves. A critical communication pedagogy should engage popular cultural images as they reconstruct unequal societal relations, sometimes challenge existing social standards, and confirm or legitimate a consumer-oriented form of social action. A critical pedagogy for television production courses consequently posits knowledge as socially constructed and encourages students to engage in television production as responsible political beings: as co-creators rather than merely replicators of a public sphere. Freire's (1981) claim that "Knowledge emerges only through invention and reinvention, through the restless, impatient, continuing hopeful inquiry that [human beings] pursue in the world, with the world, and with each other" (p. 58) can be taken up in critical praxis when critical communication pedagogues refuse an uncritical acceptance of the predominant educational teaching and learning forms.

Furthermore, accenting the significance of critically engaging with the world, critical communication pedagogy is interested in the process of learning how to learn. The contrast between the critical pedagogy and mainstream assumptions, based on a transmission model of education, is no less than the struggle between adaptation and transformation. Where mainstream approaches to teaching television production accentuate efficiency, conformity, consumerism, job preparation, reproduction, and a transmission model of communication, the critical communication pedagogy will emphasize experimentation, negotiation, dialogue, creativity, citizenship, exploration and an active participatory model of communication that promotes tolerance and respect for what are routinely marginalized voices in society.

A critical communication pedagogy provides a powerful vehicle with which to engage the social world in order to understand and change it, rather than unthinkingly participate in it. Golding and Murdock (1991) argue that it is important to see "how the making and taking of meaning is shaped at every level by the structured asymmetries in social relations" (p. 18). For students in television production courses, Golding and Murdock's commentary provides an avenue of critique as they participate in the construction of their own meanings. However, becoming aware of the nature of the world around them is insufficient insofar as it does not, by itself, produce a will to act. It is also necessary for a critical communication pedagogy to provide the space for students to examine the always political nature of the knowledge society produces and how knowledge production is always implicated in relations of power over who gets to tell the social story and with whose interests in mind: "Television remains a medium which is more rigidly controlled by the forces dominating modern society, whether economic or ideological. Hence education in television is necessary as an essential corollary to democratic education" (Tarroni, 1962, p. 62).

Fagan (1991) has argued that knowledge production situates women in a particular social space and that, as political beings, women need to empower themselves to ask: "How are we as women involved in the social process? . . . What role do we play? . . . What needs to be changed? . . . What changes do we need to make?" (p. 71). Fagan argues the case that all education is political: that the shortest route to understanding society and how it works is to analyze how our individual selves have been shaped by social forces and informed by experiences in the world and exposure to mediated knowledge, and that classroom materials must make contact politically with current social issues. Fagan is arguing for a politicized notion of education that recognizes the implicit power relations embedded in the production of and engagement with knowledge. It is crucial that critical communication pedagogues recognize the distinct voices of historically marginalized persons and groups within the institution of higher learning; specifically, the history of television production has tended to be male-centered and highly patriarchal in its orientation. Women, although claiming ground within the field, continue to encounter resistance and obstruction—especially when refusing to conform to the dominant commercial language of television. In fact, women in undergraduate television programs in higher education are very often scripted (and sometimes script themselves) into stereotypical, narrow roles that reflect the ideological framework of the mainstream media. This is a serious issue that can be ruptured merely by raising significant questions in the media production classroom that lay the groundwork for more reflective, enlightened student engagements with the technology and with each other. Critical communication theory covers this ground relentlessly in the form of political, economic, and cultural studies that uncover the unequal relations of power in communication industries: Importantly, this perspective can inform the television production courses in university communication departments. The alternative, of course, is ironic: The same unjust and unequal relations of power we critique in our scholarship, we cultivate and accommodate in our teaching practices.

As issues of gender, class, and race are engaged critically in the television production classroom—as students are invited to participate in social critique as an essential aspect of cultural production—spaces are provided for resistance to dominant media formations and creative student alternatives. It is here that a critical communication pedagogy might intervene and inform student knowledges. Kellner (1991) has argued similarly, although in another context:

> Surely education should attend to the new image culture and should teach a critical pedagogy of reading images as part of media literacy. Such an effort would be part of a new radical pedagogy that attempts to get at the root of our experience, knowledge, and behaviour and that aims at liberation from domination and the creation of new, plural, enhanced and more potent selves. (p. 64)

Critical readings are clearly not sufficient: One does not become free simply by thinking one is free. For example, a critical ethnographic study of children and television revealed that the potential for radical transformation is possible when critical communication theory is taken up through a critical pedagogy in social critique.[4] However, the activity taken up by a number of students in the study took place a year after the research project had been completed: the engagement with a critical reading of sexism and stereotyping of women in a popular cultural form had contributed to the eventual activities in which the students engaged. Interestingly, the students in this study chose to create the first alternative newspaper in their high school and contributed to a politicization of the student body during their remaining years there.

A pedagogy that provides space for critically "reading" images is fundamental to a pedagogy for television production, for it imagines a potentially active and engaged student citizenry. Reading against dominant cultural artifacts can provide students with the ability to engage critically in producing against the status quo. In this instance, producing against the mainstream is equivalent to seeking a discourse free from distortion in that the dominant media industries are inextricably linked to a patriarchal and heterosexual discourse, the logic of the market, and the accumulation of profit. Critical reading is also essential to the developing global economy as citizens around the world view each other through mediated lenses: Media have a powerful influence on how we come to know and understand each other (Bailie & Frank, 1992). Nevertheless, without the ability to act—to put into practice—transformation becomes difficult. A critical education is education for critical citizenship, and critical citizenship is an active, rather than passive, condition. As Giroux (1983) has argued:

> If citizenship education is to be emancipatory, it must begin with the assumption that its major aim is not "to fit" students into the existing society; instead, its primary purpose must be to stimulate their passions, imaginations, and intellects so that they will be moved to challenge the social, political, and economic forces that weigh so heavily upon their lives. (p. 201)

CRITICAL COMMUNICATION PEDAGOGY AND TELEVISION PRODUCTION IN PRAXIS

Critical communication pedagogy for television production courses in higher education must retrieve the concepts of "skill" and "professionalism" that have been appropriated in the service of maintaining the status quo. A critical

---

[4] I participated in "critical readings" of mainstream popular films with students while a graduate student at the University of Oregon in 1991. A number of the young high school women in the study went on to become politically active in their highschool. They produced an alternative student newspaper in their high school (see Bailie, 1993).

pedagogy for television production education is not a repudiation of television production "skill," nor antagonistic to a developed notion of "professionalism." To the contrary, a critical approach to television production practices revitalizes students and enhances their enjoyment and critical understanding of the medium. Paulo Freire (1981) provides a useful conceptual framework for understanding the differences in approach between mainstream and critical education practices. Freire calls the dominant system of teaching and learning a "transmission" or "banking" model and explains it as:

- The teacher teaches and the students are taught.
- The teacher knows everything and the students know nothing.
- The teacher thinks and the students are thought about.
- The teacher talks and the students listen.
- The teacher disciplines and the students are disciplined.
- The teacher chooses and enforces the choice, students comply.

This banking model sees students as merely receptacles into which information is deposited, only to be retrieved at some later date when the teacher applies the correct inducement in the form of tests and so forth. It is not difficult to see how, under such conditions, a distinct line can be drawn between the holder of knowledge and the one who lacks. However, a critical approach to teaching and learning television production provides students with an opportunity to understand what they are doing, within what context they do it, and with what aim. In regard to the critical dimension of skills and professionalism, it is worth returning to one of the television production texts critiqued earlier as a way of suggesting how the critical enterprise can engage with the world fully, and encourage students to do likewise. A critical communication pedagogy for television production, to fulfill its objective of empowering student citizens who can act in the world so as to affect fundamental and democratic change, necessarily encourages the development of sophisticated skills in the pursuit of that goal. What is at issue is the process, the content, and the context within which students struggle, as well as the development of a curriculum that includes the voices and visions of multiple communities of persons.

Zettl's (1990) text rests on the critical assumption that media students are empowered to act for themselves and society through the effective use of technologies of communication. Zettl's concern is with the aesthetic dimension of production, and although he tends to bracket the political and economic problematic—seeing television as an art rather than as a business—he nevertheless argues that in order to articulate visions and stories through the medium of television, it is necessary to perceive, order, clarify, intensify, and interpret the world. This speaks directly to the socially constructed nature of mediated communication and echoes Enzensberger (1970):

Every use of the media presupposes manipulation. The most elementary processes in media production, from the choice of the medium itself, to shooting, cutting, synchronization, dubbing, right up to distribution, are all operations carried out on the raw material. There is no such thing as unmanipulated writing, filming, or broadcasting. (p. 20)

Zettl holds that art is the intensification of life: "Instead of isolating art from the ordinary pursuits of life," he argues, "in applied media aesthetics, art and life are mutually dependent upon each other and essentially interconnected" (p. 2). This concept allows students to think of their lives and the meanings they produce in their television productions as interconnected: Their work speaks to their integrity, to their values, and to what they aspire. Zettl explains that as we attempt to stabilize our environments in order to make life manageable, we see "selectively" and thus tend to avoid seeing what does not conform to our developed worldview. Again, this is an important conceptual tool that provides students with a way of thinking about their own preconceived notions and received mediated images of the world. Within this context, students are enabled to articulate their own understandings and to begin to critique their own taken-for-granted assumptions about society. As students begin the process of conceptualizing programming as a result of their critical reflection on society and their place within it, it will become increasingly important to have the "skills" to articulate their concerns through the medium of television. In other words, the interest in developing skills will be in relation to their having something they want to say. Few of the texts examined here provide for the kinds of examples I have been able to draw from Zettl, and those that do provide critical assessments or promote critical pedagogical perspectives that tend to focus on the consumption, rather than the production, of media.[5] Retheorizing critical communication pedagogy is essential if critical communication scholarship is to be realized in educational practice. Although there are media educators exploring the possibilities of critical media studies (Denski, 1994; Scholle, 1994), promoting a feminist pedagogy (Fisher, 1992; Lafky, 1994; Luke, 1994), and combining critical pedagogical perspective with journalism practices (Hochheimer, 1992), much is left to be done. Critical communication pedagogy faces substantial resistance from students previously drilled in a transmission model of education, from institutional pressures and time constraints, and from the instrumental knowledge that drives the production and uses of communication technologies: This is the climate within which such a project necessarily begins. However, as Shor (1988) has argued: "Critical teachers do not have to wait for everything to change before anything can be changed. What goes on in each classroom is significant. Critical learning is by itself a form of social action because of its transforming potential, it's challenge to the dominant culture inside and outside us" (p. 195).

---

[5]A recent media text exploring the possibilities for a media pedagogy argues: "We concluded that the pedagogy ultimately was in the receiving process rather than the production process of media culture" (Schwock, White, & Reilly, 1992, p. x).

There is clear recognition that mainstream pedagogical practices in communication studies counteract the potentially liberating possibilities of critical communication theory: It is time to take the discourse on pedagogy seriously as a legitimate area of concern in critical communication studies. One alternative is that we may well be facilitating today the social conditions we take up so conscientiously in critique tomorrow.

REFERENCES

Aldridge, H.B., & Liggett, L.A. (1990). *Audio/video production theory and practice*. Englewood Cliffs, NJ: Prentice-Hall.

Apple, M. (1981). On analyzing hegemony. In H.A. Giroux, A.N. Penna & W.F. Pinar (Eds.), *Curriculum & instruction: Alternatives in education* (pp. 112-123). Berkeley: McCutchan.

Apple, M. (1990). *Ideology and the curriculum*. Boston: Routledge.

Armer, A. A. (1990). *Directing television and film*. Belmont, CA: Wadsworth.

Aronowitz, S., & Giroux, H. (1985). *Education under siege: The conservative, liberal and radical debate over schooling*. London: Routledge.

Bailie, M. (1993). Childrens' perceptions of the woman in "Teenage Mutant Ninja Turtles." *Jumpcut*, No. 38, 4- 95.

Bailie, M., & Frank, D. A. (1992). Media, madness and the Muslim world. In J. Wasko & V. Mosco (Eds.), *Democratic communication in the information age* (pp. 75-87). Norwood, NJ: Ablex.

Bazalgette, C. (1986). Making sense for whom? *Screen, 27*(5), 30-37.

Bowles, S., & Gintis, H. (1976). *Schooling in capitalist America*. London: Routledge.

Burns, G. (1991). Production theory as administrative research. *Journal of Film and Video, 43*(3), 30-40.

Burrows, T.D., Wood, D.N., & Gross, L.S. (1989). *Television production disciplines and techniques*. Dubuque, IA: Wm. C. Brown.

Chomsky, N. (1988). *Necessary illusions*. Boston: South End.

Compesi, R.J., & Sherriffs, R.E. (1990). *Small format television production*. Boston: Allyn and Bacon.

Cook, J. (1975). Teaching the industry. *Screen Education, 16*, 4-18.

Denski, S.W. (1991). Critical pedagogy and media production: The theory and practice of the video documentary. *Journal of Film and Video, 43*(3), 3-17.

Denski, S. (1994). Building bridges: Critical pedagogy & media studies. *Journal of Communication Inquiry, 18*(2), 65.

Enzensberger, H.M. (1970). Constituents of a theory of the media. *New Left Review, 64*, 18-27.

Fagan, H. (1991). Local struggles: Women in the home and critical feminist pedagogy in Ireland. *Journal of Education, 173*(1), 65-75.

Fielding, K. (1990). *Introduction to television production.* New York: Longman.

Fisher, B. (1992). Enhancing feminist pedagogy: Multimedia workshops on women's experience with "the newspaper' and "home." *Feminist Teacher, 6*(3), 9.

Freire, P. (1981). *Pedagogy of the oppressed.* New York: Continuum.

Funkhouser, E., & Savage, A.L. Jr. (1987). College students' expectations for entry-level broadcast positions. *Communication Education, 36*(1), 23-27.

Garnham, N. (1990). *Capitalism and communication: Global culture and the economics of information.* London: Sage.

Giroux, H.A. (1981). *Ideology, culture, and the process of schooling.* Sussex, England: Falmer.

Giroux, H.A. (1983). *Theory and resistance in education: A pedagogy for the opposition.* Granby, MA: Bergin & Garvin.

Giroux, H.A. (1988). Schooling, popular culture, and a pedagogy of possibility. *Journal of Education, 170*(1), 9-26.

Giroux, H.A. (1992). Introduction. In J. Schwoch, M. White, & S. Reilly, (Eds.), *Media knowledge: Readings in popular culture, pedagogy and critical citizenship* (pp. ix-xxxiv). New York: State University of New York Press.

Golding, P., & Murdock, G. (1991). Culture, communications, and political economy. In J. Curran & M. Gurevitch (Eds.), *Mass media and society* (pp.15-32). New York: Edward Arnold.

Gouldner, A. (1979). *The dialectic of ideology and technology: The origins, grammar, and future of ideology.* New York: Seabury.

Gramsci, A. (1971). *Selections from the prison notebooks of Antonio Gramsci.* New York: International Press.

Henderson, L. (1994, Summer). Communication pedagogy and political practice. *Journal of Communication Inquiry, 18*(2), 133-153.

Hochheimer, John L. (Feb. 1992). Toward liberatory pedagogy for journalism students: adapting Paulo Freire's praxis to the non-poor. *College Literature, 19*(1), 12-28.

Hudson, J.C. (1987). Broadcasters want experience, skills and liberal arts. *Educator, 41*(4), 36-38.

Kellner, D. (1991). Reading images critically: Toward a postmodern pedagogy. In H. Giroux (Ed.), *Postmodernism, feminism, and cultural politics: Redrawing educational boundaries* (pp. 60-82). New York: State University of New York Press.

Lafky, S.A. (1994). Teaching the ideologically unreliable: A challenge for mass communication educators. *Journal of Communication Inquiry, 18*(2), 108-121.

Luke, C. (1994). Feminist pedagogy and critical media literacy. *Journal of Communication Inquiry, 18*(2), 30-48.

Lusted, D. (1986). Introduction: Why pedagogy? *Screen, 27*(5), 2-15.

Richards, R. (1992). *A director's method for film and television.* Boston: Focal.

Roosenraad, J., & Wares, D. (1983). Academics vs. experience. *Journalism Educator, 38,*(2), 17-18.

Schiller, H. (1973). *The mind managers.* Boston: Beacon.

Schwoch, J., White, M., & Reilly, S. (1992). *Media knowledge: Readings in popular culture, pedagogy, and critical citizenship.* New York: State University of New York Press.

Sholle, D. (1994). The theory of critical media pedagogy. *Journal of Communication Inquiry, 18*(2), 8-30.

Shor, I. (1988). Working hands and critical minds: a Paulo Freire model for job training. *Journal of Education, 170*(2), 102-121.

Simon, R.I. (1989). Empowerment as a pedagogy of possibility. *Language Arts, 64,* 370-382.

Smith, J.R. (1983). Industry speaks: Four perspectives on media research in the 1980s. *Journal of Broadcasting, 27*(2), 185-190.

Stephens, M. (1981, April). Don't imitate professionals: In broadcast news training, who's calling the kettle black? *Journalism Educator, 36*(1), 49-50.

Swanson, G. (1985). Independent media and media education. *Screen, 27*(5), 62-67.

Tarroni, E. (1962). *The aesthetics of television: Screen education: Teaching a critical approach to cinema and television* (Reports and papers on mass communication) Paris: UNESCO.

Trent, D. (1990, November). Critical pedagogy and cultural power: An interview with Henry Giroux. *Afterimage,* pp. 14-18.

Wasko, J. (1994). *Hollywood in the information age: Beyond the silver screen.* University of Texas.

Whitlow, S. S. (1983). Teaching tips: Students can fire . . . or be fired in creative course. *Journalism Educator, 38*(2), 19-20.

Whittaker, R. (1989). *Video field production.* Mountain View, CA: Mayfield.

Whittaker, R. (1993). *Television production.* Mountain View, CA: Mayfield.

Zettl, H. (1990). *Sight sound motion: Applied media aesthetics.* Belmont, CA: Wadsworth.

Zettl, H. (1992). *Television production handbook.* Belmont, CA: Wadsworth.

Chapter 3

The Communication Revolution: The Market and the Prospect for Democracy

Robert W. McChesney

There are two striking and epoch-defining trends that dominate U.S. and global media and communication. On the one hand, there has been a rapid corporate concentration and commercialization of media industries. On the other hand, new communication technologies have emerged that undermine the ability of communication to be controlled in a traditionally hierarchical manner. The trend toward concentrated, for-profit media control violates the canons of democratic political theory, whereas the trend toward inexpensive, mass, interactive communication offers the promise of an era of unprecedented popular access to communication. Although these developments are concurrent, the trend toward corporate concentration and domination has been developing over a longer period and is most clearly ascendant. A veritable library of research has been produced examining and delineating the crisis for democracy created by having what Ben Bagdikian (1992) terms a capitalist "media monopoly." The key question then is to what extent can the communication technological revolution override the antidemocratic implications of the media marketplace and foster a more democratic media and political culture?

That will be the question I address in this chapter. I approach the issue as a matter of communication policymaking and concentrate on the U.S. experience. I examine U.S. communication policymaking *historically* to see what past experience suggests for the present and future. I also examine contemporary communication policymaking *critically*, as part of the broader contours of capitalist society. In this context, I produce an answer to the question that is pessimistic, but that suggests possible directions for scholars and citizens to pursue to generate a more favorable outcome. In particular, I argue that the rise of the new communication revolution presents a special challenge for the discipline of communication in the United States and globally. Just as the global economy and the communication system are in the throes of turbulent transformation, so it is that U.S. communication research and education finds itself at a crossroads. The stance communication scholars assume toward communication policymaking in the coming years may determine the status of the field for generations.

COMMUNICATION POLICY-MAKING

There are two sets of fundamental political questions that emerge when discussing the development of any major communication technology. The first set of questions deals with the actual control and purposes of the communication technology itself. In short, who will control the technology and for what purpose? The corollary to this question is who will not control the new technology and what purposes will not be privileged. In the case of U.S. television, for example, it was determined that a few enormous corporations would control the medium for the purpose of maximizing profits. The superior manner to maximize profits was by selling advertising time. Thus, by answering this set of questions in the manner it did, the United States put the development of television on a very distinct trajectory, a path rather unlike that which was adopted in most parts of Europe.

The second set of questions deals with the social, cultural, economic, and political impact of the new communication technology on the overall society. These questions go directly to the heart of the matter; in short, why are new communication technologies important? Regardless of how a communication technology is owned and operated, it will have consequences that are often unintended and unanticipated, and only related in varying degrees to its structural basis. Thus, television dramatically altered the domestic culture of U.S. households in the postwar years (Spigel, 1992), and it has arguably had a strong effect on the nature of journalism (Baughman, 1992) and public discourse (Postman, 1985).

The process by which society answers these questions can be regarded as policymaking. The more a society is genuinely democratic, the more that society's policy debates concerning the application and development of communication technologies will be open, informed, thoughtful, and passionate. But regardless of how democratic the policymaking process may be, these questions still emerge and will be answered in one form or another.

The United States is in the midst of a fundamental reconfiguration of communication media, often characterized as the information superhighway or the era of the interactive telecomputer. The most dramatic development has been the Internet because it has permitted mass *interactive* communication and access to information at lightning speed, relatively minimal cost, and on a global basis. This is a *not* a truly revolutionary era because of the awesome and bedazzling developments in technology, although these technologies are indeed staggering even to the most fertile human imagination. It is a truly revolutionary era because these new digital and computer technologies have broken down the traditional communication media industries and called forth a reconstitution of the communication infrastructure across the board. In short, the first set of policymaking questions have reemerged, and the answers we find to them may well set the course of development for generations.

Moreover, the current communication revolution continues, rather dramatically, the historical process whereby mediated communication has become increasingly central to the political economies and cultures of the world's peoples. Global capitalism, for example, is built to no small extent around the new communication technologies, and politics, culture, and education, to mention but a few examples, are being reconstructed in this era of the information highway. The entire manner in which individuals interact with the world is in the process of being transformed; hence, the second set of political issues concerning the social implications of the new communication technologies are of the utmost importance.

Much of the U.S. scholarship addressing the Internet and the related communication revolution has been so enamored with the technology that it has been uninterested in the fundamental political questions outlined earlier, or it has dealt with them in an ahistorical and uncritical manner. In current debate, for example, the rule of corporations over communication for the purpose of profit maximization is sacrosanct; accepting it is the ante for admission to policymaking forums. This has not always been the case in the United States, and our present lack of a more wide-ranging debate reflects not the will of the populace as much as the power of capital. In the next section I provide an historical perspective on the first set of political questions—who will control the new technology and for what purposes—that will draw on the legacy of AM radio broadcasting, facsimile, FM radio, VHF and UHF television, satellite broadcasting, and cable. I argue that presupposing corporate rule determines the outcome of the policy debates before they have even taken place, thus removing politics from policy and making democratic control of communication more a formality than a reality. This point was well understood by public service advocates in earlier communication revolutions.

As for the second set of fundamental questions—the overall social impact—the literature here, too, has tended to be decontextualized. The emphasis has been on the extraordinary advance in options available to the individual both in business and pleasure. As with previous communication technologies, grandiose claims have been made regarding the immense positive cultural and political implications of these new technologies. The market is presupposed to be a legitimate, democratic, fair, and rational regulator of communication. From this vantage point, the information highway is regarded as being a boon for democracy and individual freedom.

I take up some of these claims from a critical perspective. By critical, I mean that the communication technologies are not regarded as some exogenous gift to society that just landed in our laps as if dropped from outer space. To the contrary, the communication technologies are characterized as the consequence of a particular type of social order that produced them and into which these technologies will develop. Accordingly, the existing power relations of society are not accepted as natural or benevolent or exogenous to social analysis, but, rather, these social relations will be viewed with the same skepticism scholars have made when evaluating regimes historically or when looking at different types of social orders, such as communist societies. Therefore the rhetoric of the dominant interests in the United States are not taken at face value any more than scholars accepted the rhetoric of Stalinist ideologues as truth in years past. I argue that when one looks at the communication revolution critically, in the context of a globalizing capitalist economy, the democratic potential of the new technologies seems more stifled than encouraged. Indeed, I believe that on balance the new technologies may better be regarded as part of a process fundamentally opposed to democracy, unless the new technologies are consciously redirected away from the current pattern of development.

HISTORICAL PERSPECTIVE[1]

The current communication revolution is not unprecedented. It corresponds most closely to the 1920s, when the emergence of radio broadcasting forced society to address the two sets of political questions mentioned at the outset of this chapter. Radio broadcasting was a radically new development, and there existed great confusion throughout the 1920s concerning who should control this powerful new technology and for what purposes. Much of the impetus for radio broadcasting in the first decade came first from amateurs (Douglas, 1987) and then from nonprofit and noncommercial groups that immediately grasped the public service potential of the new technology (Feldman, 1996; Frost, 1937; Godfried, 1996). It was only in the late 1920s that capitalists began to sense

---

[1]Much of the historical material in this section is drawn from McChesney (1993) and is not cited otherwise.

that, through network operation and commercial advertising, radio broadcasting could generate substantial profits. Through their immense power in Washington, DC, these commercial broadcasters were able to dominate the Federal Radio Commission such that the scarce number of air channels were effectively turned over to them with no public and little congressional deliberation on the matter.

It was in the aftermath of this commercialization of the airwaves that elements of U.S. society coalesced into a broadcast reform movement that attempted to establish a dominant role for the nonprofit and noncommercial sector in U.S. broadcasting. These opponents of commercialism came from education, religion, labor, civic organizations, women's groups, journalism, farmer's groups, civil libertarians, and intellectuals. They looked to Canada and Britain as providing the groundwork for workable public service broadcasting models for the United States. The reformers attempted to tap into the intense public dislike for radio commercialism in the years before 1934 when Congress considered permanent legislation for the regulation of radio broadcasting annually (Smulyan, 1994). These reformers were explicitly and nonnegotiably radical; they argued that if private interests controlled the medium and their goal was profit, no amount of regulation or self-regulation could overcome the bias built into the system. Commercial broadcasting, the reformers argued, would downplay controversial and provocative public affairs programming and emphasize whatever fare would sell the most products for advertisers. It was a sophisticated critique of the limitations of a capitalist communication systems for a democratic society, anticipating much of the best media criticism and scholarship of recent years.

The reform movement disintegrated after the passage of the *Communications Act of 1934,* which established the Federal Communications Commission, and which was the reigning statute until the passage of the U.S. Telecommunications Act of 1996. The reformers did not lose to the commercial interests, however, in any fair debate on a level playing field. The radio lobby dominated because it was able to keep most Americans ignorant or confused about the communication policy matters then under discussion in Congress through their control of key elements of the news media and sophisticated public relations aimed at the remainder. In addition, the commercial broadcasters became a force that few politicians wished to antagonize; almost all the congressional leaders of broadcast reform in 1931-32 were defeated in their reelection attempts, a fate not lost on those who entered the next Congress. With the defeat of the reformers, the industry claims that commercial broadcasting was inherently democratic, and American went without challenge and became internalized in the political culture.

Thereafter, the only legitimate manner to criticize U.S. broadcasting was to assert that it was uncompetitive and therefore needed aggressive regulation. The basis for the "liberal" claim for regulation was that the scarce number of channels necessitated regulation, not that the capitalist basis of the industry was fundamentally flawed. This was a far cry from the criticism of the 1930s broadcast reformers, who argued that the problem was not simply one of a lack of competition in the marketplace, as much as it was the rule of the marketplace per se. It also means that with the vast expansion in the number of channels in the current communication revolution, the scarcity argument has lost its power, and liberals are at a loss to withstand the deregulatory juggernaut (Avery, 1993). It has left contemporary public service communication advocates arguing over extending access to an untouchable system rather than changing the control and purposes of the communication system. Although universal access is an extremely important and necessary policy aim, in a more wide-ranging political culture it would be ancillary to larger measures, not the gist of public service communication policy in itself.

This constricted range of policy debate was the context for the development of subsequent communication technologies including facsimile, FM radio, and television in the 1940s. That the communication corporations had first claim to these technologies was unchallenged, even to such public service minded New Dealers as James Lawrence Fly, Clifford Durr, and Frieda Hennock. Even in comparison to radio in the 1930s, there was almost no public debate concerning alternative ways to develop these technologies. By the 1940s and thereafter, liberals knew the commercial basis of the system was inviolate and merely tried to carve out a nonprofit sector on the margins. This was always a problematic stance because whenever these nonprofit niches were seen as blocking profitable expansion, their future was on thin ice. Thus, the primary function of the nonprofit sector in U.S. communications has been to pioneer the new technologies when they were not yet seen as profitable—for example, AM radio in the 1920s, FM radio and UHF television in the 1950s, and the Internet in recent times—and then be pushed aside once they had shown the commercial interests the potential of the new media.[2]

The emergence of the Internet and related technologies has forced a reconsideration of media policy unlike, for example, television or FM radio because the nature of digital communication renders moot the traditional distinctions between various media and communication sectors. It is clear that the broadcasters and newspaper chains that have ruled for generations will not necessarily rule—or even survive—in the coming age, although the companies that own them will fare better if they move strategically into the new digital world. This theme dominates the business pages of the press and the business-oriented media. The key question then is which firms and which sectors will dominate and capitalize on the communication revolution, and which firms and which sectors will fall by the wayside. This is the tale being told in our business press and, by prevailing wisdom, this is the key "policy" battle concerning the

---

[2]I discuss the sad history and current fight over U.S. public broadcasting in McChesney (1995a).

Internet and the information highway. The primacy of corporate control and the profit motive is a given; the range of legitimate debate extends from those who argue profits are synonymous with public service, like Newt Gingrich, to those who argue there are public interest concerns the marketplace cannot resolve, but they can only be addressed once the profitability of the dominant corporate sector has been assured, like Vice President Al Gore (1995; "Too fast," 1995).

This situation exists for many of the same reasons the broadcast reformers were demolished in the 1930s. Politicians may favor one sector over another in the battle to cash in on the highway, but they cannot oppose the cashing in process, except at the risk of placing their political careers in jeopardy. Both the Democratic and Republican parties have strong ties to the large communication firms and industries. The only grounds for political courage in this case would be if there were an informed and mobilized citizenry ready to do battle for alternative policies. But how would citizens get informed, except through the news media, in which news coverage is minimal and restricted to the range of legitimate debate, in other words, to no debate at all. That is why this is covered as a business story, not a public policy story, and that is why the critical congressional hearings have passed virtually without public notice, although the consequences of the decisions that emerge from these hearings will dwarf in significance all but a handful of other news stories in importance over the coming generation. In short, this is a debate restricted to elites and those with serious financial stakes in the outcome. It does not reflect well on the caliber of U.S. participatory democracy. The "debate" culminated in the U.S. Telecommunications Act of 1996, a law that was written by and for communication corporations. Its primary accomplishment is to eliminate even the paltry public interest standards of the 1934 law.

Those forces that benefit from this situation claim that the market is the only truly democratic policymaking mechanism because it rewards capitalists who "give the people what they want" and penalizes those that do not. When the state or labor unions or any other agency interferes with the workings of the marketplace, this reasoning goes, they produce outcomes hostile to the public interest. These were also the precise claims of the commercial broadcasters as they consolidated their hold over the radio spectrum in the 1930s. This ideology of the infallible marketplace in communication and elsewhere has become a virtual civic religion in the United States and globally in the 1990s.

This argument remains infallible to the extent it is a religion based on faith and not a political theory subject to inquiry and examination. Under careful examination, the market is a highly flawed regulatory mechanism. Let me provide three brief criticisms along these lines. First, the market is not predicated on one person, one vote as in democratic theory, but, rather, on one dollar, one vote. The prosperous have many votes and the poor have few. Is it any surprise that the leading proponents of the market are invariably the well-to-do, and that markets invariably maintain and strengthen class divisions in society? Second, the market does not "give the people what they want" as much as it "gives the people what they want *within the range of what is most profitable to produce.*" This is often a far narrower range than what people might enjoy choosing from. Thus, in the case of broadcasting, many Americans may well have been willing to pay for an advertising-free system, but this was a choice that was not profitable for the dominant commercial interests so it was not offered on the marketplace. Third, markets are driven solely by profit considerations and downplay long-term concerns or values not readily associated with profit maximization. One need only think of the global ecology to see the disastrous consequences of a blind embrace of the market. Yet the blind embrace is precisely the situation at hand.

 Is the situation therefore hopeless for those who believe there are public interest concerns outside the market? In the historical sense, the immediate answer is an unequivocal yes. There are certainly those making excellent and thoughtful arguments for a dominant nonprofit logic to guide the communication highway (Guma, 1994; Kranich, 1994; Schiller, 1994; Telecommunications Workers Union, 1995). It seems obvious to ask this fundamental question: If the information highway and the interactive telecomputer are to become the nervous system of the new age, effectively responsible for education, journalism, and culture, is it rational to permit them to be guided by the profit dictates of a handful of transnational corporations? One former Microsoft executive asked precisely this question and concluded that "the information highway is just too important to be left to the private companies" (quoted in Flores, 1995, p. D1). But in general questions like these—not to mention the pursuit of workable answers—are marginalized, effectively censored, having less resonance in our political and media culture than, say, the ideas of the various far-right militias that have emerged in the 1990s.

 At the same time, it will certainly be possible for nonprofit niches to survive and perhaps prosper even in a regime of thoroughgoing corporate domination due to the abundance of the technology. The sheer magnitude of channels and possibilities brought on by the new technologies is, indeed, overwhelming by historical standards. In addition, given the interactive nature of the technology and the relative affluence of the present user group, the user lobby may have somewhat more power to protect its specific interests, under the condition that the general primacy of corporate rule is acknowledged. Finally, as long as the identity of the eventual corporate masters of communication is being fought over, there are possibilities for concessions that will not exist once the industry is stabilized. So, in this sense, there might be some hope to promote and protect a nonprofit sector, and in the current political culture that may well be the only immediate option. Nonetheless, by historical standards, there is little reason to believe the nonprofit sector could survive a sustained commercial assault.

 In fact, by historical standards, the emergence of the Internet and the communication highway could not have come at a more inopportune moment. In the 1930s, there was an impressive array of civic organizations willing to argue that it was inappropriate for communication media to be directed by the profit motive. Many of these groups, most notably labor, have been decimated in the past two decades. We live in an era in which the very notion of public service has become discredited unless a function of noblesse oblige, in which even the commercialization of education, a notion regarded as obscene only a decade ago, is now proceeding full steam ahead (De Vaney, 1994; Wollenberg, 1995). In this context, it should be no surprise that the private sector, with its immense resources, has seized the initiative and is commercializing cyberspace—transforming it into a giant shopping mall—at a spectacular rate (Donaton, 1995; Goldman, 1995; Sandberg, 1995; Wallace, 1995). Without any public directive to the contrary, commercial interests will proceed with their feast, and nonprofit interests will continue to scramble for the crumbs that fall off the table, hoping for some big ones.

CRITICAL PERSPECTIVES

In the preceding discussion, I adopted a critical stance, assuming that the corporate domination of communication and its commercialization are problematic for a democratic society. In my view, the market is not a neutral or value-free arbiter of culture and ideas (Herman, 1993b; Murdock, 1992). These presuppositions grow out of my more general conviction that the relationship of capitalism to democracy is a rocky one: On the one hand, capitalism tends to generate a highly skewed class basis that permits a small section of society—the wealthy—to have inordinate power over political and economic decision making to the detriment of the balance of society. On the other hand, capitalism encourages a culture that places a premium on commercial values and downplays communitarian ideals. Capitalism thereby undermines two prerequisites for genuine democracy.

Most observers of the Internet and the communication revolution do not take a critical stance. Some of the analysis is made by those who exult in capitalism and see the Internet and the information highway as elevating existing capitalism to an even higher level of sheer perfection (Gilder, 1994). In this view, capitalism is synonymous with democracy; therefore, the more social affairs that can be turned over to private interests the better. The function of the government is to protect private property and not much else. Indeed, some marketphiles take a technological deterministic stance, asserting that the new communication technologies, because they eliminate the monopolies on knowledge that large corporations have, will lead to a new global economic regime of small entrepreneurs and flexible production. The transnational corporations that presently dominate the global economy will eventually appear like so many clumsy dinosaurs on their way to rapid extinction. This will be especially true in communication industries, in which size will prove to be a competitive disadvantage. In this perspective, the information highway will be the basis for a new golden age of competitive capitalism and an accompanying renaissance in culture and politics.

The problem with this argument is that there is no empirical evidence to support it. The dominant trend in communication as elsewhere is for a relative handful of enormous transnational corporations to dominate. Ever-increasing concentration, not fragmentation, is the order of the day. In global communication, in particular, the convergence of all media brought on by digital technologies makes it ever easier for firms to extend their empires into new realms (Bagdikian, 1989; Murdock, 1994). Hence, this "return to competitive capitalism" perspective would seem to exaggerate the importance of technology as being the factor responsible for the emergence of large transnational corporations and underestimate the fear of competition in spurring a strong anticompetitive impulse in successful capitalists. In short, large corporations are the logical result of markets, not a function of technologies. They use technologies; technologies do not use them.

Other mainstream observers may not revel to such a degree in capitalism, but they see the market as the natural order of things and pliable enough to permit the technological revolution to work its magic for both business and the public (Negroponte, 1995; Toffler & Toffler, 1994; criticized in Scheer, 1995). In either approach, the market is presupposed to be innately wonderful, or at least neutral, so it is not subjected to any further analysis. If the information highway fails to deliver the goods, it will not be the fault of the market.

In fact, the capitalism one finds described superficially in the literature on the Internet and the communication highway is an intoxicating one: It is comprised of venture capitalists, daring entrepreneurs, and enterprising consumers. There is no cheap exploited labor, no environmental degradation, no graft or corruption, no ingrained classes, no economic depressions, no social decay, and no consumer ripoffs. There are bold, open-minded winners and hardly any losers. It is capitalism at its best. Even to the extent there is a grain of truth in this sanitized version of capitalism, the notion that the communication system is a consequence of the "free market" is bogus. For example, many of the communication technologies associated with the revolution, particularly the Internet, grew directly out of government, usually military, subsidies. Indeed, at one point fully 85% of research and development in the U.S. electronics industry was subsidized by the federal government, although the eventual profits accrued to private firms (Chomsky, 1994).

We need a broader notion of capitalism, one that is somewhat more detailed, theoretical, historical, and critical than the one appearing in most discussions of the Internet and the information superhighway. It is no coincidence that the communication revolution appears at the same historic moment as the current globalization of capitalism. The tremendous desire to expand globally by corporations and capitalists has provided much of the spur to innovation in computing and telecommunications, and with striking effect

(Sullivan-Trainor, 1994). In the early 1970s, only 10% of global trade was financial, with the remaining 90% being trade in goods and services. The percentages flip-flopped in the subsequent two decades and grew at a rate far greater than global economic activity (McChesney, 1995b). Communication- and information related industries are now, by near unanimous proclamation, at the very heart of investment and growth in the world economy, occupying a role once played by steel, railroads, and automobiles.

This explains why an analysis of global capitalism needs to be at the center of any study of communication systems in the coming years. Only then can we begin to grapple with the second set of political questions mentioned at the beginning of this chapter: What will be the social consequences, intended and unintended, of these new communication and information technologies? My primary area of concern is with the argument that these new technologies will permit a revitalization of democracy both in the United States and globally. After all, if the information highway, Internet, and communication revolution do not deliver in this area, given their eventual scope, it will be difficult to make the case that their overall development is especially desirable.

Why do I use the term *revitalization* when referring to the status of democracy in the United States? Because, in the critical tradition, political democracy is always a problem for a capitalist society like the United States, in which a minuscule portion of the population makes fundamental economic decisions based on their self-interest. This becomes an acute problem when a mature, corporate-dominated capitalist society also grants near universal suffrage. There is the constant threat, inherent to democracy, that the dispossessed might unite, rise up, and demand greater control over basic economic decisions. The system works best, therefore, when the crucial political and economic decisions are made by elites outside of the public eye, and the political culture concentrates on superficial and tangential matters. Moreover, the tendency of capitalism to commercialize every nook and cranny of social life renders the development or survival of nonmarket political and cultural organizations far more difficult. These independent associations form the bulwark of democracy, making it possible for individuals to come together and become informed political actors (Mills, 1956). In the critical tradition, therefore, political apathy is rational behavior for those outside the inner circles, and this has been and is the reigning characteristic of U.S. politics (Macpherson 1977). As Chomsky (1987) noted, it is considered a "crisis of democracy" in conventional thinking when the long-dormant masses rise up and begin to pursue their own interests. Therefore, it is not surprising that a major development in the 20th century has been the rise of public relations—or propaganda—to promote elite interests and to undermine ideas and groups that might oppose corporate rule (Carey, 1995). The role of the masses is to ratify elite decisions.

Although the record is certainly mixed, for the most part, U.S. commercial journalism and media have failed to provide the groundwork for an informed and participatory democracy (Lasch, 1995). In Habermasian terms, media became sources of great profitability in the 20th century and have been colonized by the corporate sector, thereby losing their capacity to provide the basis for the independent public sphere so necessary for meaningful democracy (Habermas, 1989; Murdock & Golding, 1989). The upshot of most critical media research is that the commercial news media tend to serve elite interests and undermine the capacity for the bulk of the population to act as informed citizens (Herman & Chomsky, 1988). Recent scholarship suggests that increasingly concentrated corporate ownership of the media and commercial support have further destroyed the capacity of the press to fulfill a democratic mission (Bagdikian, 1992).

So what are the observable, new, and important tendencies of this global capitalist order? At least five related points are accepted by most observers, although how they are framed and their relative importance are subject to fierce debate.[3] First, the ease of transborder capital flows has lessened the capacity of national governments to determine economic policies that might promote any interests aside from those of transnational business, as capitalists can quickly move to more profitable climes. It has been long forgotten in mainstream commentary that John Maynard Keynes once noted that democracy would be impossible if capital could move beyond national borders (in Bernstein, 1987). Second, it has also had the effect of giving the international business community far greater leverage in its dealings not only with government regulations and policies, but with labor as well. As a result, the global trend is toward deregulation, in the hope of luring capital, and toward a reduction in the power of labor and labor unions, because if they are too effective business will invest elsewhere. Environmental regulation is an immediate casualty of globalization, as are most government services, which must be eliminated due to the need to reduce taxes on the well-to-do (capital flight) and economic stagnation (Barkan, 1995).

Third, this process of globalization has not led to more rapid economic growth. The rate of economic growth in the United States and globally has declined each decade since the 1960s. In fact, globalization emphasizes one of capitalism's basic flaws: What is rational conduct for the individual capitalist is utterly irrational and counterproductive for the system as a whole. Rational investors seek out low wage areas and use the threat to keep domestic wages low even if they do not move abroad (Albo, 1994; Panitch, 1994). The consequence is that there is a strong downward pressure on buying power (i.e., economic demand), which leads to a decline in profitable investment possibilities (i.e., continued economic stagnation; MacEwan, 1994). Moreover, governments are incapable of exercising the traditional Keynesian policies to stimulate economic growth as these measures run directly counter to those policies necessary to attract and keep investment. Indeed, stimulative economic

---

[3]All of the following points, although written in a critical voice, appear frequently in the business press. See, for example, "Twenty-first century capitalism" (1995).

measures are no longer even a legitimate policy option; if the World Bank and International Monetary Fund do not veto them, the global capital markets will.

Fourth, investment in information and communication tends to destroy existing jobs almost as well as it creates new ones; unlike steel and automobiles, these new paradigm-identifying industries cannot seemingly resolve the crisis of unemployment that afflicts the global working class. In this sense, the immediate consequence of the information revolution is not liberation from drudgery, but a sentencing to a life of sheer destitution (Noble, 1995). Fifth, due to the wildfire growth of enormous transnational global financial markets that are well beyond the powers of any effective national or international regulation, there is an element of overall instability to the global economy unknown since the 1930s (Sweezy, 1994). In sum, the economic thrust of global capitalism is one of deteriorating public sectors, environmental recklessness, stagnation, instability, and widening economic stratification (Cowling & Sugden, 1994). For those lucky few that sit atop the global pyramid the future never appeared brighter; for the bulk of humanity the present is grim and the future an abyss. Nothing on the horizon suggests any other course.

The implications of the global order for political culture are almost entirely negative (Herman, 1993a). Capitalism's two inherent and negative traits for democracy mentioned at the outset of this section—class stratification and the demise of civic virtue in the face of commercial values—are enhanced in the new global regime. There is nothing short of a wholesale assault on the very notion of democracy, as the concept of people gathering, debating, and devising policy has been supremely truncated. This is often presented as a crisis of national sovereignty, but, in fact, it is a crisis of sovereignty writ large. There is nothing really left to debate in the new world order because nations are required to toe the global capitalist line or face economic purgatory. Hence the *range* of legitimate debate has shrunk considerably, with socialists and conservatives alike effectively pursuing the same policies. The great paradox of our age is that formal democracy extends to a greater percentage of humanity than ever in history, yet, concurrently, there may well be a more general sense of political powerlessness than ever before. And since the democratic system seems incapable of generating ideas that address the political economic crises of our times, the most dynamic political growth in this age is with antirationalist, fundamentalist, nationalistic movements that blame democracy for capitalism's flaws and threaten to reduce humanity to untold barbarism.

The communication revolution is implicated in these developments. On the one hand, the transnational communication corporations have been leading the fight for NAFTA, GATT, and other institutional arrangements advantageous to global capital (Glaberson, 1994). These firms are among the greatest beneficiaries of globalization, and they have set their sights on dominating world communication and information (Schiller, 1995). The past decade has seen a wholesale dismantling of public sector broadcasting and communication across the planet and its replacement by capitalist, often transnational, communication systems (Pendakur & Kapur, this volume). In particular, the great public service broadcasting systems of Europe—so crucial to generating some semblance of journalism and culture not dominated by commercial values—have been either eliminated or required to adopt commercial principles in order to survive in the global marketplace (Blumler, 1992). This new world order of communication for profit has the tendencies one might expect: It tends to be uncritical of capitalism and commercialism and to be preoccupied with satisfying the needs of the relatively affluent, a small sector of the world's population (Nordenstreng & Schiller, 1993). In short, the new world order of global communication, among the most profitable consequences of global capitalism, tends to reinforce the status quo.

In this gloomy scenario, what are the prospects that the Internet, the information highway, and the communication technological revolution might break down oligarchy and lead to a revitalization of democratic political culture? The positive responses to this question emphasize the attributes of the Internet that make it so special: It is relatively cheap, easy to use, difficult to prevent access to it, and almost impossible to censor. The responses emphasize how these technological traits permit users of the Internet to make an "end run" around the existing institutional barriers to communication.

The most thoughtful arguments—and the most concerted activity—on behalf of the Internet revitalizing democracy tend to emphasize how the new media can empower individuals and groups presently ignored or distorted by the existing media industries. In effect, the Internet, especially the bulletin boards, can provide democracy's much needed public sphere, that has been so corrupted by the market. Moreover, given the instantaneous and global nature of the Internet, proponents of the "Internet as public sphere" argue that this permits the creation of a global public sphere all the more necessary in light of the global political economy. By this line of reasoning, the key fight should be to gain access to computers for everyone and to teach computer literacy. In addition, government censorship and commercial encroachment should be fought tooth and nail. Progressives point to the significance of computer networks in Mexico, for example, in permitting people to bypass the atrocious media system, thereby permitting dispossessed groups to communicate with each other and sympathizers around the planet (Frederick, 1995). These computer networks may well have permitted the pro-democracy forces in Mexico to survive and prosper, whereas in earlier times they would have been crushed. As evidence to support the belief that this is a viable alternative to commercial media, supporters point out that conservative forces appear quite upset by the existence of these uncontrolled networks of communication and obsessed with their elimination or regulation (Simon, 1995).

Although this is a convincing argument, and the prospects for computer networks are encouraging, I believe the following three qualifications are appropriate. First, assuring universal access and computer literacy is far from a certainty, and without it the democratic potential of the information highway seems supremely compromised. In an era of deregulatory, market frenzy, how can this goal possibly be made a reality, particularly on a global basis? This hardly seems like the time to exact concessions from capitalists; in fact, it is an era marked by commercial expansion, not curtailment.

Second, aside from the question of access, bulletin boards, and the information highway, more generally, do not have metaphysical powers. If there is little semblance of political culture in the society at large, there is little reason to expect the Internet to produce it. Given the dominant patterns of global capitalism, it is far more likely that the Internet and the new technologies will adapt themselves to the existing political culture rather than create a new one. Thus, it seems a great stretch to think the Internet will "politicize" people; it may just as well keep them depoliticized. In particular, having mass, interactive bulletin boards is a truly magnificent advance, but what if nobody knows what they are talking about? This problem could be addressed partially if scholars and academics shared their work and analysis with the general public, but that runs directly counter to the priorities, attitudes, and trajectory of academic life.

This is precisely where journalism, broadly construed, and communication policymaking enter the picture. Journalism provides the oxygen for democratic discussion; it provides the research and contextualization necessary to understand politics and to see behind the official proclamations of those in power. Journalism does not constitute the range of debate; rather, it provokes it, informs it, and responds to it. It is not something that can be done, as a rule, piecemeal by amateurs. It is best done by people who make a living at it, who have training and experience. Although journalism per quo is justly criticized for its failures, mostly due to commercial constraints, journalism per se is indispensable to any notion of democracy worth the paper it is written on. Quality journalism seems mandatory if the "Internet as public sphere" is to be a viable concept, and current theories along these lines are at a loss to address this problem.

Moreover, journalism is presently in the midst of a deep and profound crisis. The corporate concentration of ownership and the reliance on advertising have converted much of U.S. journalism into a travesty of entertainment, crime, and natural disaster stories. Journalism, real journalism, is not profitable, and the amount of resources dedicated to it has been cut back sharply (Kimball, 1994). Without resources, U.S.—and increasingly this means global—journalism is unable to do any investigative work and must rely on the (generally corporate) public relations industry and official sources (mostly politicians and government officials) for news stories. Morale for U.S. journalists is arguably at an all-time low (Mazzocco, 1994; McManus, 1994; Squires, 1993; Underwood, 1993). In this context the battle for public and community broadcasting is crucial both in the United States and globally; it is not about the survival of Big Bird as much as it is about the survival of an institutional basis for journalism (McChesney, 1995a). In sum, the Internet can only reproduce part of the public sphere, and its part will not necessarily be worth much if there is not the institutional framework for a well-subsidized and independent journalism.

The third qualification to the "Internet as public sphere" hypothesis is that it often seems to exhibit an unchecked enthusiasm for these technologies, and technology in general that is unwarranted. At its most extreme, some argue that the quantitative improvement in communication technology is leading to a truly qualitative shift in human consciousness. By this reasoning the computer networks are liberating humanity from the material chains that have kept human imagination and creativity locked up (Rushkoff, 1994). Some argue that cyberspace has created genuine communities that offer a glimpse of how we might truly become a global human family (Rheingold, 1993). Both these utopian views recognize that commercial and government forces seek to undermine the transcendental potential of the Internet and the information highway, yet both emphasize the revolutionary power of the technologies to liberate humanity. This perspective emphasizes cyberspace as a spawning ground for counterculture and often hearkens back to the 1960s and other eras of communitarian ideals. As appealing as this line of reasoning may be, it really is nonsensical as any sort of notion about how history is going to unfold.

I would not characterize the adoption of the "Internet as public sphere" so much a grand victory as it is a case of making the best of a bad situation. On the one hand, the motor force behind the development of these technologies is business and business demand; Walter Hale Hamilton noted 60 years ago that "business succeeds rather better than the state in imposing restraints upon individuals, because its imperatives are disguised as choices" (quoted in Rorty, 1934, p. 10). We did not elect to have these technologies, nor did we ever debate their merits. They have been presented either as some sort of product of inexorable natural evolution or as a democratic response to pent-up consumer demand, when, in fact, they are here because they are profitable and a market was created for them. Now that they are here, people can ignore them only at the risk of jeopardizing their careers and their ability to participate in society. As Neil Postman (1995, p. 4) noted, "New technologies do not always increase people's options; just as often they do exactly the opposite." I am not advancing a Luddite argument; I merely point out that a central part of democratic communication policymaking is to evaluate the effects of a new technology before adopting it, to look before we leap. That has not been the case with the Internet or the information highway.

All communication technologies have unanticipated and unintended effects, and one function of policymaking is to understand them so we may avoid or minimize the undesirable ones. The digitalization and computerization of our society are going to transform us radically, yet even some closely associated with these developments express concern about the possibility of a severe deterioration of the human experience as a result of the information revolution (Deitch, 1994; Stoll, 1995). As one observer noted, "Very few of us—only the high priests—really understand the new technologies, and these are surely the people least qualified to make policy decisions about them" (Charbeneau, 1994, pp. 28-29). For every argument extolling the "virtual community" and the liberatory aspects of cyberspace, it seems every bit as plausible to reach dystopian conclusions. Why not look at the information highway as a process that encourages the isolation, atomization, and marginalization of people in society? In fact, cannot the ability of people to create their own "community" in cyberspace have the effect of terminating a community in the general sense? In a class-stratified, commercially oriented society like the United States, cannot the information highway have the effect of simply making it possible for the well-to-do to bypass any contact with the balance of society altogether? These are precisely the types of questions that need to be addressed and answered and precisely the types of questions the market has no interest in. At any rate, a healthy skepticism toward technology should be the order of the day.

CONCLUSION

The nature of contemporary communication policymaking in the United States is only superficially democratic, and there is little reason therefore to believe that the results of such a system will do much more than satisfy the interests of those responsible for the decisions. Communication policymaking follows the contours of political debate in general (Brenner, 1995). This is a business-run society, and the communication system is tailored to suit corporate interests. There is no time to stop and consider the social consequences or possible alternatives when there is very good money to be made. By this logic, the role of the citizenry is to conform its ambitions and goals to satisfy the needs of business; it is not the responsibility of those directing the economy to make their activities meet the democratically determined aims of the citizenry, as democratic theory would suggest (Meiklejohn, 1948). In fact, the market is hardly a substitute for democracy; at most, it is a tool, like technology, to be thoughtfully employed in a democracy. And the immediate consequence of the market for global communication is one of increasing private concentration and commercialization, hardly the stuff of democracy.

It is also appealing to think that the new communication technologies can solve social problems, but they cannot. Only humans, acting consciously, can address and resolve problems such as poverty, environmental degradation, racism, sexism, and militarism. As Daniel Singer (1995, p. 533) noted, our task is to overcome "the contradiction between our technological genius and the absurdity of our social organization." So can the communication technologies save democracy from capitalism? No, not unless they are explicitly deployed for public service principles.

Is that possible? Given my argument about the nature of the global economy and the demise of sovereignty, one might assume the situation to be nearly hopeless, and that the only rational course would be to try to eke the best possible reforms out of the existing regime. And because even minor public interest reforms within the existing corporate communication system have proven nearly impossible, some may therefore regard the overall situation as hopeless for the foreseeable future.

In fact, I believe the exact opposite is the case. The current "pro-market" policies are going to be little short of disastrous for the quality of life for a majority of people both in the United States and globally. In the coming generation there will be a pressing need for alternative policies that place the needs of the bulk of the citizenry ahead of the demands of global capital. We are entering a critical juncture in which no social institutions—including corporations and the market—can remain exempt from public scrutiny. The challenge for those committed to democracy is, as William Greider (1992, p. 403) noted, "to refashion the global economy . . . so that it enhances democracy rather than crippling it, so that economic returns are widely distributed among all classes instead of narrowly at the top." The tension between democracy and capitalism is becoming increasingly evident, and communication—so necessary to both—can hardly serve two masters at once. From a critical perspective, in which democracy is privileged over profit, this is the context for communication policymaking. Given the centrality of communication to global capitalism, the move to reform communication must be part and parcel of a movement to reform the global political economy, as Greider suggests. It is unthinkable otherwise.

By this reasoning, there is a special role for communication scholars to play in debating and devising democratic communication policies, but the academic context for critical research is in turmoil. The rise of the Internet and the information highway places the future of communication research and education at U.S. universities in jeopardy. It demands a restructuring, or at least a rethinking, of the very field of communication, precisely at a time when many U.S, universities are "down-sizing" as a consequence of the global economic trends outlined earlier, specifically stagnation and the collapse of the public sector. This is putting considerable pressure on universities to redirect their activities to elicit support from the corporate sector. In effect, there is increased pressure to move away from the traditional standard of intellectual and scholarly autonomy and to link education and research explicitly to the needs of business. This has clear implications for the nature of the scholarship that the new "lean and mean" university will produce, which perhaps explains why the pro-market political right is most enthusiastic about the elimination of academic autonomy. The stars on campus are the departments and individuals who attract the most grant money; departments and scholars who fail to do so face an uncertain future.

Nowhere are these pressures more apparent than in communication. It is a paradox that precisely at the historic moment that communication is roundly deemed as central to global political economy and culture those academic departments expressly committed to communication research are facing severe cutbacks or even elimination. This can be attributed to the historic weakness of communication on U.S. campuses; when cutbacks need be made, communication is easier to attack than more established disciplines. The pressures are doubly strong therefore to link up communication research and education to the masters of the corporate communication order, to opt for what Paul Lazarsfeld (1941) termed the "administrative" rather than the "critical" path for scholarship.

Although cultivating ties to the capitalist communication sector may appear a logical "management" move, it will probably lead to the demise of communication as a viable discipline. On the one hand, the "administrative" turn is morally deplorable; it takes communication away from what Harold Innis (quoted in Carey, 1978) termed the "university tradition," a source of honest independent inquiry in service to democratic values. At a practical level, too, business schools are far better suited to conduct research along these lines, especially as communication is now a central business activity. Who needs departments predicated on public service and professional principles such as journalism when the whole idea is to maximize profit? There is no alternative then but to do honest independent scholarship and instruction, with a commitment first and foremost to democratic values, letting the chips fall where they may. The field of communication needs to apply the full weight of its intellectual traditions and methodologies to the daunting questions before us. They desperately require scholarly attention. The lesson of the last 50 years on U.S. campuses is clear: If communication does not do it, nobody else will. It will make for a rocky road—if it does not, that probably means the research is not any good—but what other choice is there?

REFERENCES

Albo, G. (1994). "Competitive austerity" and the impasse of capitalist employment policy. In R. Miliband & L. Panitch (Eds.), *Socialist register 1994* (pp. 144-170). London: The Merlin Press.

Avery, R. K. (Ed.). (1993). *Public service broadcasting in a multichannel environment.* New York: Longman.

Bagdikian, B. H. (1992). *The media monopoly* (4th ed.). Boston: Beacon Press.

Barkan, J. (1995, Winter). *Dissent*, pp. 71-76.

Baughman, J. (1992). *The republic of mass culture.* Baltimore: The Johns Hopkins University.

Bernstein, M. A. (1987). *The Great Depression: Delayed recovery and economic change in America.* New York: Cambridge University Press.

Blumler, J. G. (ed.) (1992). *Television and the public interest: Vulnerable values in West European broadcasting.* London: Sage.

Brenner, R. (1995). Clinton's failure and the politics of U.S. decline. *Against the Current, 10*(3), 26-31.

Carey, A. (1995). *Taking the risk out of democracy.* Sydney: University of New South Wales.

Carey, J. (1978). A plea for the university tradition. *Journalism Quarterly, 55*, 846-855.

Charbeneau, T. (1994). Dangerous assumptions. *Toward Freedom, 43*(7), 28-29.

Chomsky, N. (1987). *On power and ideology: The Managua lectures.* Boston: South End.

Chomsky, N. (1994). *World orders old and new.* New York: Columbia University Press.

Cowling, K., & Sugden, R. (1994). *Beyond capitalism: Towards a new world economic order.* New York: St. Martin's Press.

Deitch, J. (1994). Post human. *Adbusters Quarterly, 3*(1), 20-27,

De Vaney, A. (Ed.). (1994). *Watching Channel One: The convergence of students, technology, and private business.* Albany: State University of New York.

Donaton, S. (1995, April 10). Not your father's magazine. *Advertising Age,* p. 13.

Douglas, S. J. (1987). *Inventing American broadcasting, 1899-1922.* Baltimore: Johns Hopkins University.

Feldman, A. (1996). *Staking a place in the ether: The politics of public service broadcasting in Wisconsin, 1918-1940.* Unpublished doctoral dissertation, University of Wisconsin-Madison.

Flores, M. M. (1995, May 25). Show offers inside look at Microsoft, Gates. *The Seattle Times,* p. D1.

Frederick, H. H. (1995). *North American NGO computer networking: Computer communications in the cross-border coalition-building (Research rep.for Rand Corporation/Ford Foundation).* Washington, DC: Rand Corporation/Ford Foundation, Program for Research on Immigration Policy.

Frost, S. E., Jr. (1937). *Education's own stations.* Chicago: University of Chicago.

Gilder, G. (1994). *Life after television* (2nd ed.). New York: Simon & Schuster.

Glaberson, W. (1994, December 5). Press: A dispute over GATT highlights the complex links between newspapers and their corporate parents. *The New York Times,* p. C8.

Godfried, N. (1996). *The rise and fall of labor radio: WCFL, Chicago's labor station, 1926-1978.* Urbana: University of Illinois Press.

Goldman, K. (1995, April 5). Now marketers can buy a service to track Internet customer usage. *Wall Street Journal,* p. B5.

Gore, A. (1995, February 25). Remarks by Vice-President Al Gore to G-7 Ministers Meeting on the Global Information Initiative. Brussels, Belgium.

Greider, W. (1992). *Who will tell the people? The betrayal of American democracy.* New York: Simon & Schuster.

Guma, G. (1994, December). The road from here to media democracy. *Toward Freedom,* p. 2.

Habermas, J. (1989). *The structural transformation of the public sphere* (Thomas Burger, Trans., with the assistance of Frederick Lawrence). Cambridge, MA: MIT Press.

Herman, E. S. (1993a, September). The end of democracy? *Z Magazine,* pp. 57-62.

Herman, E. S. (1993b). The externalities effects of commercial and public broadcasting. In K. Nordenstreng & H. Schiller (Eds.), *Beyond national sovereignty* (pp. 85-115). Norwood, NJ: Ablex.

Herman, E.S., & Chomsky, N. (1988). *Manufacturing consent: The political economy of the mass media.* New York: Pantheon.

Kimball, P. (1994). *Down-sizing the news: Network cutbacks in the nation's capital.* Washington, DC: Woodrow Wilson Center.

Kranich, N. C. (1994). *Internet access & democracy: Ensuring public places on the Info Highway.* Westfield, NJ: Open Magazine Pamphlet Series.

Lasch, C. (1995). *The revolt of the elites and the betrayal of democracy.* New York: W. W. Norton .

Lazarsfeld, P. F. (1941). Remarks on administrative and critical communications research. *Studies in Philosophy and Social Science, 9,* 2-16.

MacEwan, A. (1994). Globalization and stagnation. *Monthly Review, 45*(11), 1-16.

Macpherson, C. B. (1977). *The life and times of liberal democracy.* New York: Oxford University Press.

Mazzocco, D. W. (1994). *Networks of power: Corporate TV's threat to democracy.* Boston: South End Press.

McChesney, R. W. (1993). *Telecommunications, mass media, and democracy: The battle for the control of US broadcasting, 1928-1935.* New York: Oxford University Press.

McChesney, R. W. (1995a, December). Public broadcasting in the age of Communication Revolution. *Monthly Review,* 1-19.

McChesney, R. W. (1995b). On media, politics, and the Left, Part 1: An interview with Noam Chomsky. *Against the Current, 10*(2), 27-32.

McManus, J. H. (1994). *Market-driven journalism: Let the citizen beware?* Thousand Oaks, CA: Sage.

Meiklejohn, A. (1948). *Political freedom.* New York: Harper & Brothers.

Mills, C. W. (1956). *The power elite.* New York: Oxford University Press.

Murdock, G. (1992). Citizens, consumers, and public culture. In M. Skovmand & K. C. Schroder (eds.). *Media cultures: Reappraising transnational media* (pp. 17-41), London: Routledge.

Murdock, G. (1994). The new media empires: Media concentration and control in the age of convergence. *Media development, 41*(4), 3-6.

Murdock, G., & Golding, P. (1989). Information poverty and political inequality: Citizenship in the age of privatized communications. *Journal of Communication, 39*(3), 180-195.

Negroponte, N. (1995). *Being digital.* New York: Alfred A. Knopf.

Noble, D. (1995). The truth about the Information Highway. *Monthly Review, 47*(2), 47-52.

Nordenstreng, K., & Schiller, H. I. (Eds.). (1993). *Beyond national sovereignty: International communication in the 1990s.* Norwood, NJ: Ablex.

Panitch, L. (1994). Globalization and the State. In R. Miliband & L. Panitch (Eds.), *Socialist Register 1994* (pp. 60-93). London: The Merlin Press.

Postman, N. (1985). *Amusing ourselves to death*. New York: Penguin.

Postman, N. (1995, February). 1995 *Russell Lecture*. Presbyterian College, Clinton, SC.

Rheingold, H. (1993). *The virtual community: Homesteading on the electronic frontier*. Reading, MA: Addison-Wesley.

Rorty, J. (1934). *Order on the air!* New York: The John Day Company.

Rushkoff, D. (1994). *Cyberia: Life in the trenches of hyperspace*. New York: HarperCollins.

Sandberg, J. (1995, April 10). Time Warner sells ads in cyberspace via its pathfinder service on Internet. *Wall Street Journal*, p. B6.

Scheer, C. (1995). The pursuit of techno-happiness. *The Nation, 260*(18), 632-634.

Schiller, H. I. (1994). *Info highway or corporate monorail?* Westfield, NJ: Open Magazine Pamphlet Series.

Schiller, H. I. (1995, May 19). *Corporate-driven information technologies: Constructing political ungovernability world-wide*. Paper presented to International Colloquium on "Economie de l'Information", Lyon-Lilleurbanne, France.

Simon, J. (1995, March 20). *Netwar could make Mexico ungovernable*. Pacific News Service Dispatch.

Singer, D. (1995). The sound and the furet. *The Nation, 260*(15), 531-534.

Smulyan, S. (1994). *Selling radio: The commercialization of American broadcasting, 1920-1934*. Washington, DC: Smithsonian Institution Press.

Spigel, L. (1992). *Make room for TV*. Chicago: University of Chicago Press.

Squires, J. (1993). *Read all about it: The corporate takeover of America's newspapers*. New York: Times Books.

Stoll, C. (1995). *Silicon snake oil: Second thoughts on the information highway*. New York: Doubleday.

Sullivan-Trainor, M. (1994). *Detour: The truth about the information super-highway*. San Mateo, CA: IDG Books.

Sweezy, P. M. (1994). The triumph of financial capital. *Monthly Review, 46*(2), 1-9.

Telecommunications Workers Union. (1995, March 24). Presentation to the CRTC Hearings on the Information Highway, Hull, Quebec.

Too fast on communications reform (1995, April 12). New York Times, p. A14.

Toffler, A., & Toffler, H. (1994). *Creating a new civilization: The politics of the third wave*. Atlanta: Turner Publishing.

Twenty-first century capitalism. (1995, January 24). *Business Week* [Special Ed.].

Underwood, D. (1993). *When MBA's rule the newsroom: How the marketers and mangers are reshaping today's media*. New York: Columbia University Press.

Wallace, D. J. (1995, April 10). Shopping online: A sticky business. *Advertising Age*, p. 20.

Wollenberg, S. (1995, April 18). Group warns ads bombard kids at school. *The Capital Times*, p. 5B.

Section II

Industrial Imperatives and the Possibility of Democratic Spheres of Communication

Chapter 4

Communication Policy in the United States

Vanda Rideout
Vincent Mosco

Owing in part to the growing significance of the mass media in social life, communication policy research has grown substantially over the past two decades. This chapter provides a map of the research on communication policy in the United States. However, no single review can do justice to the enormous body of research on policy issues dealing with communication. Acknowledging this limitation, the chapter focuses on the perspectives that guide and organize communication research and on central trends and issues in the relationship between the state and the major participants in the policy process. Specifically, the chapter aims to introduce some balance into the discussion of communication policy research by remedying the tendency in the literature to respond to the demands of industries affected by communication policy and of the governments responsible for setting communication policy and regulation. It also seeks to balance the tendency to assess communication policy on largely economic grounds (Picard, 1989), for example, the relationship between specific policies and economic growth, by concentrating on the *political* dimension of communication policy, particularly the relationship of communication policy to democracy.

The chapter is divided into two sections; the first section provides a conceptual map as one way of understanding the state and communication policy research. The second documents and organizes recent trends in state policy activity according to different processes. The first part begins with *pluralist* and *managerial* research, which tends to be more descriptive than theoretically grounded and more likely to mount an argument in favor of a specific business or government interest than to explain a set of actions by situating them within their social, political, economic, and cultural contexts. Moreover, this research is likely to be produced in private or government-funded institutions and directed to influencing a pending issue. In the United States private companies, including large communication providers, new challengers, and large communication users (domestic corporations and multinationals), along with large government bodies, such as the U.S. Defense Department, significantly structure the policy research agenda. Nevertheless, although these characteristics constitute a frame of reference for the research agenda, they do not determine it. Communication policy research is also informed by research that starts from a social *class* analysis that is theoretically grounded, critical, oppositional, and linked to public interest and social movement organizations. It also tends to be marginalized from mainstream perspectives.

The second part provides another way of investigating state policy activity through the four processes of *commercialization, liberalization, privatization,* and *internationalization.* These policy reorganization processes raise a concern to identify the political features of communication policy, particularly to expand the discussion of communication policy on the question of democracy. The chapter takes a broad view of democracy to encompass the fullest public participation in decisions that affect social life. According to this view, democracy refers to both the process of *participation* in decisions and the value of moving toward *equality.* Moreover, it takes the view that participatory democracy is not limited to the political arena. A fully democratic society is one in which citizens actively create economic, sociocultural, and political participation and equality. Additionally, this conception of democracy underlines its public character. Democracy means more than the sum total of votes taken among isolated individuals. In fact, it flourishes only when individuals can transcend their private selves and constitute themselves, in part through communication, in public groups, organizations, and institutions (Keane, 1984).

PERSPECTIVES ON THE STATE AND COMMUNICATION POLICY

The map of communication policy research can be sorted according to three perspectives—pluralist, managerial, and class power—which numerous social scientists identify as central ways of thinking about the role of the state in developed capitalist societies (Alford & Friedland, 1985).

Pluralism

The pluralist perspective develops from the view that power is situational, that it operates in specific circumstances over specific issues. The pluralist sees the state as the independent arbiter of interest clashes among the range of societal organizations, including business, trade unions, civic organizations, and others, none of which is powerful enough to consistently shape state action. According to this view, the state itself is held together by a legal structure and an organizational culture that reflect widely held values that the state acts on to impartially manage the preferences of competing interests (Dahl, 1956).

Pluralist analyses of communication policy begin with the study of social values and concentrate on what they conclude is a shift from support for government protection of the public interest through public ownership and regulation to support for the operation of private, competitive markets (Derthick & Quirk, 1985). In essence, from the pluralist vantage point, the state oversees a marketplace of competing political interests, with no particular interest capable of determining decision making on its own. The range of competing participants marshal political, economic, and intellectual resources to back their preferred policy positions. An interest succeeds to the extent that it can convince state policymakers that it has power and that it conforms to the dominant social value preferences (Krasnow, Longley, & Terry, 1982).

Pluralist analysis of communication policy assumes a functionalist approach to social analysis, explaining the widespread introduction of deregulatory policies as a result of value shifts within society that favor reliance on private markets for settling claims. According to this view, from the postwar period until the 1970s and 1980s, societal values and public support for media policies facilitated the operation of the market by monopoly and oligopoly media providers. Pluralist research maintains that communication providers, particularly in broadcasting and telecommunications services, were regulated to meet broad public interest goals linked to democratically based principles of fairness and equity. In U.S. telephony, these goals included universal service at fair and reasonable rates. Although broadcasting is provided by private institutions, the airwaves are considered a natural resource held in common. Consequently, the issuing of private broadcasting licenses carried public trust obligations such as freedom of speech and of ideas, requirements for public information programming, limits to advertising, fairness in programming, and equal time for political candidates. According to the pluralist view, these practices proved increasingly dysfunctional, as new participants, some taking advantage of new technologies, began to tip the balance of power in favor of competition and market power over regulation. Communication policy and regulation changed from concern over the public interest to facilitating the operation of private competitive markets (Crandall, 1991).

Disillusion over regulatory protection of communication monopoly providers, particularly in telecommunications and broadcasting, unleashed forces that undercut the connections between these communications providers and the notion of the public interest. Two very different coalitions, conservatives advocating free markets and antimonopoly liberal populist interest groups, came together to support broadcasting and telecommunication deregulation (Horwitz, 1989). Liberals and public interest groups perceived that deregulation would provide a solution to entrenched corporate power. Moreover, support for cable television broadcasting technology could concurrently limit and transcend commercial network broadcasting and create a "wired democracy." Pluralist research tends to identify technology as a major source of changing values. The growth of "smaller, faster, cheaper, better" (Ernst, Oettinger, Branscomb, Rubin, & Wikler, 1993) means of communication broadens the range of choice in communications services, making it increasingly unlikely that government monopolies or regulated industries can deliver the goods better than an open marketplace of numerous suppliers (Noam, 1987). For example, in a standard work on the economics of media, Owen and Wildman (1992) maintain that technological advances in broadcasting services have resulted in a surge of new entrants that have lowered prices, expanded services, and sped up the process of innovation. For them, as for other pluralists, this provides *prima facie* evidence for a shift from reliance on state-regulated cartels (the three major U.S. television networks) for the provision of broadcasting services. Similar arguments are made about telecommunications to defend the introduction of competition in U.S. markets (Crandall, 1991).

For pluralists, the turn to market principles benefits the process of policymaking as well. Pluralists have traditionally noted that, however salutary the public interest standard may have been for maintaining a sense of inclusiveness in the media system, the principle multiplied the number of claims that could be legitimately made on the system, thereby overloading government with unmanageable demands. This problem is compounded by the tendency of regulators to use regulations to their own benefit, what Wilson (1980) called "staff capture" of a regulatory agency. The shift to market principles streamlines the process of settling claims, eliminates many as illegitimate, and undermines the power of regulatory and policy bureaucrats, thereby creating literal technologies of freedom (Pool, 1983).

This shift does not please all pluralists. It worries some, like Dahl (1982), who has moved from his now classic position in defense of pluralism (Dahl, 1956) to a fear that pluralism no longer explains American politics because the balance of interest forces has become distorted in favor of corporate power with no substantial countervailing force. In place of reliance on the market, Dahl offers an alternative, what Held (1987) describes as a neopluralist position that calls for greater representativeness, for explicit state measures to ensure fuller equality and participation for groups that would otherwise be submerged beneath the marketplace power of business. This prescription grows out of a more general concern that pluralists have tended to identify the pressures of business and a rightward shift in the intellectual climate with a *general* shift in societal values. Furthermore, pluralists have tended to place considerable stock in the capacity for social differences to even out over the range of decisions with no single institutional force capable of seizing the policy agenda for a long duration. Finally, pluralists rely on a view of the state as the chief locus of ultimate authority in policy matters and as an independent arbiter of conflicting claims, above the potential for capture or contamination by any specific interest.

Managerial Theory

Managerialism acknowledges the shortcomings of a pluralist view and replaces it with a vision of limited, elite-guided democracy (Crozier, Huntington, & Watanuki, 1975). Unlike the pluralist, who views power as situational, linked to specific events and networks, the managerial theorist sees it as structural, embodied in the rules governing the operation of organizations and institutions. A pluralist looks for power in the constellation of interests whose balance of pressures results in a policy decision, such as the agreement between the U.S. courts and AT&T to restructure the company. Managerial theory situates power in elites whose actions constitute the policy *agenda* that frames the pluralist's discrete decisions. Whereas the pluralist perspective focuses on the individual case, with change resulting from shifts in values and technology, managerial approaches concentrate on changes in the control of power over the policy agenda.

According to this view, the fundamental driving force across all political regimes is the need to manage growing societal complexity brought about by technological change and the division of labor. Managerial theory draws its inspiration from the classic work of Weber (1978) and Schumpeter (1942). From this view, the 20th century is marked by the ascendancy of bureaucratic elites who play a crucial role in political and technological management, including the organization of those intellectual technologies central to Daniel Bell's (1973) conception of a postindustrial society led by knowledge workers.

Managerial research emphasizes that the quantitative increase in services has led to qualitative changes in the structure of media industries (Beniger, 1986). According to this view, old regulatory approaches based on distinct technologies and distinct services and industries do not work in an era of increasingly integrated and convergent technologies, services, and markets. Managerial theory maintains that the experience of regulatory bodies worldwide has shown that it is impossible to apply traditional regulatory categories to a new communication area in which the distinctions between print, entertainment, information, broadcasting, and telecommunications are eroding. In essence, several discrete, manageable technologies and industry sectors have merged into an increasingly integrated, but more difficult to manage, electronic services arena (Bruce, Cunard, & Director, 1986).

Managerialists maintain that an absence of fundamental structural change will result in the more powerful media interests resisting challenges from competitors and using the regulatory apparatus to maintain their power. This is the managerial version of the "staff capture" thesis, which sees the major telephone companies building alliances with regulators and other government departments to shape and influence changes in these arenas to their advantage (Noam, 1987). According to this view, changes to communication ownership and antitrust rules and deregulation stem from the development of coalitions powerful enough to undermine old powers. In all media areas, it includes conservative governments, in telecom it includes large corporate users, for broadcasting it encompasses cable television. New groups win out because they are able to apply their economic, political, and technological resources more effectively. But as Aufderheide (1987, 1991, 1992) points out, much of the cost of these conflicts shifts to other groups in society that are least able to successfully oppose.

The major concern within managerial research is that the market may not be the best long-term vehicle for effective management of the media sector. Deregulation and privatization provide the jolt to reorganize media industries that were characterized by rapid technological change and stagnating regulation. But as managerial research points out, deregulating the cable television industry in the United States resulted in little or no guidance in planning or coordination (Atkin & Starr, 1990). In fact, the 1984 *Cable Communication Policy Act* created an uncontrolled and unregulated monopoly situation in the United States, which enabled the industry to increase rates, diminish service quality, and participate in other noncompetitive activities. Deregulation led to continued complaints by cable subscribers, among others, which resulted in the reregulation in 1992 of basic cable rates and reduced cable market power vis-à-vis other communication industries (Atkin, 1994; Coustel, 1993).

Former supporters of U.S. telecommunication divestiture and deregulation now admit that the original decision was "a monumental mistake" (Huber, 1993). Competition in the long-distance market is now viewed as an illusion, dominated by oligopolistic players—AT&T, MCI and Sprint—and regulated by FCC price capping. The other mistake was reinforcing another powerful monopoly force, comprised of the seven regional Bell companies, in telephone local exchange. Concerns in telecommunications have also been raised about the economic arguments used to advance deregulation and divestiture. Oettinger (1988) describes these arguments as "fairy tales" to support political forces and the goals of the industry arena (see also Denious, 1986). Critics of the managerial perspective argue that economic justification for the telecommunications policy shift reflects the growing power of large corporate users and new communication providers, and that as telecommunications takes on greater strategic global significance, domestic and international policies must be changed, integrated, and exported to meet the needs of these international players (D. Schiller, 1982).

Class Power Theory

Class power theory sees power as *systemic* and calls for comprehending more than its manifestation in situation and structure. According to this view, understanding communication policy requires expanding the focus beyond a specific case, such as how the United States decided to roll back cable television rates in 1993, and beyond the agenda of decision making that bears the label deregulation. Class theory sees control over decisions and agendas as expressions of dynamic processes and power relations in the class system of capitalist societies. A class power analysis begins with questions of inequality, power, and undemocratic processes that are imbedded in the social, political, and economic relations of a capitalist society. This research sees the policy field as class divided and makes the case that democracy can only be sustained by overcoming these divisions.

Two major strands of class power theory—instrumental and systemic structural research—attempt to explain how the United States developed its system of corporate-controlled media, how the state works with the dominant class to advance these interests, and why it is important to examine the complex relations involved in communication policy and regulation.

Instrumental research identifies and analyzes the ways the media industries use their economic and political power to ensure that their interests and those of the larger capitalist class are met. It examines how media industries use technologies as instruments for capital accumulation and social control influencing all aspects of social life from work to entertainment. Additionally, it identifies and investigates the significance of class power by examining the dense web of connections between media entrepreneurs and the rest of the elite class through their connections on corporate boards, professional associations, and lobbying groups, and through their ties to state elites (Domhoff, 1978).

U.S. instrumental research focuses on ownership concentration, communication elite integration with other power elites, and the instrumental role the state has played in exporting deregulation policies and a private media model to other countries to the benefit of multinational business. This research has documented that massive consolidation and concentration of media ownership has taken place in two stages over the last 15 years. The first stage of domestic concentration occurred within specific sectors such as the daily newspaper, magazine and book publishing industries, among others. The second stage involved concentration and consolidation across media industries creating media conglomerates such as Time Warner with interests in print and publishing, film and video, music and cable, and so on. As a result, fewer than 25 businesses control more than 50% of the industry (Bagdikian, 1992).

Concentration and conglomeration have also been accompanied by integration among the media, big business generally, and government elites. Reliance on advertising revenues and interlocking directorates with oil companies, banks, insurance and retail, among others, creates a commonality and flow of interests and of personnel (Akhavan-Majid & Wolf, 1991). Examples include personnel flows between the media and government and overlaps of personnel from broadcasting and telecommunication, to commissioner positions on the FCC. Other examples include the mass media's reliance on the government for news information (press releases and press conferences; Herman & Chomsky, 1988). In addition, powerful lobby groups such as the American Newspaper Publishers Association (ANPA), the Motion Picture Association of America (MPAA), the National Association of Broadcasters (NAB), and the National Cable Television Association (NCTA) exert their influence on antitrust, media ownership, and deregulation policy decisions.

Instrumental research on U.S. radio broadcasting reveals the early influence of the Rockefeller Foundation and of communication research conducted by Lazarsfeld and others with the financial support of broadcasters and advertisers (Buxton, 1994). Research in this tradition reveals that telecommunication deregulation and the AT&T divestiture occurred because large corporate users banded together to form powerful industry and lobby organizations to demand new services and lower rates (D. Schiller, 1982).

Other studies highlight how the U.S. government has been an important instrument in exporting its policies of privatization and deregulation to advance U.S.-based communication and cultural multinational corporations. Policy changes have not only permitted further global expansion, but they have also allowed these businesses to appropriate more of the public sphere into the private arena. Examples include the selling off of public radio spectrum and the proposed sell off of the existing national electronic network—the Internet. Private corporate activity also includes promoting consumerism and the reorganization of state policy to accommodate it. Invariably these activities limit cultural diversity, social information dissemination, and democracy (H. Schiller, 1989).

Instrumental research explains *how* systems of corporate-controlled media and telecommunications develop and *how* the state works with the dominant class to advance its interests. This approach provides an advance over pluralism because instrumentalism recognizes that power is not equally distributed among all participants in the policy process, and that the state is not the independent arbiter of differences among these participants. In fact, by examining the process of policymaking from think tanks to largely private policy formation bodies through lobbying and media influence, this approach decenters the formal state decision-making process to open room for the full range of players and arenas that constitute the complete process of policy determination and implementation. Nevertheless, instrumentalism tends to neglect conflict and contradiction in the process of elite rule, much of which grows out of the oppositional struggles of classes and social movements. *Structural* communication policy research deepens and expands instrumental analysis by taking up these lacunae and by shifting from the *how* to the *why* of class rule. This research considers that the primary function of the state in capitalist societies is to serve the interests of dominant class fractions by advancing capital accumulation to produce and reproduce material resources and by promoting legitimation to ensure the maintenance of some degree of general popular belief in the system.

In addition, a structural approach acknowledges the contradictions in a capitalist society that arise from the state's often conflicting functions and from struggles connected to class, gender, race, and other divisions in civil society. In an attempt to constrain and control structural contradictions among classes, and between classes and civil society, the state plays an important role to ensure the survival and growth of the system. In order to create and maintain conditions of social harmony, the state produces policies and regulation to legitimize capitalist social relations. Consequently, the state is an important site of struggles and contradictions that also affect the policy formation process (Aglietta, 1979; Jessop, 1990). Concurrently, the state's regulatory agencies, such as the FCC, in the structural view are best seen as "unequal structures of representation" (Mahon, 1980, p. 157).

Structural studies of the film industry examine the relationships among producers, distributors, and exhibitors within the industry and their links to the banking industry, focusing on how and why these relationships have translated into control over finance and content (Aksoy & Robins, 1992) that extends from independent film producers to the cable television industry (Wasko, 1994). Research applying this perspective to the U.S. broadcasting system concludes that the real "media wars" (Mosco, 1992) have and continue to take place between the American people concerned over pricing and universal access, and the U.S. government and media entrepreneurs. As an example, the present U.S. commercial broadcasting system did not derive from consensus. From 1928 to 1935, the broadcasting reform movement vociferously opposed the commercial broadcasting model. An eclectic coalition, known as the broadcast reform movement, with representatives from education, labor, religious organizations, the press, intellectuals, and civil society groups, fought to have a portion of the system allocated for noncommercial and nonprofit use (McChesney, 1993). Pitted against powerful adversaries from the commercial broadcasting industry, their lobbyists, and the America Bar Association, the 1934 Communication Act supported the commercial system. With only a vague public service mandate, the Act has continued to incite conflicts, struggle, and resistance. Recent activism includes the American Civil Liberties Union and public television viewer's resistance to federal funding cutbacks to public broadcasting (Aufderheide, 1991). Other pressure groups have continued to engage in what Montgomery (1989) calls "negotiated struggles" over broadcasting policies that affect television programming. The activism of complex pressure groups has resulted in policy changes dealing with an array of issues ranging from fundamentalism and morality to violence on prime-time television or to the inaccurate and unfair representations of women, Blacks, Hispanics, indigenous peoples, unions, gays, seniors, and the physically challenged.

In a similar vein, the social relations involved in broadcasting deregulation (during the 1980s) were the result of a "new conservative hegemony" (Kellner, 1990). Until the 1980s, the broadcasting system was guided by a public service mandate. The drive to deregulate resulted in the commercialization of many public services and ended regulation in other areas. Deregulation included changing rules to eliminate the fairness doctrine, lift the commercial advertising limits for prime-time and children's programs, loosen ownership concentration regulations, and do away with previously required and publicly accessible reports on the performance of broadcasting outlets, despite strong and widespread resistance from the public.

Structural analysis also shows that deregulation, pro-competition, rate rebalancing, and reregulation are not just about policy changes. They are also forms of corporate restructuring that eliminate jobs, accelerate the deskilling of jobs, and reduce the bargaining power of communication unions. Recently some government agencies such as the Office of Technology Assessment (1990, 1991) and the National Telecommunications and Information Administration (1991) have begun to reflect on the meaning of a communication infrastructure and universality in a changing communication system. Nonetheless, much of this concern is couched in the language of economic competitiveness and consumers rights rather than the rights of citizens in a political democracy. Consequently, instead of broadening the definitions of the public interest (Aufderheide, 1992) and of universality (Calabrese & Jung, 1992), there has been a narrowing of the notion or concept of "the public" to that of "consumer." To ensure that a market form of universality (U.S. telephone universality is approximately 93%) was maintained, targeted telephone subsidization was introduced through a federal program ("Life Line") and state programs ("Link Up America"; Aufderheide, 1987; FCC, 1991), complete with means tests to keep the deserving poor on the system.

For structuralists U.S. government intervention into telecommunications to advance the interests of dominant class fractions has been an ongoing process beginning with financial and land grant assistance in the days of the private telegraph monopoly (DuBoff, 1984). Government regulation also helped AT&T achieve market dominance (Hills, 1986) and, during the Cold War, gave Comsat its backing to defeat the Soviet Union in communication satellite development (Mosco, 1989).

Much of the recent class power research aims to widen the debate about transformations in the communications industry by addressing why this has become a central priority of governments in almost every society. This research addresses the growth of communication to a central position in the capital accumulation process. Under the shaping influence of capital, with considerable state involvement, technology has been used to deepen and extend the ability to turn communication and information into marketable commodities. The communication/information/culture commodity also enhances the value of more traditional goods and services (D. Schiller, 1994).

According to a class analysis, state policies have accelerated the process of commodification by rupturing long-standing relationships among business, the state, and labor. These relationships provided a workable regulatory solution during a period of steady economic growth, national markets, and a strong labor movement. One example in the United States was the relationship that linked the three commercial television networks, the Congress, the Federal Communications Commission, unions such as the National Association of Broadcasting Engineers and Technicians, and television viewers. Another linked AT&T, the FCC, state Public Utility Commissions, the Communication Workers of America, and telephone subscribers. From a class power point of view, these relationships are diminished, when not eliminated, by the growing reliance on media and telecommunications for economic growth, the rise of global markets, and the decline of trade unions.

The stress on capital accumulation risks an overly economistic view. Communication policy is also directed to the more political interest of unleashing new instruments of social control by promoting the capacity to use the means of communication to measure and monitor information transactions (Gandy, 1993). In addition to refining the process of commodification by increasing opportunities for the economic use of information contained in and about media use, this also extends the process of social control by increasing opportunities for detailed surveillance of individual and group behavior at work, at home, in the marketplace, and in public life.

Structural approaches are also distinguished by their acknowledgment of the contradictions, tensions, and outright class struggles that arise from political economic tendencies in communication. Specifically, they suggest that the use of communication and media to advance commodification and control creates substantial problems, including breakdowns in the ability to manage markets that are subject to regular upheavals, the decline of collective purpose in societies increasingly organized around individual consumption, the decline in purchasing power among growing numbers of people whose jobs are lost or down scaled, and the likelihood of new oppositional coalitions to resist these tendencies.

In a changing communication and information environment questions are being raised and activism continues, as new democratic progressive movements devoted to social change struggle for democratic communication systems. Efforts to secure public democratic space on the "information highway", referred to in the United States as the National Information Infrastructure (NII), are being fought by a number of groups and organizations including the Center for Media Education, American Civil Liberties Union, Media Access Project, the Consumer Federation of America, Computer Professionals for Social Responsibility, the Electronic Frontier Foundation, and the Telecommunications Policy Roundtable, among others. These progressive groups have had some success in building so-called open platform universalist principle in new legislation, specifically *The National Communication and Information Infrastructure Act* of 1994 (U.S. Senate, 1993), to protect and realize the democratic potential of the information highway. The open platform's principles include universal service (a minimum level of affordable information and communication service), free speech and common carriage, privacy, and the development of public interest applications and services (noncommercial).

There are numerous areas that require more attention in the research literature on conflict and struggle over communication policy and some suggestions of potential directions on the question of democracy. One area includes the history of communication policy, involving the connection between policy history and general history. One example is McChesney's (1993) history of U.S. broadcasting policy. This research traces the participation of the American Federation of Labor (AFL) affiliate, the Chicago Federation of Labor, in the broadcast reform movement from the 1920s to the 1930s for public service broadcasting. WCFL, the Farmer-Labor nonprofit radio station, provided additional supported for the reform movement by favoring a public broadcasting model to be government controlled and operated .

Rethinking communication policy research (Mosco, forthcoming) also includes paying attention to cultural diversity. Influences that affect policy, in addition to social class, include gender, race, ethnicity, and other broadly defined social movements. These dimensions of cultural diversity may complement or conflict with a class analysis. Examples include examinations of labor hierarchies in the business of producing and distributing media and information and addressing the presence of significant gender divisions within an overall class-divided system (Gallagher, 1992). Additionally, communication research that addresses racial and ethnic divisions reveals differential access to communication. It includes research on access to ownership and control of communication companies (Tabor, 1991) to jobs in the media, communication, and informational technology industries (Honig, 1984).

RECENT TRENDS IN COMMUNICATION POLICY RESEARCH

Conceptual maps provide one means of understanding the state of communication policy research. Another is to examine recent trends in state policy activity in communication that have attracted the attention of the policy research community. Currently, four processes stand out: commercialization, liberalization, privatization, and internationalization.

Commercialization takes place when the state replaces forms of regulation based on public interest, public service, and related standards, such as universality, with market standards that establish market regulation. Commercialization applies to both public and private sector organizations, although it is more significant in the former because it can serve as a step toward privatization. In communication, this has meant greater emphasis on market position and profitability, even among state and public service broadcasting and telecommunications firms. Specifically, it leads to greater emphasis in broadcasting on audience size, advertising revenue, producing programming that anticipates an international market, and linkages to other revenue-generating media. In telecommunications, commercialization means building and organizing networks and services with a greater concern for those customers, principally businesses, likely to increase revenue, even if that means greater attention to linking metropolitan centers in global networks, rather than to extending networks into rural and generally underserved regions (Calabrese & Jung, 1992). Commercialization has led state communications authorities to separate telecommunications and other revenue-generating activities from postal and other services, which are mandated by constitution or legislation. Defenders of commercialization argue that it does not preclude and may even enhance public service goals, such as universality (Crandall, 1991; Noam, 1987). Conversely, opponents contend that it is a means of transforming the space of communication flows that, in a world of limited resources, inevitably means supporting one class of users over others and relying on "trickle-down" economics to overcome class divisions (Castells, 1989).

Extensive U.S. broadcasting deregulation began in the 1980s with the removal of most major structural constraints on broadcasting ownership, licenses, and business practices. Examples include increases in television station ownership limits, from 7 to 12; relaxed antitrust legislation governing multimedia ownership; elimination of most aspects of the financial and syndication rules; the elimination of the Fairness Doctrine; as well as the lifting of most advertising restrictions and community ascertainment rules in television (Kellner, 1990).

The cable industry was also deregulated, partly as a response to neoconservative practices that treated broadcasting and cable operations only as businesses. Passage of the 1984 *Cable Act* effectively eliminated basic cable rate regulation (only 3% of the industry remained regulated after the Act was passed). It also constrained the rights of state and local governments to control the franchising process. Additionally, FCC cross-ownership rules prohibited broadcasters and local telephone companies from owning a local cable system. These policy changes established a virtual monopoly for basic cable providers. In addition, the "must carry rules," and the setting aside of channels for public, educational, and government use, were eliminated. Moreover the Act exempted cable systems from regulations applicable to common carriers, that is, telephone companies or those governing public utilities, which weakened what little authority the FCC had over the industry (Aufderheide, 1992; Coustel, 1993). These changes strengthened the concentration of power among leading broadcasting and cable providers and gave broadcasting licenses and cable franchises near private property status. Broadcasting deregulation and the Cable Act became mechanisms to redefine the 1934 *Communication Act* by eroding its important public trust and public service inclusions.

Further changes, some would refer to these as "reregulation," in U.S. cable policy resulted from substantial rate increases that predictably followed in the wake of deregulation, specifically the lifting of local rate regulation. Over the period 1984-1992, basic cable rates increased by four times the consumer price index. One result was a leveling off of cable penetration to about 60% of American households. In light of broadcast deregulation that permitted profit-conscious network executives to trim costly news and public affairs at ABC, CBS and NBC, cable television, led by CNN, became the primary source of such programming. Consequently, 4 out of 10 American households were deprived access to the network of record for electronic news and public affairs (Auletta, 1991). Cable companies were satisfied with lower penetration rates because they would rather earn monopoly profits from basic and discretionary cable services than build systems in lower and working-class neighborhoods. According to Aufderheide (1992) and Coustel (1993), citizens' organizations took up the fight for regulation, particularly directed at the concentration of power in four multiple cable system operators: TCI, Viacom, Time Warner, and Cablevision with control of over 50% of the U.S. cable market. Television broadcasters and the local telephone companies also joined the fray with complaints of outdated and unfair constraints (cross-ownership prohibitions) which prevented them from entering the cable and video business.

In 1992, *The Cable Television Consumer Protection and Competition Act* was passed despite strong resistance from the National Cable Television Association (the cable lobby) and a veto from then-President Bush. The Act restores franchising and basic rate regulation power to local authorities (cities or states). However, it also requires local authorities to promote competition by encouraging them to grant several franchises in a given area. Additionally, the act lifts the cross-ownership prohibition between cable and broadcasting, and between cable and local telephone companies. Although the telephone companies cannot yet directly offer cable television services, they are now permitted to deliver video services on their networks and, more importantly, invest, directly or indirectly, in cable businesses. By lifting these restrictions the new cable act has served as a catalyst for further concentration across media, paving the way for the recent RBOCs' investments in cable businesses, for example, Bell Atlantic's once-proposed takeover of Tele-Communication Inc.; Bell South's investment in QVC home shopping and Prime Management (cable), NYNEX's share in Viacom, and USWest's investment in Time Warner cable operations (Andrews, 1993). Nevertheless, when the FCC responded to mounting public and congressional pressure by rolling back basic rates, the bloom came off the rose of large cable firms, and the interest in big mergers between telephone and cable firms dampened throughout 1994.

Liberalization is a process of state intervention to expand the number of participants in the market, typically by creating, or easing the creation of, competing providers of communication services. Usually, this involves establishing a private competitor in a state or private monopoly marketplace.

Unlike commercialization, which aims to make business practices the standard for the communication industry, with or without competition, liberalization aims specifically to increase market competition. Over the past 20 years, states have changed the communication industry in most parts of the world by introducing private competitors over a range of broadcasting and television services. Supporters contend that liberalization lowers prices, expands services, and generally speeds up the process of innovation (Owen & Wildman, 1992). Critics counter that it substitutes private oligopoly regulation for state regulation, carrying out price, service, and innovation mandates that advance the interests of an oligopoly cartel and its more privileged customers (Mosco, 1989).

Liberalization of the mass media includes changing legislation by opening up once monopoly areas to competition. Historically, the U.S. government has liberalized the media through the federal court system and changes to antitrust legislation (Compaine, Sterling, Guback, & Noble, 1982). In an effort to curtail domestic vertical and horizontal expansion, antitrust legislation was used to break up the vertically integrated film industry's exhibition (theaters) holdings from production and distribution. Antitrust legislation and the *Modified Final Judgement* (MFJ) was also used to break up and separate AT&T's long-distance service and manufacturing operations from local telephone service. Local telephone operations were reorganized into seven regional Bell-operating companies (RBOCs). Long-distance services offered by the new providers—MCI and U.S. Sprint—provided a more competitive environment for long-distance users. Additionally, anticompetitive charges have also been levied at the computer software corporation, Microsoft. Through its products DOS and Windows, Microsoft has established a virtual monopoly in personal computer software industry, gaining 77% of the market, far in excess of the anticompetitive criteria of two thirds of the market ("Microsoft's antitrust blues," 1994). Without admitting guilt, Microsoft did see fit to come to terms in an out-of-court settlement, which is now being challenged by stakeholders who want stronger action to rein in the software giant.

Cross-ownership rules have limited the degree of domestic vertical integration and horizontal concentration among media firms. Currently, FCC rulings and NTIA (1993) policy recommendations argue that these policies are too restrictive, and that media firms need to be flexible and to diversify into other media activities in order to compete globally. The FCC has provided temporary and permanent wavers to permit broadcast-newspaper combinations. Moreover, the NTIA recommends further modification to this cross-ownership policy in order to give the FCC broader waver authority. Similarly, national multiple-ownership rules, which prior to 1984 limited radio and television station ownership to 7 stations, was increased to 12. This policy change has resulted in increasing station sale activity, with 1993 marking a 44% increase (Zier, 1994). Cross-ownership restrictions on telco-cable linkages were eliminated in 1991. Lifting this restriction has resulted in aggressive investment activity by the RBOCs in domestic and international media, for example, in telephone and satellite systems in Australia and New Zealand and cellular systems and cable companies in European and Latin American countries (Andrews, 1993). In 1992, the FCC also modified its network-cable rule, so that a network and cable companies can invest in each others' systems to compete in larger markets. Taking advantage of these liberalized rules, CapCities/ABC combined a cable system with a major network. The corporation's subsequent global expansion includes investments in three European television production and distribution companies, major interests in World-wide Television News, and, through ESPN, a 50% ownership in European Television News (NTIA, 1993). As previously indicated, U.S. policy reorganization has lifted or eliminated most government restrictions in order to give media firms more flexibility to compete in an open international marketplace. To be successful in a highly competitive global arena, it is the view of government and businesses that policies must accommodate business activity over a wide range of media products by strengthening cross-ownership concentration and by allowing firms to expand vertically and horizontally across domestic and international markets.

A number of pending Senate and Congressional bills are also aimed at liberalizing US communications policy. For example, *The National Communication and Informational Infrastructure Act* of 1994 (U.S. House of Representatives, 1994), which received 1994 approval in one arm of the U.S. Congress, proposed to combine democratic access to the newly developing National Information Infrastructure (NII or information highway) with a free market policy approach. The Electronic Frontier Foundation succeeded in having an "open platform service" clause included in the bill. Open platform service in the NII would ensure that residential and commercial subscribers have access to voice, data, and video services over digital lines in a switched end-to-end basis at a low cost (EFFector Online, 1994). Nevertheless, although the bill would create the potential of democratic access to a delivery system still in its infancy, at the same time it proposed removing the few remaining restrictions preventing local telephone companies from providing full multimedia services. *The Antitrust and Communications Reform Act* of 1993 (U.S. House of Representatives, 1994), which also passed the House of Representatives, would lift the limitations placed on the Bell Companies (RBOCs) by the *Modified Final Judgment* (MFJ). In essence, the bill would allow local telephone monopolies to reenter the long-distance market and deliver information services. Moreover, the bill called for segmenting this market into interstate, interstate/regional, interstate resale, and nationwide networks. It also aimed to remove the barriers to manufacturing for the RBOCs.

Privatization is a process of state intervention that sells off a state enterprise such as a public broadcaster or a state telephone company. Privatization takes many forms, depending on the percentage of shares to be sold off, the extent to which any foreign ownership is permitted, the length, if any, of a phase-in period, and the specific form of continuing state involvement, typically constituted in a regulatory body, in the aftermath of privatization

(Duch, 1991). This process has accelerated for several reasons, including the rise of governments ideologically committed to private control over economic activity, the attraction, if for one time only, of fresh revenues for government coffers, and the pressures of transnational businesses and governmental organizations, such as the International Monetary Fund and the World Bank. For its supporters, privatization is necessary because commercialization is, at best, an inadequate first step toward market control. Critics see in privatization the elimination of the principle alternative to complete market regulation, the loss of sovereignty for nations selling off to foreign firms, and the consequent loss of local control over national policy. Until recently, the FCC considered spectrum a scarce public resource, allocating it in the "public interest." *The Omnibus Budget Reconciliation Act (Reconciliation Act)* (1993) authorizes the FCC to auction off spectrum, now considered private property, through a process of competitive bidding. Spectrum privatization affects wireless communication such as personal communication services (mobile or cellular telephone services) and mobile satellite services (interactive video). Government revenues from spectrum auctions are estimated to be worth billions of dollars. Furthermore, after their 1994 victory in congressional elections, Republican leaders have proposed to privatize the Corporation for Public Broadcasting, which allocates federal funding and manages the network of public broadcast facilities.

Finally, states are also creating their own wide range of teaming arrangements or strategic alliances that integrate them in different degrees of *internationalization*. These include regional trade alliances, such as the North American Free Agreement (NAFTA), "trade plus" (such as financial, political, and social links) arrangements like the European Community (EC), as well as institutionalized planning organizations, exemplified in the Group of Seven (G7). Internationalization also brings about specific state organizations, such as the General Agreement on Tariffs and Trade (GATT), World Bank, and International Monetary Fund which, although not new to the global political economy, have taken on increasingly powerful roles in managing relations among the most developed nations and negotiating the terms of development (and underdevelopment) in the rest of the world.

This process has been particularly important in the communication arena because the transnationalization of communication networks requires some degree of interstate coordination. Again, this is not new to the industry—the International Telecommunication Union (ITU) began to bring together governments to co-ordinate telegraph policy in the 1860s. In recent years, states have developed new arrangements that enable the richest nations to exert tighter control over global communications policy. These have brought about significant changes in international policymaking, including the decline of UNESCO, site of the major support for the NWICO, and the opening of the ITU to considerably greater private sector participation (Preston, Herman, & Schiller, 1989; Roach, 1993; Sussman & Lent, 1991). These organizations are either less powerful or are transformed to reflect new power balances that all but eradicate equal representation among the world's nations. It has also meant the growth of short-term, function, or technology-specific sites for meeting and planning that bring together government and corporate decision makers, who, largely outside the formal and publicly accessible traditional sites of regulatory activity, coordinate technologies, services, and pricing. The rise of associations representing large business and government users, such as INTUG, the International Users' Group, has provided one important opportunity for such activity.

Internationalization shifts communication responses from national policy applications to ones in which bilateral, trilateral, and multinational trade agreements require structural policy changes. Two trade agreements—The *Canada—US Free Trade Agreement* (FTA, 1988) and *The North American Free Trade Agreement* (NAFTA, 1992)—are significant documents that affect communications policies in Canada, the United States, and Mexico. Both agreements advance a new constitution for North America, one that institutionalizes the power of markets and multinational firms over the national public sphere (Warnock, 1988). The FTA is important because it is the first trade document to extend free trade to services. The agreement also identifies telecommunications as a key industry and facilitator for the service sector, particularly through the provision of enhanced information services. Enhanced services involve the reconfiguring of telephone messages using a computer in order to reproduce data, video, or other electronic products. Section 1408 opens free trade in enhanced and information services. Articles 105 and Section 1402 ensure that enhanced service products, among other services, are accorded a right-of-establishment or national treatment, which, for example, requires the CRTC or FCC to treat communication businesses of the other country as if they were nationals and cannot require such businesses to establish a physical point of presence within the country (FTA, 1988).

The NAFTA (1992) gives substantial treatment to telecommunications with a chapter devoted to these policy issues (see also Shefrin, 1993). The rules on trade in telecommunications services are broadened from the FTA to include investments, intellectual property licensing, standards, and transparency of rules and regulations. One of the most important aspects of the document is the right it gives to companies to use public networks to move information freely across North American borders through their own private secured databases. Examples include the guarantee of private corporate networks and value-added network services (VANs); rights to build, interconnect, and operate private leased lines; the use of dial-up access to interconnect to public networks; the ability to perform switching, signaling, and processing functions; the use of communication products of their choosing; and the ability to lease lines at flat-rate prices (NAFTA, 1992; Shefrin, 1993).

The Uruguay Round of the General Agreement on Tariffs and Trade (1994) signed in Marrakesh adds trade rules for the service sector and establishes a new institution, the World Trade Organization (WTO), to set rules and procedures and to provide a forum for dispute settlement. Trade in services are covered by the General Agreement on Trade in Services (GATS), and telecommunications receives special attention in the Annex on Telecommunications, ensuring access to and the use of public telecommunications networks and services on a nondiscriminatory basis. The document explains that the term *nondiscriminatory* means national treatment and/or most-favored-nation status. GATT, Marrakesh has two telecommunication annexes. The first is modeled on the NAFTA chapter on telecommunication services. The second, for basic telecommunications, sets up a Negotiating Group on Basic Telecommunications (NGBT), made up of Australia, Austria, Canada, Chile, Cyprus, the European Community, and their member states—Finland, Hong Kong, Hungary, Japan, Korea, Mexico, New Zealand, Norway, Slovak Republic, Sweden, Switzerland, Turkey, and the United States—to investigate and report on liberalizing basic telecommunications.

The renegotiation of trilateral and multilateral trade agreements, prompted by economic and political restructuring and reliance on new communications technologies, with aims toward internationalization, challenges national sovereignty (Nordenstreng & Schiller, 1993). The NAFTA and GATS constitutionalize neoconservatism and neoliberalism on a continental and global scale. As economic and political constitutions, both trade agreements are the result of exclusive negotiations among states, national conglomerates, and transnational businesses and their lobby organizations to extend market values and rights. Moreover, international telecommunications policy will be conducted by GATT, with the ITU playing a much smaller role (Mansell, 1993) to benefit transnational corporations and multinational telecommunication suppliers and users.

Internationalizing communications effectively places limits on the scope of public policy and national regulators. Ostensibly the telecommunication provisions in GATT and NAFTA serve as vehicles to promote liberalization, deregulation, and internationalization, despite widespread domestic opposition. GATT and WTO also establish a nontransparent trade regime for multinational firms and global service users. These trade agreements, essentially the result of undemocratic processes, are documents that make business rights and commerce the primary criteria for setting social and public policy. Of less importance are the democratic rights of citizens in developed and developing countries to retain a public service mandate and social policies through distinctive national treatment.

CONCLUSION

This chapter examined the state of communication policy in the United States through the lens of central theoretical perspectives and substantive tendencies.

Specifically, it first described how pluralist, managerial, and class power theories differ in their approach to examining and explaining communication policy. The pluralist perspective, true to its functionalist roots, concludes that communication policy results from tradeoffs among interest groups, none of which dominates the policy arena. Pluralism functions to maintain order in a complex policy arena with the direction and guidance of government policy and regulatory authorities. The managerial view maps a different terrain, one that is led by an elite of dominant powers who, with government support, maintain order in the face of complexity by steering policy decisions to advance major corporate interests. However admirable, concentrated corporate power makes pluralism unsustainable. Nevertheless, managerialism advances the long-run economic interests of society by favoring its most productive interests. Finally, a class power perspective sees the policy arena as fundamentally class divided with control concentrated in the hands of a dominant, increasingly transnational class that advances its own interests against those of subaltern classes. From this perspective, communication policy is forged out of the power of dominant class fractions, but also out of the contradictions and conflicts that arise from a class-divided society.

The chapter also addressed central tendencies in contemporary communication policy. Commercialization is the process of reshaping public communication institutions, such as the Corporation for Public Broadcasting, to operate along private business lines. Deregulation diminishes or entirely eliminates public interest requirements, such as universality in telephony and fairness in broadcasting, to permit private communication firms to more explicitly pursue their market interests. Privatization completely eliminates a public communication organization by selling it to private interests. Finally, internationalization promotes the development of transnational media markets by eliminating restrictions on corporate expansion and by establishing a global regulatory apparatus to manage the transition from national to global markets. Each of these four processes suggests the value of a class power perspective and also challenges the potential to create the conditions for democratic communication.

REFERENCES

Aglietta, M. (1979). *A theory of capitalist regulation: The U.S. experience* (D. Fernbach, Trans.). London: New Left Books.

Akhavan-Majid, R., & Wolf, G. (1991). American mass media and the myth of libertarianism: Toward an elite power group theory. *Critical Studies in Mass Communication, 8,* 139-151.

Aksoy, A., & Robins, K. (1992). Hollywood for the 21st century: Global competition for critical mass in image markets. *Cambridge Journal of Economics, 16*(1), 1-22.

Alford, R. R., & Friedland, R. (1985). *Powers of theory*. Cambridge: Cambridge University Press.

Andrews, E. (1993, November 28). From sibling rivalry to civil war. *The New York Times*, sect. 3, pp. 1-6.

Atkin, D.J. (1994). Cable exhibition in the USA: Ownership trends and implications of the 1992 Cable Act. *Telecommunications Policy, 18*(4), 331-341.

Atkin, D. J., & Starr M. (1990). The US Cable Communications Act reconsidered. *Telecommunications Policy, 14*(4), 315-323.

Aufderheide, P. (1987). Universal service: telephone policy in the public interest. *Journal of Communication, 37*(1), 81-96.

Aufderheide, P. (1991). Public television and the public sphere. *Critical Studies in Mass Communication, 8*, 168-183.

Aufderheide, P. (1992). Cable television and the public interest. *Journal of Communication, 42*(1), 52-65.

Auletta, K. (1991). *Threeblind mice: How the TV networks lost their way.* New York: Random House.

Bagdikian, B.H. (1992). *The media monopoly* (4th ed.). Boston: Beacon Press.

Bell, D. (1973). *The coming of postindustrial society.* New York: Basic Books.

Beniger, J.R. (1986). *The control revolution.* Cambridge, MA: Harvard University Press.

Bruce, R.R., Cunard, J.P., & Director, M.D. (1986). *From telecommunications to electronic services.* Toronto: Butterworth.

Buxton, W. (1994). The political economy of communications research: The Rockefeller Foundation, the "radio wars" and the Princeton Radio Research Project. In R. Babe (Ed.), *Economy and communications* (pp. 147-175). Boston: Kluwer.

Calabrese, A., & Jung, D. (1992). Broadband telecommunications in rural America: An analysis of emerging infrastructures. *Telecommunications Policy, 16*(3), 225-236.

The Canada—U.S. Free Trade Agreement (FTA). (1988). Ottawa: Ministry of Supply and Services.

Castells, M. (1989). *The informational city: Information technology, economic restructuring, and the urban-regional process.* Oxford: Basil Blackwell.

Compaine, B., Sterling, C., Guback, T., & Noble Jr, K. (1982). *Who owns the media?: Concentration of ownership in the mass communications industry* (2nd ed.). White Plains, NY: Knowledge Industry Publications.

Coustel, J.P. (1993). New rules for cable television in the USA. *Telecommunications Policy, 3*, 200-220.

Crandall, R. W. (1991). *After the breakup: US telecommunications in a more competitive era.* Washington, DC: The Brookings Institution.

Crozier, M.J., Huntington, S.P., & Watanuki, J. (1975). *The crisis of democracy.* New York: New York University Press.

Dahl, R.A. (1982). *Dilemmas of pluralist democracy.* New Haven, CT: Yale University.

Dahl, R. A. (1956). *A preface to democratic theory.* Chicago: University of Chicago Press.

Denious, R. D. (1986, September). The subsidy myth: who pays for the local loop? *Telecommunications Policy*, pp. 259-267.

Derthick, M., & Quirk, P. J. (1985). *The politics of deregulation*. Washington, DC: The Brookings Institution.

Domhoff, G. W. (1978). *The powers that be: Processes of ruling class domination in America*. New York: Vintage.

DuBoff, R. (1984). The rise of communications regulation: The telegraph industry, 1844-1880. *Journal of Communication, 34*(3), 52-66.

Duch, R. (1991). *Privatizing the economy: Telecommunications policy in comparative perspective*. Ann Arbor: University of Michigan.

EFFector Online. (1994, August 1). National communication and informational infostructure act. [electronic news service]

Ernst, M. L., Oettinger, A. G., Branscomb, A. W., Rubin, J. S., & Wikler, J. (1993), *Mastering the changing information world*. Norwood, NJ: Ablex.

Federal Communications Commission (FCC). (1991). *Monitoring report*, CC Docket No. 87-339. Prepared by the Staff of the Federal-State Joint Board in CC Docket No. 80-286. Washington, DC: Government Printing Office.

Gallagher, M. (1992). Women and men in the media. *Communication Research Trends, 12*(1), 1-36.

Gandy, O. H., Jr. (1993). *The panoptic sort: The political economy of personal information*. Boulder, CO: Westview.

General Agreement on Tariffs and Trade (GATT). (1994). *Final Act embodying the results of the Uruguay Round of Multilateral Trade Negotiations*. Marrakesh, Geneva: GATT Secretariat.

Held, D. (1987). *Models of democracy*. Stanford, CA: Stanford University Press.

Herman, E.S., & Chomsky, N. *(1988). Manufacturing consent: The political economy of the mass media*. New York: Pantheon.

Hills, J. (1986). *Deregulating telecoms: Competition and control in the United States, Japan and Britain*. London: Francis Pinter.

Honig, D. (1984). The FCC and its fluctuating commitment to minority ownership of broadcast facilities. *Howard Law Journal, 27*(3), 859-877.

Horwitz, R. (1989). *The irony of regulatory reform*. New York: Oxford University Press.

Huber, P. (1993). Telephones, competition, and the candice-coated monopoly. *Regulation, 2*, 34-43.

Jessop, B. (1990). *State theory: Putting capitalist states in their place*. University Park: Pennsylvania State University.

Keane, J. (1984). *Public life and late capitalism: Toward a socialist theory of democracy*. Cambridge: Cambridge University Press.

Kellner, D. (1990). *Television and the crisis of democracy*. Boulder, CO: Westview.

Krasnow, E.G., Longley, L.D., & Terry, H.A. (1982). *The politics of broadcast regulation*. New York: St. Martin's Press.

Mahon, R. (1980). Regulatory agencies: Captive agents of hegemonic apparatuses. In J.P. Grayson (Ed.), *Class, state ideology, and change* (pp. 154-168). Toronto: Holt, Rinehart and Winston.

Mansell, R. (1993). From telecommunications infrastructure to the network economy: Realigning the control structure. In J. Wasko, V. Mosco, & M. Pendakur (Eds.), *Illuminating the blindspots: Essays honoring Dallas W. Smythe* (pp. 181-195). Norwood, NJ: Ablex.

McChesney, R. W. (1993). *Telecommunications, mass media and democracy: The battle for the control of US broadcasting.* New York: Oxford University Press.

Microsoft's antitrust blues. (1994, April 18). *Fortune Magazine,* p. 1.

Montgomery, K.C. (1989). *Target: Prime time-advocacy groups and the struggle over entertainment television.* New York: Oxford University Press.

Mosco, V. (1989). *The pay-per society: Computers and communication in the information age.* Toronto: Garamond; Norwood, NJ: Ablex.

Mosco, V. (1992). Une drôle de guerre [It is a phony war]. *The Media Studies Journal, 6*(2), 47-60.

Mosco, V. (forthcoming). *The political economy of communication: Rethinking and renewal.* London: Sage.

National Telecommunications and Information Administration (NTIA). (1984). *The NTIA infrastructure report: Telecommunications in the age of information* (Special Pub. No. 91-26). Washington, DC: US Department of Commerce.

National Telecommunications and Information Administration (NTIA). (1991). *The NTIA infrastructure report: Telecommunications in the age of information* (Rep. No. 84-144). Washington, DC: U.S. Department of Commerce.

National Telecommunications and Information Administration (NTIA). (1993). *Globalization of the mass media.* Washington, DC: U.S. Department of Commerce.

Noam, E. (1987). The public telecommunications network: A concept in transition. *Journal of Communication, 37*(1), 30-48.

Nordenstreng, K., & Schiller, H. (eds.) (1993). *Beyond national sovereignty: International communication in the 1990s.* Norwood, NJ: Ablex.

North America Free Trade Agreement (NAFTA). (1992). Ottawa: Government of Canada.

Oettinger, A. G. (1988). *The formula is everything: Costing and pricing in the telecommunications industry.* Cambridge, MA: Harvard University Program on Information Resources Policy.

Office of Technology Assessment (OTA). (1990). *Critical connections: Communication for the future.* Washington, DC: Government Printing Office.

Office of Technology Assessment (OTA). (1991). *Rural America at the crossroads: Networking for the future.* Washington, DC: Government Printing Office.

The Omnibus Budget Reconciliation Act. (1993). Washington, DC: U.S. Government Printing Office.

Owen, B.M., & Wildman, S.S. (1992). *Video economics.* Cambridge, MA: Harvard University Press.

Pendakur, M. (1990). *Canadian dreams & American control: The political economy of the Canadian film industry.* Detroit: Wayne State University Press.

Picard, R. (1989). *Media economics: Concepts and issues.* Newbury Park, CA: Sage.

Pool, I. (1983). *Technologies of freedom.* Cambridge, MA: Harvard University Press.

Preston, W., Jr., Herman, E.S., & Schiller, H. (1989). *Hope and folly: The United States and Unesco 1945-1985.* Minneapolis: University of Minnesota.

Roach, C. (Ed.). (1993). *Communication and culture in war and peace.* Newbury Park, CA: Sage.

Schiller, D. (1994). From culture to information and back again: commoditization as a route to knowledge. *Critical Studies in Mass Communication, 11*, 92-115.

Schiller, D. (1982). *Telematics and government.* Norwood, NJ: Ablex.

Schiller, H. (1989). *Culture, Inc.* New York: Oxford University Press.

Schumpeter, J. (1942). *Capitalism, socialism, and democracy.* New York: Harper and Brothers.

Shefrin, I.H. (1993). The North American Free Trade Agreement: telecommunications in perspective. *Telecommunications Policy, 17*(1), 14-26.

Sussman, G., & Lent, J. (Eds.). (1991). *Transnational communications: Wiring the Third World.* Newbury Park, CA: Sage.

Tabor, M. (1991). Encouraging "Those who would speak out with fresh voice" through FCC minority ownership policies. *Iowa Law Review, 76,* 609-639.

U.S. House of Representatives. (1994). *The Antitrust and Communication Reform Act of 1993,* Bill HR 3626.

U.S. House of Representatives. (1994). *The National Communication and Informational Infrastructure Act of 1994,* Bill HR 3636.

U.S. Senate. (1993). *The National Public Telecommunications Infrastructure Act of 1994,* Bill S2195.

Warnock, J. W. (1988). *Free Trade and the new right agenda.* Vancouver: New Star Books.

Wasko, J. (1994). *Hollywood in the information age: Beyond the silver screen.* London: Polity.

Weber, M. (1978). *Economy and society.* Berkeley: University of California Press.

Wilson, J.Q. (Ed.). (1980). *The politics of regulation.* New York: Basic Books.

Zier, J. (1994, March 9). Station sales rebound in '93. *Broadcasting & Cable,* p. 33.

Chapter 5

Democratic Potentials Versus Instrumental Goals in Canadian Telecommunications

Dwayne Winseck

Choice manifests itself in society in small increments and moment-to-moment decisions as well as in loud dramatic struggles; and he who does not see choice in the development of the machine merely betrays his incapacity to observe cumulative effects until they are bunched together so closely that they seem completely external and impersonal. No matter how completely technics relies upon the objective procedures of the sciences . . . it exists as an element of human culture. (Mumford, 1934/1963, p. 6)

To those living in North American societies the slow, barely perceptible changes in society to which Mumford refers may appear to be being overtaken by the loud clamor of the prophets of the age of information. In these societies, daily pronouncements flow from policy circles, industry, popular culture, and academia regarding the emergence of a new democratic principle forged on the link between innovations in communication technology and the profusion of information. Information abundance now complements the historical link between communication and democracy founded on arguments from theology, natural rights, utilitarian ethics, and pragmatic concerns with truth (Keane, 1991).

Although the state in democratic theory has always been torn between competing demands to protect the supremacy of property rights versus its obligations to promote the conditions supportive of equality, liberty, and general well-being (Keane, 1991), many see new communication technologies negating such dualistic thinking by offering ubiquitous networks of communication, competitive markets, and the withdrawal of government from public life. The increased scope of private transactions, the reduced range of state intervention in public life, and enhanced networks of communication among people point toward societies fundamentally different from today. Crucial to this vision of social change is the capacity of the emerging communication infrastructure to enhance the flow of communication within society and among its major constituents.

Invoking the privileged relationship between communication and democracy and the radical language of social critique and political movements of the 1960s, the advertising messages, images, and writing of popular culture suggest that emerging technologies will democratize society by dispersing power away from its traditional institutional manifestations. Representative of such modes of thinking in popular culture are advertisements in the computer magazine *Wired*, promising technologies that will deliver "Power to the People" (see Figure 5.1). Replete with peace symbols, references to major events in the emergence of a radical culture of the 1960s, and frustrated hippies unable to translate their visions of social justice into reality, the language of critique is now being pressed into the service of promoting the diffusion of technology and securing technologically determined visions of the future.

Such visions are not confined to the images of popular culture. In the more staid context of academia similar visions abound. The Canadian communication and legal scholars Richard Schultz and Hudson Janisch (1993) suggest that authority is being transferred away from the politicized regulatory arena and concentrated, monopolies as "technological change increasingly offers the . . . possibility that all markets will be competitive in the not-to-distant future" (p. 7). Reflecting on the new *Telecommunications Act* and the long-distance competition decision (CRTC 92-12), the same two authors suggest that the full effect of these decisions could result in

> a massive power shift in . . . telecommunications . . . from a hierarchical, centralized, carrier-driven system..[towards] freedom of user choice . . . [that] elevates the user from telecommunications subject to equal partner with carriers and other service providers. Freedom to compete requires no less massive power shift in the regulatory system. (p. 7)

Similarly, the Director of Investigation and Research under the Competition Act, George Addy (1994) stated, "Technology is clearly the agent of change in global telecommunications markets. The . . . structural and economic assumptions" of telecommunication regulation "are rapidly being

**Figure 5.1. Gateway 2000 Ad. Copyright 1994 Gateway 2000, Inc.
Reprinted with permission**

undermined by technological change—not only in Canada, but around the world" (p. 2). In order to facilitate these far ranging changes, the task of regulation must change from "the regulation of individual rates and services" to ensuring that competition works (p. 3).

I agree that a fundamental shift in the social relations of communication is underway. Yet, instead of focusing on the causal relationship between technology and social change, the perspective adopted here analyzes how social forces shape the architecture, implementation, and uses of new technology. Such an emphasis reveals that regulatory and industry structures are not inscribed in technological infrastructures, but are shaped by social imperatives, competing discourses about communication and society, and the particular historical context from which they emerge. This way of seeing is not grounded in a negative theory of technology, but rather offers a way of thinking about how technological potentials are shaped by sociological realities. As Schiller (1986) noted:

> Viewed exclusively as a technological capability, it is hardly unrealistic to regard the present situation as one of...unprecedented abundance and richness of information. It seems all the more shocking therefore, to acknowledge at the same time, the deepening division of the society into informationally-privileged and informationally-impoverished sectors. What accounts for this? (p. 102)

From a political economy of communications perspective, information technologies are embedded in the historical process of extending commercial relations to greater areas of social life. This is the purpose of new technologies, not the result. For instance, Smythe (1981) showed how mass media recast leisure time and domestic space in its quest for the audience commodity. Garnham (1990) similarly points to the extension of commercial relations to the public spheres of broadcasting and telecommunications, and Schiller (1986) has pointed out the pressure to commercialize public domain, government information.

This commodification of time, space, and communication also affects the image of the state found in democratic theory, in favor of an instrumental role in the formation of national industrial policy. Although coupling state and economic interests may promote economic accumulation and reduce uncertainty in a complex international economy, this mix of interests displaces contemporary concepts of democratic politics, communication, and citizenship with efforts to legitimate the state/economy relationship through promises of global competitiveness and higher levels of material comfort for the population at large. Citizenship is defined by choice in consumption, economic progress, and periodic post-hoc ratification of government policies through the vote. Finally, democracy as industrial policy changes society by transferring the tensions of the commercial sphere to the political sphere, as particular capitalists try to sway policy outcomes in their favor (Habermas, 1975).

Based on these ideas this chapter argues that the driving forces of technological and social change in Canada are privatization, the commoditization of information, increased industry concentration, commercialization of the policy sphere, and the centralization of political authority. I also marshal evidence to show that these developments do not disturb, but extend, control along the three dominant axes of power within Canadian telecommunications: carriers, the federal government and major user groups.

Recent developments indicate a shift from regulation as social policy to regulation as industrial policy. Regulatory policy as industrial strategy promotes the economic value of telecommunications firms and large users of telecommunication services. Reconciling the sometimes contradictory interests of these two groups is the key objective of contemporary telecommunications policy, whereas concerns with democratic communication wane.

REGULATORY LIBERALIZATION IN CANADIAN TELECOMS

Regulatory liberalization originated in the late 1970s with the transfer of regulatory authority from the Canadian Transport Committee to the Canadian Radio-Television Telecommunications Commission (CRTC). This was followed by decisions in 1979 and 1982 that allowed CNCP to interconnect with the federally regulated telcos to provide competitive data services and the complete liberalization of customer-provided equipment (CPE).

The decisions revealed that the CRTC was willing to consider competition, that it considered the natural monopoly argument as circumspect, and that telecommunications companies themselves were willing to allow competition as a quid pro quo for a relaxation of public policy principles related to universal service and rigid price controls, as well as access to foreign markets. The connection to foreign markets was said to turn on the reciprocal treatment that would be given to Canadian firms in markets that were home to providers given access to Canadian markets—a point confirmed by the heavy presence of foreign equipment and service providers in both decisions. Thus, the decisions introduced the principle that domestic policy would now be partially determined in relation to questions of international competitiveness and as a weapon in international trade policy. The CNCP decision also acknowledged the government's support for the introduction of competition because CNCP was a joint venture between the private and public sector. Finally, competition in the federally regulated regions aligned the federal government and private sector in the pursuit of liberalized telecommunications policies across the country. This was an extraordinary development given that the federal regulator had been granted jurisdictional authority over all telecommunications systems almost 80 years earlier, but had refused to exercise this option given its sensitivity to provincial interests.

Why was the federal government at this particular point in history suddenly emboldened to do what it had previously avoided? This question is taken up later. First, however, a list of key decisions that have substantially altered the shape of the Canadian telecommunications industry, the nature of the regulatory legal system and the types of public policy goals that are pursued are introduced.

1979   Private line interconnect allowed for competitive data services (79-11; CRTC, 1979).

1982   Complete liberalization of customer provided equipment (82-14; CRTC, 1982a).

1984   The CRTC (1984) adopts United States' definitions of basic and enhanced services that map out where the natural monopoly concept is to be maintained and where competition will be allowed, that is, natural monopoly in public local and long-distance voice services and competition in enhanced services (84-18). CNCP challenges AGT to provide interconnection for competitive data services, beginning the constitutional challenge to provincial authority in telecommunication.

1985   Concept of competition in public long distance is accepted by the CRTC (1985), but not implemented because of CNCP's inability to maintain the principle of universal access. Bell proposes rate restructuring. Reselling and private line access for the purpose of providing enhanced services is approved (85-19).

1986   A Federal Provincial Task Force on Telecommunications considers long-distance competition.

1987   Reselling basic carriage capacity granted for enhanced services (87-1; CRTC, 1987a). CRTC exempts certain carriers and services from filing rate tariffs (87-12; CRTC, 1987b). Policy is challenged by the Telecommunication Workers' Union (TWU) in the courts and overturned. The reseller Call-Net offers basic services in violation of CRTC policy. Cabinet and DOC help Call-Net achieve compliance with CRTC policy.

1988   Another Task Force considers implications of long-distance competition.

1989   Supreme Court confirms federal authority in telecommunications, but exempts provincial, publicly owned telecommunications agencies.

1990   CRTC (1990) allows private line sharing and resale for public local and long-distance services (90-3). AGT is privatized.

1991   The Federal government and Manitoba sign a memorandum of understanding (MOU) transferring regulatory authority to the CRTC.

1992   CRTC allows facilities-based long-distance competition (92-12; CRTC, 1992a). The Federal government introduces the *Telecommunications Act* (Bill C-62; CRTC, 1992b) seeking a fully liberalized telecommunications regulatory environment and federal authority over the remaining provincially and municipal telecommunications authorities. The Bill does not receive passage. CRTC issues an inquiry into the development of new regulatory methods (92-78).

1993   *Telecommunications Act* becomes law. The DOC is shifted to Industry Canada.

TRANSFORMING THE TELECOMMUNICATIONS
REGULATORY REGIME

The new telecommunications policy could be considered as favourable to big business. The . . . government must develop a strategy to dissipate the formation of a common front. (DOC, 1985)

There are three factors driving regulatory liberalization in Canada: the relationship of telecommunications to economic development strategies, linkages between domestic communication law and international trading agreements, and the desire to quickly develop Integrated Broadband Networks (IBN). Crossing each of these themes is the desire to use regulatory liberalization as a means to realize the economic value of telecommunications. As representatives of the former DOC stated, "the economic infrastructure provided by telecommunications services and networks is essential to local, regional, and national economic growth and international competitiveness" (Racine, Mozes, & Kennedy, 1992, p. 1). Based on these views telecommunications policy has increasingly been associated with efforts to liberalize financial trading, investment and energy regulations. Given the import of telecommunications to international securities trading, and that Canada has the world's fourth largest securities market, relaxing financial trading and investment rules intensified pressure to adapt the telecommunications system to the needs of the transnational finance and investment community (Smith, 1991). These changes created one of the most "liberalized" telecommunications regulatory regimes in the world. Table 5.1 illustrates this point in comparison to the United States, Germany, United Kingdom and France.

Although regulatory liberalization predates the adoption of free trade agreements, there is a fundamental link between changes in Canadian communications law and the 1987 Free Trade (FTA) and 1992 North American Free Trade Agreements (NAFTA). These agreements harmonize communication, finance, and investment policies by diminishing constraints on transborder data flows, restricting the scope of public sector activity, and limiting the range of telecommunications services that can be publicly regulated (FTA, 1987; Mosco, 1990; NAFTA, 1992). NAFTA's sections on trade and investment in telecommunications equipment, network services, and information services also provided a comprehensive model for GATT negotiations. The telecommunications annexes of the two agreements are identical, except for the opening preamble to the GATT Annex, two paragraphs regarding "Technical Co-operation" and "Relation to International Organizations and Agreements," and minor rearrangements of sentence syntax in some instances and changed predicates in others (NAFTA, 1992; Trade Negotiations Committee, 1993). Thus, the liberalization and harmonization of Canada's telecommunications policies with those in the United States and

Table 5.1. Liberalization Indicators for Select OECD Countries.

Country	US	UK	France	Germany	Canada
VANS	3	3	2	3	3
> 1 International Carrier	3	3	0	0	0
Local Network Competition	2	2	1	1	2
Long Distance Competition	3	2	1	1	3
CPE	3	3	3	3	3
PTO Managerial Independence	3	2.5	2	2	3
Separate Regulatory Agency	3	3	2	3	3
Private/Public Interconnect	3	3	2	2	3
Market Pricing	2.5	2.5	2	2	2
Total (27)	25.5	24	15	17	22
Basket of Bus. Services $	1 075.6	896	896.4	1 062.6	1 023
Basket of Res. Services $	434.9	343.9	307.5	358.4	287.3
Network Invest (% of PTO Rev)	18.6%	20%	27.6%	41.8%	25.6%
Lines/100 Res.	48.5	38.9	44.6	44.5	51.5
+/- Labor	-25%	-25%	+18%	+9%	-2.5%

Note. The table attempts to systematically synthesize and compare the advance of "competitive" regulatory regimes in the countries surveyed. The 0-3 scale indicates the degree of liberalization: 0 represents no competition, whereas 3 represents no restrictions. The material is derived from OECD (1990, 1991b). When these sources did not provide information on the surveyed measures, data were obtained from regulatory sources in the countries surveyed, that is, the CRTC, FCC, OFTEL, CNCL, etc.

Mexico links pressures for domestic regulatory change to the global economic system and served as a model for the international organization of telecommunications markets.

Also intensifying the linkage between domestic and international communications regulatory regimes is the push toward the development of nationwide, Integrated Broadband Networks (IBN). Popularized in the United States as the information super-highway, in Canada the program for a nationwide system of IBNs is not yet well defined. However, the view being promoted by government and industry is that the development of the IBNs will be predicated on the principles of competition, private sector initiatives, network interconnection, and the goal of universal service (Industry Canada, 1994).

Yet, the stated principles for the development of broadband communication networks remain confused and even contradictory. For instance, although the program relies on the enforcement of *Competition Act* provisions designed to regulate excessive market power, mergers, and acquisitions, these restrictions are weighed against the cost of regulation, possible efficiency gains, and the effect of enforcement on technological innovation and the international competitiveness of the telecommunications industry. Thus, the *Competition Act* does not rule out monopolies or concentrated market power, and its application appears to be very discretionary (Addy, 1994). Likewise, although the program for IBN is said to rely on private sector initiatives, the government provides much of the technological push behind such programs by sharing the costs of network development and research, procurement policies, promoting the development of an "information age" culture through educational reform and the application of high technology to the classrooms and by shifting the focus of regulation away from questions of equity toward the creation of communication markets. Such interventions fundamentally affect the shape of new technologies and their relationship to society. For instance, although developments in technology point toward network convergence and ubiquitous supplies of information, existing restrictions in communication law compel the separation of network technologies and proposals to revise copyright laws aim to control the public dissemination of electronic communication by enforcing the economic value of information (Addy, 1994; Industry Canada, 1994).

Obviously, the development of IBNs and regulatory liberalization does not eliminate the role of the state in organizing communication policy. Instead, the state "promot[es] the application of communications technology" and acts "as a forcing house for change" (Communications Canada, 1987, p. 85). Such actions construct an "information age" culture intended to overcome public ambivalence toward new communication technologies in favor of an uncritical embrace. This is problematic because as the state alters the conditions of society, it simultaneously refuses to acknowledge its role in the determination of public life or to allow for full democratic participation in these determinative processes.

PRIVATIZATION

Illustrative of the government's emerging perspective on communication is the policy of privatization. Privatization is the act of selling public assets to the private sector, thereby opening new areas for private investment and the appropriation of value. The general policy of privatization has been central to the Canadian economy and a key plank in the former Conservative Government's agenda since the early 1980s. The centrality of privatization policy to the Canadian political economy during these years was emphasized by the creation of the Minister of State in 1986 to manage privatization and restructuring programs. In eight years, 15 Crown corporations were sold, including Air Canada, Petro Canada, de Havilland Aircraft, and Canadair, and public sector employment cut by 50% (Pugliese, 1992).

In communication the policy of privatization targets three areas: government-held information, the resources of communication held in common under national and international communication law such as the radio spectrum, and publicly owned telecommunications operators. Although the first area has yet to experience the full pressure of privatization, extensive commercialization of information by government agencies for sale to the public, increased reliance of the government on private information vendors for information about Canadian society, and discussions about the sale or reselling of government information by the private sector suggest that the commoditization of public information is imminent (Industry Canada, 1994). The privatization of such information affects the public in several ways. When public agencies such as libraries, universities, or government departments buy access to private information services, they are often required to sign exclusionary contracts that limit the number of users to those associated with the institution. Others outside the agency or department are, at least contractually, prevented from accessing these resources. Such arrangements transform the role of public institutions and personnel away from encouraging access to information to restricting it. Thus, although new technologies make it possible to enhance public access to information, economic relations and legal restrictions constrain such possibilities.[1]

The privatization of telecommunications firms is prominent at both levels of government. In 1987, Teleglobe, Canada's signatory to INTELSAT, was sold. The government claimed privatizing Teleglobe would allow it to pursue commercial goals and "contribut[e] to deficit reduction," despite the fact that the company's "annual profits averaged some $50 million, on an asset base before privatization of . . . $300 million" (Dept. of Finance, 1987, p. 1; Communications Canada, 1992, p. 3). Despite these aims the sale increased

---

[1]The author experienced such restricted access to government information about the telecommunication industry during the course of research for this chapter. Yet, interestingly, the adherence of the current generation of librarians to the notion of information as a public good helped overcome these legal barriers.

corporate concentration by allowing BCE (1991) to obtain controlling interest in the company and by extending the company's monopoly over international telecommunications traffic for 10 years. In 1988, the privatization of Terra Nova Telecommunications and NorthwesTel similarly benefited BCE (Babe, 1990, p. 30). The following year government shares in CNCP Telecommunications were sold, eventually acquired by Rogers Communication Inc., the third largest communications conglomerate in Canada, and AT&T, the world's second largest telecommunications operator (Communications Canada, 1992). In 1992, the government sold its 53% interest in Telesat, the national satellite telecommunications carrier (Dept. of Finance, 1992; Telesat, 1991). The privatization of Telesat further concentrated the telecommunications industry, as it was bought by a consortia including the telcos[2] and the Canadian satellite manufacturer, Spar Aerospace. The government also extended Telesat's monopoly in satellite communication for 10 years (Dept. of Finance, 1991). In the prairies AGT was privatized and offers made to MTS, but not accepted (Birdwise, 1992).

Although privatization has failed to affect overall government spending, it has shifted control over telecommunications from the public sector toward the private sector. In 1981, the private sector accounted for about 68% of industry revenues; now it accounts for 81%. This is paralleled by an overall increase in industry concentration. Through an intense process of amalgamation, the number of telecommunications companies has fallen from 183 at the beginning of the 1980s, to 87 in 1987, and to 62 in 1990. The remaining 62 companies provide service to almost 99% of Canadian households, a rate second in the world only to Sweden and far ahead of the rate in the a United States, where only 93% of the households have telephones (Statistics Canada, 1990-92, p. 54). These 62 companies had revenues of $21 billion in 1992, 3% of the GDP, and employed 125,000 people. The industry is also the country's most significant site of research and development (R&D), comprising 24% of total R&D. In contrast to a 3% rate of growth for the rest of the economy, the telecommunications industry is currently growing at 8.6% per year.

Although the presence of 62 companies providing telecommunications services creates the image of an unconcentrated industry, the fact that only 14 firms account for 98% of all revenues, and only 9 carriers for 83%, suggests otherwise. The two largest holding companies, BCE and Anglo Canadian Telephones, maintain service for 78.3% of all subscribers and control about 73% of all network and service revenues, opposed to 63% 12 years earlier. The largest provider by far is Bell Canada, with 58% of the subscribers, about 55% of industry revenues, half of the industry's employees and a subsidiary of BCE,

---

[2]The government privatized its 53% interest in March 1992, when it sold its shares to Alouette Telecommunications Inc., which is the Stentor group with the addition of the Canadian satellite manufacturing corporation, Spar (Department of Finance, 1992). The largest participant is Bell Canada.

the second largest corporation in Canada.[3] Thus, regulatory liberalization and privatization have resulted in the highest levels of concentration since the expiration of Bell patents in 1893.

Although alternative carriers like Telesat, Teleglobe, Unitel, two cellular networks, and resellers provide competition in some services, such as CPE and now long distance, it is also true that competitors comprise no more than 7% to 8% of the industry.[4] Even these alternative networks are dominated by Bell and already existing companies, such as Rogers and AT&T. The historical pattern of vertical integration within the telecommunications industry is being supplemented by horizontal integration, as the telcos establish their presence in new areas of the industry, consolidate their position through mergers and acquisitions, and jockey for position in the global telecommunications market. The concentrated nature of the telecommunications industry is shown in Table 5.2.

These observations indicate that an IBN based on a "network of networks" is not coequal with competition. The acquisitions of alternative network providers by dominant telecommunications operators illustrates that new network technologies do not substitute for, but complement, the existing infrastructure. The emerging communication network and industry structure suggest that the contradictory principles expressed by the new *Telecommunications Act* and *Competition Act* are being resolved in favor of efficiency and international competitiveness rather than more local concerns. The result is a shift in industry structure from regional monopolies toward national and international oligopolies.

Rather than furthering the radical decentralization of economic power and the diffusion of information and cultural production, contemporary regulatory policies promote the "competitiveness of the economy as a whole" (Racine et al., 1992, p. 6). Reconciling the sometimes contradictory interests between the telecommunications firms and large users who incorporate communications services as intermediary inputs into their primary products is the key aim of contemporary industrial policy in the telecommunications sector, whereas concerns with democratic communication and universal service wane (as will be shown later).

For the most part, the differences between network operators and large users are minimal. Telecommunications carriers see regulatory liberalization as increasing access to new communication markets and end-users see such

---

[3]Adjusted to incorporate recent purchases of Northwestel and Terra Nova.

[4]Sixty percent of the industry is now open to competition, including CPE, network services and public long distance. However, the incumbents still dominate each area. Data do not reveal the extent to which competition has eroded the telcos' market in the areas like CPE and network services. However, its still appears to be rather small, with resellers, for instance, only receiving $100 million in revenues from approximately $15 billion in total network and service revenues (Mozes, 1992a, Appendix).

Table 5.2. Leading Telecommunication Firms in Canada.

Name of Company	Type of Ownership	Total # of Subscribers (000s)	Total Revenues (000,000s)	Total # of Employees
BellCanada[a]	Private	9,024	7,729	54,632
MT&T	Private	580	527.4	4,044
NBTel[b]	Private	377	324	2,592
NfldTel[c]	Private	230	265.6	2,012
(AngloCan.Tel[d]	Private	3,050	2,212.4	7,000
B.C. Tel.	Private	1,729	1,985	15,157
Quebec Tel.	Private	550	232.6	1,799
Telus[e]	Private	1,128.7	1,227.2	10,201
SaskTel	Public	569.8	541	3,981
MTS	Public	528.8	541.7	5,626
EdTel	Public	N/A	237	2,015
Unitel[f]	Private	N/A	319	3,113
Rogers Comm.	Private	N/A	366.5	N/A
Telesat	Private	N/A	154.2	700
Teleglobe[g]	Private	N/A	404.1	1,051
NorTel[h]	Private	N/A	8,183	49,000
Microtel	Private	N/A	170.6	N/A
TOTAL		17,653	25,321.3	122,923

[a]BCE has controlling interest (33.6%) of Maritime Telephone and Telegraph (BCE, 1991, p. 46). Subsequent to BCE's purchase, MT&T obtained a 51.4% controlling interest in the Island Telephone Company of P.E.I. (Disclosure Inc., 1992).
[b]NBTel is 31.4% owned by BCE subsidiary, Bruncor (Communications Canada, 1992, p. 17).
[c]NfldTel is also owned and controlled by BCE (Disclosure Inc., 1992).
[d]Anglo Canadian Telephone Co. is owned primarily by the US GTE Corp. It owns both BCTel and QuebecTel (Disclosure Inc., 1992).
[e]AGT became Telus Corporation upon its privatization in 1990-91 (Telus, 1991).
[f]80% of UNITEL is owned by Canadian Pacific Limited (approx. 50%) and Rogers Communications Inc. (30%) (Communications Canada, 1992), while AT&T acquired 20% of the company in 1993.
[g]BCE received controlling interest (22.2%) in Teleglobe through a series of transactions after the initial privatization (BCE, 1991, p. 46).
[h]BCE owns 52.8% of Northern Telecom (BCE, 1991, p. 13).

changes as bringing reduced telecommunications costs. As the DOC/Industry Canada notes, this convergence of thought is predicated on the growing importance of the communications dependent, service sector of the economy. According to DOC/Industry Canada officials, up to 5% of large "businesses total expenditures are on telecommunications services" (Mozes, 1992, p. 2). Canada's six largest banks alone spend $470 million annually on telecommunications services, about 3% of the carriers' approximately $15 billion in revenues (Communications Canada, 1992). The Royal Bank has $100 million in annual telecommunications expenditures (Mosco, 1990), the Toronto Dominion Bank $50 million (Gates, 1992), and Manulife, a large insurance and financial institution, spends $5.2 million per year on long-distance services (Gates, 1992a). According to these firms, Canada must import U.S.-style deregulation. Representatives from the Royal Bank note that:

> AT&T has introduced more new services in the past five years than during the entire century. Many of these services are new export products, both goods and services. Prices for long distance services are about one-half of what Canadian carriers charge our businesses. And in the case of high speed data lines the cost differential is an incredible seven to one! All this has occurred without jeopardizing Americans' access to affordable basic telephone service. (Grant, 1991, p. 45)

Large user groups, the telcos, and government also a share the idea that changes in domestic regulatory policies are necessary for continued access to foreign markets. This concern is especially pertinent given the global scope of companies like Northern Telecom, and that 37%, or $2 billion, of total domestic telecommunications equipment manufacturing in 1989 was exported. Joint government/industry reports consistently encourage "Canada . . . to proceed with deregulation, to unleash its . . . companies to compete both at home and abroad . . . [and] press International regulatory bodies, such as the International Telecommunication Union . . . to deregulate . . . international telecommunications markets to the maximum" (SCC, 1991, p. 24).

TELECOMMUNICATIONS, ECONOMIC VALUE, AND COMMUNICATIONS LAW

As regulatory policy turns toward realizing the economic value of communication, there are increasing challenges to the conventional political and legal framework governing telecommunications. These developments impinge on issues of industry structure and directly on questions of democratic communication.

Currently, the expansion of telecommunications network operators into new information markets is restricted by prohibitions against the convergence of network technologies and legal principles requiring the separation of carriage functions from the provision of information services (Addy, 1994; Industry Canada, 1994). Although eliminating such distinctions would allow network operators into additional communication markets and create further pressure for technological convergence, it would also project concentrated market power into new domains and extend this power into the sensitive areas of editorial control. Eroding the distinction between conduit and content threatens to introduce broadcast and cable-type structures into telecommunications and, consequently, raises questions pertinent to vertical integration, freedom of communication, the status of different speakers in electronic space, and the location of censorship powers. Does allowing network operators to control the technological infrastructure and the supply of information establish the potential for private sector and commercial censorship in the emerging networks at the same time that the state's ability to exercise control over the flow of information is being challenged? Although the use of the *Competition Act* and "structural separation" regulatory mechanisms are offered as panaceas to these potentials, the discretionary nature of competition law, the history of vertical integration and market power in the communications industry, and the ability of dominant firms to shield themselves from regulatory oversight suggest caution (see Babe, 1990, for a discussion of some of these issues).

Similar questions arise in regard to those reselling network capacity or offering Value Added Networks (VANs). Two questions are important with respect to this tier of service providers. The first pertains to the relationship of network operators to service providers in terms of ownership, control, and editorial discretion. The second concerns the relationship between network service providers and end-users in terms of equitable access and editorial control. Recent examples in Canada and the United States demonstrate the immaturity of free speech and communication law in relation to these issues. In the United States, the electronic information service provider, Prodigy, prohibits politically related discussions, and an electronic database associated with Dun and Bradstreet refused access to labor unions. In Canada, a value-added network recently cut service to a controversial, sex-related service despite the fact that the service had not transgressed any laws.

The fact that some groups within civil society find it advantageous to limit the free flow of communication while others seek to enhance it compounds these difficulties. As a result, certain actors try to restrict access through copyright and pricing mechanisms, whereas others such as marketers try to extend free speech protections to the new technologies in order to further commercialize domestic space, time, and personal information, and still others argue for the removal of all commercial and state restrictions on the flow of information except for those pertaining to economic and governmental surveillance of the population. The tensions between the economic value of information, the value of the free flow of communication to democratic societies, and the value of privacy and control over personal information are central to the emerging networks and legal issues related to free speech. How these competing values are resolved will have significant implications for democratic communication in Canada and elsewhere.

Changes in key legal concepts are mirrored by changes in the type and number of agencies responsible for administering the telecommunication regulatory regime. Indicative of changes in the relationships among administrative agencies is the ascendancy of the DOC/Industry Canada over the CRTC as a source of policy inspiration. DOC officials played key roles in negotiating the FTA and NAFTA, briefing foreign governments and industry officials about the Canadian telecommunications environment, visiting provincial agencies to promote competitive telecommunications regimes and the link between telecommunications and economic development, and elaborating domestic regulatory policy (Kincaid, personal communication, July 7-10, 1992; Mozes, personal communication, July 30, 1992).

An increasingly powerful alliance is also being forged between the DOC, come adjunct of Industry Canada, and the Cabinet, although this abrogates the arms-length arrangements designed to inoculate the industry and legal process from political pressures. The increasing politicization of telecommunications was revealed in 1985 when a confidential Cabinet briefing document prepared by the DOC was leaked to the telecommunication unions. Instead of explicitly introducing new legislation to replace the Railway Act, the DOC (1985) recommended that:

> The government should undertake a public consultation process, publishing a consultation document in autumn 1985 and possibly a white paper at a later date. . . .

> Release a speech in June, to be followed by consultations with interested parties and lobbying groups, and continuing discussions with the provinces.

> The government would authorize the Minister to spend $1 million from the economic envelope for public information, studies and consultation. (p. 1)

> The DOC envisioned the proceedings concluding that

> Canada should move to cost based pricing. . . .

> Canada should introduce competition gradually. . . .

> If Canada's policies don't change, international bypass and higher costs for Canadian industry could have severe consequences.

This is one of numerous recent examples in which the regulatory authority of the CRTC has been superseded. For instance, in 1987, after finding Call Net, the largest reseller, violated regulatory policy by offering basic public long-distance services, the CRTC allowed the telcos to refuse network access to the company. However, Call Net successfully petitioned the Cabinet twice for a reprieve from the CRTC decision and secured the assistance of the DOC to help bring it into compliance with CRTC regulations (CRTC, 1987b; Call Net, Telecommunications, Inc., 1987, 1988; Communications Canada, 1988). In the end, rather than Call Net altering its operations, the CRTC changed its regulatory policies to correspond with the operations of Call Net and the desires of the government by allowing resale and private line sharing for public telephone services (CRTC, 1990). Thus, the CRTC executed the government's implicit policy absent a legislative mandate. Similar actions were also apparent in matters regarding Telesat Canada and dubious activities on the part of the Minister of Communications in a rate case involving Bell (Telesat, 1991, p. 2). As an article in the Financial Post pointed out, the Minister of Communications had intervened more times "in 20 months than all her predecessors in the past 20 years" ("MacDonald's record," 1988, p. 1).

The new *Telecommunications Act*[5] retains Industry Canada and Cabinet powers given by the *Railway Act* to "vary or rescind" CRTC decisions, and it extends their authority by giving the Minister of Communications exceptional discretionary power regarding consultations with the provinces, exemptions from the regulatory framework, interventions in CRTC matters, and ability to issue policy directives to the CRTC on matters of broad policy, national security and international telecommunications policy (Bill C-62, 1992). The CRTC remarked that these proposals could undermine its status as "an expert, quasi-judicial tribunal, accessible, public, . . . independent and non-partisan." It also warned that by delegitimating the regulatory process the government would find itself "beleaguered by . . . petitioners who no longer believe in . . . public proceedings" (pp. 3-4). Such excessive use of discretionary state powers undermines the legitimate politico-legal order and supports the idea that the DOC/Industry Canada and Cabinet are now the most significant sites of communication policy authority. There is an unmistakable move away from legislative sources of oversight to direct intervention by the executive with the resulting politicization of the industry.

Other agencies have also ascended in importance, including the Department of Finance, the Ministry of State (Privatization), and departments within the Ministry of Consumer and Corporate Affairs. These agencies are commercially oriented, and their solutions tend to be conceptualized in terms accessible to economics, accounting, finance, and so on. For example, divisions of Consumer and Corporate Affairs regularly participate in CRTC proceedings to promote competitive policy positions. In other instances, the privatization of Teleglobe and Telesat involved Consumer and Corporate Affairs and the application of the *Competition Act* by the Ministers of State and Communications (Department of Finance, 1992).

The increased use of private sector consultants to study the implications of regulatory changes, assist in the privatization of crown corporations, and help companies strategically important to the Canadian telecommunications industry also reflects and promotes the commercialization of the policy sphere. Complementing the use of these private sector knowledge producers are prominent industry groups, including the Canadian Business Telecommunications Alliance (CBTA), Canadian Banking Association (CBA), Communications Competition Coalition (CCC), and the Information Technology Association of Canada (ITAC). The CBTA represents 340 private and public sector interests with annual telecommunications expenditures of $4

---

[5]The analysis is based on Bill C-62. There are no material differences between this Bill and the Bill given Royal Assent in June 1993. One important change is that Bill C-62 included a licensing procedure, whereas the new *Telecommunications Act* does not.

billion, or about 20% of all industry revenues (CBTA, 1992). ITAC lobbies on behalf of 300 members from the high technology industry, whose combined revenues are about $15 billion per year, or about 2% of the GNP (ITAC, 1992; Mosco, 1990). The CCC is even smaller, but consists of 40 of the largest corporations in Canada, including the Canadian Imperial Bank of Commerce, General Motors, and Sears (Crockett, 1991). The CBA represents the six largest banking institutions in Canada with combined annual expenditures on telecommunications services and equipment in the order of $470 million. Overall, the telcos receive about 40% of their long-distance revenues from 300 of the largest corporations in Canada (Gates, 1992). Similar patterns prevail in the Prairie and Atlantic Regions (Beresh, personal communication, September 2, 1992; Gowenlock, personal communication, September 1, 1992).

A steady process of consultation through industry associations, attendance at annual conferences, and participation on government boards also reaffirms these groups' status as a community and helps to define common solutions to current and anticipated regulatory problems. In addition, these meetings contribute to the "revolving door" among the CRTC, DOC/Industry Canada, and private sector corporations, such as BCE, Call Net, UNITEL, and the resellers. As public officials put their knowledge of the regulatory process and experience in drafting legislation out for private hire, the demarcation between private and public interests is obscured, as is the claimed impartiality of the government agencies' advisory role.

Low-income people, workers, and average Canadians are represented by groups such as the National Anti-Poverty Association, Communication and Electrical Workers of Canada (CWC), TWU, Atlantic Canada TWU, Public Interest Advocacy Centre, and Consumers Association of Canada, but these groups' limited resources mitigate their effectiveness. Their efforts are mainly reactions to specific policies, rather than sustained efforts to define the issues through conferences, coordinating boards, and so on. However, each group maintains an office and stays abreast of developments by being on the mailing list of the CRTC, DOC/Industry Canada, and the Minister of Communications. A crucial role has been played by the CWC, the largest telecommunications union in Canada, in creating and maintaining the Action Canada Network (ACN), a focal point for a range of social and political action groups. The ACN maintains an office, supports the Centre for Policy Alternatives, which regularly publishes analyses of government policy, and was instrumental in distributing a leaked copy of the proposed NAFTA agreement, breaking the secrecy imposed on the negotiations by the Canadian, Mexican, and American governments.

Although unions and these other groups make valuable contributions to the regulatory proceedings, especially with respect to principles relating to access, cost, and universal services, the new telecom legislation allows the CRTC to exclude them from regulatory hearings. This suggests that conflict and overt power may complement commercial standards and Cabinet authority as methods of political and regulatory action. The result is a regulatory process squeezed by executive authority on the one side and commercial imperatives on the other, at the expense of any public space for the contemplation of new relations between telecommunications and society. In contrast, some unions suggested that the increased importance of telecommunications be reflected in "strong[er] public regulation involving a more open process in which the public has influence on the policy agenda" (CLC, 1992, p. 13; TWU, 1992, p. 11).

ECONOMIC EFFICIENCY, TECHNOLOGY, AND CONSTITUTIONAL CHANGE

The second axis of political change involved overcoming the heterogeneous nature of the Canadian telecommunications systems. Under the traditional split jurisdictional, regulatory framework, for example, reselling and private line interconnection prevailed in British Columbia, Ontario and Quebec, but not in Saskatchewan, Newfoundland and Manitoba. Likewise, network convergence between telephone and cable systems developed in the prairies, whereas it is prohibited in the federally regulated areas. As such, there was not a Canadian telecommunications network, but a heterogeneous collection of companies, loosely unified through Stentor. However, this diffuse constitutional ordering of political power had to yield to the objections of ITAC, CCC, and CBTA "that inter-provincial trade barriers . . . weaken competitiveness and effectiveness" (Canada, 1991, p. 18), especially as the economy feels the pressures of free trade (Communications Canada, 1987).

Eighty years after its powers were affirmed over telecommunications matters, the federal government attempted to assume authority over the provincially-regulated telcos (*Toronto v. Bell Telephone Co.*, 1905). The Supreme Court confirmed federal regulatory authority over telecommunications in 1989 (*AGT v. CRTC and CNCP*, 1989). The decision brought the privately owned, provincially regulated, Atlantic region telcos under CRTC jurisdiction, but left AGT, SaskTel, and MTS, as Crown Corporations, as well as a number of independent telcos across Canada, outside of federal jurisdiction. Shortly before and after the AGT decision, the government tried to obtain control through negotiations dubbed the "Edmonton Accord" and subsequently through legislation. Both attempts were rebuffed by the provinces. Playing on historical tension between the prairies and Ottawa, the *Winnipeg Free Press* ran a series of articles disparaging the legislative attempt as an unparalleled "federal raid on the jurisdiction and regulatory authority of the provinces" ("PCs put move on", 1989, p. A3).

However, the election of the Conservative government in Manitoba led to a more sympathetic relationship with Ottawa. An example of the improved relationship is the 1991 Memorandum of Understanding (MOU) between Manitoba and the federal government. The agreement transfers regulatory authority to the CRTC, institutes local representation on the CRTC, assures that policy issues will be considered with great "sensitiv[ity] to regional interests," and establishes competition and "regulatory forbearance" as priority policy goals (Canada/Manitoba, 1991, p. 2). However, it is important to note that the MOU was achieved only after business lobby groups by-passed the Manitoba legislature and regulatory board, and the Manitoba government centralized regulatory power in the hands of the newly unified, provincial Minister of Telecommunications and Policy, much to the consternation of the unions (CWC and IBEW), the Public Utility Board regulators, and other social interests (Raper, personal communication, September 1, 1992; Birdwise, personal communication, August 31, 1992).

The "prairie alliance" further deteriorated in 1990 when the Alberta government issued the first shares in the privatization of AGT. As a consequence, AGT lost its Crown immunity and came within the purview of the CRTC. The government may have privatized AGT to escape the contradictory pressures generated through local political structures by unions and residential and rural users, on the one hand, and the CRTC's competitive initiatives, the federal government's display of resolve on the jurisdictional matter, and the local, national, and transnational business's efforts to commercialize the company's operations, on the other (Desrochers, personal communication, September 3, 1992). Others suggest that privatization reflected the Conservative government's belief that the public sector should not compete with the private sector for limited economic resources, an observation that accords well with the fact that AGT was still a profitable company when sold (Panelli, personal communication, September 3, 1992).

Recent Constitutional proposals promote nationwide competitive telecom policies and the spread of VANS, reselling, alternative network development and private lines by allowing government economic, social, or cultural policies to be challenged in the name of "economic efficiency" (Canada, 1991; Communications Canada, 1987). These proposals attempt to codify the subordination of social objectives to economic imperatives and directly write the logic and centralizing pressures of the recent trade agreements into Constitutional law.

Most of these objectives are achieved by the new telecommunications law. The CBTA and other large user groups supported the federal initiatives, "emphasiz[ing] how important . . . one regulator are to the sector. . . . [A]nd . . . that jurisdiction over the sector . . . be held inviolate from provincial encroachment in the future" (CBTA, 1992, p. 4). However, Quebec, Saskatchewan, the TWU, CWC, ACTWU, among others, continued to oppose the initiative. SaskTel argued that,

> The needs of the customer in Metro Toronto are not identical to those of a farmer in northern Saskatchewan. . . . [T]here are regional sensitivities and geographic realities which the individual telcos are the best ones to address in order to satisfy the unique requirements of their own customers. (Teichrob, 1992, p. 2)

The only remaining large, nonfederally regulated telcos are SaskTel and the municipally-owned and regulated EdTel. A recent Quebec court decision suggests that the remaining 48 independents[6] that had escaped the terms of the AGT decision will also come under the CRTC's supervision. The federal government's success is also evidenced by the fact that from 1980 to 1993 the number of telecommunications companies under federal authority increased from 70% to 95%.[7] Although at the beginning of the 1980s, only 7 of the 19 largest telcos were under federal jurisdiction, by 1993, 12 out of the 14 biggest telcos were federally regulated.

A CRITIQUE OF INSTRUMENTAL REASON IN TELECOMMUNICATIONS POLICY

Although a consensus among key institutional actors in telecommunications policy has emerged over the need for regulatory reform, it is important to note the limits to this consensus and to illustrate some of the grounds on which it can be critiqued. Immediately, it can be pointed out that the examples chosen to show that Canadian businesses are at a competitive disadvantage are *unrepresentative* of business telecommunications costs in general. Data show that a "basket of national business telephone charges" in Canada are above the OECD average, but below the aggregate cost of service in the United States, Japan, and Germany. In relation to mobile communications and leased, high-speed digital lines, costs in Canada are below the OECD average and major trading partners, except for the United Kingdom in regard to certain services in the latter category. This is more impressive considering that telephone costs for Canadian residential users are among the lowest in the world, whereas those in which deregulation has occurred are relatively high (OECD, 1990).

Comparatively speaking, network investment in Canada is equal to, or higher than, the United States, United Kingdom, and Japan (OECD, 1990). By prioritizing universality over commercial values, network development in Canada has not become as uneven as in the United States, United Kingdom, and Japan. In Canada, extensive digitization programs, heavily subsidized by the local governments in the largely rural, prairie provinces, demonstrate the connection between public investment in the telecommunications network and broad social policy objectives. The rate of network digitalization and fiber-optic implementation in the prairies is more advanced than any other country (SaskTel, 1991). Stentor's efforts toward the completion of a national fiber-

---

[6]Independent telco refers to the smaller telephone companies that are not involved in Stentor. A 1992 decision by the Quebec Court of Appeals also found that the provincial government had no authority to regulate locally situated independent telcos, as has historically been the case (Ravensberg, 1992, p. D3).

[7]Measured as a percentage of subscribers under different regulatory jurisdiction.

optic network using CCS7 digital-switching equipment will provide a much more advanced technological platform to provide a wide range of services, in contrast to extensive investments in the early 1980s by the U.S. telcos in CCS6 analogue-switching equipment (Gowenlock, personal communication, September 1, 1992; Telus, 1991). Thus, Canadian systems compare favorably with deregulated environments in terms of costs, equitability, and technology.

Critical interrogation of the claim that the current pricing regime curtails the competitiveness of Canadian businesses indicates that telecommunications costs as a business expense have been vastly overstated. The 1986 Federal Provincial Task Force on Long Distance Competition concluded that, despite the difference between certain U.S. and Canadian costs, changes in the rate structure would "have only small impacts on the overall cost structure and the performance of Canadian business . . ., even for large price changes" (p. 51). The Task Force found that average telecommunications costs represented only about 0.7% of business costs. Bank and financial institutions' balance sheets support this conclusion. More recent data show that whereas Canada's six largest banks have over $470 million in annual expenditures on telecommunications services, this is a paltry sum alongside total annual operating expenses of $58.1 billion.[8]

The fact that large corporations allocate close to 1% of their disbursements on telecommunications services is similar to the levels made by citizens for telephone service. On average Canadians allocate about 1.2% of their annual family income on basic telecommunications services, an amount similar to the funds spent for electricity bills, education, health care, and recreational pursuits. However, for residential users below or near the poverty line, the cost of basic service equals about 2.7% of all expenditures. That people are willing to allocate such a sizeable portion of their income to telephone costs signifies the social importance attributed to telephone service. It is reasonable to conclude from these comparative measures, and from the perspective of social justice, that the traditional pricing regime resulted in a rough level of equality between businesses and residential users, and that if anybody needs an adjustment to offset the disadvantages of the current pricing structure they are low-income users. This is especially true since telephone penetration as a whole is 99.2%, whereas for low-income families it falls to around 86% (NAPO, 1987; Statistics Canada, 1990-2). There are no persuasive reasons to require citizens to allocate more of their budgets to telephone costs than is required of business.[9]

---

[8]Compiled from financial statements of each bank reported in World Reports, 1992 on the Lexis Nexis electronic database.

[9]Although proposals to change the price structure to favor business are justified on the basis of their function to the production of wealth, a factor presumed absent for residential users, two objections must be raised. First, although it is claimed that reduced business costs will be passed on to consumers, one must be skeptical. It is likely that reductions would go toward increasing profits rather than passed on to consumers as

Current pricing practices reflect a history of regulatory policy founded on the hithertofore bedrock principle of universality. Historically, regulatory policy has forced the cost of telephone service to fall faster than the rise of the overall consumer price index by ensuring that all rate increases were "just and reasonable" (Pike & Mosco, 1986; Statistics Can, 1970-1991). Despite the benefits of this historical approach, two important points need to be raised. First, given that the unions and groups such as NAPO, FAPG, and so on have been the most ardent defenders of affordable, universal services, provisions in the new legislation allowing these groups to be excluded from regulatory affairs could allow frequent rate restructuring proposals to be implemented. Second, although the CRTC has resisted massive rate restructuring to date, the recent long-distance competition decision and current hearings before the agency aimed at creating new regulatory procedures, pricing policy, and network cost allocation schemes will affect commitments to universal services.

Nowhere is the industrialization of telecommunications policy more evident than in the CRTC's (1992a) *Competition in the Provision of Public Long Distance Voice Telephone Services and Related Resale and Sharing Issues* (CRTC 92-12) decision. The decision introduces facilities' based competition and demonstrates the extent to which competition has achieved ideological status within the CRTC. Even with the benefit of elaborate methodological slights of hand that collapsed the analysis of economies of scale into narrowly conceived "toll-specific scale economies," the CRTC was unable to produce any conclusive evidence supporting the inherent competitiveness of long-distance services. In regard to each of the measures on which the decision was supposed to turn, the CRTC was forced to note the "inconclusive nature of the evidence" (pp. 36-40).

This is not surprising. Conclusive evidence regarding the benefits of long-distance competition has not been forthcoming since the 1984 CNCP application to provide competitive services. Yet, as early as 1979, and certainly by 1985, the CRTC had accepted the principle of competition. Although in 1985 CNCP's application was turned away, this was not because the CRTC rejected the principle of competition, but because CNCP could not achieve the price discounts it promised while at the same time offering universal services (CRTC, 1985). Thus, although the CRTC accepted the principle of competition, it also agreed that competition was merely another means to achieve important social objectives, that is, universality. In the balance of things, competition remained subordinate to social policy.

Between 1985 and 1993, the means-end relation between competition and social policy changed. Competition became an end in itself, marking the transformation of regulation from social policy to industrial policy. By

---

savings (NAPO, 1987). Second, considering that the home and people's expenditures are necessary to the reproduction of labor power, there is no compelling reason to favor business over the home for preferential pricing regimes.

overturning its commitment to universality, the CRTC negated the concerns of those who had consistently opposed long-distance competition. On the forefront of opposition was MTS and SaskTel, who contended that new entrants would concentrate their efforts on the 0.5% of the largest customers (about 175 corporations) located in the large urban areas of Winnipeg, Regina, and Saskatoon that provide 20% of the telcos' revenues (Beresh, personal communication, September 2, 1992; Gowenlock, personal communication, September 1, 1992; MTS, n.d.). Prior to signing the MOU, the Manitoba government also noted that there were more than 50 different groups representing municipalities, farmers, businesses, and social and religious organizations opposed to the CNCP application. Similarly, anticipating the CRTC's decision-making methods, AGT stated in its 1988 *Annual Report* "that competition must be *conclusively* determined to be in the best interests of Canadians, prior to introduction of major legislative or regulatory changes" (p. 12; emphasis added). In British Columbia, 52 city municipal councils, including Vancouver, passed resolutions opposing the UNITEL decision. The Ontario and Quebec provincial governments held similar positions. The telecommunication unions—TWU, CWC and ACTWU—also led oppositional campaigns across the country.

The CRTC (1992a) does not "require competitors to provide universal service as a condition of entry" (pp. 62-63). Although UNITEL promised universal service after six years, the CRTC removed this obligation, arguing that the allocation of services according to market principles was preferable to either route averaging or the goal of universality. Other competitors proposed to offer service only in the large urban areas of Quebec, Ontario, and British Columbia. The CRTC accepted these proposals, acknowledging that it could increase regional disparities in network development, access, and costs. An additional dimension that may aggravate the decline of universality on a regional basis is the decision by the CRTC to require the telcos to continue to route average intraregionally but, not on a cross-Canada basis, as previously done through Stentor's Revenue Settlement Plan. Saskatchewan and Manitoba argue that this shortage in revenue will need to be compensated by local rate increases.

Requiring the conventional telcos to preserve universal service and give new competitors expedited regulatory consideration creates a two-tiered regulatory regime. This two-tiered regulatory structure reflects the CRTC's (992a) decision to use regulation to help new competitors overcome the historically entrenched position of the telcos and actively influence the shape of the emerging market. The incumbent companies have strongly resisted responsibility for continuing to provide universal service and have suggested that this be temporary while new methods to accomplish social policy goals are considered, such as direct subsidies, local measured services, "incentive regulations, price caps or other variations" (Stentor, 1992, p. 2). Given that specific sections of the private sector cannot be made to bear the burden of government sanctioned social policy, it can be anticipated that universal service and affordable pricing will be abandoned altogether, or that market failures will be socialized through direct government subsidies. These issues are currently being taken up by the CRTC.

Finally, the erosion of universal service must be put in the context of earlier CRTC decisions (1984) and NAFTA that tightly circumscribe the range of services governed by the principles of universality and prevent cross-subsidization between private (i.e., private line interconnect and VANS) and public services (local and long distance). Each of these measures ensures that universality is a narrowly defined policy goal that does not address questions related to the new communication technologies. Even if universal service is maintained, it will certainly be far less satisfactory than current programs or the potential of new technologies. Overall, then, universal service has been diluted in terms of geographical coverage, the range of services covered, and agents responsible for achieving social policy goals.

SUMMARY

The idea that new communication technologies will radically alter social relations and democratize communication in Canada is unable to pass critical scrutiny. Although essential changes have occurred, they further concentrate power along the three main axes of power within Canadian telecommunications—telecommunications carriers, the federal government, and major user groups. Power has been extended by reconstituting the historic balance between the provinces and Ottawa; increasing the role of the private sector over the public sector through mergers and acquisitions, privatization, and increased reliance on private consultants; increased industry and market concentration; the redistribution and diffusion of authority within the federal bureaucracy, increasing the presence of commercially oriented agencies, such as Consumer and Corporate Affairs and the DOC/Industry Canada; and by extending state discretionary powers in the proxy/person of the Minister of Communications.

Recent regulatory changes increase the scope of Ministerial action and allow the CRTC to unilaterally exclude certain interveners. The extension of state powers ensures that the industrialization of telecommunications policy will be freed from the erstwhile attempts of public interest groups and unions to assert social policy objectives. This responds to successful legal action by the TWU and others that forced the CRTC to regulate the industry according to the provisions of the *Railway Act*, much to the consternation of the government, CRTC, and industry (*TWU v. CRTC et al.*, 1988).

The unbridled subordination of the public's interest to instrumental imperatives requires that we rethink ways to establish the link among communication, social action, and democracy. Part of this process of rethinking public involvement in the processes shaping the emerging technological environment must include efforts to expand the range of issues addressed beyond those dealing with universal service, competition, and the equity of various pricing formulas. At a minimum, regulatory interventions must address the pressing tensions between the economic value of information, the value of democratic communication, and the value of private space free from both state and commercial surveillance. How we order these competing values will determine the prospects for democratic communication in the emerging communication networks.

Part of the solution to these normative dilemmas depends on how we conceptualize communication: as a means of intensifying the economic value of time, space and the body; or as a means to extend democratic forms of social interaction. If we accept the latter conception, it is necessary to consider ways in which free speech principles can be extended to the emerging network technologies and information services. Unlike those presuming a technological determinist view of history and social change, such an effort entails intervention in the social construction of technology.

First of all this means that policymakers must accept the constitutive role of regulatory policy vis-à-vis industry structure, the terms of access to communication networks and information services, and the conditions of public life. Crucial to this recognition must be an acknowledgment that regulatory changes have extended the control of existing network operators into new communication markets rather than decentralized information and cultural production. To counteract this trend and to realize certain decentralizing potentials of the new technologies it is necessary to maintain the distinction between information carriers and information providers. Pushing these distinctions further at a time of media convergence offers an opportunity to break with the unsatisfactory history of vertical integration in telecommunications and the control over transmission facilities and content by broadcasters and cable operators at the expense of public communication.

The distinction between control over facilities and control over the contents of public discourse must also encompass the emerging tiers of value-added networks and information services. Regulatory policy must prohibit network operators and VANs' ability to restrict access to networks or information services or to curtail the nature of public discourse on public and commercial networks. Open network architectures must not only be technological concepts designed to facilitate network interconnection and new communication markets, but also a political legal framework for guaranteeing that citizens' right to receive and produce communication is consistent with technological potentials.

This vision of democratic communication recognizes that in modern society control is not only exercised by nation-states, but also by the private sector. Democratic communication requires prohibitions against the state and private control of the facilities and content of public discourse. These suggestions draw on the free speech tradition of negative freedoms, but expands the range of actors covered and also suggests a notion of positive freedoms that enables the public's right to communicate. These suggestions are incomplete, but they can draw inspiration from Article 19 of the United Nation's 1948 *Universal Declaration of Human Rights*, which states: "Everyone has the right to freedom of opinion and expression; this right includes freedom to hold opinions without interference and to seek, receive and impart information and ideas through any media regardless of frontiers (pp. 1959-1960). The challenge today is to turn these democratic ideas into sociological realities.

REFERENCES

Addy, G.N. (1994, March 29). *The Competition Act and the Canadian telecommunications industry.* Speech presented to the Institute for International Research Telecommunications Conference. Toronto.

Alberta Government Telephones. (1988). *1988 Annual report.* Alberta: Author.

AGT v. CRTC and CNCP, et al. (1989). *Supreme Court Reporter*, pp. 225-302.

Angus Telecommunication Management Group (ATMG). (1990). *Potential purchasers of Mitel.* Canada: Author.

Babe, R.E. (1990). *Telecommunications in Canada.* Toronto: University of Toronto.

Bell Canada Enterprises. (1991). *Annual report: Leadership in telecommunications.* Montreal: Author.

Bill C-62: An Act Respecting Telecommunication. (1992). Ottawa: Canada Communication Group.

Call Net Telecommunications Inc. (1987, October). *Petition to the Governor in Council pursuant to Section 64(1) of the National Transportation Act. To revoke PC 1987 -2349 and to vary telecom decision CRTC 87-5.* Toronto, Canada: Author.

Call Net Telecommunications Inc. (1988, January). *Petition to the Governor in Council pursuant to Section 64(1) of the National Transportation Act. To Revoke PC 1987 -2349 and to vary telecom decision CRTC 87-5.* Toronto, Canada: Author.

Canada/Manitoba (1991). *Memorandum of understanding respecting telecommunications.* Winnipeg: Manitoba Government News Release.

Canada-U.S.-Mexico North American Free Trade Agreement (NAFTA). (1992). Washington, DC: Westlaw.

Canadian federalism and economic unity. (1991). Ottawa: Minister of Supply and Services.

The Canada—U.S. Free Trade Agreement (FTA). (1987). Ottawa: Minister of Supply and Services.

Canadian Business Telecommunications Alliance (CBTA). (1992). *Notes for presentation to the proceedings of the Standing Senate Committee on Transport and Communications, fifth proceeding on: Examination of the subject matter of Bill C-62, An Act Respecting Telecommunications.* Ottawa: Author.

Canadian Labour Congress (CLC). (1992). *Submission to the proceedings of the Standing Senate Committee on Transport and Communications, fifth proceeding on: Examination of the subject matter of Bill C-62, An Act Respecting Telecommunications.* Ottawa: Author.

Communications Canada. (1988). *Regulatory impact analysis statement regarding Order in Council P.C. 1987-2349.* unpublished document.

Communications Canada. (1992). *Government extends Teleglobe Canada mandate.* Ottawa: Communications Canada News Release.

Canadian Radio-Television and Telecommunications Commission (CRTC). (1979). *CNCP Telecommunications* (Decision 79-11). Ottawa: Minister of Supply and Services.

CRTC. (1982a). *Attachment of subscriber provided terminal equipment* (Decision 82-14). Ottawa: Minister of Supply and Services.

CRTC. (1982b). *Annual report.* Ottawa: Minister of Supply and Services.

CRTC. (1984). *Enhanced services* (Decision 84-18). Ottawa: Minister of Supply and Services.

CRTC. (1985). *Interexchange competition and related issues* (Decision 85-19). Ottawa: Minister of Supply and Services.

CRTC. (1987a). *Resale to provide primary exchange voice services* (Decision 87-1). Ottawa: Minister of Supply and Services.

CRTC. (1987b). *CNCP Telecommunications -application for exemption from certain regulatory requirements* (Decision 87-12). Ottawa: Minister of Supply and Services.

CRTC. (1990). *Resale and sharing of private line services* (Decision 90-3). Ottawa: Minister of Supply and Services.

CRTC. (1992a). *Competition in the provision of public long distance* (CRTC 92-12). Ottawa: Minister of Supply and Services.

CRTC. (1992b). *Submission to the proceedings of the Standing Senate Committee on Transport and Communications, fifth proceeding on: Examination of the subject matter of Bill C-62, An Act Respecting Telecommunications.* Ottawa: Author.

Communications Canada. (1987). *Communications for the twenty first century.* Ottawa: Minister of Supply and Services.

Crockett, B. (1991, January 14). Packet switching fees under fire in Canada. *Network World, Inc.* (Nexis Lexis), p. 27.

Department of Finance. (1987). *Government shares in Teleglobe to be sold.* Ottawa: Dept. of Finance News Release.

Department of Finance. (1991, October 23). *Telesat Canada legislation tabled.* Ottawa: Dept. of Finance News Release.

Department of Finance. (1992, March 24). *Government shares in Telesat Canada to be sold to Alouette Telecommunications, Inc.* Ottawa: Dept. of Finance News Release.

Disclosure, Inc. (1992). *Corporate information on Canadian companies.* USA: CD-ROM.

DOC. (May, 1985) *Confidential brief presented to the federal Cabinet.* Author.

Federal Provincial Task Force On Telecommunications. (1986). *Examination of telecommunications pricing and the universal availability of affordable telephone service: Report.* Ottawa: Minister of Supply and Services.

Garnham, N. (1990). *Capitalism and communication.* Newbury Park, CA: Sage.

Gates, B. (1992, March 23). Consumers will be big winners in CRTC verdict. *The Financial Post* (Lexis Nexis), p. s5.

Grant, J. C. (1991). Making it to the global major leagues. In D. W. Conklin & L. Deschenes (eds.), *Canada's information revolution* (pp. 41-53). Canada: The Institute for Research on Public Policy and Canadian Workplace Automation Research Centre.

Habermas, J. (1975). *Legitimation crisis.* Boston: Beacon

Information Technology Association of Canada. (1992). *Notes for presentation to the proceedings of the Standing Senate Committee on Transport and Communications, fifth proceeding on: Examination of the subject matter of Bill C-62, An Act Respecting Telecommunications.* Toronto: Author.

Industry Canada (1994). *The Canadian Information Highway: Building Canada's information and communications infrastructure.* Ottawa: Minister of Supply and Services.

Keane, J. (1991). *The media and democracy.* London: Polity.

MacDonald's record: The readers view. (1988, February 29). The Financial Post, p. 1. Manitoba Telephone System (MTS). (n.d.). *Current issues in long distance telephone regulation* [Internal company document].

Mosco, V. (1990). *Transforming telecommunications in Canada.* Ottawa: Centre for Policy Alternatives.

Mozes, D. (1992, June 10). *Current trends in Canadian telecommunications Policy.* Paper presented at the Canada—European Community special regulatory subgroup meeting.

Mumford, L. (1963). *Technics and civilization.* New York: Free Press. (Original work published 1934)

National Anti-Poverty Organisation (NAPO). (1987). *Rate restructuring.* Ottawa: Public Interest Advocacy Centre.

Newman, P. (1985, March 11). A tight pair of Tory shoes. *Maclean's,* p. 40.

Organisation for Economic Cooperation and Development (OECD). (1990). *Performance indicators for the public telecommunication operators.* Paris: Author.

OECD. (1991a). *Country reports.* Paris: Author.

OECD. (1991b). *Universal service and rate restructuring in telecommunications.* Paris: Author.

PCs put move on phones in West. (1989, October 20). *Calgary Herald*, p. A3.

Pike, R., & Mosco, V. (1986). Canadian consumers and telephone pricing. *Telecommunication Policy, 10*(1), 17-33.

Proceedings of the Standing Senate Committee on Transport and Communications. (1992). *Examination of the subject matter of Bill C-62, an Act respecting telecommunications*. Ottawa: Canada Communication Group.

Pugliese, D. (1992, December 10). *Uncrowning achievement*. The Ottawa Citizen, p. A5.

Racine, P., Mozes, D., & Kennedy, H. (1992). *Managing competition and regulation*. Ottawa: Communications Canada.

Ravensberg, J. (1992, December 12). Strike 2 called on Quebec's claim to regulate phone firms companies. *The Gazette* (Montreal) (Lexis Nexis), p. D3.

SaskTel (1991). *Annual report*. Regina: SaskTel, Public Affairs.

Science Council of Canada (SCC). (1991). *Sectoral technology strategy series*. Ottawa: Minister of Supply and Services.

Schiller, H. (1986). *Information and the crisis economy*. New York: Oxford University Press.

Schultz, R., & Janisch, H. (1993). *Freedom to compete*. Ottawa: Bell Canada.

Smith, J. (1991). Canada's privatisation programme. In J. Richardson (Ed.), *Privatisation and deregulation in Canada and Britain: Proceedings of a Canada/U.K. colloquium, Gleneagles Scotland* (pp. 35-47). Canada: Institute for Research on Public Policy.

Smythe, D. (1981). *Dependency road*. Norwood, NJ: Ablex.

Statistics Canada (Stats Canada). (1970-1991). *Telephone statistics*. Ottawa: Supply and Services.

Statistics Canada (Stats Canada). (1990-2). *Family expenditure in Canada*. Ottawa: Supply and Services.

Stentor Telecom Policy Inc. (1992). *Petition to the Governor in Council to vary a section of telecom decision CRTC 92-12*. Unpublished manuscript.

Teichrob, C. (Minister responsible for Sasktel). (1992, October 8). *Unfinished business*. Paper presented at the annual Financial Post Conference on *Telecommunications—Telecommunications in Canada—Can you put me through to the 21st century?* Toronto, Ontario.

Telesat. (1991). 1991 *Annual report*. Ottawa: M.O.M. Printing.

Telus. (1991). 1991 *Annual report*. Calgary, Alb., Canada: Smith and Associates.

Toronto v. Bell Telephone Co. (1905). *Canadian Law Journal, XLI*, 371.

Trade Negotiations Committee (TNC). (1993). *Final Act embodying the results of the Uruguay Round (General Agreement on Trade in Services—Annex on Telecommunications)*. Geneva: Gatt Secretariat.

TWU. (1992). *Brief to the Standing Senate Committee on Transport and Communications, fifth proceeding on: Examination of the subject matter of BilC 62, An Act Respecting Telecommunications*. Burnaby, BC, Canada: Author.

TWU v. CRTC et al. (1988, October 14). Federal Court of Appeals Court File No. A 498-88, Judgement). Unpublished decision.

Chapter 6

Restructuring the Spanish Television Industry

Richard Maxwell

In this chapter I relate the conditions of the transition from dictatorship to democracy in Spain to the acceptance and legalization of private television. Private television was not an inevitable outcome of democratization of the media in Spain. Commerce and media democracy were joined together by an official cultural policy that aimed principally at solving legal, technical, and administrative problems associated with the political transition. This official "politicization" of television reform led ironically to a narrowing of participation in the debates on licensing private media; that is, in actuality, the polity depoliticized policymaking. This was necessary for political parties whose dominance was guaranteed through management of television on the legislative side. Yet, reduced political participation also ensured that debates about the future of television were framed by the commercial press on the public side. Under such conditions, the commercial press was able to wage war as a self-appointed proxy for public dissent against the state control of television and by rhetorical extension against public service models. Instead of finding a radical alternative to elite politics and corporate media control, the Spanish Socialist Workers Party (PSOE) used the law licensing private television as political capital to buy the support of the commercial press and win a reprieve for their legislative dominance.

The central government's instrumental approach, described later as a feature of liberal corporatism, could not contain all social movements, however, as small-nation nationalisms in the Basque Country and Catalonia challenged the central state's model and schedule of reform for the television industry. The nationalist regional governments confronted the centralist hold over broadcasting by opening the way for a new configuration of communication technology that extended the multinational identity of Spain and led to greater media pluralism. Nevertheless, I argue that it would be a mistake to be swept away by the influential events occurring in the periphery of the official national culture of Spain. Although small-nation nationalism in Spain furnished the decisive counterpower to the central state media, cultural nationalism opened the national market to transnational media corporations as well. Regional television and private TV legislation together helped push the Spanish television industry into the international market, in which transnational buyers have so far had the deepest pockets.

At the end of 15 years of restructuring, this dialectic of nationalism and imperialism generated two important changes in the Spanish television industry: the collapse of the national independent film and video production sector, and the deepening of transnational corporate and financial control through private broadcast and satellite services (and soon through cable too). The national state and regional TV systems retain significant influence, but gauged by standards of commercial viability and resilience within an inflationary market, the most powerful agents to emerge in the Spanish television industry are foreign investors, big banks, and commercial media promoters. A roughly drawn ranking of notables includes Silvio Berlusconi, Spanish and foreign banks, Leo Kirch, Radio-Television Luxembourg, the Spanish media conglomerate PRISA (which controls the largest daily newspaper, *El País*, and three pay television services), and the Spanish media boss Antonio Asensio.

Finally, my analysis of the Spanish television industry is limited by distance in both time and space from the events that followed the legalization of private television. With each succeeding review of the Spanish situation, new actors and new problems emerge to outpace previous conclusions or arguments (see Maxwell, 1995). What follows attempts to situate the Spanish television industry in terms of trends and patterns. For example, I show how, when, and why the socialist government—following failed attempts of its predecessor, a two term conservative government—chose to legalize private television. I can conclude generally that their interests came down to opportunistic, or if you prefer, pragmatic attempts to win the commercial media promoters to the electoral cause of the socialist party. This can be further contextualized within international processes of privatization, a process that benefits transnational corporations, the main agents in the global economy. This characteristic feature of the transition then links national political opportunism to transnational hegemony. The trend demonstrated here shows a built-in tendency toward greater foreign investment, direct and indirect, in the Spanish television industry. As I write in the summer of 1994, for instance, Bertelsmann has emerged as a leading candidate (ahead of Time Warner, Disney, ABC, and TF1) for the purchase of a 25% share of the top-ranked private television company, Antena-3. Two years before this, that same 25%share was held by Rupert Murdoch, for now absent in the Spanish market. The point is that pinning down the exact relation between corporate owners and media influence in democratic Spain is a slippery affair—who knows who will buy and sell in each round of speculation. In contrast, to demonstrate that a more general trend of transnationalism is afoot can be grasped and more easily verified by the analyst.

The problem of instrumentalism, in which media are seen as instruments of a ruling class seeking top-down control of the "masses," is complicated by the fact that the controllers of media in Spain have, at least through 1994, been using television as an instrument of investment first and foremost while legislators continue to use television regulation as political capital to service the interests of dominant political parties. Hence, this chapter focuses mostly on the consolidation of monied and vested class interests who began to take control of the media system during the transition to democracy. The chapter is less concerned with the causal ties between this elite control and its influence on TV programs and audiences. Still, when the game of buy and sell outruns political questions of communicative democracy, ordinary folks— whether defined as citizens or popular classes or others—are entirely excluded or turned once again into masses of spectators whose cultural welfare is managed from above; workers in media firms become little more than passive observers of industrial reorganization; and policymakers are reduced to making what's left of the public system competitive with the private operators. Democratic media systems, I believe, cannot be based on such a closed system of market relations, in which the defining instrument is commercial viability—an apparent relegation of power to structure, a reification of the grandest sort—and in which the terms of debate make realist phrases like "that's the way it is" sound highly reasonable. Nothing could be further from the truth, for "the way it is" always hides the unified class interests of commercial business and political elites, a class in Spain of questionable loyalty to the people or the place.

In a limited normative sense, this chapter hopes to show that communicative democracy depends on more than a "free" press and a "modern" telecommunication infrastructure. It depends on an open and perpetually mutable cultural field that, in the Spanish case, could not be cultivated with a policy discourse obsessed with administrative acumen. The question is not how to make policies that "fit" democracy, but rather how to change the forms of policymaking by politicizing them so that a dialogical, participatory communicative democracy can begin.

MANY CHANNELS, FEW VOICES

When Francisco Franco died in 1975, Spaniards could watch two TV channels of Televisión Española (TVE), both operated by the state-controlled Radio Television Española (RTVE). By 1994, 80% of the population could receive at least four (TVE 1 and 2 among them) and up to eight channels from land-based stations, 1 to 3 land-based subscription services, and, if they owned a satellite dish, up to 16 other channels (Law 10, May 3, 1988). In the 1980s, TVE-1 could count on up to 27 million viewers for its top-ranked shows. In 1993, it could rarely get more than 8 million to watch even its most popular program, although it still attracted more viewers than any of its competitors. By 1993, the combined shares of private broadcasters regularly surpassed the combined shares of TVE-1 and 2, resulting in financial losses in RTVE that have totaled in the billions of dollars. Since 1982, RTVE received no state subsidy and survived by becoming the most highly commercialized public system in Europe. After the arrival of private television, however, the government was finally forced in 1993 to renew the state subsidy, which, nonetheless, could not turn back a debt that grew by 450 million dollars in that year.

Before private television, RTVE's toughest competitor was TV-3, a regional network owned and operated by the Catalan Parliament within the autonomous region of Catalonia. In the 1980s, TV-3 sold air time, to the same transnational advertisers courted by RTVE, worth about one-tenth that of the national state network. Two other, less lucrative, regional networks belonging to the Parliaments of the autonomous communities of Galicia and the Basque Country also broadcast to regional markets. These three regional networks competed for audiences, with greatly varying levels of success, against TVE and no other channels within their proscribed political region. By 1990, 11 regional broadcast organizations were approved, six of which were broadcasting on a daily basis (Basque Country, Catalonia, Galicia, Madrid, Valencia, and Andalusia, with approved companies in the Canary and Balearic Islands, Navarra, Aragon, and Murcia). In 1989, the directors of these systems agreed to merge into a national federation of autonomous broadcasters, known as the Federation of Autonomous Radio and Television Organizations, or FORTA, creating a network of public broadcasters to rival RTVE. RTVE and FORTA, a de facto public oligopoly of advertising-funded, not-for-profit television, dominated the market until 1991, when they were challenged by three privately owned, advertising-funded, for-profit, national networks: Telecinco, Antena-3, and the subscription service, Canal+.

According to El País (August 15, 1993), the national register of viewer attention throughout 1993 indicated that TVE-1 decreased its share to 31% (down a point from 1992) and TVE-2 fell to 10.8% (down almost 4 points). By December 1993, TVE-1 held on average about 29.1& of the national audience, Antena-3 was attracting 26.3% followed by Telecinco's 19.3%, whereas TVE-2 had sunk to 8.8 percent (Crain Communications, 1994). FORTA companies saw a slight reduction to 14.3% of the national total for 1993. In the first quarter of 1994, Antena-3 rose to the top of the ratings. Its advance in 1993 represented a 65% increase in advertising revenues over figures for 1992, and in the first four months of 1994 this channel registered a further 47% surge in advertising revenues ("Spain: Antena 3," 1993). Of the estimated 4 billion dollar television advertising billings in Spain for 1994, first quarter earnings showed that over 67% was going to Antena-3 (35.2) and Telecinco (32) combined ("Television advertising," 1994).

For obvious reasons, when the state was the only television broadcaster, the private media promoters, regional Parliaments, advertisers, and the advertising agencies saw RTVE's hold over the airwaves as a monopoly over audience attention—a monopoly, moreover, with tremendous economic and political value. In 1983, the regional autonomous systems broke this monopoly, and by the late 1980s, with three regional television networks and an expanded national network, the total investment in television advertising had already risen 1,200% over investment in 1975 (Bustamante, 1989). Why did the Spanish state let private companies loose into this market? What conditions were necessary to force open what was a relatively protected market for the publicly held oligopoly?

OUT OF DICTATORSHIP: TELEVISION IN QUESTION

From the outset of the transitional period in 1975, there was little disagreement that the state broadcasting system was the direct and most visible institutional descendent of the Franco dictatorship. Starting as early as 1977, when official channels for reform were ostensibly opened, governmental investigations of the corrupt and mismanaged RTVE began. Although these investigations had little official impact, their findings became ammunition for the private press who waged war against the state system and, by association, against the idea of public service television. Most of the articles appeared in popular and trade journals and focused on the lack of democratic control, internal sabotage, inept personnel, bumbling administrators, and financial mismanagement.

The press war against the public system subsided with each governmental promise of private television and resumed when it was evident that legislation was not forthcoming, which was usually within a few days. A dizzying rise of expectation among major economic, informational, and political forces peaked as the press hyped the promise of new channels, whereas the mostly baffled population showed little interest in private television (Bustamante & Villafañe, 1985). Like other press wars in Britain, Germany, France, and Italy, this one was waged with calls for expressive freedom as part of a strategy to gain a foothold in future, private TV channels. The links between this rhetoric of expressive freedom and corporate media interests should have been clear because the same scenario had by that time been played out in most of Western Europe. But at the time in Spain, such press attacks were hard to disentangle from frontal assaults on francoist institutions and thus hard to dissociate from the transitional movement toward democracy.

With Eurocommunism and social democratic platforms defining official politics of the left in Spain, radical proposals for a transitional state were absorbed by political game rules in line with evolutionary, rather than revolutionary, political practice. The political means (or game rules) of this evolutionary practice were characterized by the leader of the Communist Party of Spain (PCE) as the ruptura pactada, or negotiated break, with the francoist past (Carr & Fusi, 1984). For the right, the ruptura pactada offered a solution to the growing social tensions created by the political impasse that followed Franco's death. In 1976, the Spanish working class struck for 150 million working hours; in 1977, for 110 million hours (Maravall, 1981). Throughout 1975 and 1976, the Minister of the Interior called repeatedly for the violent repression of all strikes and demonstrations. The most tragic incidence occurred in 1976 ,when police were ordered to fire into a crowd of demonstrators in Vitoria (Basque Country), murdering five workers. Daily reports of police torture were common; journalists, filmmakers, and theater groups were continually harassed by censors and police. Demands for reform were mounting on both the left and right. The military finally acquiesced to politicians and businessmen who were forced to accept the reformist conditions of the transition in order to avoid what some feared would lead to a return to a closed and stagnant economy or, worse, to civil war. Not to be underestimated, the King of Spain strongly encouraged the reformist alternative, which he saw as the only viable route to maintain the monarchy (Carr & Fusi, 1984; Maravall, 1981).

The reluctant reformers needed a coherent political organization that could negotiate democratic changes within the existing legal framework and, in turn, forge some semblance of stability. The leader chosen by the King to head the new coalition of self-proclaimed centrists was Adolfo Suárez. As a young, ambitious technocrat within Franco's political alliance known as the Movimiento Nacional, Suárez had served as the Chairman of TVE between 1969 and 1973. He projected an image of a serious, reform-minded politician and quickly proved to be skillful at bridging the gap between the past regime and the transitional government. Among the achievements credited to Suárez are the legalization of the leftist opposition, partial amnesty of political prisoners, legal toleration of nationalist symbols in the regions, and a democratic election arranged within the confines of francoist law.

Suárez headed the Union of the Democratic Center (UCD), a coalition of 14 miniparties broadly divided between Social and Christian Democrats. With only a relative majority after the 1977 elections, the UCD presided over the Spanish government until 1982, when it finally dissolved for good. Like

Suárez, one third of the UCD leadership were identified as politicians previously associated with the Movimiento Nacional (Maravall, 1981). On the whole, the UCD was a loosely formed bloc of ruling-class interests tied variously, and in contradictory unity, with national financial, industrial, and military elites. The credibility of the UCD, under Suárez's leadership, hung precariously between the extremist right wing of the party, who advocated continuity of existing institutions, and the Social Democrats, who encouraged reforms such as legalized divorce, media democratization, and greater civil freedoms. In contrast, the left opposition, headed by the Spanish Socialist Workers Party (PSOE) and the PCE, proposed at first the complete sociopolitical rupture with the past regime, what they called "democracy without adjectives."

In this context, the *ruptura pactada* can be understood as an outgrowth of early impasse resolution and of the historical compromise of revolutionary forces. It was emblematic of a time characterized by pacts and deals. The most important social compromise of the period was signed in October 1977 in the so-called Moncloa Pacts. The left agreed to wage ceilings, credit restrictions, and a conservative fiscal policy. In exchange, the government was supposed to reform, among other things, regional policy, the structure of the general economy, and the police forces; loosen restrictions against public protest; legalize contraceptives; and decriminalize adultery. This "contrived unanimity" (Hooper, 1987, p. 43) sought to ensure political peace and protection for the UCD's legislative package until a new constitution could be written, approved, and enacted. To many activists, workers, and members of the popular opposition, however, the Pacts were evidence that the left leadership had betrayed democracy and progressive principles. Moreover, in signing the deal the leftist reformers recalled the style of ex-francoists reformers who sought to "bestow" democracy from above.

A statute of reform for RTVE was developed as a result of the Moncloa Pacts, but did not emerge from its paper existence until 1980 under the second UCD government. In fact, no reform for television came out of the first UCD government. Meanwhile, anti-RTVE sentiments continued to rise in the press and among opposition parties and intellectuals. Nevertheless, the *ruptura pactada*, inscribed in such deals as the Moncloa Pacts, led quite easily to the subsequent reduction of participation in media reform for democratic Spain. It set the stage for the depoliticization of cultural policy by making the cultural transition to democracy a matter of normative procedures that could be contained and planned from above.

As noted earlier, TVE was the most visible incarnation of the francoist past, referred to by the popular and trade press at the time as the "bunker," the epithet commonly used for francoists. TVE was a readymade apparatus of power and functioned as the primary ideological arm of the state. This power was reserved for the majority party alone and explains both UCD's lack of interest in liberalization and the opposition's push for change. More generally, to separate the ruling party from TVE symbolized a break with the past and a move toward democracy and a pluralistic political order. Thus, when the Statute of Radio and Television (RTVE statute) was passed in 1980, the symbolism of TV reform crystallized as a call for clear and precise norms regarding control over the state system. Among other things, the statute stipulated that the administrative council of RTVE should be reorganized to reflect the mosaic of political parties in Parliament (Article 7, Law 4 1980, January 10), which nevertheless benefited the majority parties, UCD and PSOE, who jointly authored the legislation. It was noted at the time that most observers saw the statute as a sign that the state-controlled media were going to be democratized, even though implementation of it was conspicuously slow. The PCE and Catalan minority in Parliament, however, criticized the statute as a setback for disenfranchised people and minority parties, whom the statute explicitly excluded from cultural policy and the social means to cultural and political expression (Torrents, 1984). The RTVE statute notwithstanding, the UCD failed to consolidate its control over TVE while an internal battle (over a divorce law and the statutes of autonomy) started to split the Social Democrats and Christian Democrats apart.

In March 1981, a new executive committee of the UCD presented a bill to legalize private television. The crisis of the government that preceded this action had ended with Adolfo Suárez's resignation as president of Spain in January 1981, followed by an attempted military takeover of the government that resulted in a failed *coup d'etat* on February 23, 1981. Already evident after the elections of 1979, growing discontent over Adolfo Suárez's leadership caused a "revolt of the barons" in UCD and a rightward shift to the so-called mono-color governments of Suárez and of his successor Leopoldo Calvo Sotelo (Carr & Fusi, 1984). In such a climate, it would appear that the proposal for private television could not have come at a more inappropriate moment in the government's history. Yet the preemptive tactic by the UCD executive was clear: When demands for administrative reform of television signified the end of the ruling party's political control over the medium, the leadership of the moribund party rushed to legalize a privately controlled television (Costa, 1986; on Italian similarities, see Pavolini, 1980).

Many influential members of the ruling party, caught off guard by the proposal, fumed publicly that the authors of the bill had not consulted anyone and, worse, were planning to push the bill through Parliament by means of a simple decree. A decree, or ordinary law, does not require two thirds of the Parliamentary vote for passage, as does an organic law. The tacit accord of the *ruptura pactada* would be violated if passage of the bill were pursued in this manner. Consensus politics had already been lost within the UCD, and it was obvious that consensus would be impossible to achieve in an open Parliamentary debate. This indeed was the case, as the bill met with opposition from both the left and, more damaging, from the Social Democrats within the UCD.

The instability of the UCD government contrasted sharply with their subsequent bold maneuvers, as the following episode demonstrates. In the spring of 1982, the Constitutional Tribunal passed judgment on a lawsuit in which Antena-3 radio claimed that RTVE's control of Spanish TV violated the free speech rights stipulated in article 20 of the Spanish Constitution. In their decision, the Tribunal said that the Constitution neither prohibits nor mandates the existence of privately controlled television networks. However, if such networks were proposed by Parliament, the law regulating them must attend to issues of freedom of access, reply, expression, and other rights that the Tribunal interpreted as necessary in a democratic culture. The Tribunal insisted that such legislation can only be "adopted within the framework of the Constitution by means of an organic law" (*El País*, April 4, 1982). In order to fit the proposal of private TV to this constitutional clarification, the members of the UCD who wrote the bill removed all but the technical aspects from the proposal by decree, exploiting the fact that the Tribunal had said nothing about the installation of transmitters and receivers. By doing this, the UCD hoped to negotiate passage of a bill that would establish privately held TV technology in Spain. They would then submit an organic law covering the aspects of freedom of expression, right to reply, access, and so on.

This political maneuver critically transformed the discourse of TV reform within the polity. The mode of transitional politics that had served to promulgate some semblance of stability through consensus among political forces—namely, the *ruptura pactada*—had been jettisoned by the idea of a law by decree. The UCD had broken the rules of the game and thereby redirected the attention of the opposition from the question of private television as a suitable, desirable alternative in itself to the question of the legislative process per se. With the second proposal, the UCD split technical aspects and social aspects of television in order to link technology with principles of free enterprise and tie separate legislation of an organic law of private television to principles of free expression. The effect was to make TV-as-free-enterprise the new rhetorical frame: Building business exclusive of the social rights of expression was a position buttressed moreover by article 38 of the Spanish Constitution, which instructs the state to defend and promote free enterprise.

Only a minority of the Parliament spoke out against the actual premise of the first proposed bill, whereas all were furious at the impropriety of the proposal of a decree law. The PSOE even accepted the idea of private television as an alternative on the condition that certain restrictions be placed on advertising. The socialists exposed their lack of a developed cultural politics when they offered no reason for supporting private television nor any indication what the nature of the restrictions on advertising would be. Only the PCE opposed the idea on the grounds that economically privileged groups would be the sole beneficiaries of private channels.

Although the second UCD-sponsored bills were presented to the Parliament at the end of April, 1982, they were never debated. The Parliament soon after dissolved in an open crisis, and elections were held in October of that year. In those elections, the PSOE won the absolute majority of seats in the government; the socialist leader, Felipe González, became president of Spain; and the agenda for TV reform was repackaged.

FROM RUPTURA PACTADA TO LIBERAL CORPORATISM

The PSOE attacked the UCD TV bill as bad etiquette for a ruptura pactada, although they neglected the fact that private television had been placed on the political agenda while the long-term moral, social, and political effects of private television were never debated. More important to the PSOE was the project of winning and maintaining consensus about the proper administration of the political transition to democracy, a very loose rhetorical frame in which privately owned technology had been naturalized as a feature of a democratic culture. Nevertheless, the PSOE garnered credibility through their adherence to a politics of negotiation of TV reform and used the issue to gain momentum for their electoral victory. Thus, they inherited an environment in which the language of private versus state TV was legitimated as the basis for the debate on broadcast reform. This hackneyed debate was fostered by the commercial press for whom the opposing sides were represented basically as freedom or francoism. Nowhere on the public agenda was the obvious alternative of nonstate, publicly controlled, commercial free television.

Still, in early 1983, the PSOE declared that there would be no private television or additional channels of any kind. Other social democracies in Europe were still resisting multiplication of channels, and so should Spain, said the socialist leader Felipe González. González cited election poll data that, he said, showed unequivocally that the people of Spain were not interested in more TV channels. He also invoked an election promise—that had developed in the wake of the UCD proposal for private television—to fight cultural imperialism. For the first time, the socialist leadership argued that private television would lead to the colonization of Spanish culture.

Rhetoric aside, the same old media power motivated the socialists. After all, they had inherited the state television system and held a majority of seats in the Parliament, meaning that the opposition faced a ruling party whose control of the national television company was more firmly entrenched than the previous government's had been. Thus, the socialists issued many normative declarations demonstrating reticence to act on the issue of broadcast reform, but it would soon become evident that the PSOE position was merely symbolic, although no less effective for being symbolic.

The PSOE never produced a coherent media policy of the left, one that would interpret the needs of politically and culturally disenfranchised groups as the basic building blocks for a democratic broadcasting policy. Instead, and to their benefit, the PSOE developed a politics of acquiescence vis-à-vis dominant political and economic groups. This reactive stance transformed the informal and often porous containment of political participation characteristic of the ruptura pactada into procedures for implementing a "democratic" cultural policy that were more formal, technocratic, and explicitly tied to the needs of a narrow group of "experts," professional broadcasters, big money interests, and the conservative opposition. What the PSOE did not count on was that the nationalist agitation in the Basque Country and Catalonia would effectively spite the nascent hegemony of the socialist party in the national power structure and reopen the issue of TV reform in Spain in unanticipated ways.

By the end of 1983, the Basque regional government was broadcasting regularly on *Euskaltelebista* (ETB), or Basque TV, whereas the Catalan authorities had initiated the construction of their own television channel, TV-3. No national law existed at that time allowing the regional governments to build transmitters or use the airwaves; these technical conditions for broadcasting were the sole property of RTVE and the central state, as stipulated by a 1908 Royal Decree. It was impractical for the PSOE, nevertheless, to challenge the actions of the regional authorities because already some vague form of autonomous regional television had been guaranteed by the 1978 Constitution, by the 1980 Statute of Radio and Television, and by the regional Statutes of Autonomy. When the Basques and Catalans successfully overturned 70 years of exclusive centralist control over the airwaves, they pushed the PSOE into accelerating TV reform. The PSOE faced the effects of regionalism without having as yet effected a regional policy.

The PSOE enacted a new law in early 1984 that legalized and regulated the new regional stations a posteriori. This law, known as the Third Channel Law, provided the legal means by which all the autonomous regional governments might eventually create their own broadcasting system, albeit dependent on both the RTVE infrastructure and central government. The Parliaments of the autonomous regions of Galicia, Catalonia, and the Basque Country took an antagonistic position against this national regulation. Rather than abide by the letter of the Third Channel Law, which established the norm of one network within each autonomous region, the authorities in these three regions said their networks functioned "allegally." They contended that the Third Channel Law only pertains to the central state allotments and not to their own allotments. By 1994, the Basques and Catalans operated two channels but argued, along with the Galician Parliament, which operated only one channel, that these have always been independent of existing law. They still hold the position that one additional channel within the framework of the Third Channel Law is coming to them, raising the potential number of land-based channels controlled by the regional governments to three, as opposed to the central government's stipulation of one.

The scramble to produce the Third Channel Law forced the PSOE to confront an unknown political and economic situation created by the regional governments. The new competition for the Spanish political imagination and for advertising revenues gave new clout to the promoters of commercial media. Within a month of enacting the Third Channel Law, the leadership of the PSOE announced that they were considering the issue of private television for internal debate. The polity already treated private TV as the primary alternative form of television, and, despite the powerful regional governments, the major force that the PSOE had to contend with were the private media promoters whose relentless press war was damaging the socialist's credibility. The socialists hoped that discussion of private channels would reduce external pressure on them in the same way that passing the Third Channel Law had, that is, by manufacturing expectation of more channels. This release would, in turn, furnish a reprieve to the socialists by protecting their control over RTVE. At this time, not surprisingly, the PSOE leadership diluted their demands for cultural sovereignty and suggested that democracy and the free in-flow of foreign cultural products were not incompatible.

By 1984, the socialists had furnished new means for political transition to democracy with a mode of political reform associated with a liberal corporatist state. A ruling social democratic party, best suited to liberal corporatism, is able to maintain a high level of negotiation between a reduced number of significant political and economic actors because "they fuse several major roles into one political organization" (Jessop, 1979, p. 207). In this case, with limited participation from both the communist-led union and the opposition parties (left and right), the socialists and their affiliated labor union met alone with the major business association to set, for instance, wage levels and labor market controls. The liberal corporatist state, organized on a principle of induced class collaboration, also furnished the socialist party with a paradigm for negotiations in broadcast reform. When the socialists proceeded to frame legislation for private television in 1984, they opted to eliminate the participation of less powerful political forces and to favor representatives from the most powerful political and economic sectors.

The major economic forces to enter this phase of policy formulation were multinational electronics and information industries, as revealed by the proposal of a new telecommunications reform law known as the Ley de Ordenación de las Comunicaciones (LOC). Initiated in March 1984, this law was the first major attempt to merge the entire communications infrastructure into one system (integrating post, telephone, broadcasting, satellite, digital systems, etc.). The LOC survived in many versions until it was discarded in 1986, when it was replaced by the Ley de Organización de las Telecomunicaciones (LOT) and separate norms dealing with private television (discussed later). This proposed reform reflected a shift in the politics of transition to a technocratic management of multinational and national business interests, which resulted from the PSOE's earnest implementation of economic policy to entice Spanish capitalists and multinational firms to invest in electronics and information technologies in Spain (it should be noted that this came on the heels of the failure of the UCD to implement similar economic policy).

The socialists connected the legalization of private television to this all-encompassing law of telecommunications in a cautious move based mostly on imitation. The French and British governments had already pegged the telecommunications industry as the cornerstone of economic recovery. The Spanish socialists, following the lead of the French socialist party, refused to allow Spain to miss the train to the information society or to become second-class citizens of the European information economy. But in Spain, which lacked both a basic telecommunications industry and the national financial base to build one, this policy shift meant increased participation of multinational industries. The pursuit of foreign investment, in turn, required dismantling the remaining relics of protectionism, carried out within a policy of assisted capitalism as an "appropriate strategy for integration" into the international market (Vazquez Barquero & Hebbert, 1985, pp. 290-291).

The political reasoning behind this strategy draws on the experience of the UCD, which was caught in the middle of the "historical accident [when the] onset of and adjustment to the economic crisis happened to coincide in Spain with the critical transition from dictatorship to democracy" (Vazquez Barquero & Hebbert, 1985, p. 285). Primarily due to the global recession, to outdated economic development models, and to the oil shock of 1973-74, Spain suffered a dramatic reduction in economic growth throughout the 1970s and early 1980s. The annual average growth rate of the Gross Domestic Product (GDP) dropped from the 7% of the boom years (1961-74) to only 2.3% in the first three years of the transition. Inflation jumped over 10% between the same two periods. By 1977, inflation had reached a high of 26.4% whereas growth stagnated. Under this "stagflationary" strain, unemployment began to rise sharply, and by the early 1980s, it rose to the highest level in Europe, over 20%. By that time the rate at which the GDP was expanding had diminished to almost nothing, with a low of 0.3% in 1981 (Gunther, 1986; Vazquez Barquero & Hebbert, 1985).

The effects of political and economic crises on the agenda for broadcast reform are hard to disentangle, although decisive economic pressures evidently limited the socialist's thinking. On the one hand, political forces who backed broad economic liberalizations, including the privatization of television, faced a conservative national elite of investors, manufacturers, and employers. Franco had ensured Spanish capitalists a level of protection for their goods and markets, so calls for liberalization and increased investment with unknown prospects seemed to many investors to put fortunes in jeopardy. On the other hand, the remaining vestiges of the dictatorship, including protectionism, were seen as unnecessary by many of the reformist parties and younger entrepreneurs. This led to a political stalemate in the midst of the stagflationary period. Spanish capitalism was caught between an ineffective political class that had just recently begun to redefine itself and a conservative capitalist class that balked at institutional change.

The old alliance of state and business elites faced an emerging group of younger reformers in the PSOE leadership who were willing to make decisions and forge new alliances and a new hegemony. Continuist options posed by the francoists were unacceptable, whereas most attempts by the UCD to make modest liberalizations in the economy, private television among them, were resisted by traditional business elites who considered that a form of assisted capitalism should be maintained at all costs (Vazquez Barquero & Hebbert, 1985). By withholding state support to the ailing economy, the UCD projected an image of incompetence that alienated the Social Democrats within the UCD coalition. This schism eventually caused leading members of the Social Democrats to join the socialists in the 1982 election. The alliance generated a "new" PSOE that claimed a "realistic" economic policy was one that combined notions of competitive and assisted capitalism in order to bring national investors into the process of modernization. This shift in position offered perhaps the best fit to the residual policy agenda on private television: It sanctioned free enterprise within the social controls of a liberal democratic state (the same agenda the distrusted UCD proved incompetent to sell).

Another part of the "appropriate strategy for integration" into the international market, and a crucial impetus to tie TV reform to a larger telecommunication law, was entry of Spain into the European Economic Community (EC, now the European Union). If Spain were to be European, said the socialists, its communication system would have to achieve compatibility (capacity and standards) with systems throughout the EC. Yet much skepticism lingered among national manufacturers. For instance, *El País* (February 7, 1985) published a summary of a study conducted by the association of employers of the electronics and informatics industries (ANIEL), which showed that modifications in the tax structure related to EC policies would crush what was left of the national electronics sector. The government confronted such pessimism by limiting discussions of television and telecommunications systems to the role that new structures would have in economic development and growth in employment. Again, this rhetoric of modernization was more positively interpreted by the commercial press and leading segments of the corporate sector.

There was consequently a sharp rise in meetings, roundtable discussions, colloquia, and interviews between the private TV promotion companies and political parties. The press enjoyed publicizing these meetings and showed a penchant for finding internationally known figures such as Walter Cronkite, or Roy Gibson of the European Space Agency, to testify that there is nothing worse for democracy than a state-controlled television. Gibson, in particular, made the threatening prediction that "if the Spanish government doesn't accept two or three private channels, there'll be an invasion of pirate transmissions that no one will be able to stop" (*El País*, February 24, 1984).

In October 1985, the socialists agreed to work with the opposition to enforce the RTVE Statute and finish a draft law for private television. A preliminary version of the reform bill was circulated in September, and the text of discussions between the PSOE and the opposition, led by the right-wing Alianza Popular (today known as Partido Popular), finally appeared in January 1986. In April, the council of ministers passed on a bill to Parliament that proposed to authorize three new private channels and to develop a separate technical plan for them. Virtually fitted to the demands of private promotion companies, the law seemed to have the future of Spanish television well tied up. Perhaps for that reason the press then began in earnest to publicize the populist rhetoric of the bipartisan discussions calling for the end of RTVE and the rise of citizen responsibility. Such banner statements led to no practical outcome, however, as the law of private television did not reach debate in the Parliament before the next elections were called. Nevertheless, the private TV bill soon after served a purpose utterly distinct from the one it was designed for.

The government had other things to do besides legalize private television. Throughout the winter and spring of 1985, for instance, the PSOE was more concerned with its June date to sign the treaty of adherence to the EC. This precipitated a major internal crisis in the socialist party apparatus. Ministers were reassigned, and several significant resignations were announced in anticipation of the formation of the second socialist government in May. A key resignation was that of Fernando Morán, who had been the Minister of Foreign Affairs since the first socialist government was formed in 1982. Morán was a staunch opponent of Spain's participation in North Atlantic Treaty Organization (NATO); he once called for the complete withdrawal of U.S. troops from Spain and was a prominent critic of liberalization plans that opened Spain to transnational investments. The Morán resignation typified the general modification in PSOE behavior at this time—just a month before EC agreements were signed and less than a year before a scheduled referendum on Spain's membership in the NATO. Morán was replaced by the man who led the Social Democratic exodus from the UCD to the PSOE, Francisco Fernández Ordoñez. The ministerial changes of May attracted immediate approval from the United States. Shortly following Morán's replacement, the Reagan Administration gave security clearance for AT&T to begin construction of a microchip factory near Madrid, after which the socialist government channeled its energies into the national referendum on Spain's membership in NATO.

While becoming more conservative in international relations, the PSOE was simultaneously charged with a rightward turn on the domestic front by Nicolas Redondo, leader of the Unión General de Trabajadores (UGT), the socialist-affiliated trade union. Redondo denounced the government's labor record, and taking advantage of UGT's independence from party control, he publicly accused the PSOE of creating "greater unemployment, greater inequality, and greater poverty" (quoted in Camiller, 1986, p. 28). In May and June 1985, the UGT-PSOE dispute could be found sharing headlines with the revelations about the LOC and private television cited earlier. The association is curious: the PSOE promised 800,000 jobs, and delivered between 600,000 and

800,000 more unemployed; the PSOE promised private television and delivered a blinkered draft of a technical law that failed to fulfill its brief.

Hence, the practical problems of consolidating corporatist and transnational hegemony came at a time of reduced popularity for the ruling party. This was precisely the context in which the PSOE's private TV bill realized its greatest social influence. According to Villagrasa (1992, p. 346), the 1986 bill was "used" by the government "to manipulate the Spanish press" into supporting the PSOE campaign for membership in NATO and eventually the PSOE reelection. The media were encouraged to sway Spanish voters away from their significant, and well-documented, opposition to NATO. The quid pro quo for the press was the assurance that the private TV bill would not be rejected because of political caprice (the largest national dailies, *El País* and *La Vanguardia*, were part of the conglomerates owning two major private TV promoters, SOGETEL and TEVISA).

The PSOE, the government-controlled RTVE, and the private press together won a pro-NATO victory in the popular referendum, by a notably narrow margin. Forty percent of the voters abstained, whereas of the eligible votes 52.5 percent voted to stay in NATO, 40% to quit it (another 13% were disqualified); and the vote occurred with polls still showing defeat on the eve of the referendum (Mujal-León, 1986). I want to stress the role of the commercial press, given the belief that the PSOE was able to win support for NATO because they controlled the TVE (Payne, 1986). The government had used the private TV bill in such a way as to leverage the private press to the state's cause, a corporatist collaboration that brought together a pro-NATO alliance of both state and private media. The role of the private press in both referendum and national election that soon followed has too often been underestimated.

The government saw the NATO vote as a confidence vote and very quickly called for early elections. A media machine was on their side, as long as the press got what it wanted—licenses for private television. By June 1986, the PSOE and González were back in power. The private TV bill was finally approved by the government, after six amendments from the opposition, in April 1987. However, González postponed enactment of the law until 1989. The postponement was really meaningless because all the major institutional players and all the major points of law were the same as they were prior to the NATO vote and the general election. This episode recalls with force something that Jesus de Polanco said back in 1985. Polanco, who is the chairman of PRISA, the company that owns El País, said that there are only two truly important powers in Spain, "the government and PRISA," adding that "we [PRISA] appointed the government and it will last for as long as we want" (Epoca, 1985).

CONGLOMERATION AND THE TRANSNATIONAL PRESENCE

Not a single company bidding for a private TV license was allowed to be wholly owned by a single Spanish media firm or individual. The law stipulates that no person—defined as a physical person or an entity claiming rights as such (i.e., a nonnatural person or corporation)—can own, directly or indirectly, more than 25% of a company. Nor can a single "person" own, directly or indirectly, more than one private TV company. The law adds that at no time must total foreign ownership—direct or indirect—surpass 25% of the capital of the company. In addition, the private TV law suggests that there can be no hidden partners or hidden patterns of ownership, and stipulates that the company must be headquartered in Spain and have a decidedly Spanish nationality (Articles 18 and 19). In principle, monopoly ownership is outlawed, public accountability required, and transnational corporate control restricted. In practice things turned out differently.

Among the firms to play a part in the bidding were Polanco's *Promotores de Informaciones S.A.* or PRISA, Canal Plus France, *La Vanguardia* and Antena 3, Banca March, Berlusconi's Fininvest, and Grupo 16 (eventually disqualified). The TV companies that actually won a license were *Antena 3 de Televisión, La Sociedad Española de Televisión Canal Plus*, or Canal + (with PRISA and Canal Plus France each holding 25%), and *Gestevisión-Telecinco*, or Telecinco (with Fininvest—Berlusconi, the Spanish national organization of the blind, and the Grupo Anaya—a publisher—each holding 25%). The rest of the shares were distributed in smaller packages among banks, newspaper groups, and individual Spanish and foreign investors.

According to these percentages of individual holdings, no one company is controlled by a single interest. This is deceptive, however, because total bank holdings of the Canal+ group were about 40%. Overall, the total control of private television accorded directly to financial institutions was between 19% and 21%, and with interlocking directorates in Spain, bank representatives can be found sitting on boards and influencing the actions of cultural industries as diverse as newsprint, publishing, and publicity (Bustamante, 1982; Bustamante & Zallo, 1988). With a conservative estimate that accounts for direct and indirect ownership, the banks, commercial media, and publicists together hold about 60% of private television in Spain, giving them more clearance than any other sectors to control the direction of the "independent" television industry.

Some changes have occurred since the first licenses were issued. In 1990, the Anaya publishing group left Telecinco over a dispute with Berlusconi, selling 20% of their holdings to the Spanish representative of the Kuwaiti Investment Office (KIO), Javier de la Rosa. Berlusconi orchestrated this purge to get control over the company, which he did by extending ownership of Fininvest's Publiespaña in Spain to other Telecinco shareholders. In this way, the Italian Berlusconi guaranteed his Fininvest would be the dominant contractor for advertising on the Telecinco network—a direct amplification of his influence. De las Rosa eventually sold his shares to German media boss Leo Kirch. By early 1994, the ownership of Telecinco broke down as follows: Kirch (25%); Berlusconi (25%); Radio-Television Luxembourg (19%); Jacques Hachuel (10%); Bank of Luxembourg (8%); the commercial builder Angel Medrano (7%) and ONCE, the Spanish national organization of the blind (6%). The "Spanish firm," Telecinco, was clearly controlled by non-Spanish interests in violation of the law.

In the summer of 1992, Rupert Murdoch and the Spanish media conglomerate, Grupo Zeta, took over a 25% stake in Antena-3 television. Also at that time the industrial arm of the bank Banesto increased its declared holdings of Antena-3 TV to 25 percent. Mario Conde, the head of Banesto, arranged the $100 million financing for Murdoch's Grupo Zeta hostile takeover, which gave Banesto an unlisted 25% control of Antena-3 TV through a collateral charge on the loan (Banesto also held 12.5% of Grupo Zeta). Two important changes in the ownership structure of Antena-3 TV took place in 1993-94. Rupert Murdoch sold his 12.5% share in Grupo Zeta to the Banco Central Hispano in order to raise cash for other global ventures. Mario Conde was deposed after the central bank intervened to put Banesto under state guardianship. In the first months of 1994, Banesto's holdings were being investigated and where possible divested, leading to the following restructuring of the capital in Antena-3 TV: Grupo Zeta (25%), Renvir (25%), Banesto on paper (10%), Bouygues (15%), Invacor and Corpoban (25%). On paper Asensio controlled nearly 70% of Grupo Zeta, Ediciones Primera Plana owned 5%, and BCH and Banesto controlled 12.5% each. Banesto's media holdings were up for sale, and the U.S. bank, Bankers Trust, which was charged with finding buyers, courted Disney, TF1, ABC, Time Warner, and Bertelsmann (which seemed to be leading the pack; Scott, 1994a).

Canal+ ownership structure remained through 1994 much as it was in 1989: 25% belongs to PRISA, 25% to Canal Plus France, about 8% to the Grupo Eventos, 16% to the Banca March, 15% to Banco de Bilbao-Vizcaya, 5% to Bankinter, and 5% to Banco de Zaragoza. Canal+ ranked third in 1993 among pay-TV channels in Europe for audience and turnover. Its one major Spanish media investor, PRISA, has moved beyond the internal market, which it has used as a staging ground for global expansion. PRISA's international investment strategy began in earnest in 1991 with the purchase of an 18% stake in the British firm, Newspaper Publishing, which publishes *The Independent*. By 1993, PRISA had increased its holdings in Britain, Portugal, France, and Germany. More recently, PRISA joined a consortium of Mexican investors to buy *La Prensa*, the largest newspaper in Mexico. Also, Bertelsmann and Canal+ have signed an agreement to develop pay-TV and pay-per-view services in Spain, extending a partnership they started with the German pay-TV service, Premiere (El País, June 18, 1993, pp. 52-53; Fickling, 1994).

For PRISA the gold lay in the liberal policy of media acquisition created by the Spanish government. In no other country in Europe can a media company hold as much property in so many different media sectors. PRISA runs the largest daily newspaper, a popular commercial radio station (after it bought the leading competitor, Antena-3 Radio), and now Canal+ is about to make massive profits on the heels of its rising subscription rates and cable ventures (thanks to a new cable TV law).

WHAT'S LEFT OF THE PUBLIC SYSTEMS . . .?

The public systems, for their part, have been slipping nonstop into crisis since 1991. In mid- 1992, the regional firms together registered a deficit of $2 billion, quadrupling the figure of 1991. FORTA's red ink made some politicians put forward plans to sell the regional systems to private investors. Although this seems unlikely, given the political and cultural importance of television to the regional governments, it is not altogether out of the question, especially among the poorer regions.

Other strategies besides full privatization have emerged. Among the most surprising was the cooperation agreement signed between RTVE and ETB, the Basque television, in June 1993. Ten years ago when ETB was being created, many Basque politicians treated Spain as an external state, an imperial ruler. For a decade, the tensions between RTVE and ETB persisted, reflecting historic conflicts between centralism and regionalism. The agreement of 1993 is perhaps a small sign that this conflict has lost some of its defining force and highlights the influence of external economic conditions. More recently, the Basque government signed a joint agreement with TCI, US West, and Time Warner to start a cable television company, called Euskalnet, of which 51% will belong to the Basque radio and television company owned by the regional government ("U.S. West and Time Warner", 1994).

RTVE retains a privileged, if extremely tarnished, position within the industry and among political classes. Except for its decline within the internal TV market structure, RTVE holds onto this significant presence by virtue of being the national state broadcaster. As such, it continues to be the preferred target of reform, liberalization projects, or basic outrage from the opposition. It is not surprising, therefore, to discover that in 1993 the Partido Popular (formerly the Alianza Popular) was still bringing lawsuits against RTVE and the government—this time for the manner in which a general director of RTVE was appointed. The democracy of the state system is perpetually in question, a process of accountability that the privately held companies can stubbornly avoid.

. . . AND PROGRAM PRODUCTION?

In 1991, the euphoria in the TV industry that came with the startup of private television was especially prominent in the film and video production sector. The tripling of demand between 1988 and 1990 created great new opportunities for suppliers, even though no one could fill the orders. Still, production companies that had till then only served clients for advertising and corporate communications were, as one excited trade writer put it, "springing up all over the country, keen to satisfy the demand for programs" (Fickling, 1994, p. 4). It is true that at first there were a number of startups that allowed large film processing and editing companies to move out of the declining film industry and into video. Overexpansion led to a crisis in Spanish production facilities, however, as the independent producers realized that they were not being hired because films and teleseries bought on the international market tended to take the place of job orders. As one trade magazine put it, Spain suffered the "European paradox of more television hours, but less work" (Ibid. p. 4).

In Spain, RTVE was the greatest patron of indigenous production, although by 1991 the cash crisis of the state company brought commissions (and its own production) to a standstill. RTVE commissioned no new projects in 1991 or 1992, and finished only 157 hours of old orders (demand in the Spanish TV economy had risen to 57,000 hours by 1990). Despite all the euphoria in 1991, the share of television hours filled by independent producers barely reached 2%. One telling symptom of the collapse was the rising percentage of repeats of dramatic broadcasts on TVE—54% in 1991, double the figure for 1989, triple for 1982. The cash crisis throughout the system of buying, commissioning, and production has forced the independent producers back into commercial and corporate communications. Some have sought out foreign co-production partners, whereas others have been lucky enough to get work in the rare telefilm drama. It appears as though independent program production in Spain has been abandoned without significant institutional support.

NEW GADGETS, OLD STORY

The newest players in 1993 are the satellite channels. Among the major satellite broadcasters have been Galavision, from Mexico's Televisa, Eurosport, TVE International, Super Channel, and the subscription services controlled by PRISA. On Spain's first satellite, Hispasat, a new five-channel package with one encryption system, was established in the summer of 1994 by a consortium called Cotelsat. Cotelsat partners included terrestrial rivals, TVE, Canal+, Telecinco, and Antena-3 TV; Cotelsat's first president was Antonio Asensio. Although they will compete with other satellite packages that are on the established Astra system, Cotelsat was counting on profits to start once new cable systems were approved and built (Scott, 1994b). Besides the Euskalnet system mentioned earlier, a cable network agreement was also arranged in Galicia that included the major regional newspaper, La Voz de Galicia; the national phone company, Telefónica; and Grupo Zeta, among its partners ("Ten companies," 1994). In Catalonia, too, a company called Multimedia Cable, partly held by the city of Barcelona and the Catalan government, agreed to form a cable venture with Time Warner and US West to lay a fiber-optic cable network in and around Barcelona ("U.S. West," 1994). Otherwise, there are no national cable providers in Spain. Once again, the regional development of media services together with the expanding commercial operations of private (and public) television companies have extended the influence of transnational capital in the Spanish television market.

SUMMARY

During the transition to democracy, the private press made themselves the primary targets of whatever remnants of cultural autocracy they identified, linking their "struggle" with those struggles seeking access to multidimensional spheres of public expression (regionalism, feminism, movements for artistic and informational freedom, marginalized political groups, etc.). Official politics had already reduced the participation of extra-Parliamentary movements through the *ruptura pactada*, which made feasible the ventriloquism of public opinion performed by the private press. On their terms, the commercial press held the monopoly on complaint and the power to publicize the problems with broadcast reform. The socialists contained the tensions within the cultural field with the game rules of liberal corporatism, leaving the commercial press alone in voicing opposition, with one notable exception. Small-nation nationalism in the regions spoke out through the conservative nationalist parties in Catalonia, Galicia, and the Basque Country, and through the increasing presence of these parties in the national Parliament.

The short-term economic gains pursued by the socialists have made the Spanish economy one of the most productive in Europe. But this does not reflect the internal traumas of unemployment (still the highest in Europe) or the vicissitudes of uneven regional development (*Economía Regional*, 1988a, 1988b). Likewise, industries of new information technologies have made large investments in Spain and added to the growth of the service sector, the largest contributor to national productivity (Banco de Bilbao, 1988). But this infusion of capital has not significantly altered either unemployment or development inequalities. Multinational information and electronics firms continue to locate near major cities, primarily in Madrid and Barcelona, reproducing geographical inequalities. Furthermore, they have not been the great protagonists of increased employment that the socialists promised (Castells et al., 1986).

CONCLUSION

There is a clear class alliance in the ownership structure of commercial television that stands in sharp contrast to the rhetoric of democratic reform, which said that Spain's transition beyond francoism should lead to greater freedoms of civil society. Civil society was defined in the negative—that is, it was not francoism, it was not dictatorship, it was not the state; and until the UCD proposal for private television, democratic media would also be defined in this negative way. Two Spanish governments, and the PSOE in particular, made it feasible for the commercial press to put political freedoms of civil society (of speech and thought and action) in the same frame with commercial freedom. Given the ownership patterns discussed earlier, the responsibility of television to support Spanish civil society seems to have devolved to the banks, advertisers, and multinational, multimedia firms. Against this observation stands the private TV law. Yet even according to the law's best intentions, it represents a mere paper fragmentation of the dominant bloc of investors. Contrary to president Felipe González, who once resisted TV reform on the grounds that new channels would bring a combined U.S. and Soviet invasion of Spanish culture, the threat to national sovereignty brought by new TV channels in Spain has been entirely Western and capitalistic. The bridgehead for this "invasion" was established from within and, to no small degree, by the "pragmatism" of the PSOE's private TV law.

REFERENCES

Banco de Bilbao. (1988). *Renta nacional de España y su distribución provincial 1985* [Spanish national income and provincial distribution for 1985]. Madrid: Servicio de Estudios del Banco de Bilbao.

Bustamante, E. (1989). TV and public service in Spain: A difficult encounter. *Media, Culture & Society, 11*, 67-87.

Bustamante, E. (1982). *Los amos de la información en España* [The lords of information in Spain]. Madrid: Akal.

Bustamante, E., & Villafañe, J. (1985, March 2). *La larga marcha de la televisión privada* [The long march of private television]. Liberación, pp. 2-4.

Bustamante, E., & Zallo, R. (1988). *Las industrias culturales en España* [The cultural industries in Spain: Multimedia groups and transnational corporations]. Madrid: Akal.

Camiller, P. (1986, March/April). Spanish socialism in the Atlantic. *New Left Review, 156*, pp. 5-36.

Carr, R., & Fusi, J. P. (1984). *Spain: Dictatorship to democracy.* London: Allen & Unwin Publishers.

Castells, M., Barrera, A. Casal, P., Castaño, C., Escario, P., Melero, J., & Nadal, J. (1986). *Nuevas tecnologias, economia, y sociedad en españa* (Vols. I & II). Madrid: Gabinete de la Presidencia del Gobierno/Alianza Editorial.

Costa, P.O. (1986). *La crisis de la televisión pública*. Barcelona: Ediciones Paidós.

Crain Communications (1994, March, 21). Correction. *Advertising Age*, 00.

Economía Regional: Hechos y Tendencias. (1988a). *Papeles de Economía Española* (Series 34) [Regional economy: Facts and trends]. Madrid: Fundación Fondo para la Investigación Económica y Social.

Economía Regional: Ideas y Políticas. (1988b). *Papeles de Economía Española* (Series 35) [Regional economy: Ideas and politics]. Madrid: Fundación Fondo para la Investigación Económica y Social.

El País. *Anuario 1985, Anuario 1986, Anuario 1988*. Madrid: Prisa.

Fickling, J. (1994, April 19). Spain: From broadcast backwater to one of the most exciting markets in Europe. *Broadcast*, p. 4.

Gunther, R. (1986). The Spanish Socialist Party: From clandestine opposition to party of government. In S. Payne (Ed.), *The politics of democratic Spain* (pp. 8-49). Chicago: The Chicago Council on Foreign Relations.

Hooper, J. (1987). *The Spaniards: A portrait of the New Spain*. London: Penguin.

Jessop, B. (1979). Corporatism, parliamentarism and social democracy. In P.C. Schmitter & G. Lehmbruch (Eds.), *Trends towards corporatist intermediation* (pp. 185-212). London: Sage.

Maravall, J. M. (1981). *La política de la transición* [The politics of transition]. Madrid: Taurus Ediciones.

Maxwell, R. (1995). *The spectacle of democracy: Spanish television, nationalism, and political transition*. Minneapolis: University of Minnesota.

Mujal-León, E. (1986). The foreign policy of the Spanish Government. In S. Payne (Ed.), *The politics of democratic Spain* (pp. 197-245). Chicago: The Chicago Council on Foreign Relations.

Pavolini, L. (1980). Communicazioni di masa e democrazia: Una nuova fase della reforma. In G. Vacca (Ed.), *Communicazioni di massa e democrazia* [Mass communication and democracy]. Rome: Editori Riuniti.

Payne, S. (1986). The elections of June 1986. In S. Payne (Ed.), *The politics of democratic Spain* (pp. 245-255). Chicago: The Chicago Council on Foreign Relations.

Scott A. (1994a, May 27). Disney poised for stake in Spain's Antena 3, *Broadcast*, p. 11.

Scott, A. (1994b, June 24). Spain's satellite channels make debut as a package. *Broadcast*, p. 10.

Spain: Antena d de Televisión Makes Profits for 1993. (1994, June 7). *Gaceta De Los Negocios*, pp. 1, 18.

Ten Companies Form Cable Television Firm for Galicia. (1990, August 3). *Gaceta De Los Negocios*, p. 28.

Torrents, N. (1984). Cinema and the media after the death of Franco. In C. Abel
    & N. Torrents (Eds.), *Spain: Conditional democracy*. London: Croom
    Helm.

U.S. West and Time Warner set up Basque Production Centre. (19 , June 4).
    Cinco Dias, p. 10.

U.S. West, Time Warner in Spanish Cable TV Venture with Multimedia Cable.
    (1994, May 26). Agence France Press, AFX News, Company News
    Section.ws

Vazquez Barquero, A. & Hebbert, M. (1985). Spain: Economy and state in
    transition. In R. Hudson & J. Lewis (Eds.), *Uneven development in
    southern Europe: Studies in accumulation, class, migration and the state*
    (pp. 284-308). London: Methuen.

Villagrasa, J. M. (1992). Spain: The emergence of commercial television. In A.
    Silj (Ed.), *The new television in Europe* (pp. 337-426). London: John
    Libbey.

Chapter 7

New Communication Policies and Communication Technologies in the Caribbean

Aggrey Brown

Communication policies can be thought of as efforts to shape and direct technologies toward certain ends. The ends served by communication policy are usually quite contested, with people in general, government bodies, communications corporations, or some combined interaction of these forces seeking to influence the types of policies adopted. As is the case elsewhere, this interaction between policymaking and new communication technologies is shaping the communications systems and environment of the Caribbean. The purpose of this chapter is to consider the interaction between policy and technology in the Caribbean to discern the ends that are being pursued and the prospects for more democratic forms of communication in the region.

Policymaking involves making choices between alternatives; setting the parameters within which action or behavior will be considered legitimate within a given environment. It is not a value-neutral activity, nor does it take place in a vacuum. In fact, it is axiomatic that to be relevant, policymaking must be context specific. In the sphere of political economy, policymaking involves making choices between often conflicting goals and values, for example, making choices between what is efficient versus what is meritory, what is expedient versus what is equitable, what is contemporary versus what is appropriate, what is practical versus what is desirable, and so on. In the final analysis, at the national or macro level, policymaking is usually designed to enhance a people's performance capacity—their competence or ability to achieve their objectives utilizing their own or others' resources.

Where democracy informs policymaking, it is an end in itself as well as a means to an end. That is, under ideal conditions, the choices made by decision makers are informed by the tenets of democratic practice, and the ensuing choices themselves should aim to enhance the democratic process. Practice, however, often varies from the ideal. Concretely then the environmental context, the goals of policy, and the structures that emanate from policymaking all affect the dynamics of evolving human relationships in any society, including, of course, the policymaking process itself.

Apart from the inherent difficulties involved in making choices between competing and often conflicting alternatives, the task of the decision maker is further complicated when policymaking has to do with technologies—the physical and intellectual tools that extend our capacity to relate to our environment. The choices are not simply between one piece of technology and another, between one tool and another, but also between ways of doing things. It is a characteristic of all technologies that they not only affect the way in which people relate to their environment, but that they simultaneously structure relationships in that environment. In fact, it can be argued that the ultimate test of the appropriateness or inappropriateness of technologies is how they affect relationships between people.

Given the centrality of communication within human affairs, whether we agree that the world has become a "global village" as a result of the introduction and application of new information/communication (infocom) technologies, there is virtual universal consensus that the introduction and convergence of telecommunications, computers and video technologies—the so-called "information superhighway"—is altering human relationships. Precisely because the process of transformation is still evolving and trends are already discernible, the most that can be said with any certainty is that globally human relationships are in transition.

THE CARIBBEAN POLICY ENVIRONMENT

In the present context, the *Caribbean* is defined geo- and sociopolitically to include all those countries within the Caribbean Basin that were former colonies of England and that comprise the formal grouping: Caribbean Community (Caricom). These 13 geographically dispersed countries are all island nations with the exception of Belize in Central America and Guyana in South America. The Bahamas in the North is over three hours flying time from Trinidad in the South but it is a mere half-hour from Florida. At the opposite end, Trinidad in the south is only 15 minutes from Venezuela on the South American mainland, whereas almost 3 hours from Jamaica.

The countries of the grouping vary in size from smaller than 200 square kilometers to over 214,000 square kilometers. Jamaica, the most populous, has over 2.5 million citizens—equal to the number of inhabitants of all the other members of the group combined. Montserrat with fewer than 12,000 inhabitants has the smallest population. Historically a migratory people, it is estimated that there are more persons of Caribbean ancestry living outside of the Caribbean than within it. North America and England have been the traditional hosts of the migrant population.

Ethnically, the Caricom countries are a polyglot. Guyana and Trinidad and Tobago have almost equal numbers of inhabitants of African and (East) Indian ancestry, whereas all the others with the exception of Belize are of predominantly African ancestry. The citizens of Belize are a mixture of Mayans, Africans, and Mestizos. There are also significant minorities of Chinese, Syrian, European and Lebanese in many of the countries. The region is a veritable melting pot. Although the dominant (official) language of Caricom is standard English, the majority language varies from country to country. Thus, in Jamaica, the majority of citizens speak Jamaican English, whereas in St. Lucia and Dominica, for example, the majority language is French Creole (or kweyol). Politically all Caricom countries are Parliamentary democracies that gained their independence from England between the early 1960s and mid-1970s. With few exceptions they have sustained stable multiparty political systems for prolonged periods.

Although the Republic of Trinidad and Tobago has significant reserves of oil and Guyana and Jamaica major reserves of bauxite, with Guyana having gold, diamonds and timber as well, historically, the Caricom countries have been monocultural economies dependent for the most part on the export of sugar and its derivatives as well as on bananas. Since the 1980s, and with few exceptions, tourism has emerged as a major industry throughout the region. In his seminal work, George Beckford (1972) characterizes the region as the classic plantation economy. For all that, and in spite of many commonalties, the Caribbean is not a homogenous entity. It is a complex region consisting of many scattered islands and continental countries varying in size, language, resources, forms of government, and culture.

Plagued by severe balance of payments problems, a number of countries of the region have relied increasingly on support from the International Monetary Fund (IMF) and the World Bank. Indeed, from the mid-1970s, following the first oil shock of the early part of the decade, Jamaica has been an IMF client. Trinidad and Tobago, Guyana, and Barbados became clients subsequently. As clients of these multilateral financial institutions, governments of the Caribbean have had little room to maneuver within the strictures laid down by them. More to the point, there are four linked planks within the ideological armor of these multilateral lending institutions that are applied with formulaic precision regardless of national idiosyncrasies.

Couched in terms of the "structural adjustment" of their clients' economies, the IMF/World Bank insist on: First, *macroeconomic* policies that require cutbacks in public spending or the raising of taxes and a reduction in public borrowing and the maintenance of competitive exchange rates that invariably means currency devaluation, and second, microeconomic measures that include abolishing price controls, deregulating markets, reducing tariffs on imports, and encouraging the free movement of capital. In short, governments "must define and protect property rights, to create an environment within which commerce can flourish" ("Survey," 1988, p. 47). The third plank of lending policy is *trade liberalization* that includes the elimination of protection for domestic industries, opening economies to imports and foreign investments and encouraging export-led growth. Fourth, and in keeping with the second measure, the IMF/World Bank insist on what they call *social investments*— investments in services such as health care, education, and telecommunications. Under this dispensation, what were once considered the legitimate social responsibilities of governments now become the profitable prerogatives of the private sector.

The policy environment of the Caribbean is therefore characterized by small, widely geographically dispersed, shrinking, and fragmented economies that are immersed in a wider global environment that is itself characterized by emerging trading and economic blocs such as the EEC and NAFTA. It is an environment in which the multilateral lending agencies, the IMF and World Bank in particular, serve to define the ideological parameters of action of debtor governments in keeping with the economic orthodoxy of the industrialized world. In such a context and combined with sociohistorical and cultural factors, it is hardly surprising that the quest for regional integration is a consensual imperative of political leaders and policymakers within the region. Formation of the Association of Caribbean States in 1994, which widens the English-speaking Caricom grouping to include Columbia, Mexico, and the Dominican Republic, is but one tangible manifestation of that imperative.

INFOCOM POLICY GOALS AND SERENDIPITY

An aphorism of our epoch is that the media are ubiquitous, which has given rise to the cliché that we are now living in a "global village." However, what the cliché obscures is that the village is not a community, if by community we understand a collective of individuals with shared ideals that foster mutual self-actualization. Of course, the McLuhan concept, properly understood, draws attention to altered temporal and spatial relationships that result from the ubiquity of infocom technologies. Self-evidently, those altered spatial and temporal relationships are also profoundly cultural in their impact.

From its inception, for example, radio broadcasting, introduced under the colonial regime in the mid-1930s in the Caribbean, remained essentially a government monopoly for over 50 years. The Reithian model of broadcasting that informed the development of the BBC was applied with little modification by the colonial regime in the West Indies. In that model the medium (relatively new at the time) was used paternalistically as an essential tool of "enlightenment" and for the maintenance of the status quo in Britain and within the colonies. Naturally, within that status quo, a small, largely expatriate elite were the arbiters of "good taste" for Caribbean society.

With the coming of political independence, control of radio broadcasting passed from the colonists to the local leadership of the independence movement but the policy of government ownership and control of the medium with its inherent paternalistic assumptions, was never seriously questioned by the local elite. What changed were the values propagated by the medium under the aegis of nationalist leadership. Under the new regime nationalist development became a goal of policy and to that extent local cultural expression began to get systematic exposure in a number of countries. In Jamaica, for example, the establishment of the Jamaica Broadcasting Corporation (JBC) by the government in 1959, just prior to independence, enhanced public access to the medium and with it the unleashing of creative musical talent that subsequently resulted in the emergence of reggae as a musical form and such exponents of the form as the late Bob Marley.

Television broadcasting introduced in Trinidad, Jamaica, and Barbados at the time of political independence followed a similar trajectory in terms of ownership and control. In each instance, the license for television broadcasting was given to the government-owned national radio broadcasting corporation. Initially, although less widely distributed than radio, television was perceived to be a far more potent information transmitting medium—a fact that simply strengthened the resolve of regional governments to pursue and maintain monopoly control of it. In short, the unstated goals of early broadcasting policy of Caricom governments were nationalistic, in keeping with the advent of political independence. But well meaning as those goals might have been, they were also paternalistic and pursued within clear boundaries of government ownership and control of the media.

On the grounds that the values propagated by the medium were inimical to the socialist path of development being pursued by the government at the time, the government of Guyana under the leadership of Forbes Burnham was the only Caricom government to adopt a deliberate policy of foregoing the introduction of television. That policy was only rescinded in the latter half of the 1980s after technological developments had made it redundant. In other instances, such as in Belize, St. Lucia, Grenada, Montserrat, and so on, the development of the medium by governments was constrained by pragmatic economic considerations. Notwithstanding, for political reasons, these governments refused to grant operating licenses to private operators: a policy that was also overtaken by technological developments beginning in the early 1980s.

Given the region's geographical location, beginning in the early 1980s, signal overspill from U.S. domestic geostationary satellite transmissions virtually incorporated the Caribbean into the North American cultural orbit. It took very little time for the economically privileged and cosmopolitan segment of Caribbean society to discover that with the appropriate receiving equipment access could be gained to the program feeds of North American television networks, which had adopted the new transmitting technology for the delivery of services transcontinentally.

Privately owned Television Receive Only Antennae (TVROs)—the "dish"—numbered upwards of 40,000 in Jamaica alone by the mid-1990s. As a Northerly island the strength of the signal overspill in Jamaica allowed for the use of relatively small dishes for signal reception, whereas in the Southern Caribbean the investment in receiving hardware was initially considerably higher. Thus, in the Southern Caribbean, MATV and cable technologies were the technologies of choice used by private entrepreneurs to provide citizens with as many as 145 channels of mostly entertainment television programs from the same source. The dish is also a reservoir of audio programming that includes at least one radio station—ZGM FM—which has a transmitter based in Montserrat specifically to serve Eastern Caribbean countries with programs originating from the U.S. mainland.

By the early 1990s, every country within Caricom had some form of television service that by-passed the official regulatory ambit of governments, thanks to the vagaries of geography and the stealth of satellite technology. However, in spite of the global reach and the pervasiveness of these technologies within the Caribbean, not all citizens of the region have access to them or for that matter even to some of the "old" technologies. The distribution of television is still largely an urban phenomenon in the larger countries (Guyana, Belize, and Jamaica), and cable does not reach all the citizens of the territories in which it is present.

As Table 7.1 shows, the telephone—the basic communication technology on which the newer convergent infocom technologies build and rely—is a relatively inaccessible technology in most countries. On the other hand, radio remains the most potent and widely distributed mass medium in the Caricom. It is the medium through which the majority of citizens, many of whom are illiterate, receive public information. In short, in spite of increasing use of state-of-the-art infocom technologies in most Caricom countries, there still is an uneven distribution of these technologies throughout the region, with the consequence that participation in mainstream media activities is skewed in favor of urban dwellers. With few exceptions, differential access to and participation in mainstream media have led to the emergence of alternative forms of communication such as popular theater to meet citizens' needs (Brown & Sanatan, 1987).

Table 7.1. Telephone Penetration Rates in CARICOM, 1993.

COUNTRY	LINES/100 of pop
Antigua	15.5
Barbados	30.6
Bahamas	25.5
Belize	13.3
Dominica	9.9
Guyana	4.0
Grenada	15.1
Jamaica	3.7
Montserrat	25.9
St. Kitts	15.7
St. Lucia	8.3
St. Vincent	9.1
Trinidad & Tobago	17.5
CARICOM Average	14.9
USA Average (1982)	78.4

Note: From "A call for competition: A call for regulation," by H. Dunn, 1994, *Intermedia*, 22(2), p. 23. Reprinted by permission.

General acceptance at official levels of and compliance with IMF/World Bank policies and loan conditionalities in the 1980s let to the divestment of some government-owned media and to the liberalization of the media environment, particularly in Jamaica and Trinidad and Tobago and to a lesser extent in St. Lucia, Belize, and Barbados. The government of Jamaica divested three regional government-owned radio stations to the private sector; granted an additional national radio and two television licenses to private operators; granted a national radio broadcasting license to Jamaican religious institutions; and granted the University of the West Indies (UWI) Mona campus both low-power radio and television licenses. However, up to the end of 1994, the Jamaican government had not yet legitimized the over 100 MATV and cable television services operating extralegally in the country, although it was in the process of determining what its CTV policy should be.

In the case of Trinidad and Tobago, the liberalization process was even more expansive. The government of that twin-island republic issued six new television broadcast licenses: five cable television and eight new radio station licenses. Market forces would determine the viability of these. More to the point, then, throughout the Caricom deliberate self-serving, paternalistic, and conservative government, media policies gave way to externally imposed market- and technology-driven structural adjustment policies resulting in the breaking up of some government media monopolies in both radio and television broadcasting and with some surprising consequences.

In the new liberalized regional media environment, the privately owned Helen Television of St. Lucia pioneered the routine use of geostationary satellite for the regional transmission of its programming, including some domestically produced material. This development was followed subsequently by the Caribbean Broadcasting Union (CBU)—a pan-Caribbean organization—which began transmitting regionally produced programs via satellite in 1993.

IMF/World Bank strictures notwithstanding, geographic and cultural factors, including regional consumption patterns, are also major contributors to the preponderance of U.S. satellite-transmitted materials within the Caribbean (Brown, 1987). The proliferation of visual media technologies has seen a commensurate proliferation of imported content, primarily from North America. That is to say, even though there is some increase in local content, expanded local ownership and increase of visual media outlets has not led to a commensurate increase in the production and transmission of local (regional) media materials in the Caribbean. On the contrary, the importation of visual media content originating primarily from North America has increased as a result of the breaking of the government monopoly and governments' liberalization policies.

THE INFOCOM "SUPERHIGHWAY" AS SUPERSTRUCTURE

The telecommunications sector is dominated by an oligopoly comprising the British-based Cable and Wireless (C&W), ATN, and GTE, with C&W having monopoly privileges for external and internal telecommunications in 9 of 15 countries (see Table 7.2).

This state of affairs was a direct consequence of structural adjustment policies pursued by governments of the region and applied to the telecommunications sector. Up until the mid-1980s, the so-called more developed countries of the region (Jamaica, Trinidad and Tobago and Barbados), as well as Guyana, Belize, and the Bahamas, all had controlling interests in their external telecommunications carriers. With acceptance of, if not agreement with, the notion of private, sector-led growth propagated by the multilateral lending institutions, all these countries, with the exception of Belize, divested the telecommunications sector to TNCs. With access to the enormous amounts of capital required for the modernization of the sector, the takeover of the telecommunications sector by TNCs has led to the expansion and modernization of services throughout the region. Interestingly, however, the technical expertise required to undertake plant modernization existed within the region with very little of it being imported.

Table 7.2. Cable and Wireless Ownership of Caribbean Telecommunications Organizations.

COUNTRY	% of Local Telco	C&W Ownership in Overseas Carrier (%)
Anguilla	100	100
Antigua	0	100
Barbados	85	85
Bermuda	100	100
Br. Virgin Islands	100	100
Caymen Islands	100	100
Dominica	100	100
Grenada	70	70
Jamaica	79	79
Montserrat	100	100
St. Kitts	80	80
St. Lucia	100	100
St. Vincent	100	100
Trinidad & Tobago	49	49
Turks Island	100	100

Note: From "A call for competition: a call for regulation," by H. Dunn, 1994, *Intermedia, 22*(2), p. 23. Reprinted by permission.

As a result of huge infusions of capital by the TNCs, in most countries of the Caribbean today there are fully digitized telecommunications services including, in the case of Barbados, ISDN. According to one researcher: "There is no doubt that the English-speaking Caribbean has access to some of the most advanced technologies available to modern telecommunications. . . . On line hotel reservations systems, boat phones, mobile and cellular networks and a new generation of digital exchanges are among the services already in place" (Dunn, 1994, p. 23). The region is connected via undersea fiber-optic cable to a globe-spanning network stretching from Florida on the U.S. East Coast to the Dominican Republic, Puerto Rico via Jamaica, to Colombia in South America. The transatlantic connection to the "superhighway" is in Bermuda. All the islands of the Lesser Antilles in the Eastern Caribbean are integrated into the network by the Eastern Caribbean Fiber (Optic) System (EFCS) commissioned into service in 1994.

High-speed data transmission services via packet-switching technology has been available in Montego Bay, Jamaica since the early 1980s and since the late 1980s also in St. Lucia. In both instances, however, the facilities were put in place to provide "offshore U.S." data entry and processing services with the "digiports," as they are called, delinked from the respective national telecommunications networks. More precisely, the monopoly privileges granted to C&W by the governments of Jamaica and St. Lucia, respectively, were protected from competition from the preexisting digiports. In essence, the digiports are technologically driven export zones within the two countries—quite in keeping with the conditionalities for export laid down by the IMF/World Bank. The region is, therefore, fully served by multiple distribution systems comprising microwave, fiber optics, and satellites.

Of course, C&W's colonial presence within the Caribbean gave it an advantage over other bidders as the preferred regional common carrier. To be sure, although there have been some discernible benefits of its presence in the region, there have also been some obvious disadvantages, including high service costs, selective introduction of new services, and other monopolistic practices inimical to the rapid development and equitable distribution of services in otherwise open market conditions. So, for example, when Telecommunications of Jamaica (TOJ, the C&W company) discovered that a number of persons within a localized area of the country were able, through technological means, to make and receive overseas collect calls without having to pay for the calls, the company arbitrarily froze all incoming collect calls to its over 300,000 subscribers islandwide until it was able to solve the fraudulent practices of a few.

Furthermore, telephone penetration rates in the region are misleading to the extent that the provision of basic telephone and other value-added services, such as call waiting and call forwarding, are skewed in favor of urban subscribers. Although fixed, portable, and mobile cellular services are available throughout the region, the C&W monopoly allows it to offer these services as high-end services so that only high-income subscribers—including drug dealers—have access to them. Given the mountainous topography of many Caribbean countries and the sparse distribution of rural dwellers in some cases, social utility is not a factor in the C&W strategy of telecommunications development.

The over 50 million U.S. dollars pretax profits generated by C&W in Jamaica alone in 1994, and its carte blanche license courtesy of the Jamaican government, do not motivate it to adopt a strategy of development based on low-cost and high-penetration delivery of services. On the contrary, they encourage the development of a strategy that meets the requirements of the TNC's global operations. One plank of that strategy, among others, is to maintain its monopoly privileges by preventing the entry into the Caribbean of competing service providers. Yet, technological developments, not government policies or regulatory practices, are likely to force the TNCs operating in the telecommunications sector in the Caribbean to provide inexpensive, need-based services to the citizens of the region. Already, such competition is beginning to be applied by U.S. based, computer-assisted call-back services that offer cheaper long-distance telecommunication service than C&W by exploiting the monopolistic billing practices of C&W. In those practices, C&W bills users by the minute for long-distance calls. So, for example, a 2-minute, 10-second call, is billed at 3-minutes. On the other hand, call-back services bill users per six seconds. A 2-minute, 10-second call is therefore billed at 2-minutes and 12-seconds. Needless to say, call-back services are making inroads in C&W's bailiwick as the dominant regional external common carrier. It is therefore likely that greater responsiveness to local needs by regional monopolies in the telecommunications sector will develop over time.

ANALYSIS AND CONCLUSION

Although multiparty democratic electoral practices and a Parliamentary form of government have existed for over 50 years and are entrenched in Caricom countries, in an economic environment defined by scarcity, strategic decision making is invariably undemocratic. From as early as 1984, Jones (1984) noted that telecommunications arrangements in the Caribbean "operate in a context of dependent, weak, small, open economies with skewed distribution of income, where the private sector is dominant in the policy sphere" (p. 19). The tendency toward autocratic decision making, which such an environment nurtures, is further exacerbated by the external constraints imposed on policymakers by the multilateral lending agencies whose policies themselves are the ideological pincers of the industrial countries. In that ideology, a colossal abstraction, "the free market," is the arbiter of all. In that market, instrumental rationality rather than social and distributive justice is the primary objective of economic action. In the words of Time Warner's first Annual Report

> In the eighties we witnessed the most profound political and economic changes since the end of the Second World War. As these changes unfolded, Time Inc., and Warner Communications Inc. came independently to the same fundamental conclusions: GLOBALIZATION was rapidly evolving from a prophecy to a fact of life. No serious competitors could hope for any long-term success unless, building on a secure home base, it achieved a major presence in all of the world's markets. (Wasko, 1991, pp. 187-188)

In this global arena, countries whose individual GNPs are dwarfed by the annual revenues of infocom TNCs stand little chance of formulating independent infocom policies. To be sure, whereas before some reliance could be placed on the regulatory influences of international organizations, such as the ITU, to help define acceptable policy goals, today those organizations are themselves captives of the TNCs. Furthermore, in the Caricom, electronic media policies were initially informed by British prewar practices, in which government paternalism played a decisive role in determining the structure of the media landscape. Even the most charitable interpretation of the role of government vis-à-vis broadcasting in these societies would have to conclude that it limited access of broad sectors of society to media as well as to participation in media. Manifestly, the virtual monopoly of governments in the broadcast sector within the region ensured a degree of political control of internal information flows, even as in rare but important instances it also provided a vehicle for indigenous creative cultural expression.

Given the Caribbean's proximity to North America, the introduction of satellite broadcasting there and the subsequent explosion of new infocom technologies have virtually incorporated the region into the U.S. cultural orbit, all but eliminating the decision-making power and influence of regional governments over the infocom sector as a whole. Coupled with the adoption of IMF/World Bank structural adjustment policies, the consequent unleashing of market forces as a substitute for home-grown regional policy within the sector was inevitable. The delinking of the Jamaica and St. Lucia digiports from the respective national telecommunications networks is but one example of the resulting policy incoherence.

Contemporarily, regional infocom policy and policymaking are characterized by serendipity, the uncertainties of global technological developments and acquiescence in the strategic plans of the monopoly telecommunications service providers. Because the objectives of the latter are to maximize profits in an increasingly global competitive marketplace, social utility concerns are secondary to concerns for profit maximization. The existing monopoly structures within the telecommunications sector and the convergence of infocom technologies, including the electronic media, merely consolidate the power of the TNCs to determine developments within the sector across the region. Differential access of urban vs. rural, literate versus illiterate, and privileged versus deprived citizens to the information superhighway is perhaps the most insidious manifestation of this consolidation. Only in Barbados and Belize have governments deliberately eschewed the imposition of taxes on the importation of computers with the objective of encouraging their widespread use and consumption among the citizenry. However, in these societies as elsewhere throughout the region, such token gestures are no substitute for integrative infocom policies that embody a comprehensive vision of Caribbean society in the age of cyberspace.

Predictably, therefore, the commoditization of information is already exacerbating and will continue to exacerbate the growing cleavage between the information rich and the information poor. The paradox is that the paralysis of policy within the region and the lack of transparency in decision-making processes are allowing the deepening of an infocom crisis that the new technologies have exacerbated if not helped to create, but which, if consciously and creatively managed , could help to resolve. The formation of a Caribbean Telecommunications Union (CTU) in 1989, bringing together national, technical, telecommunications government advisers and bureaucrats, provides a useful forum for disinterested regional experts to undertake the kind of continuous research and analysis that may allow for more consideration and rational decision making and development within the sector in the future.

Because the monopoly licenses already granted to the telecommunications TNCs operating in the region by governments represent long-term agreements, they cannot be rescinded and renegotiated without risking severe repercussions from an array of powerful transnational forces. However, given the volatility of technological developments within the sector globally, as yet unforeseen technologies are likely to emerge that will provide windows of opportunity for regional policymakers to make the sector as a whole more responsive to the needs of the majority of people of the region. Already, computer-assisted call-back services are an augury of the possibilities. That C&W attempted to protect its monopoly against these services through litigation would indicate that the TNCs are themselves aware of the fragility of their status within a competitive global environment whose major characteristic is rapid technological obsolescence.

Contemporarily, therefore, what is important for regional policymakers is to recognize that the context or environment of policymaking presents both constraints and opportunities; that the goals of policy must be to minimize the constraints and maximize the opportunities so that the infocom structures that evolve from the policymaking process will be responsive to the authentic communications needs of the people of the region. That the determination of authenticity is a function of democratic practice within civil society, should at this point be self-evident.

REFERENCES

Beckford, G. (1972). *Persistent poverty.* New York: Oxford University Press.

Brown, A. (1987). *Television programming trends in the Anglophone Caribbean* (Occasional Paper No. 2). Kingston: Carimac.

Brown, A., & Sanatan, R. (Eds.). (1987). *Talking with whom: A report on the state of the media in the Caribbean.* Kingston: University of West Indies.

Dunn, H. (1994, April/May). A call for competition: a call for regulation. *Intermedia.*

Jones, E. (1984). Regional realities determining the context for communication policy making. In C. Hamelink (Ed.), *Telecommunications policy in the Caribbean region.* The Hague: ISS.

Survey: The entertainment industry. (1988, December 23). The Economist.

Wasko, J. (1991). Hollywood, new technologies and Europe 1992. *Telematics and Information, 8*(3).

Chapter 8

Discourses of Democratic Communication and the Archaeology of Information Technology in South Korea

Sunny Yoon

The purpose of this chapter is to explore a theoretical framework that helps to explain the power relations involved in technological deployment. To accomplish this task the chapter highlights human interactions with technology in its material and knowledge forms. I elaborate a new methodology to examine the complex process of technological deployment and its relationship to human life in Korea. An argument is presented that conventional theories, including liberalism-positivism and Marxism-structuralism, do not adequately explicate the complex factors shaping technological power in societies such as Korea.

I portray the conventional domain of political economy from the perspective of human practice. Using a Foucauldian framework, I analyze power relations by looking into everyday practices inside bureaucracy, legislative bodies, and business organizations. Conventionally, these institutions are considered to be rational and coherent power centers. However, I argue that human practices, fragmentation, and the discontinuous exercise of power transforms the development and adaptation of new communications technology by government and business institutions into something less than a rational and coherent process. This case study of Korea illustrates that complex interactions between the strong political authority of the Korean State, international power relations, and diffuse bodies of knowledge and practices within the microcontexts of Korean society shape the formation and implementation of information and communication technologies

TECHNOLOGICAL FANTASIA

"Technological fantasia" is a perspective that assumes that technology provides an impetus for social development and promotes human welfare. This perspective rests on the notion that technology will create a new world that will satisfy people's material needs and dispense with physical limitations such as depletable natural resources.

Alvin Toffler (1980) represents this idealist outlook on technology, arguing that new communication technologies are creating a new civilization based on decentralization rather than centralization, knowledge workers rather than manual workers, and flexibility over rigidity. He calls the movement toward this new civilization the Third Wave, a movement displacing cultures built on the Second Wave (industrialization) and/or the First Wave (agrarian societies). Toffler believes that technological development brings about diversified and decentralized lifestyles in all areas of life, from the workplace, to the home, and to leisure activities. In this view, technology functions as a "saviour," relieving humans of strenuous labor and alleviating conflicts that are rooted in the very structure of industrial society. According to another proponent of this view, Daniel Bell (1973), the structural basis of class conflict typical of industrial capitalism is extinguished as the information economy pushes its industrial predecessor into the annals of history.

Theorists of the information society also suggest that new communication technologies promise solutions to the problems of environmental degradation as they no longer rely on the resource-intensive processes of industrialism. Communication technology has advantageous environmental benefits in that it consumes few natural resources in the production process, instead relying on the nondepletable resources of human knowledge and information. As such, communication technology contributes to natural conservation as it produces high economic value.

TECHNOLOGICAL ASURA[1]

Another perspective on communication and social change is that offered by marxist political economy. Marxist political economy is consistent with the

---

[1]*Asura* is a Buddhist term similar to Hades or hell. Asura is occupied by a very belligerent ghost who tries to exterminate justice.

earlier perspective insofar that it characterizes human history as the successive movement through different modes of production. Although the focus on the means of production is an important part of historical materialism, Marxist political economy does not view technology in its material form only. Instead, the emphasis is on the social relations of technology and how technology structures the relations between different classes in capitalist societies.

In contrast to the "technological fantasia" perspective, political economists suggest that the history of technological development is related to the amplification of social inequality. A common theme is that technology degrades labor power, especially in industries that are capital and technology intensive. According to Marx, capitalism promotes the displacement of labor by machines in the production process. As a result, labor increasingly appears to be auxiliary to the production process, even though labor continues to be the primary source of "surplus value" (Marx, 1967). Yet, despite the severity of this fact, and that current patterns of growth in many economies are occurring with decreasing amounts of labor, Marx suggested that the relations between technology, work, and surplus value remains a mystified one because of the tendency for machines to become admired, even fetishized. In the process human beings are alienated as their labor power is degraded and the fetishization of technology obscures the true nature of social power relations. Contemporary political economists, such as Vincent Mosco (1989), argue that this is precisely the logic at work as computerization is introduced across the economies and bureaucratic structures of modern societies, with the result that there is often, simultaneously, an overall increase in unemployment rates amidst the celebration of the new informatics.

Political economists also suggest that technology not only displaces labor, but it obscures class conflicts by reorganizing labor power. In late capitalism, society is reorganized as white-collar workers increase and blue-collar workers decrease. White-collar workers, or the middle class, stay away from class confrontation because they are often segregated from the production process. In technologically developed societies, as compared to early capitalism, the working class has less chance to gather together and grieve their working conditions. In early capitalism, working conditions were certainly unpleasant and harmful for workers' health and welfare but, paradoxically, the compact space and unpleasant working conditions provided a common arena for labor to organize collective actions and a shared working-class culture. In late capitalism, one of the most powerful features of the new means of communication is the ability to further isolate the labor class as they eliminate the common space for labor.

Yet rather than merely focusing on questions of class confrontation in the workplace, political economists also pay attention to the total control of capitalism over the labor class outside the workplace as well as the production process itself. In late capitalism, class relations are amalgamated with cultural and political matters. Just as on the factory floor, the domestic space and leisure time of the labor class is dominated by technology. By providing distribution conduits for commercialized "culture," goods, and entertainment, communication technology facilitates the control of the human psyche. One of the early critical theorists to take up this line of thinking was Herbert Marcuse (1964), who argues that all-encompassing technological development has brought about a "one-dimensional society" and "one-dimensional man." According to Marcuse, technology is a form of "cultural terrorism" that promotes a totalitarian way of life.

COMMUNICATION TECHNOLOGY AND THE DESPATIALIZED RELATIONS OF CAPITALISM: THE INTERNATIONAL DIMENSION

In late capitalism, technology loosens the spatial confinement of the workplace; computerization and automation of factories and offices allow for the creation of dispersed work spaces. Due to this re configured geography, the labor class has less human interaction in the work process. As technology develops, workers interact with anonymous "colleagues" through computer networks more frequently than face-to-face interactions. As workers lose a common place to confer about collective bargaining, labor becomes de-unionized. This is detrimental for the labor class as a whole, not only for specific labor groups in the computer and telecommunication industries. Furthermore, as the production process is internationalized through the global assembly lines of the multinational corporation, "homogeneous human labor" takes place on a global scale. This coupling of labor, the multinational corporation, and communication technology creates conditions in which the value of commodities are determined by the "labour time socially necessary" as calculated on a global basis (Marx, 1967, p. 39). Consequently, the impact of communication technology on labor does not stop at the communication industry but includes many industries across the globe.

Capitalism has expanded internationally and formed class relations at the global level. Although underdeveloped countries adopt and develop technology for industrialization, this process does not mitigate social inequality. The underclass in the global society is persistently exploited in world capitalism because social inequality is reproduced by unequal exchange between countries. Due to the neglect of international factors in Marx's own time, some radical theorists revise the Marxist framework to explain inequality at this global level. Dependency and world-system theories are the most prominent models that attempt to explain international social relations. According to these theories, technological adoption through industrialization does not lead to universal development. Even if some industrializing countries achieve a certain level of development, like South Korea and other "semi-peripheral countries," the dependent structure of the world system as a whole is intact (Wallerstein, 1979).

Critique does not rest at the unequal structure of the world system: Some neoMarxian theorists look into the internal structure of new industrializing countries by addressing the phenomena of their strong States. They argue that the State in industrializing countries appears to be strong and autonomous, but is actually controlled by the international capitalist class, if not by domestic capitalists (Evans, 1979; O'Donnell, 1973). In the third world, as the State develops technology, its power becomes stronger. For technological development, third-world States often exercise repressive and exploitative power to create a favorable investment environment. These States concentrate on technological development at the expense of social welfare and humanistic values for the public.

A CRITIQUE OF MARXIST POLITICAL ECONOMY

Although Marxist political economy provides a useful framework for examining the power dimension of technology, it offers only a limited understanding of the complex power relations involved in technological deployment, particularly in non-Western societies. Marxist political economy characterizes technological power only in the context of class conflict. It assumes that class relations dominate every aspect of human life. As such, Marxist political economy only explicates the intervention of "repressive power" involved in technological deployment. In historical materialism, as technology develops the capitalist class consolidates its means of control and is able to further exploit the labor class by degrading the labor value. Based on the assumption that humans and technology are separate entities in confrontation, Marxist political economists tend to assert only the negative effects of technological development. However, such negative effects are only a portion of all the power relations involved in technological deployment. By concentrating on class dominance, Marxist political economy oversimplifies diverse aspects of human engagement in technological deployment.

TECHNOLOGY IN EVERYDAY LIFE

In contrast to Marxist political economy and the "technological fantasia" perspective, this study portrays how technological power is sustained by human engagement in practice. In order to do so I look into people's engagement with technological power during the course of their everyday practices inside political and economic institutions. People are not separated from technological power but are in fact integrated into it. It is not only the power center, or the capitalist class, that enforces the deployment of technology in political and economic arenas. In reality, people are voluntarily involved in the process of technological deployment and in producing the very conditions that sustain the presence of power in society. According to Foucault (1980):

We must cease once and for all to describe the effects of power in negative terms: it excludes, it represses, it censors, it abstracts, it masks, it conceals. In fact, power produces; it produces reality; it produces domains of objects and rituals of truth. The individual and the knowledge that may be gained of him belong to this production. (p. 194)

As this quote indicates, Foucault refuses the idea that a transcending force controls human history behind empirical processes, instead perceiving that history is constructed through human practices. According to Foucault, human history consists of fragmented and discontinuous practices in everyday life that generate discrepancies between rationality at the macro level and human practice at the micro level. In order to detect this discrepancy we need to look at the empirical process at the local level, as in the present analysis of information and communication technology development in Korea.

Individuals and social organizations engage in constructing reality by practicing power and power-based discourse at the micro level. Discourse analysis produces a unique methodology that sees statements and discourses as events, or human practices—practices that do more than merely represent objective relations between thought and objects in language. By being uttered in nonrandom and repetitive patterns, discursive formations produce meanings that reflect the historical, social, economic, geographic, and linguistic context in which they are produced (Foucault, 1972). Such "discursive productions" allow us to understand how people observe objects in their environment and how these objects are drawn into the net of everyday practices and normalized.

There is no power behind discourse that manipulates human life. Discourse channels power as it is spoken, heard, and read. By going beyond structuralism and hermeneutics, discourse analysis does not allow researchers to judge truth beyond the empirical process, nor to interpret discourse in people's everyday life from a transcending position. By starting with concrete, empirical processes discourse analysis does not presume a transcendental force, a kind of presumed structure, that controls human history behind the scene. This means getting down to the ground level by looking at how power and social relations are reproduced through the discourses people use in their everyday lives. As Foucault (1972) remarked:

We shall not pass beyond discourse in order to rediscover the forms that it has created and lift behind it; we shall remain, or try to remain, at the level of discourse itself. . . . I would like to show that "discourses" in the form in which they can be heard or read, are not, as one might expect, a mere intersection of things and words. . . . It is neither by recourse to a transcendental subject nor by recourse to a psychological subjectivity that the regulation of its enunciations should be defined. (pp. 48, 55)

By refusing to engage in the search for transcendental forms of rationality and the hidden exercise of directed power, Foucault refuses to see modern technology as janus-faced machines, simultaneously expressing a dialectical relationship between the powers of control and the possibilities of human liberation. As all objects, technology forces people to account for its existence and to relate it to the cultural contexts in which life proceeds. This all-encompassing incorporation of technology into every nook and cranny of people's lives results in incessant and pervasive forms of self-imprisonment and surveillance as people monitor their relationships to one another and to the machine. Thus, unlike other critical scholars such as Marx and Habermas, Foucault does not imagine that modern technology can lead to the emancipation of individuals and the social system through critique and social transformation. What he clearly perceives in the genealogy of technology is that modern technology provides a docile means of controlling people and training them as if people are in a global prison.

Under these conditions there need be no repressive monarchs, cruel executioners, or exploiting capitalists to imprison individuals—individuals discipline themselves according to scientific criteria and willing subjection to the demands of technique. Through this technique of subjection, a new "docile body" is formed ready and willing to reproduce the discipline underpinning the factories, schools, hospitals, and communication systems of contemporary society. As a result, there is no essential self, but rather a subject whose body and soul is constructed by historically specific discourses of power or knowledge (Foucault, 1978, 1980). Applying these insights, one can attempt to discover the nature of power constructed through the discourses of science and technology that have guided technological development and computerization in Korean society. This is particularly useful for the present study because it permits inquiry into the multiple discourses of diverse cultures rather than the search for universalist concepts of structure, power, and rationality presumed by the "technological fantasia" or Marxist political economy perspectives.

HISTORICAL BACKGROUND OF TECHNOLOGICAL ADOPTION IN SOUTH KOREA

Since the early 1980s, the Korean government has developed communication technology. Yet it would be an oversimplification to interpret the process of technological adoption in Korea as primarily a technical matter. In adopting technology, the technical process and market principle are subordinate to political power and economic development strategies of the government. Due to the involvement of a strong State in the development of Korean computerization, political and cultural factors strongly affect the computerization process. Furthermore, in Korea, economic classes are far from autonomous from State power, in fact they are often dependent on the State. The State creates and transforms economic classes based on political power. As a result, the Korean economic system is much more politicized and complex compared to that of Western society. The resulting distinctive social formation of the Korean political economy means that conventional political economic analysis as well as neoclassical economic theory cannot be easily applied to the analysis of technological evolution in Korea.[2]

In Korea, the strong State has played the most important role in leading industrialization. By studying the computerization process in Korea we can illustrate how the Korean government uses development strategies to direct this process. In early industrialization during the 1960s and the 1970s, Korea played an active role in integrating its economy into the international market system by focusing on labor-intensive industries, the development of an export-oriented economy, and the supply of a cheap labor force to the international market. Economic development plans were designed by technocrats on the Park administration's Economic Planning Board, one of the highest authorities in the Blue House responsible for developing five-year development plans that began in 1962. Through economic planning, technocrats controlled the entire realm of the Korean economy from private investment projects to market prices. In this process, Korean capitalists became heavily dependent on governmental power. Given the historical integration of Korean society into the world system through colonialism and the cold war, Korea did not have a strong internal social force that could stand up against the strong political authority of the state.

Taking advantage of the high tide of the world economy during the 1960s, the Park government was able to achieve rapid economic development. The United States was the primary trade partner for Korea, and Korea was heavily dependent on the U.S. economy. Although the Korean economy kept growing, changes in the international system resulted in the country facing a major crisis during the 1970s. The Park administration attempted to cope with the economic crisis by designing a new plan. From the Third Five-Year Plan, Korea moved from a purely export-oriented economy to import substitution for intermediate manufacturing products (Amsden, 1989; Haggard & Chung, 1983). The government planned to domestically produce intermediate resources, such as steel and chemicals, instead of importing these products. In the early 1970s, the giant steel company, Pohang Iron and Steel Company (POSCO), and the world's largest ship builder, Hyundai Shipbuilding Industry, were established to carry out these objectives (Amsden, 1989).

---

[2]Social formation is a concept that explains the concrete class relations in a specific society. In Marxist historical materialism, society evolves through five modes of production—from primitive to socialist. In the contemporary world, the majority of societies are characterized by the capitalist mode of production. However, Marxism does not define society as a universal model. Mode of production is only an abstract, conceptual model. In reality, despite conceptually belonging to a particular mode of production, each society differs from another by containing its own social formation. Social formation reflects diverse social relations within a mode of production (Hindess & Hirst, 1975).

Despite the Park government's new economic strategy, the Korean society once again experienced an economic crisis. Korea could not repeat the easy phase of rapid economic development it had enjoyed in the 1960s. In 1980, Korea showed negative economic growth rates and exports decreased. The dependence on export markets meant that the recession in the international market severely affected Korean society. Korea was experiencing the paradoxes of the international political economy, and since the late 1970s the international political economy has no longer favorably worked for Korea.

In early industrialization, labor was the main source of economic growth and exports in Korea. In the 1970s, although the government suppressed wages to a certain level, wages increased due to rapid economic growth. As labor costs increased in Korea, international business started to move to countries less industrialized than Korea, such as Southeast Asia and Central America. Once Korea lost the comparative advantage of cheap, quality labor, the government attempted to regain international competitiveness by developing high-tech industries. The development of the information industry became the focus of the government's new industrial policy.

During the Chun government, people heavily criticized the earlier industrialization and export strategies of the Park government, especially in relation to the development of the heavy chemical industry. The Chun government integrated these criticisms into its development plans by turning attention from labor-intensive and heavy industries to high-tech industries. Information technology was Chun's strategic industry for promoting economic development as well as avoiding political criticisms and labor disputes, a strategy consistent with the views of the "technological fantasia" perspective.

In the early 1980s, in order to accelerate the development of telecommunications, the Chun government established various new agencies, including KTA (Korea Telecommunication Authority, presently named Korea Telecom, KT), Dacom (Data Communication Corp.), and ETRI (Electronic and Telecommunications Research Institute). During the 1980 to 1987 period of the Chun government, the supply of telephones increased from less than 10 per 100 to 30 (Korea Telecom, 1991). Moreover, Korea started to invest in advanced telecommunication technology including computerization, CATV, and satellite. Communication technology provided a number of advantages to reduce the economic and political crisis. Consistent with the views of Marxist political economists, the application of communication technologies mitigated labor disputes by segregating the labor force. Through automation of factory and office, laborers were separated from each other. Furthermore, the information industry is less labor intensive compared to heavy chemical and light manufacturing industries. Communication technology needs less "muscular" labor power than other industries and changes employment and working conditions by multiplying white-collar and service workers.

Yet, more than just instruments of economic policy, since the Rho government communication technology has been integrated with public demands for democratization. By developing communication technology, the government frequently makes claims for local development and decentralization. President Rho was more sensitive to the discourse of democracy than the previous two presidents, emphasizing the effect of computerization on equal development and decentralization. Distribution of computers to schools, the establishment of "small government" and democratic use of computerization became specific objectives of government policy.

INTERNATIONAL POWER AND TECHNOLOGICAL ADOPTION

As Korea promotes technological development, it increasingly becomes involved in conflicts with the United States. The United States demands the opening of the Korean telecommunication market and the elimination of "protectionism" in the telecommunication market. Trade conflicts between the United States and Korea have been aggravated partly due to the differences in the two economic systems. In Korea, the free market system has never worked without modification. The strong State has played an active role in forming class relations and the economic system, whereas the United States considers this activity "protectionist" and attempts to change it through trade negotiation.

The United States claims that Korea has developed enough telecommunication technology to compete with foreign technology. From 1985, Korea had a trade surplus in the telecommunication area, and the surplus rate was increasing. In 1986, when Korea developed its own TDX, imports decreased, and the balance of payment increased 270% (KISDI, 1991). In 1988, the U.S. trade deficit in telecommunications was $1,383 million. With a trade surplus, Korea contributed to U.S. trade deficits by $415 million, which reflected 9.1% of total imports, whereas Japan had a $2,174 million trade surplus in telecommunications (Korea Telecom, 1991). Since 1989, the United States has employed the political mechanism to overcome its trade deficits, engaging Korea in telecommunication trade negotiations with the demand for specific plans and procedures for regulatory liberalization.[3]

Korea responded to these trade conflicts ambivalently. From the perspective of conventional political economy, the trade conflict between Korea and the United States is one of imperialist interests in controlling a dependent

---

[3]In the meeting the United States insisted that the current 15% tariff be reduced to 7.5% immediately. The United States wanted to set up a negative system that specifies nonimportable goods, while criticizing Korea's positive system, which specifies importable telecommunication products. Second, the United States wanted the Korean government to abolish certain regulations, such as those involving registration and a permit system. Third, the United States demanded to guarantee foreign business participation in supplying telecommunication equipment for the government and its agencies, including KT and Dacom, and in determining technical standardization. Fourth, the United States asked Korea to eliminate government restrictions on foreign investment.

country. However, from the Foucauldian perspective, "imperialism" does not exist as a universal form, but is discursively practiced at the local level. In Korea, the U.S. trade pressure brings about double-edged responses. On the one hand, Korea wants to take advantage of its technological development in order to enhance international competitiveness. For instance, the Korean government is eager for more technological development in order to break through the present problem of economic growth and exports. On the other hand, Koreans resist the technological dominance of international power by experiencing frequent trade conflicts with the United States.

The government, as well as the people in general, acknowledge that Korea no longer has a harmonious relationship with technologically advanced countries due to changes in the international system and the economic recession in the international market. As the United States loses its hegemonic power in the international system, its government becomes more insistent that Korea open its markets. European countries also develop more aggressive trade policies to protect their markets. As Korea develops its technology further it must engage in more conflicts with technologically advanced countries because it will no longer be specialized in labor-intensive industries: It must compete with technologically advanced countries in the capital-intensive, industrial market. In this context, Korea attempts to develop technological self-determination by both soliciting and resisting the dominant system.

However, Korean people's resistance to international power does not depart far from the dominant ideas—or discursive formations—of technologically advanced countries. Instead, Koreans contribute to the discursive formation of technological power by conforming to the idea that technological development is necessary for economic growth and international competitiveness. Koreans believe that international competitiveness will eventually provide Korea with the power to determine its own direction. The Korean government believes that the best strategy for overcoming international dependence and gaining self-determinism is to adopt advanced technologies. Yet, Korean people do not blindly worship technology and obey international power. People engage in resistance in their everyday lives, even if their form of resistance is not radical enough to break up the frames of power/knowledge established elsewhere. When diverse channels of the discourse come down to a society, the society employs a strategy to accommodate discourses into practice. Facing technological power, Korea has adopted a strategy to pursue technological development even further.

Computerization is one of the most ambitious Korean government projects for establishing technological self-determinism. The Korean government deliberately developed a domestic computer system through its computerization plan. Even though the domestic computer system is more costly and less efficient than foreign systems, the Korean government endeavors to localize computer technology for the purpose of establishing international competitiveness and technological self-determination. The strong State plays the most important role in proceeding with this project. Korea struggles against the technological power of advanced countries by adopting more technologies instead of discarding them.

TECHNOLOGICAL FORMATION

Beginning in 1983, the Korean government planned and implemented computerization. Unlike other countries, Korean computerization was not developed primarily by the market principle, but initiated by the government. Relying on the strong authority of the government, Korea successfully enhanced the computer industry and promoted the use of computers through a national computerization plan.

The Korean government is establishing five networks based on this plan: public administration, banks, education and research, military, and police networks.[4] Computerization of the public administration network is the most important and comprehensive project among the five networks. The Korean government believes that the development of the public administration network will establish a more efficient and productive system of bureaucracy and enhance Korea's international competitiveness by supporting the information industry (CCC, 1992; MOC, 1989, 1990, 1991). The government claims that computerization can contribute to enhancing efficiency in production systems and to democratization in political institutions.

However, bureaucracy seldom ensures the efficiency and public interest considerations intended in the government's plan. As with other institutions, bureaucratic organizations have their own interests and compete with one another. Yet despite this well-known tendency, the government established an alternative bureaucratic institution to coordinate the diverse interests existing between bureaucracies: the Computerization Co-ordination Committee (CCC). The CCC was established in 1987 through the *Law of Expanding Distribution of Computer Networks and Promoting Their Use*. In its Annual Report, the Ministry of Communication (MOC) described the purpose of the new legal framework for computerization as follows:

> Although we urgently need to establish a law for advancing an information industry, we have had difficulties in establishing an appropriate law due to the diffusion of governmental administration and a conflict of interest between ministries. . . . As a result, we established *The Law of Expanding Distribution of Computer Networks and Promoting Their Use*. (MOC, 1988, pp. 271-272)[5]

---

[4]Although the government planned for the computerization of office networks, government reports usually describe plans for four networks, excluding the police network. In 1991, the government added the health and social welfare network, which is sometimes included in the five network plan (CCC, 1992; KISDI, 1991).

[5]The MOC report defines the purposes of the Law as follows: First, the government

In addition to establishing the CCC for the purpose of cross-organizational coordination, the government also established the National Computerization Agency (NCA) to administer the technical standardization required for nationwide computerization. Another bureaucratic organization, KITI (Korea Informatics Telesis Incorporated), was also set up to provide financial support for carrying out the national computerization plan.

According to *The Law of Expanding the Distribution of Computer Networks and Promoting their Use* (*The Law of Computer Networks*, hereafter), the CCC has ultimate authority over the computerization project. According to Section 4 of the Law, the CCC approves the basic plan of computerization submitted by the Minister of Communication. Section 14, Article 2 states that the CCC also recommends technical standards to computer producers when the Minister of Communication consults with the CCC in this matter. The Presidential Decree further provides a legal basis for CCC authority. According to Section 4 of the Decree, the CCC makes decisions for financing technological standards and selecting those who will implement computerization. The CCC consists of one Chairperson and no more than 30 members. According to Section 5 of the Decree, the Chairperson is appointed by the President of the ROK from ministers or those who have an equivalent position. In the revised Law of 1991, the Chairperson is the Minister of Communication. Members are recommended by the Chairperson and appointed by the President. The CCC members' term of office is two years, and the membership is renewable once.

Under the strong authority of the State, the CCC contributed to national computerization, both negatively and positively. Korean computerization was rapidly developed with the support of the highest authority of the presidential office at the Blue House. The CCC controlled the process of Korean computerization from a transcendent position over diverse ministries. However, the Blue House exerted its own normalized procedures through a top-down pattern of communication. The CCC did not integrate feedback from implementing agencies into the planning process. Using its authority, the CCC impeded the bottom-up pattern of communication that was recommended by implementing agencies (An, 1991). The excessive power of the Blue House thus thwarted the computerization process. At the implementation stage it is necessary to respond flexibly to feedback from implementors. The power of the CCC as a bureaucratic organization halted the process of national computerization.

---

makes plans for national basic computerization and directs policies on the information industry; second, business sectors establish their own management plans following the government's direction and participate in implementing the national development plan; third, the National Computerization Agency develops standardization, provides technical support for the industry, and researches the feasibility of national computerization plans; fourth, Korea Informatics Telesis provides business information, channels demands of the business sector to the government, and encourages information exchange between business members; and fifth, research institutes cooperatively develop technology with industries and teach new technology to industries.

The Korean government subsequently restructured the bureaucracy and established new bureaucratic organizations. According to a CCC report (1992), in 1989 the CCC was integrated into the Ministry of Communication. The change in the bureaucratic structure of computerization reflected political changes. Because the Rho administration showed less willingness to push the computerization plan than the former government, the CCC was moved from the Blue House. Through restructuring, the Minister of Communication became the chairman of the CCC. In 1991, the MOC established the Department of Information and Telecommunication as a new full-time executive office containing the CCC (1992). Yet, having restructured the CCC, the Korean government was caught in a dilemma: a conflict of power between different bureaucratic organizations. After its transfer into the MOC, the authority of the CCC diminished, and it became difficult for the CCC to coordinate the various needs and power conflicts between ministries.[6] Power conflicts are particularly severe between the MOC, the Ministry of Science and Technology, and the Ministry of Commerce. Not only are all these ministries concerned about their political power, they also have different perspectives and different standard procedures for implementing the computerization plan.

The *Law of Computer Networks* and various regulations following this Law illustrate that the process of Korean computerization is totally bureaucratized. It created an extended series of laws and numerous bureaucratic organizations. The Law encourages cooperation between bureaucracies while checking any abuse of power by any institutions involved. Although the bureaucratic expansion is justified by the new Law, the Law does not specify how to coordinate different positions of government organizations. The general outcome has been a bureaucratization of the computerization project, under the presumption that bureaucracy can serve the public good through the pooling and efficient organization of resources. Yet, the implementation of computerization has been far from rational. In practice, the discourse of technology contains multiple dimensions of struggle, resistance, and deviance. Although the government owns and controls the implementing agencies through personal interlocks as well as financial control, many technicians indicated that relationships across the government bureaucracy are often not harmonious and thus hinder the implementation of rational planning. In Korea, computerization is not implemented according to technological rationality because of the rupture of power by bureaucracy.[7]

---

[6]In my interview, S.S. Lee at KISDI described the diminishing power of the CCC as "taking its teeth out." Y.S. Yeom at the MOC also talked about the MOC's difficulty in implementing computerization.

[7]In an interview, one of the managers at Dacom, Hyun, stated that Dacom often had to revise programs and sometimes totally change the system itself because the bureaucrats had not properly directed their computerization plans. Moreover, when there were changes in bureaucratic positions, new bureaucrats demanded different things, so Dacom had to change the implementation process to correspond to changes in bureaucratic power.

From the Foucauldian framework, the Law represents a discourse that reproduces power in the everyday practices of bureaucratic institutions. In daily practice, the information industry and consumers have to conform to the rules and normalized standards of the government. The law promotes further normalization and fragmentation of bureaucracy in the process of computerization. The process of computerization is fragmented so that it does not coalesce with other social issues in a comprehensive manner. As the process of computerization becomes more professionalized, the objectives of national computerization tend to be limited to those consistent with technocratic rationality and business interests.

The Law of Computer Networks demonstrates that the normative objectives of the national computerization plan are eliminated from the process of establishing the law. Even at the ritual level, the government does not make an effort to promote the computerization plan as a means of creating public goods. In the same MOC annual report, the MOC does not even symbolically mention the public welfare and democratization in computerization plans. This shows that in the implementation process, the power dimension becomes more transparent. Earlier, in the planning stage, the government declared the democratic value of computerization, but that part has been eliminated as it is institutionalized through laws (MOC, 1987, 1988). In the report, the government now solely emphasizes the economic contribution of computerization.

DECENTRALIZING INFORMATION?

The government claims that computerization of the public administration will establish a democratic, "small government," meaning fewer numbers of bureaucratic workers with higher productivity and overall gains in efficiency. In official reports, the Korean government frequently contends that bureaucratic supervision ensures efficiency, the public interest, and fairness of the total process of computerization (CCC, 1992; MOC, 1989, 1990, 1991). Ostensibly the government has designed a computerization plan that extends public services by establishing a "small" government. However, the idea of small government changed between the planning and the implementation stages.

In an interview, a response by one of the officials at MOC confirmed my observation that the new arrangements had yet to coordinate the competing interests of the various bureaucratic agencies involved in the computerization project. Contrary to the blueprint for "the one-stop service," he stated that "we are developing computer networking within an organization, but it is not possible to share information between different ministries due to the problems of responsibility, information control and security." (S.S. Lee, personal interview, July 25, 1992). In another interview, a technician at Dacom, who was in charge of implementing computerization of the public administration network, also pointed out that "technically, there is no problem in connecting computer networks between ministries, but there is a political problem" (J.Y. Hyun, personal interview, July 20, 1992) Dacom has established technical facilities for interconnecting the computer network of public administration through the cable network at the regional level and the space network at the national level. He stated that "two-way communication is technically possible through these networks, but politically problematic." Unlike the claims of the government, in reality, national computerization does not seem to promote either decentralization of power or horizontal two-way communication.

The Korean government has recently established local municipal governments for the purpose of more geographically even development and democratization. The government emphasizes advancement of public administration through computer distribution to local administration offices and education for local administrators. The Korean government has distributed mainframes, workstations, and PCs to local administrative offices through computerization of the public administration. According to a CCC report, computers have been installed in 4,300 local district offices nationwide. The government spent $29 million for central and local administration office PCs (CCC, 1992). The government has also arranged computer education programs as part of its computerization plan. These programs are designed to mitigate the problem of insufficient levels of computer literacy among government officers. Addressing this need the government has trained civil servants, in order that they will be able to use the public administration networks once they are in place.

However, local administrators do not seem to have equal opportunities to take advantage of computerization. I have conducted open-ended, in-depth interviews with several local district administrators who use the public administration computer system daily. In these interviews, and contrary to the government's blueprint for computer education, local administrators revealed their concerns about insufficient knowledge of computers. Kim, a local administrator at the district office of Seo Kim Nyoung Ri, said that she had no experience or computer education when she started to use the computer network at the local administration office.[8] According to her, the central government has provided no training for those who enter into local administration since it finished its first training sessions. Due to limited knowledge of computers, local administrators cannot flexibly utilize computer networks to fit the demands of local people. Lee, a local administrator at one of the district offices of Seo Gui Po, pointed out that the job was limited to simply punching in resident information data. Most local administrators do not have knowledge of the network system, nor do they know how to use computers to communicate with each other. Kim, at Seo Kim Nyoung Ri, contended that local administrators

[8]Interview with Kim, a local administrator at Seo Kim Nyoung Ribranch office of Ku Jwa Eup district administration office in Cheju Province on August 3, 1992, in Cheju Province. Ri is the small district in the local areas. Seo Kim Nyoung Ri does not have its own administration office, but has a branch office under the direction of a larger district office of Ku Jwa Eup.

rely totally on maintenance companies when they have minor problems, such as the need to decipher computer messages with which they are not familiar.

These two local administrators suggested that the computerization of public administration may contribute to centralized control. For instance, computerized information on residents is more accessible than written documents. Kim, at Seo Kim Nyoung Ri, said that governmental offices were allowed to get information about residents by requesting copies of formal documents, but frequently government officials ask for information by telephone without submitting formal requests. According to Kim, police and tax offices make the most frequent requests for information about residents. Consequently, although the government is proceeding with the decentralization of the political system by establishing local governments, this does not seem to lead to the decentralization of power. The central government dominates local governments. Because the central system controls budget plans and distribution, it can intervene in local administration through subsidies. In this situation, it is hard to execute autonomous local politics.

The local information system is not an exception. Although the government has developed computerization of local administration, the central government has dominated the plan and implementation process of computerization. In the bureaucratic process, computerization seems to strengthen central power instead of decentralizing it. Localization of information does not support local politics because the budget and resources for its plan are very limited. Local administrators are not encouraged to represent local interests, their jobs being limited instead to the input of technical data. Thus, computerization does not change the basic structure of the centralized Korean political system and geographic inequality.

This is true not only in the political arena, but also within industry. Industries have not been decentralized in accord with the development of information technology. Unlike the technological fantasia of the information society, computerization in Korea does not change the industrial structure and decentralize the production system. As discussed earlier, the proponents of the "technological fantasia" perspective tend to emphasize changes in the pattern of production, from the mass production of manufacturing industry to a more innovative and professionally oriented production system. However, in Korea, despite the development of information technology, the preexisting industrial structure remains intact. Business practices in the information industry and related public projects, such as the computerization plan, are conducted in the same manner as those that have been implemented in manufacturing industries. Chaebols (big conglomerates) monopolize the market as well as research and development (R & D) of computer networks and hardware. Small companies work under their direction, only obtaining a small profit determined by the chaebols.

Because the government does not support innovative small and medium-size companies that concentrate on software production, the mass production system remains the model for the information industry. As a result,

Korean computer software is not internationally competitive. In fact, the software industry reflects the highest import rate in Korea's information industry, importing, in 1987, $29 million worth of goods while exporting only $7.2 million worth of software (*Computer Yearbook,* 1992). In 1990, the Korean software industry was even further dependent on imports, spending six times more on imports than it received for its exports.

While directing computerization, the MOC selected companies that manufacture computer systems and personal computers: companies that provide hardware for the computerization of the public administration network. Most of these companies are big conglomerates. On the contrary, Dacom competitively selected software companies and telecommunication equipment companies through newspaper announcements. These companies included medium and small-sized companies. It shows that the government favors chaebols for developing computer networks and hardware instead of equally distributing business opportunities to small and medium-sized companies, even though computerization is a public project. Throughout the industrialization process, the government has created and supported chaebols in accordance with the assumptions of the economic theory of uneven development. Now when the government changes its policy by promoting decentralization and localization, bureaucracy still promotes the information industry based on normalized procedures that were employed to support manufacturing industries. Also, the business sectors, particularly chaebols, manage the information industry using old modes of production that reinforce inherited industrial structures.

The Korean government does not seem to proceed with its policy of localization enthusiastically, even though it is included in the grand plan of Korean computerization. Government agencies have established local PR (public relations) centers to provide information technology facilities to the public. KT, Dacom and ICC (Information Cultural Center) participate in the PR business. KT and Dacom, established local PR centers mostly for business purposes. They contribute to spreading the "information culture" to the public in the hope of inducing consumption of information technology. The ICC provides local computer education by operating computer classes in agriculture and fishing areas. In 1992, the ICC established two local computer classes in all provinces but Cheju and one in Cheju Province.

I interviewed H.Y. Kim, who teaches the computer class in Seo Gui Po in Cheju Do (Province).[9] The computer class of Cheju Do was first established in Hanrim, a rural area, before moving a year later to Seo Gui Po, where it acquired more students. The computer class is open to the public and provides free computer lessons. Seo Gui Po is the second largest city in Cheju Province. In Kim's class most students are company employees, civil servants, and

[9]Interview with H.Y. Kim, July 31, 1992, Seo Gui Po, Cheju Do. In the interview, Kim stated that although Dacom set up a data information base about agricultural and fishing production through Chunrian II, "farmers and fishermen are not inclined to invest in computers because they do not find the information useful."

housewives. There are no farmers or fishermen in the computer class. In Hanrim, according to Kim, "there were several farmers, but most farmers and fishermen were not interested in computer education, nor did they have time to learn about computers."

Although the computer class was established for the purpose of localization of information, it does not seem to encourage local development. First, at the economic level the computer class does not provide a business opportunity for local people. The computer class does not promote local business nor local communication channels, nor is there a localized database that farmers and fishermen can use for their business. Thus, the computer class does not introduce any local information network that might compliment the communication patterns of the local population. Instead, according to Kim, students in the computer class mainly learn how to use MS-DOS and word processing programs.

CONCLUDING REMARKS

Applying Foucault's theory, I have analyzed the interconnection between the discourse of technology and the process of computerization in South Korea. From the Foucauldian perspective, it is meaningless to discuss whether technology in general and computerization in particular enhances democracy and serves the public until the discourse is contextualized at the local level. From this perspective, computerization can only be assessed in terms of how it is incorporated into people's everyday lives.

Computerization can be a channel to carry the multiple voices of people if it integrates their everyday life at the local level. In this sense, localization and decentralization are important criteria for the democratic construction of computerization. In most societies, however, computerization is unilaterally directed by technological rationality. Korea is no exception. Although politicians and technicians praise the function of computerization as a service to the public, they implement computerization without integrating the diverse interests of the public. In Korea, computerization of public administration does not appear to promote decentralization of power. The government does not emphasize the importance of horizontal communication for enhancing democracy through computerization. Instead, it focuses on technocratic concepts of democracy that emphasize efficiency and productivity. Although the total process of computerization is bureaucratized and politicized, there are few channels that provide for diverse voices at the local level.

Although computer networks are localized, the role of local administrators is limited to technical work. They are not trained to utilize the computer network for horizontal communication among local people. The computer class does not promote communication through a network—education is limited to technical training. Most people in the rural areas are not likely to be interested in computerization because it usually does not provide information regarding local business and local political life or any communication channels that supplement those already available.

The Korean government has made a positive effort to distribute the benefits of information technology more evenly to local areas through the national computerization plan. However, it mainly serves to consolidate the power of the central government and business interests. Localization of information is constructed in a one-way communication system that integrates local residents into one systematic database. The public exists only as a form of written data, or as consumers of computer information. As a result of the exclusion of a public discourse from the computerization process, people in general have little interest in utilizing computers. Consequently, computerization in Korea does not contribute to promoting horizontal communication.

REFERENCES

Amsden, A. (1989). *Asia's next giant.* New York: Oxford University Press.

An, M. (1991). *Research on activating the function of the Computerization Coordination Commission.* Seoul, Korea: Korean Government.

Bell, D. (1973). *The coming post-industrial society.* New York: Basic Books.

Computer yearbook (1992). Seoul, Korea: Ministry of Communications.

Computerisation Coordination Commission. (1992). *Basic planning of national computerisation.* Seoul, Korea: Author.

Evans, P. (1979). *Dependent development.* Princeton, NJ: Princeton University Press.

Foucault, M. (1972). *The archaeology of knowledge* (A.S. Smith, Trans.). New York: Pantheon Books.

Foucault, M. (1978). *The history of sexuality* (Vol. 1, R. Hurley, Trans.). New York: Vintage Books.

Foucault, M. (1980). *Power/knowledge: Selected interviews and other writings 1972-1977* (C. Gordon, Trans.). New York: Pantheon Books.

Haggard, S., & Chung, I. M. (1983). The South Korean state in the international economy: Liberal, dependent or mercantile? In J. Ruggie. (Ed.), *The antinomies of interdependence.* New York: Columbia University Press.

Hindess, B., & Hirst, P. (1975). *Pre-capitalist mode of production.* London: Routledge & Kegan Paul.

Korea Telecom. 1991. *Telecommunications statistics.* Seoul, Korea: Author.

Korean Information Society Development Institute (KISDI). (1991). *Analysis of social effects of national computerization.* Seoul, Korea: Author.

Marcuse, H. (1964). *One-dimensional man: Studies in the ideology of advanced industrial society.* Boston: Beacon.

Marx, K. (1967). *Capital* (Vols. 1 & 3). New York: International Publisher.

Ministry of Communication (MOC). (1986). *Annual reports.* Seoul, Korea: Author.

Ministry of Communication (MOC). (1987). *Annual reports.* Seoul, Korea: Author.

Ministry of Communication (MOC). (1988). *Annual reports.* Seoul, Korea: Author.

Ministry of Communication (MOC). (1989). *Annual reports.* Seoul, Korea: Author.

Ministry of Communication (MOC). (1990). *Ministry of Communication White Paper.* Seoul, Korea: Author.

Mosco, V. (1989). *Pay-per society.* Norwood, NJ: Ablex.

O'Donnell, G. (1973). *Modernization and bureaucratic-authoritarianism.* Berkeley: University of California.

Toffler, A. (1980). *The third wave.* New York: Bantan Books.

Wallerstein, I. (1979). *The capitalist world economy.* Cambridge: Cambridge University Press.

Chapter 9

Think Globally, Program Locally: Privatization of Indian National Television

Manjunath Pendakur
Jyotsna Kapur

The liberalization and privatization of India's television, started in 1984, has moved at a frenzied pace since 1990 as an integral part of the government's economic liberalization program. Not only has television become nationally available as a source of entertainment in middle-class homes, privately owned cable networks have mushroomed all over the country, some of them pulling satellite-delivered signals from far off places. The institutional character of television has changed, in a short period of time, from a primarily state-controlled broadcast operation with all its attendant problems of staid and predictable programs, highly censored news, and public affairs programming to the shrill American-style cable network operations.

In early February 1994, Rupert Murdoch arrived in New Delhi with an entourage of managers and technical experts that was large enough to occupy a whole floor at the Taj International Hotel.[1] Having acquired a controlling

---

[1]Highly ironic an international conference on communications technology and democratization was being held at the same time in that city. Most of the academics

interest in the satellite delivery pan-Asian network called STAR-TV in 1993, which had given him access to a large part of the Asian-Pacific region, Murdoch needed to negotiate his space in the changing Indian political economy. The Rao government rolled out a red-carpet welcome to Murdoch and gave the visitor high priority befitting a foreign head of state or royalty. He was received by the President, the Prime Minister, and the leaders of the opposition political parties in private meetings. As the state embraced him, the English language press featured Murdoch on the front page. The indigenous, small capitalists who created cable television were at his feet, requesting the media emperor to help them convince the government of India to regulate the emerging cable industry in their favor.

The irony could not be missed. Here was an international capitalist whose only priority was to seek entry into the Indian economy and sell entertainment produced by his vast holdings in the United States and elsewhere, including the 20th Century Fox movie and television operations, with as few constraints as possible. The Indian capitalists went to him for help. Here also was the political establishment, which, not too long ago, had debated the issues of cultural imperialism in the Parliament, giving him a warm welcome. Here was also the Hindu right-wing leaders, led by L. K. Advani, whose concerns about Murdoch's MTV were represented as "nationalist" and anti-imperialist. Advani was reportedly assured by the king of global media that MTV would be appropriately censored to suit the Indian conditions. Following Murdoch, other international giants in the media business—Time Warner, Universal, Paramount, Disney, the Turner Group—are reportedly setting up production facilities in India (Cherian, 1994). Obviously, the whole policy context had changed in a very short period of time from one of national autonomy to the dogmas of liberalization and privatization, necessitating a different outlook, a "new" perspective on investment, including the difficult area of culture.

An analysis of the nature and course of privatization of television raises a number of complex issues linked to imperialism, both cultural and economic, the historical development of India as a dependent capitalist economy, and the political choices made by the Indian state on behalf of the indigenous bourgeoisie. We argue that the present move toward liberalization is a continuation rather than a break with the postcolonial state's policy of capitalist development in conjunction with foreign capital. It is, nevertheless, the last significant parting with the socialist rhetoric that for so long functioned as a vote-getting mechanism. We argue that the shifts in India's policy toward television should be seen in the overall context of globalization that defines the nature of capitalism as this century draws to a close. Globalization and localization are two facets of the same phenomenon. The welcome given to privatization by local audiences should be seen against the history of state

gathered there did not appear to pay attention to the negotiations that were going on between Murdoch and the government of India and others (Pendakur, 1994).

control over broadcasting. The overall story is about the spread of capitalism and capitalist culture, but it interacts with historical specificity in complex ways, holding forth the promise of democracy and links to an international culture.

TELEVISION IN INDIA—THE CURRENT SCENARIO

It may be helpful at the outset to lay out the way in which television is transmitted in India. There are currently three layers in operation—Doordarshan or the national network, regional networks, and the pan-Asian satellites. Doordarshan was conceived as an arm of government, and its operations are centered in the nation's capital, New Delhi. Doordarshan also has regional stations in each of the state capitals in order to be able to produce and distribute programming in the local languages.[2] No private networks, however, were allowed by the state until 1990, when certain key changes began to occur in national policy regarding privatization in general and television in particular. Although these layers of broadcast operations in the country have developed over the last 20 years, the most recent among them are the satellite delivery systems. We return to them later.

The most powerful among the broadcast operations is still Doordarshan, which is controlled by the Central government and transmitted off of the domestic satellite INSAT. Doordarshan claims that the total terrestrial coverage of its signal has increased to 91.8% of the population.[3] Its extensive operations included 31 production centers in 1994. Doordarshan expanded its broadcast operations in 1994 to six channels from a single national channel. These are as follows: Doordarshan 1 is transmitted terrestrially, has a viewership of 40 million TV homes. It broadcasts for 15 hours a day, and the programs include a mix of information, education, and entertainment. The second is the Metro Channel, which is available terrestrially in six cities— Madras, Delhi, Bombay, Calcutta, Hyderabad, and Lucknow. For the rest of the country, it is available through satellite. The Metro Channel has an audience of 7.2 million TV homes and is solely an entertainment channel, broadcasting 15 hours a day. Doordarshan 3 is transmitted via satellite and is terrestrially available in Delhi, the nation's capital. It is broadcast for five hours a day and is an entertainment channel. Doordarshan 4 is also transmitted via satellite and is

---

[2]These regional stations are of varying power from 100-watt stations to 10 kilowatt, depending on their strategic significance. For instance, the stations in Srinagar and Amritsar were established in 1973 for political reasons, as the signals from those stations cross the border into Pakistan.

[3]Coverage here does not mean that such a high percentage of the population can actually watch television because acquisition of a TV set is a factor of disposable income. Given that nearly half of India's population is below the poverty line, not all view television regularly.

available terrestrially in Delhi. Programming is in the southern languages of Tamil, Kannada, and Telugu for 15 hours a day. Doordarshan 5 and 6 are both transmitted via satellite and are available terrestrially in Delhi. They are to broadcast for 15 hours a day in Marathi, Gujarati, Punjabi, and Kashmiri (Agha, 1994). Although not all the channels launched are profitable, Doordarshan posted total revenues Rs. 3,800 million in 1993 and expected them to grow to Rs. 4,000 million in 1994 (Deenadayal, 1994).

Doordarshan's regional channels, which are run from the state capitals, are available terrestrially by way of a microwave network combined with low-power transmitters placed in medium-size towns of 100,000 population. Given the linguistic and other diversities in the country, regional channels are desired by the audience. Finally, the pan-Asian satellites transmit many channels into India, including the five most watched channels—BBC, CNN, ZEE-TV, Star Plus, and Prime Sports.

PRIVATIZATION OF INDIAN TELEVISION
AND THE GLOBAL ECONOMY

The most significant shift in Indian television in the 1990s was the introduction of the pan-Asian satellite which challenged government monopoly over programming and initiated Indians into an international global culture. There is a growing body of literature on globalization that discusses the issue mainly in terms of cultural imperialism or postmodernism. The former emphasizes U.S. control—both economic and cultural—reading globalization as a form of neocolonialism. This validates nationalism as a strategy of resistance. As we argue in this chapter, nationalism in India today is politicized as a hegemonic discourse linked to Hindu fundamentalism. The debate on postmodernism, on the other hand, for all its ambiguities, is centered on a North American and Western European crisis of authority that is both cultural and institutional. Both these positions center the West and colonialism in a discussion of the process, nature, and impact of globalization for the third world.

There is very little analysis that is done from within a third world perspective. Although we do not deny the significance of international capital in the privatization of Indian television we argue that it is important to see the ways in which it interacts with the historical specificities of class and state in India. Rajgopal (1993), draws attention to the ways in which globalization is resisted through the state's assertion of its regulatory function and the day-to-day workings of the bureaucracy. However, this tends to underplay the pressures of international capital as one component of the class basis of the Indian state and its historical development, which makes it a willing partner to global capital. Kishore (1994), on the other hand, in keeping with the developmentalist, modernization paradigm, hails the privatization of television as enabling technical advancement and greater choice in entertainment and information without recognizing the ideological shift in the Indian government's move towards liberalization. Although we recognize the utopian promise of international community inherent in global media culture, we critique the class basis of such a utopia in the context of increasing economic disparities in India. Second, we also point to the limitations of the democratic promise of privatization. International capital has historically made alliances with military dictatorships or religious fundamentalism to ensure national stability for capitalist expansion. It is significant that the other agency besides the government that Murdoch chose to meet with was the BJP, a Hindu nationalist party. To sum up, it is only through an analysis of the complex interaction of both internal and external factors and of the historical specificities of the development of the Indian state and class relations along with the expansion of international capital that we can understand why the privatization of Indian television is happening at such break neck speed and with such little resistance.

The most visible manifestation of globalization is the new global media culture that is marketed by multinationals such as BBC, MTV, Prime Sports, and the empire of Rupert Murdoch. As Robins (1989) pointed out, this represents the move inherent in capitalism for expansion, that is, the search for new markets and the organization of production on a world scale in order to affect economies of both scale and scope.[4] This economic expansion is not accompanied by the imperial conquest characteristic of 19th- and 20th-century imperialism. MNCs not only produce but also adapt to local markets and target local populations through what Robins (1989) called "insiderization." Nevertheless, Petras (1994), reminded us that the threat of military intervention—as in the Gulf War and Latin America—economic sanctions, and the withholding of aid is ever present.

India is attractive to international capital because of the vast market that it represents in its middle class in addition to cheap labor that it can provide. Its middle class is one with its class in Asia and Latin America. *Business Week* (1994), characterized this as "increasingly looking, living and even talking more like each other," estimating the middle class at 1.2 billion people. Popular business journals such as Fortune and Business Week carry celebratory images of smiling, upwardly mobile executives, and rags to riches stories. According to Business India (1994), the Indian middle class is growing at the rate of 5%, or 40 million people every year. Although the middle class represents only about 15% of the total population, it translates to a staggering 150 million in absolute terms. For once, the Western media is celebrating population growth in the third world with striking irony and an all too obvious class bias! Besides the sheer numbers, the Indian middle class is also attractive

---

[4]MTV, which is owned by Viacom International, at the time was being supplied in Asia by Star-TV. It may be useful to recall here that Viacom is a large U.S-based media conglomerate with assets in cable, motion pictures, broadcasting operations, and the largest video retail outlet, Blockbuster.

Rural middle class home in Karnataka with an antenna to receive the national TV channel. Manjunath Pendakur

because of its relative westernization, including English language skills and an inherent suspicion of state control.

It would be a mistake, however, to characterize the Indian middle-class imagination as land waiting to be colonized. In order to understand the appeal of globalization it is important to recognize the sophisticated terms that international capital uses to make its appeal. Instead of positioning itself as covert imposition of western culture, characteristic of 19th- and 20th-century imperialism, globalization appears to undercut western authority through the cosmopolitan culture it promises for the Indian upper middle class and a stress on the local. In fact, India offers an excellent test case of this policy of "think locally and act globally." Local production not only attracts local audiences, it is also cheaper. Murdoch repeatedly stated that he would produce locally in local languages, including a Hindi version of MTV. Numerous Indianized versions of "Dynasty" have appeared on Doordarshan as well as other networks; "Khandan" in the 1980s and "Kurukshetra" in the 1990s are two such examples. These serials feature two (or more) warring, industrial families whose primary motivations in life are greed and power, ends that justify any means, and in the midst of all this, they search for the happiness that cannot be found in their material possessions. The story, setting, characters, locale, sets, music, and cultural nuances distinguish the programs from their import inspirations. Furthermore, American series like "The Bold and the Beautiful," "The Cosby Show," Beverly Hills 90210," and various talk shows provide an insight into American middle class life that had so far been mystified and out of reach for even the middle-class Indian. These are not censored versions of the West characteristic of colonial relations and racial segregation of the 19th and 20th century. Indeed, it is with no small amount of glee that the erstwhile colonized world watches the West wash its dirty laundry in public.

The support of privatization of television also comes out of an internal history of strict government control over Doordarshan programming. We outline this history in a later section, pointing out how since its establishment television was, in the popular mind, associated with government propaganda. Privatization, by ending government control over programming, offers the possibility of a democratic debate. This can perhaps be best explained by the popularity of *Aapke Adalat* [Your Court], which stimulates public trials of important persons from public life. It is a weekly, 40-minute program aired on Sunday morning at 10 on Zee TV.

It is packaged with commercial breaks, a laugh track and live audience participation. Famous personalities, political and other, are interrogated by a very smart, real-life lawyer, named Rajat Sharma. The show is produced before a studio audience. Murali Manohar Joshi, President of the BJP; Sharad Pawar, Chief Minister of Maharastra; and Mr. Banatwala, President of the All India Muslim League were some of the political personalities that were featured in early 1994. The set looks like a court room. The show opens with a court functionary dressed in colonial garb announcing, as though in some king's court, "The Chief Minister of Maharastra, Mr. Sharad Pawar, is appearing today in the People's Court." The guest walks in, takes the chair, greets the audience, and so on. A different judge presides over the court every week, whose credentials are announced to the audience in the beginning. The announcer then goes on to list the first charge to which a graphic rolls and the words in big letters appear on the screen, "CORRUPT," or "ACCUSED OF GANG CONNECTIONS," and so on. Sharma, dressed conservatively in a dark suit, stands as the prosecuting attorney and questions the accused at rapid-fire speed. In between Sharma's questions and comments (he jokes freely to which the audience responds generously), an audience member may be given a chance to ask his or her own questions. The show is paced well and the questions well researched. The judges are well qualified and appear informed. The emphasis, however, is to create humorous situations, embarrassment to the accused, even amidst sickening political controversy. Viewers are riveted to the show because of a number of attributes of the show. They want to see the politicians who are key to certain national crisis pinned against the wall. Because political power is the domain of the rich, powerful, and/or criminal elements in society and because it touches their lives so deeply, the audience love to see the politicians unmasked, albeit briefly. Even if they wiggle out, their sweaty foreheads, embarrassment, awkward grinning, when they seem to be caught by the clever questioning and evidence presented by the attorney, are entertaining. The audience identifies completely with the host, who is smart, informed, well dressed, and clearly appears to be on the people's side. The laugh track ruptures the false idea created by the show that it is a court of law, but nobody seems to care. As the show is repeated at least twice each week at different time periods, everyone in the family has an opportunity to watch it (Pendakur, 1994). Clearly such a show could not have been conceived by Doordarshan with all the problems related to its governance. At every step of the way, there would have been political hindrance placed in its way by the Prime Minister's office or some one in the Ministry of Information and Broadcasting. As noted earlier, a show such as *Aap Ke Adalat* signals to the audience that there is real freedom here to question those that are in power, to make them uncomfortable, and to somehow hold them accountable to public scrutiny. The show's hidden motive, however, is to generate sufficient numbers of those desirable audience members with disposable income to spend on the goods that are advertised on the show.

It needs to be pointed out that in recognizing the appeal of the global media culture we are not condoning it. However, our critique of globalization is not based on the consumerism that it generates. As Sinclair (1987) has pointed out, this often translates into a condemnation of genuine third world aspirations for material improvement. Our critique is of the open advocacy of the market that accompanies the celebration of consumer choice. Neither do we critique globalization from a nationalistic versus western imperialism perspective that is characteristic of the right wing Hindu fundamentalist parties.

Our critique rests on Petras's argument that cultural imperialism empties India's national identity of substantive socioeconomic content as a Third World country. There is a glorious history of third-world resistance to cultural imperialism. Only a decade earlier (December 1983), Sinha (1994) points out that during the NAMEDIA conference at New Delhi concern had been expressed at the centralization of information technology and the role of satellite broadcasting in cultural domination. Before that, at the Conference of Heads of States of NAM countries, the following declaration had been adopted: "Non-aligned countries noted with concern the vast and ever growing gap between communication capacities in non-aligned countries and the advanced countries . . . [which] had created a situation of dependence and domination" (1994, p. 532).

A critique of television privatization and satellite broadcasting based on nationalism may have little appeal against the international and cross-class bonds that these offer along with an alternative to replays of Republic Day parades and ministerial speeches. Furthermore, as pointed out by Offe (1984), there is a sense of powerlessness experienced at an individual and national level against the force of multinationals. Unlike the national government, Offe pointed out, we cannot vote in or out multinational corporations or the international market system—yet these have more influence on our lives than the national governments we elect. This, however, does not mean that liberalization is not a political choice made at a certain historical juncture benefiting a certain class relationship. The significance of television liberalization, as Sinha (1994) suggests, has to be discussed in the same vein as the GATT agreement.

PRIVATIZATION AND LIBERALIZATION OF THE INDIAN ECONOMY—WHY NOW?

The process of privatization and liberalization was undertaken in 1991 by the Congress—the ruling party—to placate, on the one hand, the International Monetary Fund and the World Bank, and on the other, the rising bourgeois class of nearly 150 million.[5] There are both external and internal factors that explain this policy shift.

The major external reason for this was the collapse of the Soviet Union and the general worldwide capitalist media attack on planned economies. In the years following the Bolshevik Revolution, decolonization gained significant momentum in Asia and Africa, leading to the end of colonial rule. Government-led planning was seen as instrumental in economic development for many complex historical and political reasons, including the fact that private capital would not venture into high-risk, low-profit sectors of the economy. Although it

---

[5]For an an.alysis of the Indian government surrender to the IMF and the World Bank, see "Going to the IMF" (1991).

is true that Nehru, the first Prime Minister of India after British rule, talked insistently about socialism, Singh (1990) argues that the principle of socialistic redistribution, beginning with basic land reforms, was not put into practice. Instead, the emphasis on science, technology, and state planning led to the development of a "state-supported capitalism." However, it is only in recent years that the rhetoric of socialism or the "socialistic pattern of society" was finally given up.

The second pressure for opening the economy came from the United States, which, facing recession at home, initiated the two free trade agreements—NAFTA and GATT. The developing countries have increasingly become important markets for Western goods. In 1993, 42% of America's, 20% of Western Europe's, and 48% of Japan's exports, went to the Third World and the countries of the former Soviet Union ("Rich north, hungry south," 1994). In fact, the *Economist* further points out that, "for the first time developing economies were acting as a 'locomotive', helping to pull the rich world out of its recession of the early 1990s." This ahistorical statement ignores completely how colonialism plundered both material and human resources of the Third World and how the colonies were instrumental in the economic development of the West. This is yet another illustration of the image change the Third World is undergoing in the Western media.

Attached to U.S. pressure was the IMF and the World Bank linking their loans to their models of development. The formula for development pushed forth by the World Bank is, as pointed out by Jayashree Sengupta (1994), the same for developing countries all over the world, whether in Africa, Asia, or Latin America. The elements of this formula are to open up the economy through liberalizing imports, allowing foreign investment; to minimize the role of government and public sector enterprises; to deregulate the market and let market forces direct investment; to remove price support mechanisms or subsidies; to reduce taxes, particularly income tax; to give incentives to private investment; and, lastly, to stop attempts at redistribution of incomes.

In the light of these external pressures there has developed at home a configuration of politics that represents for the moment the victory of the Congress as a centrist, liberal, secular party representing bourgeois interests that quickly get translated as those of the "nation." This is to some extent an example of political astuteness on the part of the current Congress leadership, but in larger part an example of the political crisis in Indian bourgeois politics. The bourgeoisie is willing to go for economic liberalization without the accompanying efforts to strengthen democratic institutions or the classic, liberal ideal of secularism. Singh (1990) points out that since the deepening economic crisis of the 1960s, Parliamentary politics has become increasingly corrupt, criminalized, and communal. The Congress, in power most of the time since independence, is a case in point. First, with the Emergency (in 1975) and then its open involvement in the anti-Sikh riots (in 1988), its image as a liberal, secular, middle-of-the-road party was considerably eroded.[6] The opposition that is most prominent currently is the BJP-led assortment of Hindu fundamentalist parties. The Congress, by opting for economic liberalization, once again attempted to recapture its traditional political basis in the national bourgeoisie, putting the nation on the way to economic development. The Hindu fundamentalist parties, so far open to economic liberalization, seem to be forced into a corner—the Hindu neonationalist position compels them to adopt the antiliberalization stance. Ironically, this places them on the same side as the left parties, which also oppose economic liberalization. The CPI-ML, prominent among the left, opposes liberalization on the grounds that it represents a withdrawal of the commitment to a welfare state in favor of the market. It is the Congress that has emerged once again as the centrist party representing bourgeois interests and consequently the "nation" and its "secular" interests rather than those of caste, religion, or language. It for now represents the victory of the bourgeoisie in face of the painfully fragmented nature of the struggles of marginalized groups—dalits, women, farmers, workers, tribals, minority, and ethnic groups.

The privatization of television reflects the working of these internal and external pressures rather well. On the one hand, satellite broadcasting and the expansion of private cable networks made government control virtually irrelevant. The government was compelled to come up with an additional five channels and thereby more opportunities for advertisers. On the other hand, it is important to see the government not in opposition to indigenous and international capital, but working along with it right from the establishing moments of television. The two business groups whose interests are clearly linked to television are advertisers and TV manufacturers. The number of television sets in use increased from 627,000 in 1977 to 8,000,000 in 1990 (*International Marketing Data and Statistics*, 1994, Table 1306). Currently, the toughest competition in the television manufacturing industry is over the top segment, that is, color television with Matsushita, Sony, and the German multinational Grundig all entering the Indian market in alliance with Indian manufacturers ("Indian middle class," 1994). The state and private capital (both national and international), however, are at odds over the monopoly that the state continues to enjoy over certain primary goods' markets such as steel, aluminum, and coal, and key service sectors such as transport and communications. It is not clear yet as to how long the state can monopolize these sectors. If putting profitable state-owned corporations such as the Bharat Heavy Electronics Limited on the sale block becomes a trend, then privatization of the Indian economy will reach new heights.

---

[6]More than 2,000 Sikhs in Delhi were murdered in a pogrom in 1984 as a reprisal for the assassination of Mrs. Gandhi, the then Prime Minister, by her two Sikh bodyguards. Some key members of her Cabinet were implicated in the heinous assault on the Sikhs, but went unpunished by Rajiv Gandhi's government that came to power.

Ad for a color TV set shows a Japanese woman signifying the collaboration with a Japanese company and the "high" quality that consumers associate with Japanese electronics. Manjunath Pendakur.

DEVELOPMENT OF INDIAN TELEVISION: THE BALANCE BETWEEN PRIVATIZATION AND GOVERNMENTAL CONTROL

Governmental control and broadcasting are so intimately linked in popular consciousness because the postcolonial state kept intact the imperialist strict censorship and control over broadcasting. Pendakur (1991) points out that under colonial rule the central government was vested with the power to control the communications sector—post and telegraph, railways, airlines, radio, television, and documentary film. Each of the services was organized into a centralized bureaucracy vulnerable to abuse by the ruling party.[7]

The control, however, was focused internally and not against international capital. In fact, as Pendakur (1991) points out, the initial thrust toward the development of television came from globalization processes in the 1970s and was strongly tied to transnational electronic firms and international "aid" agencies. Black and white television technology arrived in India as part of the 1955 Industrial exhibition in New Delhi (Duggal, 1980). It was here that Phillips (Holland) and the Radio Corporation of America (United States) displayed their transmission, camera, and other television studio technology and donated it to the government at the end of the exhibition. The first television station in New Delhi went on the air in September 1959 under a UNESCO grant to study the impact of television on farm practices.

SITE (Satellite Instructional Television Experiment), launched on August 15, 1975, a landmark in Indian television history, grew out of an alliance between international agencies such as UNESCO and USAID and the Indian Space Research Organization. It began as a collaboration between NASA and India's Department of Atomic Energy. In six states, 2,330 villages were chosen for this experiment based on certain characteristics, including common socioeconomic conditions and infrastructure, and so on. ATS-6, a communication satellite borrowed from NASA for a year, assisted in beaming the programs, all produced indigenously, direct to receive-only dishes placed in these experimental villages. The SITE village had an augmented TV set, a 10-meter receive-only dish located in a community hall, a school, or some such place in which rural people could gather to view TV programs that were beamed to them via satellite.

So centered was this approach on media technology's ability to affect social change that television was introduced without even the basic infrastructure needed for television operation, such as electricity, a building without a leaky

---

[7]The most hopeful time for breaking control over broadcasting was in 1977, when for the first time since Independence, the Congress party was defeated because of the Emergency, in which fundamental rights of citizens and freedom of the press was suspended. In the "White Paper on the Misuse of Mass Media," the new government reported large-scale misuse of the official media and the excesses of the emergency. Although the coalition government appeared keen to restructure broadcasting and allow relative autonomy, it never came through with it because of internal contradictions in the regime.

Students and teachers in a SITE village watch Prime Minister Indira Gandhi's speech inaugurating the experiment in 1975. Manjunath Pendakur.

roof, or a road connection to a nearby town and maintenance center. Chander and Karnik (1976) mentioned that 70% of the Indian villages were not electrified in this period. In Orissa, television sets were run on batteries. In May 1974, state governments and electricity boards had undertaken "Operation Electricity" to electrify the public buildings in which the sets were to be installed and insured against power cuts during the transmission hours. Building an infrastructure that would make the development programs advocated on television have any relevance, such as a primary health center, a primary school, farmers and youth clubs, or a post office, became the least of the priorities in this scenario.

It is important at this juncture to point out the political climate of the decade before SITE was launched in order to see how television in popular memory came to be strongly associated with state control. The period 1965-67 was the first time in which India imported food grains from the United States. In the general elections in 1967, the Congress party lost its majority substantially. These were also years of strong leftist and civil rights movements. In outlining these turbulent years Shah and Gandhi (1991) point to the Bihar Bandh (which united 400 labor unions) and the *Lal Morcha*, or the Redmarch, in Bombay, attended by 20-30,000 people including students, labor, and peasant unions. Between 67 to 70 armed peasant rebellions joined by students were brutally suppressed in Bengal, Andhra Pradesh, and Kerala. In the urban areas Jayaprakash's antiprice increase and anticorruption movement was gaining ground. Finally, in 1975, the railway workers' strike paralyzed the nation amounting to civil disobedience not seen since the twilight years of the British Raj. It was against this growing unrest and loss of popularity that Indira Gandhi imposed a state of national emergency in June 1975. All civil and fundamental rights of citizens, including the freedom of the press, were suspended. Thousands of labor leaders, social activists, and other dissenters were arrested. Even major opposition leaders were put under house arrest.[8] Part of this draconian scheme to establish hegemonic control by the state was the USAID-funded population control program that was put into practice under the ruthless leadership of Sanjay Gandhi, the Prime Minister's younger son. Family planning was on the top of the SITE programming agenda as well. It is against this that we must read Chander and Karnik's (1976) comments about the difficulties of pretesting programs in the rural areas:

> In some cases, farmers had to be brought to the Block headquarters (administrative centers at the district level) for an exposure to the programs. This brought some other *problems* in its wake. A rumour went around that showing of these programs was a ruse to take the villagers to the block headquarters for vasectomy operations. Perhaps the jeeps provided to transport villagers were taken to be the proverbial Trojan horse! At one place, to reassure the villagers, the Project Director offered to stay back in the village till the party returned from the Block headquarters. (p. 29; emphasis added)

---

[8]For a detailed discussion of the Emergency's impact on the country's media, see Pendakur (1988).

In programming choices these early educational programs continued talking down to people, defining their audiences as individuals whose behaviors needed to be changed. This was based on certain assumptions that are clear from the research design of these early experiments. In testing programs great care was taken to insure that individuals did not discuss the program among themselves. This is, of course, in direct contrast to how television was and is watched collectively in neighbors' houses, and meaning or sense is made of what is shown. Chander and Karnik explained how they had to place one monitor outside the room in which the test was being conducted "in order to pacify the crowd" (p. 29). The following conclusions were drawn about programming: Totally unambiguous presentations in real-time sequence were essential for full understanding. Education was seen as contradictory to entertainment, and the latter's only purpose was to hook the audience. Therefore, discussion raged on about where to put the entertainment package— at the beginning, the middle, or the end. The results were, in Chander and Karnik's own evaluation, dull programming, which was nevertheless suitable for an unsophisticated rural audience. This has been a central problem with education packages on Indian television. Entertainment, storytelling, and popular forms were suspect and served only as a bait.

The next impetus to the development of Indian television came with the Asian Games in 1982. The single technical advance was the introduction of color television and an expansion of television outreach through the building of transmitters in major metropolitan centers such as Bombay, Srinagar, Calcutta, Madras, Lucknow, Amritsar, and Jalandhar (Government of India, 1982-83).

Significant expansion continued to take place from 1983 to 1985, when 133 new transmitters were added. Between 1983-1988, the number of television sets had increased from 2.8 million to 27 million, and the audience increased from 30.3 million to 216 million, which was approximately 25% of the population (Audience Research Unit, 1985). Analysis done elsewhere (Pendakur, 1991) points out that the government abandoned its policy of indigenous development, research, and production of television technology by large-scale import of television sets and television kits to be put together in India, relaxation of customs regulations, reduction on export duties, and a special provision allowing relatives abroad to send television sets home. The links between the open-arm policy toward foreign capital and the IMF loans, at a time when the country's total debt had more than doubled between 1985-1989, have also been noted (Pendakur, 1991). It was at this time that ITT, GE, Northern Telecommunications of Canada, Plessey of Britain, and L. M. Ericsson of Sweden entered the telecommunications market (Pendakur, 1991).

Furthermore, advertising on television continued to increase, and advertisers demanded more entertainment on television, seeing the rural, education-based programs as impediments to entertainment-based programs, which attracted the largest audiences. It was in 1980 that advertisements were first allowed on television, and by 1984 the revenue from advertising had gone up from US $8.5 million to US $52 million (Contractor, Singhal, & Rogers, 1986). So the government continued to choose between its own needs for propaganda and the demands of foreign as well as indigenous capital.

STAR-TV AND THE STAR CONSUMER

The advent of pan-Asian satellite networks controlled by multinationals such as Star-TV, however, changed the scenario, giving the final push toward privatization. Star-TV was founded in 1991 by Li Ka-Shing, an entrepreneur from Hong Kong and a regional conglomerate, owned by Hutchinson Whampoa. It was launched from the AsiaSat1, whose footprint extends over the Asia-Pacific region to cover over 38 countries, with a potential audience of 1.5 billion. As this Asia-Pacific region's economies are growing at an annual rate of 8% compared to 2-3% in the rest of the world, transnational corporations turned their attention to this region. An estimated 300 million households in the region have TV sets, a market as large as that of Western Europe. Considering the fact that another 300 million households in this region potentially will join the ranks of TV owners in the next few years, coupled with the fact that these households will have disposable incomes to spend on consumer goods, the Western consumer goods manufacturing giants, the ad industry, program exporting corporations, and other allied industries are salivating over the prospect of benefiting from this region (Davies, 1994).

Rupert Murdoch of NewsCorp was the first major Western media corporation to stake out this region. In July 1993, Murdoch paid a hefty $525 million for a controlling interest in the fledgling Star-TV, thereby gaining access to a potentially profitable market (Marich, 1993). India is so lucrative to a transnational like NewsCorp, not only because of the size of its market, but also because of the open-arm policy of the Indian state in contrast to the Chinese. One Star-TV executive noted, "With China looking doubtful thanks to the clamp down on backyard dishes along with the Chinese policy of generally controlling foreign broadcasts, India has to be the main platform for Star" (Davies, 1994, p. 36).

Star-TV was also welcomed by the local cable industry that was already in place in the metropolitan areas, particularly in Gujarat and Maharashtra. The cable operators were primarily showing pirated Hindu film videos and welcomed more program choices for which they paid nothing, at least thus far. Satellite television first came under public attention during the Gulf War when cable operators hooked up to CNN International. With Star-TV the local cable operators could buy an indigenously made dish and provide five free channels—BBC, MTV, Star Plus, CNN, and Prime Sports—to their subscribers.[9] The initial investment for an operator could be as low as Rs. 5,000

---

[9]What each cable operator offers their subscribers depends entirely on the competitive

and, lacking any rudimentary regulations, it was an open field for entry by small capitalists. By 1993, the number of private cable operators had risen to 50,000 according to Alyque Padamsee, the head of Lintas, a prominent Indian advertising agency (*Business Week,* 1994, p. 181). This thriving small cable operator business, however, may only have a short life left. Foreign capital is tightening its control. Star-TV, keen to introduce pay channels, is pushing for the regulation of the cable industry, through specialized billing systems and sophisticated decoders that may make it difficult for the small cable operators to stay in business. This would, of course, open the way for those with greater capital to consolidate the business and exert a greater degree of control over the cable operators.

The increasing popularity of Star-TV translated into greater advertising, taking the audiences away from Doordarshan. Between January 1993 and December 1993, the penetration of Star-TV in Indian households had risen from 3,300,500 to 7,278,000 (Palmer, 1994). According to Palmer, four-week audience totals in Bombay, Bangalore, and Delhi in November/December 1993 gave Star-TV between 3.4 million and 5.3 million viewers per week. In fact, it was cheaper to buy a pan-Asian spot on Star than an India-only spot on Doordarshan. A 30-second spot on Star-TV (with no volume discount) cost $2,062 as compared to $11,785 on Doordarshan (Raliman, 1992). *India Today* reported that Star-TV attracted 9% of the total advertising pie in 1993, with 11% going to Zee TV and the rest going to Doordarshan's regional Metro and Network channels. Clearly, Doordarshan's monopoly is still considerable, with Star-TV appealing only to a small minority. *India Today* reports that the three most popular programs on Star—*Bold and Beautiful, Santa Barbara*, and *The Wonder Years*—had a combined viewer ship of only 4.9% in January 1994 (Agha, 1994). But the 9% share in advertising can be explained by the higher purchasing power of this class. It is this class that the government is competing for, even as it continues to hold a monopoly over the non-English-speaking population.

The success of Star-TV saw the inauguration of Zee-TV, also to be broadcast over AsiaSat1. A group of institutional investors from abroad co-financed Asia Today Ltd., the parent of Zee-TV, along with a group of Indian expatriates in Asia and elsewhere. Based in Bombay, Zee-TV is primarily a Hindi-language channel showing reruns of Hindi Films, serials, and music-based programs.[10] Consequently, it had an appeal beyond the English-speaking

situation and consequently varies greatly all over the country. For instance, an operator may be able to pick up seven channels, but will supply only four of them to limit distribution costs. In a Karnataka small town, an operator told me that he could receive Pakistan-TV along with BBC, and so on. He, however, chose not to supply it because of the "political" bias against India in its news (Pendakur, personal communication with D. Manjunath, Ramanagara, August 3, 1994).

[10]Subhash Chandra, the founder of Zee-TV, headed the group of Indian expatriots who co-financed Asia Today Ltd. His group controlled 50.1% of the company, and the rest was controlled by the General Oriental Group of Britain (15%), the Jardine Select

audience and came into direct competition with Doordarshan. Particularly popular in the north and the west, Zee TV is available in 43% of TV homes in the North and 25% of all TV homes in the West (Agha, 1994). Zee-TV appeared to command a much bigger audience in 1993, 11% of the audience per week compared to 2% for Star-TV. Given its rising popularity, Murdoch decided to buy an interest in the company. He acquired 49.9% of Asia Today Ltd., the parent of Zee-TV, in January 1994, for a substantial increase over the approximately $16.5 million invested to launch Zee-TV. The Indian expatriates retained control over the rest of the company (Davies, 1994).

Other private networks that emerged in the same period are Sun-TV, based in Madras, and Jain-TV, in New Delhi. Both are delivered by satellite and show reruns of old, Hindi- and regional-language feature films. As Doordarshan and Zee-TV compete with each other by using serials and Hindi language feature films, the other two networks focus on regional-language programs.

Realizing the popularity of regional-language entertainment programs, certain interesting initiatives have been undertaken by the central and state governments. Doordarshan signed an agreement during October 1994 with Viacom International to telecast MTV on its Metro Channel. It will carry "MTV's Most Wanted," the five-day-a-week request show with exclusive sponsorship from Coca Cola India. Although revenues for MTV from this reportedly run into several millions, the joint venture is significant on two counts. MTV has successfully cracked the citadel of public broadcasting in India for transnational capital. There was hardly any presence of imported programming on Doordarshan, as that was considered undesirable for the last 20 years. The version of the program telecast in India by MTV will apparently be far more "decorous than its Western counterpart, with a good mixture of Indian music and dance numbers" ("It's the real thing for MTV India," 1994, p. 51). It will also feature Rahul Khanna, the son of the major movie star Vinod Khanna, as the veejay.

This development clearly signifies a major shift in policy toward foreign capital in the cultural arena, which hitherto was one of suspicion and rejection. We may see this development as part of the continuum that started with allowing privately produced TV serials and other programs on Doordarshan in 1984. It, however, is not an unproblematic policy for national capital as it became clear last year when serious concerns existed in the privately controlled printed media about allowing foreign competition. This issue was settled recently when K. P. Singh Deo, the Minister for Information and Broadcasting, announced in the Parliament that the central government forbids the entry of transnationals into the printed media industry in the country. He was emphatic when he noted, "There is no change in the view in the matter

---

Investment Fund of Hong Kong (10%), the W. I. Carr Investment Group (5%), and APAC, an associated company of IndoSuez Bank, subsidiary of Suez Asia Capital Management Ltd. (20%). See Davies (1994) for further details.

of entry of foreign print media in the country. The government continues to be guided by the 1955 policy decision which provides that no foreign owned newspaper or periodical should be permitted to be published in India" ("Foreign media ban," 1994, p. 1). As the newspaper conglomerates in the country are closely tied to certain political parties and they are the conduit to reach the elite readers, the government may be reluctant to invite foreign transnationals, who may not be easily controlled. There are, however, some applications pending for joint ventures between national and international print media corporations. Those decisions may change this scenario effectively.

An example of a state government initiative in producing for local markets is the Asianet channel broadcast off the Russian satellite, Ekran. Sponsored by the Kerala State Industrial Development Corporation, it planned to broadcast in Malayalam a way to capture the several zonal markets that exist in India and overseas in the Persian Gulf. Although scheduled to be launched in 1992, it was delayed until 1993, ostensibly because of the lack of software. This clumsy footed development of the gap between technology and software planning has characterized government planning since the early days of Indian television.

CONCLUSIONS

The recent scenario of satellite television expansion sketched in this chapter poses, according to Rajgopal (1993), a serious limit to the Indian state. However, in attempting to develop a "state-society" perspective in contrast to an American centered one, Rajgopal reasserts the importance of the state, arguing that eventually the multinationals will have to negotiate with the state. Although it is legitimate to look at internal formulations of state control over television and the way it has translated into actual practice through the bureaucracy, our argument is that it all happens within a world economy, and at no time are the links as sharp as in these global times. At present the welcome given to transnationals and overall liberalization of the economy points to the state's acquiescence to globalization.

As Berbergolu (1992) has pointed out, countries emerging out of colonialism that chose state-sponsored capitalism have been unable to escape neocolonial domination within the world capitalist system. Our argument so far has been that the Indian state has always represented the interests of the bourgeoisie and business, although in the initial years the rhetoric of socialism may have had a greater sincerity than the post-1960s period. Consequently, the current phase of liberalization has greater continuities than breaks with the past. The resounding welcome given to Murdoch by the government at all levels, including his statement that Star TV would definitely get the uplinking facility from India, is a case in point.

From the point of view of audiences, the current welcome given to Star TV and Zee TV and American programming cannot completely be explained by a craze for American media. The appeal lies in its being different, free of government control, and holding what is perceived to be a mirror to Western society. This radical impulse can too easily be appropriated by the likes of Murdoch, who now come across as the real democrats offering a choice where none existed before. Rupert Murdoch, when asked what he would like to be remembered for, answered, for giving people choice, "for giving people the power to make up their own mind" (Chengappa & Agarwal, 1994, pp. 50-52). It is important not to underestimate the power of this appeal if one is to avoid getting lost in the hopeless scenario of a middle class consumerist culture. The Indian press, largely a bourgeois institution, in spite of its biases continues to be a pillar in the Indian democracy. Murdoch in the same interview said that he would not take over Indian newspapers that although "good are very political" (p. 28).

Therefore, any analysis of the privatization of television is necessarily a complex one and must deal with both the external pressures of the world economy as well as the historical role of the state in controlling media programming and its subsequent rejection by popular opinion that cuts across class. It is significant that in the current euphoria over third-world markets it is the middle class that is the star consumer. Yet, the middle-class support to privatization of television cannot simply be explained away by a desire for consumer goods, but has to be seen in the context of the state's continuation of monopoly over public broadcasting. This is the radical impulse that can be the basis for negotiating for more democratic programming, at least the setting up of local-access channels as in the United States and creating forums for discussion of government policy and activities by politically independent groups in the country. Programs such as "Aapke Adalat" provide opportunities for viewers to create spaces within the overall thrust of globalization that is taking shape on Indian television, but cannot be substitutes for an organized, open space for debate by all sectors of Indian society, especially the voiceless.

REFERENCES

Agha, Z. (1994, April 15). The opposition: Damning Dunkel. *India Today*, pp. 27-30.

Audience Research Unit, Doordarshan Kendra. (1985). *Television in India*. New Delhi: Author.

Berbergolu, B. (Ed.). (1992). *Class, state and development in India*. New Delhi: Sage.

Chander, R., & Karnik, K. (1976). Planning for satellite broadcasting: The Indian instructional television experiment. In UNESCO (Ed.), *Reports and papers on communications* (No. 78). Paris: UNESCO.

Chengappa, R., & Agarwal, M. (1994, February 28). Rupert Murdoch: I am an Opportunist. *India Today*, pp. 50-52.

Cherian, V.K. (1994, June 14). Satellite TV: A boom for entertainment industry. *The Hindu*, p. 4.

Contractor, N. S., Singhal, A., & Rogers, E. (1986). *Satellite television and development in India: A utopian, dystopian, neutral and contingency view of a communication technology.* Paper presented at the IAMCR, New Delhi.

Davies, S. (1994, January 3). Star TV takes half of Indian programmes. *Multichannel news* (Lexis Nexis), p. 36.

Deenadayal, M. (1994, July). I & B Expenditures pegged at Rs. 349 crore. *Screen* (Bombay), p. 35.

Duggal, K. S. (1980). *What ails Indian broadcasting?* New Delhi: Marwah.

The emerging middle class: The good life, getting and spending. (1994). *Business Week,* [Special Issue], p. 181.

External debt: Long and short of it. (1989). *Economic and Political Weekly,* 24, 26-29

Foreign media ban continues in India. (1994, December 8). United Press International (Lexis Nexis).

Going to the IMF. Dr. Ashok Mitra on its economics and politics. (1991, July 20 - August 2). *Frontline.*

Government of India, Ministry of Information and Broadcasting. (1982-83). *Annual report.* New Delhi: Publications Division.

Indian Middle Class. (1994, June). *Business India,* p. 56.

International Marketing Data and Statistics (1994). Chicago: London & Euromonitor International Inc.

It's the real thing for MTV India. (1994, December 12-18). *Variety,* p. 51.

Marich, R. (1993, November 10). Asian Pacific region riches in emerging cable markets. *Hollywood Reporter.*

Offe, C. (1984). *Contradictions of the welfare state.* Hutchinson: London.

Palmer, R. (1994, September 5-11). Dear diaries wooing doubting Asia adverts. *Variety.*

Pendakur, M. (1988). Mass media during the 1975 national emergency in India. *Canadian Journal of Communication, 13*(4), 32-48.

Pendakur, M. (1991). A political economy of television: State, class and corporate confluence in India. In G. Sussman & J. A. Lent (Eds.), *Transnational communications: Wiring the Third World* (pp. 234-262). London: Sage.

Pendakur, M. (1994, August 7). *Field notes on ethnography of TV audiences.* Karnataka: Host.

Petras, J. (1994). Cultural imperialism in late 20th century. *Economic and Political Weekly, 29*(32), 2070-2073.

Rajgopal, A. (1993). The rise of national programming: The case of Indian television. *Media, Culture & Society, 1,* 91-111.

Raliman, M. (1992, November 15). The new TV super bazaar now at your fingertips. *India Today,* p. 23.

Rich north, hungry south. (1994, October 1-7). *Economist,* p. 15-16.

Robins, K. (1989). Global times. *Marxism Today,* pp. 20-27.

Sengupta, J. (1994, July 17-23). The Indian report card. *Sunday,* pp. 62-63.

Shah, N., & Gandhi, N. (1991). *Issues of state: Theory and practice in the contemporary women's movement in India.* Delhi: Kali For Women.

Sinclair, J. (1987). *Images incorporated: Advertising as industry and ideology.* London: Croom Helm.

Singh, R. (1990). *Of marxism and Indian politics.* Delhi: Ajanta Publications.

Sinha, D. (1994). Media tycoon as development guru. *Economic and Political Weekly, 29*(10), 531-532.

Chapter 10

The Evolution of China's Media Function During the 1980s: A New Model in a New Era?

Junhao Hong

The issue of communication and development has been discussed for more than three decades. In many third-world countries, communication was expected "to convey useful information from government programs to their intended audiences, in order to persuade them to plan their family size, educate their children, adopt improved health practices, follow better nutritional practices, and raise their productivity and income" (Rogers, 1973, p. vii). Like other nations, China has also regarded communication as "fundamental to all social processes" (Schramm, 1964, p. 44) and is one of those countries that have derived its communication and media practices from the modernization theories adopted by many scholars in the 1960s and 1970s (Lerner, 1958; Pool, 1973; Rogers, 1973; Schramm, 1964).

Although this dominant paradigm of mainly one-way communication flow did not lead to widespread development in most third-world nations, the Chinese experience is often cited as an example in which it has been more successfully applied. According to UNESCO, the Chinese model is being introduced to some other developing countries ("China's development plan," 1991). However, the Chinese experience suggests that communication alone cannot bring about social change, but rather that communication can function well for development under the appropriate political, economic, and cultural conditions. It is thus instructive to consider the context of Chinese media practices and to ponder their relevance for others wishing to use communications media in development projects. Such an investigation also has wider theoretical implications for the continued viability of the modernization theory that underpins Chinese media practices.

In the past few years, evidence of changes throughout the communist world has been plentiful. As Baum (1991) states, these developments have represented significant changes of kind, rather than mere variations on old, familiar totalitarian themes. This is also the case for China. During the last 15 years or so, China has undertaken a nationwide mobilization for development, known as large-scale reform (Harding, 1986). In support of the wide-ranging project of reform, the nation's media have changed drastically. The media institutions/information systems have been used extensively and effectively to propagate, support, promote, and consolidate the reform (Hong, 1993).

Among China's media, television has grown most rapidly and become a dominant medium in terms of popularity and powerfulness ("China's television," 1993; "Broadcasting industry," 1993; Song, 1985; Zhou, 1988; Zhuang, 1984). Television plays a particularly significant role in the daily lives of the Chinese, because the Chinese are home-oriented due to their traditional way of life. They do not frequent theaters, concerts halls, pubs or parties. Instead, they spend most of their spare time watching television, especially the people in the rural areas (Li, 1991). Capitalizing on this, the Chinese authorities use television heavily to serve their development plan. As Lull (1991) described, "endorsed by the Deng Xiaoping regime as a 'bridge' between government and the people, television became at once the official mouthpiece of the Communist Party and the most popular form of entertainment for Chinese people" (p. 1). The years following the Cultural Revolution (1966-1976) have seen the arrival of television as part of China's effort to "modernize" and "open up" to the West.

It is true that, as Lee commented as early as 1979, the lessons that third-world nations can learn from China are obviously controversial and range from total admiration to total rejection (Lee, 1979). However, no one would deny that, for whatever reasons and purposes, China's mass media/information system did experience major changes in the past decade. Taking television as a case, this chapter examines the evolution of China's mass media/information system during the country's reform period in the 1980s. The changes in the function of the media institutions/information system from pure political propaganda to a multipurposed social development tool are discussed. The questions include: What changes have occurred in China's mass media/information system during the reform period in the 1980s? What were the major factors causing the changes? What effects have the changes produced? And, what are the future trends? Although the study primarily focuses on the media, the nation's political, economic, and social contexts, which played important roles in the process of the media evolution, are also analyzed.

NEW POLICIES AND THE RAPID GROWTH OF MEDIA

After the Cultural Revolution, China embarked on a massive development effort toward industry, agriculture, science and technology, and defense modernization (known as the Four Modernizations) to construct anew the material and spiritual culture (also called the Two Civilizations) of the country. All these projects were based on knowledge and electronics (Ganley & Ganley, 1989; Ming, 1987). The changes in economy and politics also brought about many consequences for the nation's media, television, in particular. The 1980s in China represented what Womark called the "third wave" of electronic media development, a period when nearly every family bought a TV set—a phenomenon similar to what happened in the United States during the 1950s (Lull, 1991).

Aiming at realizing the four modernization's and building the two civilizations, three new policies were issued and implemented. The most well-known new policy was the open policy, in which China pledged to terminate its isolation from the rest of the world, open its door to other countries, and create a cooperative international environment for its economic development. The second policy was the decentralization policy, which meant that the central party leadership and government would give some freedom and power to regional and local governments. The third new policy was the pluralist policy, which implied that the party would relinquish monopolistic control over power and permit alternative ways to reach reform goals (Hong, 1993).

These new policies were real breakthroughs in the Chinese Communist Party's history. Many significant changes—economic, political, social, and cultural—resulted. The rapid growth of the mass media/information system was also caused by these policies. The three general policies led the Chinese authorities to ratify a number of specific policies designed to develop the country's mass media/information system and to create conditions for their expansion (Li, 1991). By the end of 1985, there were a total of 2,327 newspapers in China, 65% of them opened after 1980. From 1980 to 1985, a new newspaper was published at least every two days (Reng, 1987).

Similar conditions were also present in the development of television. The features accompanying the swift growth of television were twofold. First, there were increases in the amount of television stations, production capacity, technology advancement, broadcasting hours, TV sets, transmission scale, and audience size. Second, there were improvements in programming format and content. In the 1950s, China only had two TV stations, Beijing TV and Shanghai TV, and it took the country 20 years to add 28 more. But during the reform period of the 1980s, the number of program-originating TV stations proliferated from 52 in 1983 to 422 in 1988. By 1992, a total of more than 600 programming-originating TV stations were in operation. As a result of the decentralization policy, a four-level TV system—national, provincial, regional, and local—was been formulated ("China becomes," 1992; *Radio and television information*, 1989; Zhuang, 1984). Table 10.1 shows the growth of China's television stations from the 1950s to the 1990s.

Besides terrestrial broadcasting, China also launched its first telecommunications satellite in 1970 and developed its first ground-receiving station in 1972. In 1984, China launched its first experimental television communication satellite. The satellites, together with more than 41,000 ground relay installations, have brought TV programs to even the country's most remote and mountainous areas, such as Tibet and Xinjiang. Because of the widespread network of television broadcasting, by 1993, 81.3% of China's total population received television broadcasts, compared to less than 50% in the 1970s (Li, 1991; "China's television," 1993; Wang, 1988).

While importing advanced television equipment and facilities from Japan, West Germany and the United States, made possible because of the open policy, China also quickly developed its own communication technology during the reform period. By the early 1990s, 90% of the country's TV transmission facilities were made by China itself ("China speeds up," 1991). The technological advancement remarkably enhanced TV production capabilities. For example, in the 1950s, only two TV plays were produced per year; in the 1960s and 1970s, fewer than a dozen plays were made annually, but during the reform period production proliferated swiftly: in 1988, 800 TV plays were produced; in 1990, the number jumped to 1,500. Dramatically in 1992, 5,000 TV plays were produced ("Changes in TV play," 1988; "China becomes," 1992; "TV plays," 1991).

Nevertheless, the most significant change is the explosion of TV set ownership, symbolizing the public's increased access to the mass media/information system. In 1960, there was one TV set per 70,000 people. Ten years later, it was one per 16,400. By 1980, the ratio changed to one set per 280 people. However, in 1988, it became one set per 7.5 people nationwide. This represented a 35 fold increase in less than 10 years. Moreover, by 1992,

Table 10.1. Television Stations in China (1958-1995).

Year	TV Station
1958	2
1968	23
1978	30
1988	422
1993	614
1994	682
1995	980

the ratio became one set for only four people. The percentages of Chinese households owning a TV set in 1978, 1987, and 1990 was 2%, 48%, and 70%, respectively. As early as 1986, 95% of all urban families owned at least one TV set. According to Qin (1993), China's output of TV sets increased 55.4 times from 1978 to 1992. By 1993, China had 230 million TV sets, which had surpassed the U.S. total of 200 million sets, becoming the country with the largest number of TV sets in the world ("China becomes," 1992; "China's television," 1993; "Progress over," 1989).

Another rapid growth area was in the production and distribution of color TV. In 1978, there was less than one color TV set for every 100 urban families—only 0.59 color TV sets per 100 households. During the reform period, the number increased 100 times to become, by the end of the 1980s, 59.04 sets for every 100 urban families. This occurred despite the fact that the price of one color TV set could equal a year's wage for workers ("Changes in living," 1991).

The effectiveness of communication is first determined by how many people can be reached by the information senders. The previously mentioned rapid growth of different aspects of television has brought about a steep increase in the size of TV audiences. By the end of the 1980s, the estimated viewers equalled about 80% of China's total 1.1 billion population—900 million (Chen & Er, 1989). The huge number of viewers, relatively easy access, and advanced communication technology have made television an effective instrument for reaching the massive Chinese population. These are the main reasons the Chinese authorities identified television as their most important communication vehicle for conducting political propaganda and as a vital tool for pursuing economic development. Table 10.2 shows the changes in China's TV viewers in the past two decades.

THE UNCHANGED NATURE OF MEDIA:
A VEHICLE FOR PROPAGANDA

Although the rapid growth of China's mass media/information system has boosted the government's ability to inform, educate, and entertain people, it should be stressed that the fundamental role of media, even during the reform period in the 1980s, has remained unchanged; their most important function is still as a vehicle for propaganda (Chu, 1986). Specifically, the first priority of media has always been to propagate the party's guidelines and policies. As the authorities have repeatedly claimed, the media are "the mouthpiece of the government and the Communist Party" (Peng, 1987, p. 23). Under this principle, the first task of the media has always been to channel the population into the Party's political orientations.

Table 10.2. TV Audience in China (1975-1995).

Year	Viewers (million)
1975	18
1976	34
1977	47
1978	80
1979	120
1980	210
1981	270
1982	340
1983	400
1984	470
1985	540
1986	580
1987	590
1988	600
1989	650
1990	700
1991	750
1992	800
1993	900
1994	900
1995	1,020

Over the past decade or so, television, as well as all other Chinese media institutions, mainly conducted two propaganda campaigns. The first was to propagate the four modernization's and two civilizations. The authorities emphasized that all media's most important role was to be a loyal and effective vehicle to help realize the party's goals and to make the government's corresponding policies known to everyone. This requirement was clearly stated in a speech of Wu Lenxi, former Minister of Radio-TV-Film: "[Radio and television] must function to propagate the Party line, its principles and policies, and serve the main Party objectives of the time. It should voluntarily keep in line with the Central Party Committee politically and avoid deviating from it" (Chang, 1989, p. 164).

According to this doctrine, the three main categories of TV programs—news, education, and entertainment—should inform, educate, and entertain, respectively. They should make their first priority the diffusion, explanation and interpretation of "the Party's general task and objectives for the new historical era" (*The work of the ministry of radio*, 1984, p. 13). In other words, all TV programs as well as all other media/information content should be the Party's vehicle to propagate the Party's goals. This should not be a short-term function, but a permanent one. In 1985, Hu Yaobang, the former General Secretary of the Chinese Communist Party, stressed this viewpoint once again when he said, "No matter how many reforms are introduced, the nature of the Party's journalism cannot be changed" ("Hu Yaobang," 1985, p. 1). In 1992, Jiang Zeming, the current General Secretary, reaffirmed this stance at the 14th National Congress of the Chinese Communist Party. He emphasized that China's reform, including its media reform, must be implemented under the leadership of the Party because the reform "is not intended to change the nature of our socialist system but to improve and develop it" (Jiang, 1992, p. 10).

In order to guarantee that the four modernization's and two civilizations are achieved, four cardinal principles were erected: adherence to Marxism-Leninism and Mao Zedong Thought, the proletarian dictatorship, the socialist road, and the Party leadership (Wang, 1989). The Party emphasized that the four basic principles are the bedrock upon which the reform campaign must rest (Wiedeman, 1986). Thus, to diffuse, explain, and interpret the four fundamental principles was the Chinese media's second major task, and the four cardinal principles were the basic rules for the media's daily operation.

NEW MEDIA FUNCTIONS: A MULTI-PURPOSE TOOL FOR SOCIAL DEVELOPMENT

In addition to achieving these goals, China's mass media/information system has been used during the reform period as a tool for social development. Specifically, media/information were used to mobilize the population for economic development, political advancement, and technological innovation, as well as to assist in solving practical short-term problems. To succeed in a large-scale development project, a major priority is to raise the level of social and political consciousness of people because development goals acquire significance only in the context of a developed and motivated consciousness (Jayaweera, 1988; Midgley, 1986). During the reform period of the 1980s, China's media institutions or information systems, TV news programs in particular, were chosen by authorities to be the main instrument to raise the public's consciousness of the Party's goals and government policies. As a result, the content, structure, format, technology, and quantity of TV news programs were changed substantially (Hong, 1991).

For a long time, China's TV news coverage, like the country's other news reporting, was narrow and limited. There was no such thing as "pure information"—everything contained clear political messages (Lee, 1979). Television news programs were more like a political course than a news program (Y. Zhang, 1986). As MacFarquhar (1986) explains, the Party put emphasis on the supremacy of politics in all things. News reporting was therefore not based on objective facts, but on the intention and will of the authorities. This functioned as a self-serving ideological straitjacket (Chu, 1978). Consequently, the major part of news programs was the simulcasts of Party instructions, and the rest usually introduced the accomplishments of advanced workers, peasants, and soldiers (Yu, 1986). The images monopolizing TV news programs were primarily of two types: officials addressing various meetings, or people working in different scenes. As for China's international television news, as Chu (1978) states, it was essentially an extension of the domestic news. The selection of international news was centered around China and its relationships with other countries. They were chosen not for their inherent information value, but more for China's need of ideological indoctrination. Given this orientation of news programming, viewers quickly became tired of the format and seldom watched. Obviously, this did not help Chinese authorities achieve their purposes.

During the 1980s, television news programming broadly expanded its coverage. Economic reporting gradually became the staple of the news program and eventually occupied the most prominent position. From 1978 to 1992, China's gross domestic product (GDP) increased from 358.8 billion Chinese yuan to 2,402 billion yuan, a rise of 233% calculated in terms of comparable prices (Qin, 1993). Many of the Party's and government's newly issued economic policies, decisions, trends, experiences, and problems with the ongoing reforms, and both positive and negative examples of economic development projects, were often reflected on the screen. Through reports, commentaries, and panel discussions, the restructured TV news program promoted the public's awareness of the reform's current situations, progress, problems, and long-term goals (Shi & Zhang, 1990).

Besides the expansion of economic coverage, reporting of cultural affairs, various social activities, science and technology, education and sports, and family life also appeared on television news (Si, 1987). Moreover, as a breakthrough, news stories regarding the outside world, mainly the West, also entered the long-time isolated country. Thus, the multidimensional expansion of news coverage made TV news programs both a popular and effective channel to convey the top's intentions to the bottom and to deliver up-to-date information to the public, despite the fact that the information was still selective, filtered, and controlled.

Due to these changes, the TV news program became more watchable and useful to the public. The changes in the ratings were an indication. For instance, in a 1984 survey shortly after the expansion of economic reporting, 51% of the respondents chose economic reporting as their favorite news item (*China Journalism Yearbook 1983*, 1984). One interesting and significant change came from rural viewers. Traditionally, news programs interested very few farmers. However because the reform from the "big-pot system" (everyone gets the same no matter how much he or she does) to the "responsibility system" (one only gets what s/he makes), millions of Chinese farmers now turn to news programs for stories concerning economic policies, development directions and guidelines, production improvements and technological innovations, as well as market information (Shi & Zhang, 1990). In the survey mentioned earlier, 58.4% of the farmers liked economic reporting, showing an even higher percentage than the 51% of the general viewers reporting that they found such programs enjoyable (*China Journalism Yearbook 1983*, 1984). Some farmers even bought video cameras and VCRs to record and exchange economic information ("Elder farmer," 1992).

As many scholars have pointed out, to mobilize the masses in China is to mobilize the peasants because peasants represent more than 80% of the country's 1.1 billion population. In addition to their huge number, the peasants are important because they comprise the basic economic infrastructure, produce the major part of the GNP, and support the country's living. However, the peasants have traditionally been poorly organized and received little education. Mao Zedong, the founder and late Chairman of the Chinese Communist Party, clearly saw the importance of mobilizing the huge body of peasants, but was also keenly aware of the difficulties in doing so. Throughout his life, Mao's efforts centered around the farmers. He was successful most of the time. Since Mao's death in the late 1970s, China's reformers led by Deng Xiaoping were also successful in using the mass media/information system, particularly television, to raise the consciousness of the country and its 900 million peasants.

REDUCING KNOWLEDGE GAPS THROUGH EASY ACCESS TO PUBLIC TV EDUCATION

Although many factors contribute to producing knowledge gaps, the chief one may be the difference in education. As Schramm (1964) states, any social change in the direction of modernization requires an education program. To reduce knowledge gaps through education is therefore crucial because it is one of the preconditions for reducing behavior gaps. Realizing the importance as well as the difficulty of reducing knowledge gaps, especially among hundreds of million of peasants, the Chinese authorities made great efforts and invested a tremendous sum of money building an electronic public education network to fulfill this objective. Television education proved the most fruitful of all media efforts at education and directly facilitated the largest education campaign in the nation (Terrell, 1986; S. Zhang, 1986).

Television education in China was first experimented with in the early 1960s, but its growth was stunted during the Cultural Revolution (Shi & Zhang, 1990). Since the 1970s, the country developed its space technology rapidly. In less than two decades, the nation has launched nearly 40 satellites of various types, becoming a world leader in the field ("China launches," 1990; "China's television," 1990; "Software error," 1994). Although these applied satellites were mostly used to facilitate telecommunications services, they were also used for educational purposes, mainly in the rural areas. The swift development in this aspect greatly assisted the popular use of satellites to promote public education. Television thus became an extremely important supplement to public education.

In 1986, China aired its first TV education program on a specialized channel. In 1987, the State Education Commission established the China Educational TV Station (CETV). In 1988, the second specialized educational TV channel was put in use. Since then, more rigorous progress has ensued, and the largest satellite TV educational network in the world has been formed in the country. By 1992, China had constructed a comprehensive web consisting of more than 1,000 educational TV stations and transmission stations, 6,100 ground satellite stations, and more than 53,000 video centers (Feng, 1994). Besides, the nation opened a number of television universities. For instance, using three channels, which cumulatively transmit 30 hours of programming a day, China's Central Television University broadcasts education programs via satellite to the whole nation ("A rapid growth," 1990). Currently, around 60 specially designed education programs are transmitted to train teachers, give continuing education, and provide youth with practical or professional skills. Now, every province and major city has its own television university, airing more specific, purpose-oriented, education programs to the public (*China Education Encyclopaedia 1949-1981*, 1982; Feng, 1994).

The most significant result of the rapidly expanded public television education was the increase in receivers. From 1985 to 1989, 20 million people, mostly in rural areas, received TV education. In recent years, 3 million people registered in television universities annually. From 1986 to 1990, 1.2 million students graduated from TV universities. This number accounted for 37% of the country's total university graduates in the same period. From 1986 to 1991, after receiving a public TV education, 6.5 million people in rural areas became professionals, working as leaders in administrative or technological positions in their hometowns. For example, from 1990 to 1992, nearly 2 million farmers in the Chende Region of Hebei Province were trained by TV education, and 4,000 of them obtained technician licenses. Presently, it is estimated that there are more than 30 million viewers of educational programs (Feng, 1994; "4,000 farmers," 1992; "The great achievements," 1991; "Ten years," 1989).

The reduction of illiteracy was another important aim of the TV public education campaign. China was a country of high illiteracy. However, through a variety of means, including extensive use of public TV education, the nation managed to eliminate illiteracy. From the founding of the People's Republic China in 1949 to the end of the Cultural Revolution in 1976, a total of 11.5 million people became literate, an average of 0.4 million a year. From 1977 to 1981, 2.6 million people became literate, an average of 0.65 million a year. But in 1991 and 1992, an annual average over 5 million individuals became literate, hitting an historical record (*China Encyclopaedia Yearbook1982*, 1983; Cui,

1993). According to Cui (1993), thanks to sustained efforts over the last 40 years, China's illiteracy rate declined to 15.88% from 80%. In the past few years, the provinces of Sichuan, Shandong, Jilin, Hunan, Guizhou, and Heilongjiang, and Xinjiang Uygur Autonomous Region have received international anti-illiteracy prizes from UNESCO for their outstanding endeavors (Cui, 1993).

Public TV education has been used fruitfully. Not only has it provided hundreds of millions of less educated people with easy access to up-to-date knowledge and skills and broadened their visions, but, more importantly, it has also made them more organized. Education has not only reduced the knowledge gaps among the people, but has also made it easier to mobilize the less organized groups. This step was very important to China because the nation's development project is operating on a large scale, involves a huge population, and lasts for a long time. For example, a nation-wide and decade-long anti-illiteracy campaign has therefore been set by the authorities. It aims at dropping the illiteracy rate to at least 10% by the year 2000 to keep up with international literacy levels. The level among the 15-40 age group should be down to 5% or lower. Meanwhile, by late 1995, 70% of China's more than 2,000 counties will have set up educational TV stations. Before the year 2000, two more transmission devices will be added to the educational network to enable broadcasting of four channels, providing a total of 70 hours a day. In addition, the Chinese Academy of Sciences seeks to systematically use television to popularize science (Cui, 1993; Feng, 1994; Wei, 1993).

PROVIDING PARTICIPATION OPPORTUNITIES VIA TWO-WAY COMMUNICATION PROGRAMS

According to Schramm (1964), the communication tasks behind social change and national development include three "musts": (a) the populace must have information about national development; (b) the needed skills must be taught; and (c) last, but maybe most importantly, there must be opportunities to participate. During the 1980s, the Chinese authorities began to pay attention to providing the people with participation opportunities, although the opportunities were still very controlled and limited.

Although raising consciousness and reducing knowledge gaps may create the necessary conditions for behavior changes, these conditions may not be sufficient for receivers to act. One of the reasons is that these two things normally are done through the top-down approach and still resemble a one-way communication model. They may neither hit the target exactly, nor really meet people's needs appropriately. Another reason is that one-way communication not only lacks feedback from the receivers, thus reducing the effectiveness of communication, but it fails to involve receivers in the process, and thereby making them passive and not action-oriented.

Compared to other media, television can play a more efficient and effective role for providing people with opportunities to participate in development projects. Getting viewers to appear on television, either as panel members or interviewees, not only provides some people with opportunities for direct participation, it also gives people more opportunities for indirect participation. Taking the advantage of the rapid development of television and the drastic increase of viewers, a number of programs have adopted forms of interactive, two-way communication strategies to encourage the public to participate in political, economic, and social activities. As Goulet (1989) put it, "different kinds of development require different forms of participation" (p. 167). During the reform period of the 1980s, China opened several kinds of TV programs based on a two-way communication model. Among them at least two are worth noting: panel discussions and telephone inquiries and opinions from viewers.

Panel Discussions and Telephone Inquiries

Because of long-time political restrictions, the media were like a "forbidden city" to ordinary Chinese people. The media did not adopt the format of public discussion, nor did they invite ordinary people to voice their opinions about the Party's guidelines and government policies on the air. Even in the 1980s, halfway through the reform period, political deliberation and decision making had virtually nothing to do with ordinary people (Li, 1991). In recent years, this situation has changed to a certain degree. Television at all levels—central, provincial, regional, and community—opened panel discussion programs. Viewers appeared on the screen to discuss the Party's decisions and government policies concerning economic development plans, marketing and pricing, future strategies for education, as well as cultural affairs, such as whether China should shut its door when confronting the massive importation of foreign TV programs (Hong & Cuthbert, 1991).

What was historically significant was that, very often, opinions were quite critical; facing hundreds of million of viewers, Party and government officials were sharply questioned by panelists or calling viewers. Compared to the fact that the Chinese mass media were never willing to publish any news items that might embarrass the Party and government, this was really unprecedented (Chang, 1989). Although not all the opinions from the audience were accepted, this activity did help the "top level" to be more people-oriented when making policies, adjusting directions, and considering alternatives. Also, by participating, the audience now shares some common interests with the policymakers, becoming part of the project and thus acting more positively (Lerner, 1958). In the late 1980s, when China's reform was in full swing, some local officials were even asked to make public speeches during elections. Prior to the 1980s, the public could know nothing about the leaders until the officials' appointments were announced. Now, ordinary people got involved in political activities as well as economic development.

Opinions From Viewers

In addition to panel discussions and telephone inquiries, opinions from viewers also began to be broadcast by most of China's TV stations. Using different names such as *Letters from the Audience* and *Viewer's Forum*, those programs were specially designed to make the audience's opinions known to the public by interviewing members of the audience on camera or airing their letters. This format allowed the "bottom level" to use media to communicate with each other as well as with the "top level."

One of the pioneers was Shanghai Television (STV), China's second largest TV station with 100 million potential viewers. In 1982, STV set up a program entitled *From Our Viewers*. At first, it broadcast only once a week for just five minutes. The content of the program was the viewers' opinions on some "nonsensitive" topics. However, this was the first time that ordinary people had a media forum to express their feelings and complaints ranging from housing problems to TV programs (Dong, 1988). Like similar programs in many other countries, viewers were encouraged to write, and their letters were usually read during a following program, thus bringing problems to the notice of the authorities (Katz & Wedell, 1977). As soon as this program appeared, it immediately became a hit. Although the show was short and the subjects limited, it was the most popular program at that time. By the end of the 1980s, it had been expanded to a half-hour prime-time show in response to the audience's strong petition. Furthermore, topics were broadened, ranging from economic concerns to political issues.

This type of program was not only used to expose the problems ordinary people had with reform, but was also used to publicize the viewers' reactions to the Party's guidelines and government policies. For example, TV reporters and editors sometimes conducted investigative reporting using information provided by the viewers to expose a case further and bring public opinion to bear on the problems involved. Problems could be either practical or policy-related. When a problem was solved, a followup story and responses from both the audience and authorities were delivered to the public. Although this format, a large number of people participated in a two-way communication process. Though it is hard to precisely evaluate the effectiveness of these viewer-centered programs, this kind of program does appear to be workable. In the past few years, letters and phone calls from the public increased substantially at almost every TV station across the country.

One important feature of the China case is that the three approaches— raising consciousness, reducing knowledge gaps, and providing participation opportunities—not only functioned in an integrated way, but also affected each other very much. For instance, the easier the public's access to media, the higher the probabilities of dialogue and participation; the better the dialogue, the more useful the access to media and the greater the impact of participation; and the more and better the participation, the more the probabilities of occurrence of dialogue and access (Beltran, 1980). Although the examples used thus far in this discussion suggest the benefits of the programs for the viewers, in fact, the authorities benefited much more from it. The Party and government have gained considerable political advantages from opening up their agenda and plans to the public through the mass media/information system. In doing so the authorities got an opportunity to explain their policies as well as to be informed of how policies operated in practice, what problems were encountered, and what opinions and suggestions people had to offer.

THE DUAL EFFECT OF THE MEDIA'S NEW FUNCTION

Any medium, when used as an authoritarian institution, has the power to serve the political and economic interests of the rulers by creating a narrow agenda and monopolizing opinions. However, even if television seemed to be a very effective communications medium for the perpetuation of autocratic rule in the restrictive environment of China, it still presented "a multiplicity of meanings rather than a monolithic dominant view" (Newcomb & Hirsch, 1987, p. 62). It is because the power of television rests not only in its ability to influence people by exposing them to particular ideas, thereby serving the interests of those who control programming, but also in the personal evaluations, interpretations, and uses of program content that are made by viewers and the ways audience-initiated actions engage and transform political, economic, and cultural realities. As Lull (1991) commented, "programs can never foster a single understanding or response on the part of the audience" (p. 214). How viewers interpret television's messages does not simply reflect the aims of the producers or the senders, and the apparent implications of programs do not necessarily reveal the meanings that audiences take away from viewing.

This was true to China's experience. The changes in television caused dual effects: Some were expected by the authorities, some were not anticipated. As a result, progress and problems came hand in hand. Raising consciousness, reducing knowledge gaps, and encouraging participation have not only promoted economic development and social changes, but also produced some danger to the authorities—the "bottom-level" people began to demand more than before. Probably, the first side-effect was that the country's ordinary people became unsatisfied with their lives. As Lull wrote:

> Television has become the main reference point which Chinese people use to compare and evaluate their own national status, a development that has inspired viewers to dream of a better future while at the same time they have become frustrated and angered by the barriers that stand in the way. Television has irreversibly altered the consciousness of the Chinese public. (p. 170)

Moreover, the three approaches led people to become more politically as well as economically aware. This consequently made them want to be more involved in "decision making," if not "power sharing," although more or less the two are interrelated. This political effect of the media's new function as a "mind opener" was more apparent in the countries that were politically closed and isolated from the outside world. Certainly, China is one of those countries that has been radically undermined by television in recent years. As Wicke (1991) put it, the shocking dissolution of communism in Eastern and Central European countries, particularly former East Germany, was directly traceable to a cultural upheaval that resulted in part from Western television. The difference between China's case and that of Eastern European countries is that, whereas the European communist-bloc nations were intruded on by Western television, the television signals that opened the Chinese audience's political mind were transmitted by the nation's own ideological apparatus.

Nevertheless, it should be emphasized that it is not because the Chinese authorities failed to foresee media's dual effect to inspire resistance to official ideologies, but because they failed to prevent that dual effect. The extensive use of the mass media/information system in implementing the three new policies— the open policy, decentralization policy, and pluralism policy—for the four modernization's and the two civilizations campaign, perhaps more than anything else, has also greatly raised viewers' consciousness of freedom and democracy, especially among the younger generation. The authority of the Party and government, which had never been challenged before, has now been strongly challenged. One of the most unexpected (although not so surprising) results was the student pro-democracy movement in 1989, which the Chinese authorities could not tolerate, as it was a threat to its control over ideas (Appadurai, 1990).

Another example of the government's loosening grip on the ideological contours of the public was apparent in its response to the television series *River Elegy*—first highly praised, then banned, and finally meeting with severe criticism. *River Elegy* is a six-part TV documentary series that appeared in 1988 on China Central Television Station (CCTV), the country's official and only national TV network with 800 million regular viewers. The program was shown and highly praised by the authorities during the first few weeks, it was then banned from being rerun on TV or distributed on videotapes. The assault culminated in the series being heavily criticized. The main content of the documentary is a narration of China's 5,000 years of history, with a focus on modern times. The chief point of the program is that traditional culture is a heavy burden, hindering the nation from becoming modernized like western industrial countries. The series claims that some of China's most revered symbols, such as the Yellow River, the Great Wall, the dragon, and Confucianism, actually represent the nation's backwardness and passivity, not its greatness. The documentary argues that what caused the country to fall behind advanced nations was a persistent inward orientation, a fixation on the land, which led to isolation from the rest of the world (Lull, 1991). The program suggests that China should abandon its traditional culture's negative aspects and absorb the West's positive aspects.

At first, the authorities thought the program was good material to raise the audience's consciousness while mobilizing them to pursue the modernization campaign. After all, the themes of the program were consonant with attempts to construct a public culture supportive of science and technology. As such, the documentary was approved and broadcast in prime time. The series was very well received, drawing an enormous, adoring audience. Many wrote to CCTV to ask for a rebroadcast. *River Elegy* was therefore shown again and regarded as a milestone in Chinese television programming.

Nevertheless, soon after the airing, the hardliners of the Party felt the strong side-effect of the documentary: It not only raised the audience's consciousness of China's economic backwardness, but also stimulated their awareness of political backwardness in terms of the nation's social system and ideological restrictions. Because the Chinese Communist Party's control over the country is essentially based on the principles of the traditional culture, the authorities realized that the criticism along with the demand for abandoning the traditional culture would eventually affect their ruling position. It was therefore no surprise that, not long after the series was treated as a masterpiece even by the authorities themselves, *River Elegy* was banned both on television and on video. Moreover, since the 1989 Tiananmen Event, the series was frequently blamed for helping stir up the unrest, giving theoretical and emotional preparation for the turmoil and rebellion. The writers, producers, and directors of the documentary were severely condemned for intentionally setting out to use television to transmit subversive ideology. The authors were searched for across the country as "most wanted criminals" for committing "anti-revolutionary propaganda crimes." Some of the program makers were eventually forced to flee China.

The impact of *River Elegy* was so strong that authorities tried to use another carefully designed television series to counteract the influence. In the wake of the 1989 military crackdown, under the instruction from the Party's topmost leadership, CCTV produced another TV documentary series entitled *One Hundred Mistakes of River Elegy*. This series was designed to refute every major claim or criticism that had been made in *River Elegy*. Unfortunately, as Lull (1991) observes, the remedial program may have actually extended the influence of the original by calling attention to *River Elegy* once again.

CONCLUSION

The authorities have tested both the great power and the great danger of the media. As an old Chinese saying goes: "Gentle water contains great powerfulness as well as great danger; no matter how heavy a ship is, the water makes it float, yet no matter how big, the water can also make it sink." Perhaps the student pro-democracy movement would not have developed without television and *River Elegy*. The tiny screen may be capable of mobilizing 1 billion people to pursue great achievements, but it could also be capable of stirring the masses to cause chaos. Not surprisingly, when the student pro-democracy movement occurred, one of the first actions taken by the authorities was to shut down television transmissions to the outside world and clear out all content related to the event in domestic television broadcasting. This was not an invention of the Chinese government, but a common practice of authoritarian regimes. As Goulet (1989) sharply remarked:

> Most national development strategies can tolerate considerable participation in micro arenas, provided it poses no threat to the rules of the game operative in macro arenas; thus a highly dictatorial and technocratic development pattern may allow considerable participation at local, problem solving levels. (p. 168)

After learning a lesson from the student pro-democracy movement, the Party and government resumed their tight control over the media. Although reform is said to be continuing, it appears to be proceeding in a more cautious manner. Once again, the authorities claim that the mass media of a socialist country must not allow the expression of opinions contrary to the Communist Party's principles and political standpoint (Yan, 1991). Politically and ideologically, the Chinese authorities are now controlling the media more tightly than before. As Lull (1991) observed, some steps were taken to exercise greater control over media since the period of martial law in 1989.

Despite the unsettling effects of China's reform, it is unlikely that the mass media/information system can return to being a pure Party mouthpiece again. As remarked by Cohen (1987), there are good reasons to believe it is impossible for the country to turn back the clock and revive previously discarded techniques of ideological exhortation. Furthermore, as Baum (1991) stated, "Globalized markets, information flows, and cries for popular empowerment have already conspired to render autarky, self-reliance, and Neo-Maoist ideological mobilization obsolete;" what the Chinese authorities want to do is to try "to shift that country from a typical Soviet-style command economy to a typical East Asian type of economic miracle" (p. 186). As Sun (1994) states, they have been trying to find a path that combines entrepreneurial flexibility with political stability. These comments suggest that standards for media and culture loosen when the economy is going well, but that crackdowns in culture and politics are again instigated once the economy stumbles (Lull, 1991). The Party's two national campaigns against "spiritual pollution" and "bourgeois liberalization" during the 1980s, allegedly from the West, are examples of such variable politics.

As China entered the 1990s it substantially widened its door to the outside world and quickened the pace of reform. However, it appears that authorities may have loosened controls over companies a lot, but not as much over citizens; over prices, but not as much over the press (Kristof, 1992). Thus, as an overall conclusion, we might venture the thought that, in the near future, more changes in the media's practice may be expected, but few changes in the media's fundamental nature are forthcoming.

REFERENCES

Appadurai, A. (1990). Disjuncture and difference in the global cultural economy. In M. Featherstone (Ed.), *Global culture: Nationalism, globalization and modernity* (pp. 295-310). London: Sage.

Baum, R. (Ed.). (1991). *Reform and reaction in post-Mao China: The road to Tiananmen.* London: Routledge.

Beltran, L. (1980) A farewell to Aristotle: Horizontal communication. *Communication, 5,* 5-41.

Chang, W. (1989). *Mass media in China: The history and the future.* Ames: Iowa State University.

Chen, C., & Er, M. (Eds.). (1989). *A perspective study of media effects in China.* Shengyang, China: Shengyang Publishing.

Hu Yaobang on the Party's Journalism. (1985, April 15). *China Daily,* p. 1.

China Education Encyclopedia 1949-1981. (1982). Beijing: China Encyclopedic Publishing House.

China Encyclopedia Yearbook 1982. (1983). Beijing: China Encyclopedic Publishing House.

China Journalism Yearbook 1983. (1984). Beijing: People's Daily Publishing House.

Chu, L. (1978). Flow of international news on China's television. *Asian Messinger, 3*(2), 38-42.

Chu, L. (1986). Revolution becomes evolution: China's communication across 30 years. *Media Development,* No. 1.

Cohen, B. (1987, April 13). Interview. *Television/Radio Age,* pp. 38-39.

Cui, L. (1993, December 20-26). Goal for 2000: Aiming to reduce illiteracy to five percent or below. *Beijing Review,* No. 51.

Dong, M. (1988). Being a proxy of the audience. *Radio and Television Research* (Shanghai, China), No. 3, 13-16.

Feng, J. (1994, April 25-May 1). *Satellite TV education network.* Beijing Review, No. 17.

Ganley, O., & Ganley, G. (1989). *To inform or to control?* (2nd ed.). Norwood, NJ: Ablex.

Goulet, D. (1989). Participation in development: New avenues. *World Development, 17*(2), 165-178.

Harding, H. (1986). Political development in post-Mao China. In A. Barnett & R. Clough (Eds.), *Modernizing China: Post-Mao reform and development* (pp. 13-38). Boulder, CO: Westview.

Hong, J. (1991). Changes in China's TV news program in the 1980s. *Media Asia, 18*(2), 109-115.

Hong, J. (1993). China's TV program imports 1958-1988: Towards the internationalization of television? *Gazette, 52,* 1-23.

Hong, J. (1994). CNN over the Great Wall: Transnational media in China. *Media information Australia,* No. 71, 60-69.

Hong, J., & Cuthbert, M. (1991). Media reform in China since 1978: Background factors, problems and future trends. *Gazette, 47,* 141-158.

Jayaweera, N. (1988, July) *Four experiences in people's communication.* Paper presented at the Assembly of the International Association for Mass Communication Research (IAMCR). Barcelona, Spain.

Jiang, Z. (1992, October 14-20). Accelerating the reform, the opening to the outside world and the drive for modernization, so as to achieve greater successes in building socialism with Chinese characteristics. *Beijing Review* No. 42, 1-14.

Katz, E., & Wedell, G. (1977). *Broadcasting in the Third World: Promise and performance.* Cambridge, MA: Harvard University Press.

Kristof, N. (1992, October 19). Chinese Communism's secret aim: Capitalism. *The New York Times,* p. 1.

Lee, C.C. (1979). *Media imperialism reconsidered: The homogenizing of television culture.* Beverly Hills, CA: Sage.

Lerner, D. (1958). *The passing of traditional society: Modernizing the Middle East.* New York: Free Press.

Li, X. (1991). The Chinese television system and television news. *The China Quarterly,* No. 126, 341-356.

Lull, J. (1991). *China turned on: Television, reform, and resistance.* London: Routledge.

MacFarquhar, R. (Ed.). (1986). *China under Mao: Politics takes command.* Boston: MIT Press.

Midgley, J. (1986). Community participation: History, concepts, and controversies. In J. Midgley (Ed.), *Participation, social development and the state* (pp. 126-154). London: Methuen.

Ming, A. (1987, July). *China's mass communication: For the two civilizations—some aspects of the transformation of the mass communication system in China.* Paper presented at the Annual Conference on International Communication, Spain.

Newcomb, H., & Hirsch, P. (1987). Television as culture forum. In H. Newcomb (Ed.), *Television: The critical view* (pp. 23-48). New York: Oxford University.

Peng, Z. (1987). Speech at the forum of Beijing journalists. In H. Xiaoguang (Ed.), *News and legislation* (pp. 1-3). Beijing: CCTV Publishing House.

Changes in TV play production. (1989, September 14). *People's Daily,* p. 4.

Progress over the past 40 years in China. (1989, October 2). *People's Daily,* p. 3.

Ten years of China's radio and television university. (1989, October 24). *People's Daily,* p. 4.

China launches satellites for other countries. (1990, February 7). *People's Daily*, p. 7.

A rapid growth of TV education. (1990, February 14). *People's Daily*, p. 1.

China's television reaches a new level. (1990, July 19). *People's Daily*, p. 1.

TV plays show a rapid increase. (1991, October 9). *People's Daily*, p.8.

Changes in living standard. (1991, October 12). *People's Daily*, p. 4.

China's development plan introduced to the world. (1991, October 29). *People's Daily*, p. 4.

China speeds up in building radio and TV facilities. (1991, October 26). *People's Daily*, p. 3.

The great achievements of the rural development plan. (1991, October 31). *People's Daily*, p. 4.

China becomes a TV giant. (1992, November 20). *People's Daily*, p. 3.

Elder farmer uses video camera for production. (1992, December 22). *People's Daily,* p. 8.

4,000 farmers receive technician licenses. (1992, December 22). *People's Daily*, p. 3.

China's television develops rapidly. (1993, August 30). *People's Daily*, p. 1

Broadcasting industry expands unprecedentedly. (1993, October 21). *People's Daily*, p. 3.

Pool, I. (1973). Communication in totalitarian society. In I. Pool & W. Schramm (Eds.), *Handbook of communication* (pp. 275-292). Chicago: Rand-McNally.

Qin, H. (1993, October 25-31). China: 15 years of reform. *Beijing Review,* No. 43, 20-23.

Radio and television information. (1989). Shanghai Radio & Television Institute, China.

Reng, Z. (1987). How many newspapers are there in China? *Shanghai Journal of Journalism*, No. 10, 10.

Rogers, E. (1973, August). *Communication for development in China and India.* Paper presented at East-West Institute, Hawaii.

Schramm, W. (1964). *Mass communication in national development.* Stanford, CA: Stanford University Press.

Shi, H., & Zhang, Y. (1990) Communication and development in China. In F. Casmir (Ed.), *Communication in development* (pp. 98-110). Norwood, NJ: Ablex.

Si, T. (1987). *Theory of radio and television.* Shanghai: Fudan University Press.

Song, S. (1985). TV grabs masses in China. *Media development*, No. 1.

Sun, L. (1994, May 28). Renewal of China's trade status could open 'historic opportunity'. *Washington Post Electronic Service.*

Terrell, R. (1986). Modernization and the media in China. *Media Development,* No. 1, 4-7.

Software error caused crash of India's most powerful rocket. (1994, January 3). *UPI.*

Wang, R. (1988). Major developments in Chinese telecommunications: An assessment. *International Communication Bulletin, 23*, 3-4.

Wang, Z. (1989, May). New developments in the Chinese mass media. *The Democratic Journalist,* 18-20.

Wei, L. (1993, December 13-9). TV Popularizes Science. *Beijing Review*, p. 29.

Wicke, P. (1991). The role of rock music in the political disintegration of East Germany. In J. Lull (Ed.), *Popular music and communication* (Rev. ed., pp. 131-+150). Newbury Park, CA: Sage.

Wiedeman, K. (1986). China in the vanguard of a new socialism. *Asian survey, xxvi*(7), 774-92.

The work of Ministry of Radio and TV in 1984 and the propaganda work requirement in 1985. (1984). China: Radio-TV-Film Ministry of China.

Yan, H. (1991). *Understanding the political system of contemporary China.* Occasional paper published by Princeton Center for Modern China.

Yu, J. (1986). News reform in Shanghai television station. *Media Development,* No. 1, 20-22.

Zhang, S. (1986). Solving problems of national development through communication technology. *Media Development*, No. 1, 6-7.

Zhang, Y. (1986). On Shanghai TV's news program. *Radio and television research* (Shanghai, China), No. 5, 16-18.

Zhou, J. (1988). On the role of TV news programming. *Journal of Journalism* (Beijing, China), No. 1, 16-18.

Zhuang, C. (1984). *Chinese television.* Beijing: China Radio and Television.

Section III

Constituents of Civil Society: Media Freedom, New Technologies and the Role of the Church

Chapter 11

Broadcasting in Transition: Media Freedom Between Political Freedom and Economic Pressures in Eastern and Central Europe

Wolfgang Kleinwaechter

The transition of the broadcasting system was one of the key issues in the building of new democratic societies in Eastern and Central Europe after 1989. The media system in the socialist societies was an integrated part of the old power structure. With the disappearance of the communist state, a process of fundamental changes in the media started. Five years after the changes began, the media landscape in Eastern and Central Europe has totally changed. The old censorship has gone, but the new media freedoms are sandwiched between growing political and economic pressures.

Looking back to 1989, the five years of transition in broadcasting can be subdivided into four different stages. It started with an enthusiastic awakening of the new media freedoms, followed by a disillusionment in stage two. The third stage, in which broadcasting laws were drafted and debated by Parliaments, was overshadowed by a growing power struggle. Different political groups tried to get control over broadcasting and, in particular, over national television. Stage four brought the Eastern radio and television system back to "normality": political and legal disputes over the "frontiers" of the media freedoms, and struggle for economic survival, that comes with competing in a free broadcasting market for high viewing rates and conditioned by the process of integrating into transnational European broadcasting frameworks and structures.

Although all Eastern and Central European countries had more or less the same starting position—the burden of the inherited media system and the timing of the beginning of the changes—and followed the same line according to the previously mentioned four different stages, the speed of the transformation has been rather different from country to country. Some countries have reached the fourth stage, whereas others are lagging behind. As in policy and economy, so it is in the media field: The former uniform "Eastern Bloc" is no longer a block as it becomes more and more diversified.

STAGE ONE: THE SWEETNESS OF UNLIMITED FREEDOM

The call for media freedom was at the center of the "velvet" and "singing" revolutions from Warsaw to Sofia. The old media system, and in particular broadcasting, was state owned and under the control of the politburo of the Communist Party, in which journalists were seen as "Party workers" who had to instruct the "masses." There was no media legislation in these countries: Radio and television worked on the basis of Party directives. Personnel and program policy was decided by the central committee of the Party. As a rule, the director general of the national broadcasting company was a member of the central committee of the Communist Party.

The majority of the people in Eastern and Central Europe did not trust these radio and television stations. Acceptance of national media was very low (the viewing rates of the daily national news bulletin was sometimes below 5%). Foreign shortwave broadcasters such as the BBC or the Voice of America became the most reliable sources of information, not only about world affairs, but also about domestic issues. But regardless of this situation, when the political changes started in Eastern and Central Europe in the end of the 1980s, the democratic restructuring of the undemocratic media system did not begin from ground zero. Long before 1989, "information questions" were among the most discussed items in Eastern and Central Europe, both within and outside dissident circles.

The concept for a new media model went far beyond the wish to "reform" the existing media. It was basically determined by and aimed at a total denial of the "old system." These involved monopolistic state-owned media systems under Party control, with instrumentalized journalists and passive recipients as targets for a one-way flow of one-sided propaganda. New proposals were for the development of a pluralistic media system, which should be independent from the government and without any involvement of political parties. It was further suggested that journalists should have comprehensive rights for co- and self-determination and that the audience should actively participate. It was anticipated that this would result in a broad diversity of voices in interactive public debates on all issues of general interest. New democratic media, and in particular new broadcasting institutions, were seen as a "fourth estate," as important as a new Parliament, a new executive, and a new judiciary. The "emancipated citizen" was seen as the "key player" of a new media model.

The conceptual ideas for a new media system were rooted in classic Western media philosophy. They were inspired by the originators of the First Amendment to the U.S. Constitution and the founders of the BBC. The main legal sources for the concept were article 19 of the Universal Declaration on Human Rights (from 1948) and other international human rights documents adopted by the United Nations, UNESCO, the Council of Europe or the CSCE. Although, generally speaking, the "Western media model" provided the overall guideline for the process of change, there were also ambitions among the different dissident and reform groups to go even beyond the existing Western media systems. Many of the scholars who became a driving force in the first stage were critical not only of the socialist media system, but they also had some reservations concerning media practices in the West. Proposals were introduced that aimed to block negative developments, such as overcommercialization of the media and concentration of ownership. The individual was seen as the owner of the right to freedom of expression, of whom the media, free from governmental and commercial control, should serve. The "right to communicate," as an individual and collective human right that guarantees access and participation for everybody, should become the backbone of a new democratized media system.

This "participatory model" played a central role in the first stage of the discussions on new media legislation after 1989 because it was the most radical challenge to the old system. There was a broad consensus among all opposition parties, including the reformist wing of the old Communist Party, to replace the existing media system with a totally new one; one serving first and foremost the citizen. Within weeks after the collapse of communism, broadcasting began to change. New director generals, mainly from former dissident groups, took over national radio and television. For the first time the audience in the East could follow controversial political discussion in their national radio and television programs. Live coverage of Parliamentary debates got the highest viewer ratings. Censorship disappeared within days. New forms of investigative journalism were developed. An incredible diversity and variety of opinions could be found in the media. There were practically no barriers to the right to freedom of expression, and in particular journalists enjoyed the sweetness of the limitless new media freedoms. As a side effect, Western radio stations lost their audience in Eastern and Central Europe.

THE SECOND STAGE: GROWING DISILLUSIONMENT

The idealistic "participatory model" soon reached its frontiers. The new political forces rediscovered the power potential of the media. With the development of a free market society, economic pressure and financial restraints played an ever-increasing role. The practical life, with policy and economy in the center, defined the new boundaries for media freedoms.

After the first free elections, the original media consensus among the former opposition groups, united until 1989 in the struggle against communism, began to disappear. The new governments developed their own media concepts, which were very different from the idealistic participatory model. For the new power elites, more pragmatic politicians than visionary intellectuals, media freedoms were seen less in the context of the right to communicate and more as an instrument of power. Their understanding of the role of the media in society was defined not by theoretical textbooks on human rights but by practical experiences. For these groups, media, and in particular television, was first of all an instrument of power. Although the general concept was also based in liberal Western media theory, their approach to a new media policy was defined by a very simple and practical notion: In the old system it was "their" television, now it is "ours." 'They' were no longer legitimized to use the media because they were not elected in free elections, but "we" can legitimately use the media for the distribution of our "right ideas" because we were elected in free elections.

This inherited "structure of thinking," to see the media first and foremost as political instruments, serving the government, determined more and more the national media debates. The concrete changes in the broadcasting systems concentrated more on persons and programs instead of structures and mechanisms. For the new governments the most important questions became whether the director general of the national radio and television stations is on "our side." New ideas such as access or participatory rights were seen as disappearing props of a "revolutionary romanticism," critical television coverage of governmental actions was labeled a "dangerous effort to reestablish communism" and governmental guidance to radio and television was justified as needed to promote the "development of democracy and free market principles."

Another key factor involved the financing of broadcasting. The "participatory model" had no clear concept of how to finance radio and television. Nobody had developed a financial plan that would guarantee that the new public broadcasting stations could really become independent from governmental subsidies. Before 1989, broadcasting was financed both by license fees as well by state subsidies. The money was there; nobody asked where it came from. The license fees were mostly on a low level and did not really cover the costs—additional money came from the state budget or directly from the central committee of the Communist Party. After 1989, when these mechanism of subsidizing broadcasting disappeared, public radio and television were confronted with growing financial pressure. The national stations were overstaffed, equipped with old technology (which called for new expansive investment) and confronted with exploding program production costs. Although advertising had been introduced in all the countries since early 1990 (earlier in Hungary and Poland), the rising costs never were balanced by the new income. As such, the East European broadcasting stations remained highly dependent on state subsidies.

The new political and economic pressure introduced new boundaries for the exercise of media freedoms. Certainly, there was no reintroduction of direct censorship practices, and legally these freedoms were guaranteed in constitutions and laws like never before in the history of these countries. But the fear journalists had of loosing their jobs, and the financial limitations for expensive investigative journalism, reduced the practical exercise of media freedoms. This reinvented the "scissors in the head" mode of journalism and redefined the "real role" of the media in the society.

To take the example of Hungary: The government, which came into power in the first free elections in 1990, was not satisfied with the work of Hungarian Television (MTV) and its director general, Elmar Hankis, a famous intellectual from the dissident movement. In 1991, the Parliament stopped the transfer of several million Forints to the budget of MTV. In 1992, Prime Minister Antall decided to recall Hankis, although he failed to reach the legally needed confirmation of president Gîncz for the removal. Nevertheless, after one year of political pressure, Hankiss resigned in January 1993. One year later, in Spring 1994, more than 100 critical radio journalists were fired before the elections on May 1994. Regardless of the guaranteed media freedoms in the constitution, political and economic pressure interfered with the daily lives of journalists. As an irony of life the government coalition lost the elections.

In this stage, the calls for "legal protection" of the new freedoms, for the elaboration of a media law, and, more specifically, for a broadcasting law got high priority on the political agenda. In all Eastern and Central European countries the work on drafts for media bills started immediately after the beginning of the political changes. Media legislation was seen as a needed instrument to block any backlash and to guarantee the new media freedoms. But the drafting of media and/or broadcasting laws, after an enthusiastic beginning, became immediately subject to political power struggles between the government and the opposition in and outside the Parliament. First drafts, discussed in expert and Parliamentary commissions in early 1990, were postponed or rejected. No single broadcasting law was adopted until the end of 1991. The first new law was the Law on Radio and Television of the Czech and Slovak Federal Republics, adopted on October 31, 1991, followed by the Rumanian Law on Radio and Television Broadcasting in May 1992.

Progress in broadcasting legislation remained limited during the second stage. The first drafts, mainly inspired by the "participatory model," were no longer acceptable for the new ruling elites who had won Parliamentary majorities after the first free elections. Only in the Czech and Slovak Federal Republic did the adopted broadcasting laws (October 1991) reflect the spirit of the first stage. In Poland, all governments—Mazowiecki, Pawlak, Olszewski, and Bielecki—failed to bring the various drafts of the broadcasting law through the Parliamentary bodies and the office of the President. In Hungary, the constitutional provision that a media bill needs a two-thirds majority for adoption, produced a deadlock situation and blocked the law. In Bulgaria, a Temporary Statute for Radio and Television, which transferred the authority over the media from the Party to the Parliament in December 1990, was not transformed into a broadcasting law. And the Law on Radio and Television Broadcasting, which was adopted in Rumania in May 1991, did not include the basic elements of the participatory model, but had a lot of vague formulations, such as the prohibition against defaming the nation and its symbols, including the president of the republic. Obviously such formulations were wide open to subjective interpretations by the government.

The early expectations that a new media system, independent from state power, and serving first and foremost the "emancipated citizen," remained a vision. The disillusion was paralleled by a tremendous shift in the priorities of the national media discussion from the human right to freedom of expression to the political and financial conditions for national radio and television. The audience, on the other hand, frustrated by endless and fruitless controversial political disputes and confronted with growing social and economic problems, also had other priorities. The burden of daily life became more important than the right to have access to the media and to participate in communication. A new wave of depoliticization was combined with a partial return of the old mistrust against national broadcasting. The discussion about media issues, once an open national debate, moved into very sophisticated expert circles in which mainly politicians redefined the new legal frameworks for national radio and television.

THE THIRD STAGE: POWER STRUGGLE
OVER THE CONTROL OF TELEVISION

All Eastern and Central European countries were—two or three years after the changes started—confronted with an intensive political "television war." After the first free elections, the new governments tried to keep or get back control over broadcasting. In particular television was seen as the most influential medium, as an instrument to promote governmental policy. The revolutionary romanticism in broadcasting, as it was pointed out by the former state secretary for information in the Prime Minister's office of the Czech Republic, Jiri Kovar, was seen as an "outdated concept" and a barrier to "governmental efficiency."

The power struggle circled around questions concerning which new model should be introduced to guard the new broadcasting system: On the one hand, all parties agreed to introduce media legislation compatible with "European standards." For example, all sides wanted to introduce a "dual system" (public plus private broadcasting). On the other hand, when it came to concrete details, there were no consensus. Individual Party interests, not national ones, dominated the media debate.

In Hungary, the parties of the government coalition and the opposition were unable to research a two-thirds majority compromise on a broadcasting law. When the draft was tabled for adoption in the Parliament at the end of 1992, it did not receive a single "yes" vote. The opposition abstained; the government voted against it.

In the Czech Republic, television became a central political issue after the split of the country. The independent Czech broadcasting bodies, established under the Federal Law on Radio and Television (in October 1991), became a target of growing governmental pressure after it made decisions (e.g., the licensing of the private NOVA TV) that were seen by the Klaus government as "wrong." The Annual Report of the Czech National Broadcasting Council for 1992 did not receive Parliamentary approval, and the chairman of the Council, the reformer Daniel Korte, was pushed to retire. The director general of the federal television, Kantourek, also a former dissident, lost his job after the federal television network was eliminated.

In the Slovak Republic, the Meciar government revised the federal broadcasting law and adopted a set of amendments that nearly totally revised the "participatory approach" of the Federal Law from October 1991. According to the amendments adopted in July 1993, the government could now hire and fire members of the three national broadcasting councils (public radio, public television, and licensing of private broadcasters). All that it would involve would be a simple majority in the Parliament at the request of 10% of its members. Critical television coverage of governmental policy was answered by public announcement of officials from the Ministry of Culture that the public Slovak radio and television, which is highly dependent on state subsidies, could also be reorganized as a state organ. In April 1994, five members of the Slovak Television Councils were fired because Parliament was unsatisfied with the television coverage of Parliamentary debates and governmental decisions.

In Bulgaria, each new prime minister fired the old director general for broadcasting and nominated a new one more favorable to the policy of the government. In Rumania, the national broadcasting system remained under strict control of the government, and the private sector remained rather dependent on agreements with the state-controlled radio and television stations.

In Poland, there was a three-year struggle over the broadcasting bill. In Fall 1991 a draft was adopted both by the Sejm and the Senate; President Walesa refused to sign the Bill. Only after another two years of complicated negotiations among the Sejm, the Senate, and the President could a compromise be reached that passed all stages and entered into force in March 1993.

The power struggle for television centered on the following four issues:

- the establishment of broadcasting authorities and advisory bodies;
- the nomination procedure for senior officials in radio and television;
- the procedures for licensing of private broadcasters; and
- the introduction of quota systems for domestic (and European) program production and foreign ownership in broadcasting.

Although the discussion was different from country to country, the arguments of the opposing groups, at least in the first three questions (councils, nomination procedures, and licensing policies), were more or less the same. On the one hand, the governmental representatives in the media law commissions were in favor of more politically oriented broadcasting councils, in which the government could have a decisive or at least most influential vote. They preferred a procedure for the nomination of the senior broadcasting officials in public radio and television, either by a vote with a simple majority in the Parliament or by a council friendly to the government. They also wanted to keep state control over the allocation of frequencies to private broadcasters. On the other hand, the opposition parties were in favor of independent broadcasting councils, composed of distinguished members of the public who would have no direct connections to political parties. They proposed that such independent councils should elect the senior broadcasting officials for a period that was longer than the interval between Parliamentary elections. They also proposed the establishment of independent broadcasting authorities for the management of the frequency spectrum.

Only on a limited number of questions, for instance, in the introduction of quota systems, could a compromise between government and opposition be reached. Evidently, a general "national consensus" on broadcasting failed. With some exceptions the adopted laws, the established procedures, and the composition of the new broadcasting authorities followed more or less the governmental proposals.

THE FOURTH STAGE: LEGAL DISPUTES
AND FINANCIAL BOTTLENECKS

By the end of 1993, the new legal framework for broadcasting in Eastern and Central Europe, with the mentioned differences in speed and design, had been more or less established. Media freedoms have been incorporated into the Constitutions. Broadcasting legislation has been adopted, with some exceptions. New broadcasting authorities have been created. State broadcasting institutions have been transformed into public corporations, or are on the way. Private broadcasting has been legalized, and for the most part, although more so in radio than in television, practiced. Efforts have been made to promote national broadcasting television production as well as international cooperation, particularly with European partners.

In Poland, the Broadcasting Act was adopted on December 29, 1992, and it entered into force on March 7, 1993. In the Czech and in the Slovak Republics, the Federal Law on Radio and Television, from October 1991, remained in force, but was substantially changed via the adoption of Amendments made by the two Parliaments (in the Czech Republic December 22, 1992, and in the Slovak Republic on July 14, 1993). In Rumania, the Law on Radio and Television Broadcasting was adopted on May 22, 1992. A second law that transformed the state broadcasting company into a public institution followed in Spring 1994. In Bulgaria, the Temporary Statute from December 1990 remained in force, and no special broadcasting law was adopted. In Hungary, the adoption of the broadcasting Bill failed on December 30, 1991. A new draft is under discussion after the elections of 1994, in which the new government coalition of three socialists and the liberals have a two-thirds majority.

In nearly all Eastern and Central European countries new broadcasting authorities have been established. In Poland, there is only one broadcasting authority. The new National Broadcasting Council is the highest body for radio and television in the country. It is composed of nine members. Four members are appointed by the Sejm, two by the Senate, and three by the President of the Republic. The President also has the right to appoint the chairman of the council. The council has far-reaching competencies. It is the highest authority for the new public Polish Radio and Polish Television companies. It is the licensing authority for private broadcasters, and it has the task of drawing up, in consultation with the Prime Minister, directions of state policy in matters of broadcasting (Article 6, paragraph 2.a).

In the Czech Republic, there are three councils. The National Council for Radio and Television is responsible for the licensing of private broadcasters. Both Czech public radio and Czech public television have their own councils. All three councils are composed of nine members elected by Parliament.

The situation in the Slovak Republic is similar. There are also three councils for public radio, public television, and private broadcasting. Each council has nine members, who are elected by the Parliament. As mentioned earlier, after the adoption of the amendments in July 1993, the nine members of each council are not only elected by the Parliament, but they can also be withdrawn by the Parliament by a simple majority at the request of 10% of its members.

In Rumania, the Law on Radio and Television Broadcasting established a National Council of Radio and Television. The Council has 11 members: 6 are nominated by the two chambers of the Parliament, 3 by the government, and 2 by the President of the Republic. According to article 72, paragraph 2 of the law, the council is responsible for the licensing of broadcasters.

In Bulgaria, the Standing Committee for Radio and Television, a Parliamentary body, is for the time being the highest broadcasting authority in the country. The Committee is responsible both for public/state broadcasting as well as for private broadcasting. There are no special regulations for the composition of the Standing Committee. Its recommendations have to be confirmed by the Parliament. The failure of the Hungarian broadcasting law has prevented the establishment of new broadcasting authorities, and the Radio and Television Act remains, for the time being, under the old regulations set up within the general constitutional framework.

A comparison of the councils shows the interrelationship between political power structures and the media. Indeed, after the adoption of the laws, their implementation remains a permanent political tug-of-war, particularly when the new broadcasting authorities do not fulfill the expectations of the government.

An interesting illustration is the political media development in the Republic of Poland, in which media legislation has reached European standards. In Poland, the new broadcasting authority was confronted with criticism by President Lech Walesa, who has the right to delegate three candidates to the council and to nominate the chairman. One of the first decisions of the council was to elect the new Director General for public television. The election of Mr. Walendszak, a former director of the private Polish satellite television service POLSAT, was attacked sharply by Walesa. Also the second decision, to give the first national private television license to POLSAT, was seen by Walesa as a big mistake. He removed the chairperson of the Council, Mr. Markeiwicz, and nominated Mr. Bender as his successor. The removal was seen by opponents as an illegal reaction because the law gives only the president the right to nominate the chairperson. There is nothing in the law concerning the removal of the chairperson. The case was brought before the Constitutional Court, which decided that the president has no right to remove the chairperson, but it did not call for a replacement of Mr. Markiewicz. Regardless of this decision, in Fall 1994, after the conflict surrounding the licensing of POLSAT, Walesa removed two other members, and after the resignation of Mr. Bender, he nominated Mr. Zaorski as the new chairperson of the broadcasting council. Zaorski has served from 1990 to 1993 as the director general of Polish Television under president Walesa.

This case is interesting for two reasons: First, it shows how intensive politicians try to influence media decisions and how limited is the independence of the media. Second, it shows how much progress has been made: The new broadcasting authorities develop their own policies, ignoring guidelines from the "top." And, in cases of conflict, independent courts make decisions that can and do go against the President of the Republic.

Although the political pressure against the media makes headlines, the economic pressure is less visible. The new public stations are confronted with a deep financial crisis. They have to reduce their programs. The privatization of the "second public channel" is under discussion in nearly all countries. The personnel has to be reduced. Independent, self-directed program production becomes rare. In competition with the new private sector, income from advertisements is dropping drastically. For example, in the Czech Republic, the rapid success of the new NOVA TV has put the future of the public sector in peril.

Yet, even the emerging private sector is economically still in troubled water. The licensing policies of the broadcasting authorities, particularly in the radio field, has produced tremendous competition among small advertising markets, which blocks the development of strong national private broadcasters and the production of high-quality programs. Against this background the call for "joint ventures" with strong foreign media giants is unavoidable. Cross-ownership, bringing newspapers, radio, and television stations under one private umbrella, is not yet excluded in the laws, and the danger that such conglomerates will reintroduce a monopolistic media situation cannot be excluded. Thus, the Eastern and Central European media landscape provides ripe terrain for the big transnational media corporations.

CONCLUSION

The five-year transitional period, and the development of a new legal framework for broadcasting in Eastern and Central Europe, can be described as an exciting and exhausting process that is producing a fascinating and frustrating "two step forwards and one step backwards" scenario. Compared with the aims and hopes at the beginning of the changes in late 1989, there were two steps forward. All countries, with some minor differences, now have a free broadcasting system, based on constitutional guarantees for the right to freedom of expression. Censorship is forbidden, private broadcasting is permitted and there is a growing media diversity and pluralism in radio and television.

On the other hand, the reinvention of stronger governmental linkages and growing commercialization represent steps backwards. The original ideal of broadcasting stations independent from both governmental and commercial control remains unfulfilled. It seems that the new broadcasting systems in the former East Bloc, confronted with the realities of daily life, now have the choice between domestic governmental control or foreign commercial control. For the time being it remains open whether there is a way between Szylla and Charibdis that will lead to a democratic broadcasting system, serving the communication rights of citizens in a civil society.

Chapter 12

Mexican NGO Computer Networking and Cross-Border Coalition Building

Howard H. Frederick

The growth of global interdependent communication relations has been greatly accelerated by the advent of decentralizing communication technologies such as computer networking. Global civil society, as represented by the NGO movements (nongovernmental organizations) now represents a force in international relations, one that circumvents the hegemony of markets and of governments.

This chapter reviews the role of computer communications technology in the emergence of "global civil society." It describes the rise of nongovernmental computer networks that connect social movements throughout the globe. It then focuses on a case study of Mexican nongovernmental computer networking during 1993-1994, a period of the debates on the North American Free Trade Agreement (NAFTA) and the Chiapas uprising of the Zapatista National Liberation Army. It concludes with a description of the current status of Mexican internetworking and prospects for the future.

COMPUTER NETWORKS AND GLOBAL CIVIL SOCIETY

Elsewhere I have described how the concept of "community" has changed in the information age. In the present era communications technologies have woven parts of the world together into an electronic web. No longer is community or dialogue restricted to a geographical place. Under such conditions, the traditional understanding of civil society as an imaginary philosophical and juridical space for private citizens to realize their interests free from government interference and market corruption is expanding beyond the boundaries of nation-states to assume global proportions. This corresponds to a view of electronic communication networks as producing forms of social organization—social networks, communications networks, and especially the emergence of multiorganizational networks—that allow people and groups to play an increasingly significant role in international relations as governmental and market hierarchies are eroded by the diffusion of power to smaller groups (Frederick, 1992a, 1993a, 1993b).

We now speak of the emergence of a global civil society, and that part of our collective lives, which is neither market nor government, is so often inundated by them. Still somewhat inarticulate and flexing its muscles, global civil society is best seen in the worldwide—NGO movements— nongovernmental organizations and citizens' advocacy groups uniting to fight planetary problems whose scale confounds local or even national solutions. From the industrial age to the present, mercantilist and power-political interests have pushed civil society to the margins. In many countries, civil society even lacks its own channels of communication. It is speechless and powerless, isolated behind the artifice of national boundaries, rarely able to reach out and gain strength in contact with counterparts around the world.

The development of new decentralizing communications technologies has vastly transformed the capacity of global civil society to build cross-border coalitions. They are decentralizing in the sense that they democratize information flow, break down hierarchies of power, and make communication from the top and bottom just as easy as from horizon to horizon. New communications technologies facilitate communication among and between national civil societies, especially within the fields of human rights, consumer protection, peace, gender equality, racial justice, and environmental protection. From the Earth Summit to GATT, from the United Nations General Assembly to the Commission on Human Rights, NGOs have become an important embodiment of this new force in international relations. Many people, organizations, and technologies are responsible for this development, but one organization, the Association for Progressive Communications (APC), has distinguished itself by specializing in the communication needs of the global NGO movements. This organization is also influencing the course of politics within North America (see Figure 12.1).

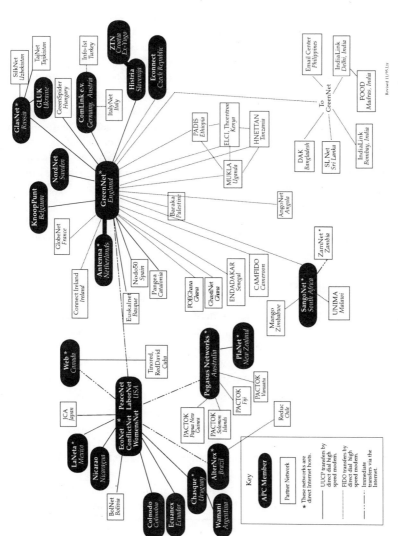

Figure 12.1. Map of the Association for Progressive Communications (APC)

Today there are APC partner networks in Brazil (serving South America), Uruguay (serving also Paraguay), Germany (serving German-speaking regions of Europe), Ecuador, Colombia, New Zealand, Russia (serving the Commonwealth of Independent States' countries), Ukraine, Great Britain (serving Europe, Africa, Asia, and the Middle East), Slovenia, Mexico, United States (serving also Japan and China), Nicaragua (serving Central America), Sweden (serving also Nordic and Baltic States), Australia (serving Pacific Islands and Southeast Asia), South Africa, Argentina, and Canada (serving also Cuba). There are partner systems in the Czech Republic, Ethiopia, India, Italy, Kenya, Papua New Guinea, Philippines, Senegal, Thailand, Uganda, Zambia, and Zimbabwe. The APC now even has a partner network in Cuba and can boast of providing the first free-flow of information between the United States and Cuba in over 30 years. Dozens of FidoNet systems (single-user bulletin board systems—BBS) connect with the APC through "gateways" located at main networks.[1]

The APC's largest computer is located in Silicon Valley, CA. Altogether, more than 22,000 subscribers (individuals and organizations) in 133 countries are fully interconnected through personal computers. These groups constitute a veritable honor role of NGOs and form the world's largest computer system dedicated to peace, social justice, human rights, and environmental preservation (see Table 12.1). The APC networks can now set up complete electronic mail and conferencing systems on small, inexpensive microcomputers for between $5,000 and $15,000 with software developed since 1984 and available to partner systems at no charge. Individual users make a local phone call to connect to their host machine, which stores mail and conference postings until contacted by a partner computer in the network, typically about every two hours. Aside from its low cost, this technological configuration is appropriate for countries whose telecommunications infrastructure is still poor. For example, the file transfer protocols used between the computers have a high level of resiliency to line noise and satellite delays, and if an interruption does occur, they are able to resume a transfer at the point the connection was interrupted. This is particularly important for transporting large binary files, when the chances of losing the connection over poor quality telephone lines is significant.

Within the APC, main nodes at London (GreenNet), Stockholm (NordNet), Toronto (Web), and San Francisco (IGC Networks) bring in the communication flow from regional nodes. Messages are then exchanged and distributed around the world so that a message from Australia can end up on a screen in Estonia in two to four hours. Messages can be sent through these

---

[1]There are small Fidonet systems connected to the APC in Angola, Austria, Bangladesh, Basque Country, Belgium, Cambodia, Cameroon, Chile, Cuba, Eritrea, Ethiopia, Fiji, France, Gambia, Ghana, Hungary, India (Delhi, Bombay), India (Madras), Indonesia, Ireland, Italy, Japan, Jordon, Kazakhstan, Kenya, Malawi, Malaysia, Morocco, Nigeria, Palestine, Papua New Guinea, Philippines, Romania, Senegal, Sierra Leone, Solomon Islands, Spain, Spain (Catalonia), Sri Lanka, Sudan, Tanzania, Tajikistan, Turkey, Uganda, Uzbekistan, Vanuatu, Western Samoa, Zambia, and Zimbabwe.

Table 12.1. APC Member Networks Address List (August 4, 1995).

(* These networks are direct Internet hosts.)
(+ These networks have WWW sites.)

AlterNex * +
  Rua Vicente de Souza, 29
  22251-070 Rio de Janeiro, Brazil
  Tel: +55 (21) 286-0348
  Fax: +55 (21) 286-0541
  Email: suporte@ax.apc.org
  wwwW: http://www.ax.apc.org

Antenna * +
  Box 1513
  NL-6501 Nijmegen, Netherlands
  Tel: +31 024 32-35-372
  Fax: +31 024 32-36-798
  Email: support@antenna.nl
  www: http://antenna.apc.org

Chasque *
  Casilla Correo 1539
  Montevideo 11000, Uruguay
  Tel: +598 (2) 496-192
  Fax: +598 (2) 419-222
  Email: apoyo@chasque.apc.org

ColNodo * +
  Avenida 39 No. 14-75
  Santafe de Bogota, Colombia
  Tel: 57-1-3381277
  Fax: 57-1-2861941
  Access numbers: 57-1-2871806 / 2324246
  Email: soporte@colnodo.apc.org
  www: http://www. colnodo.apc.org/colnodo/

ComLink e.V. * +
  An der Lutherkirche 6
  D-30167 Hannover, Germany
  Tel: +49 (511) 161 78 11 (Voice)
  Fax: +49 (511) 165 26 11
  Modems: +49 (511) 165 22 11 (5 lines)
  Email: support@oln.comlink.apc.org
  www: http://comlink.apc.org

Table 12.1. APC Member Networks Address List (August 4, 1995) (cont.).

Econnect * +
  Ceskomalinska 23
  Prague 6 ZIP CZ-160 00 Czech Republic
  Tel: +42 2 31-18-170, +42 2 24-31-17-80
  E-mail: support@ecn.cz
  www: http://www.ecn.cz

Ecuanex *
  Casilla 17-12-566
  Calle Ulpiano Paez # 118 y Av.Patria
  Edificio FLACSO 4to piso
  Quito,Ecuador
  Tel: +593 (2) 227-014 or 508-277
  Fax: +593 (2) 227-014
  E-mail: intercom@ecuanex.apc.org

GlasNet * +
  Ulitsa Sadovaya-Chernogryazskaya, 4, Suite 16a.
  107078 Moscow, Russia
  Tel: +7 (095) 207-0704
  Fax: +7 (095) 207-0889
  E-mail: support@glas.apc.org
  www: http://www.glas.apc.org

GLUK - GlasNet-Ukraine *
  14b Metrologicheskaya str.
  Kiev, 252143 Ukraine
  Tel: +7 (044) 266 9481
  Fax: +7 (044) 266 9475
  E-mail: support@gluk.apc.org

GreenNet * +
  393-395 City Road - 4th Floor
  London EC1V INE United Kingdom
  Tel: +44 1 (71) 713-1941
  Fax: +44 1 (71) 833-1169
  E-mail: support@gn.apc.org
  WWW: http://www.gn.apc.org

Histria & Zamir Transnational Net (ZTN) * +
HISTRIA, ABM d.o.o.
  Mestni trg 9
  61000 Ljubljana Slovenija
  Tel: +386 61 1263565, +386 61 1263576

Table 12.1. APC Member Networks Address List (August 4, 1995) (cont.).

Fax: +386 61 212989
Mtel (Hren): +386 61 609-615681
Email: Retina@KUD-FP.SI
www: http://www.kud-fp.si/retina

ZTN systems:
    ZAMIR-BG is in Belgrade at tel: +381 11 632 566.
    Voice support at tel: +381 11 635 813 / 626 623
    Email: support@ZAMIR-BG.ztn.apc.org
    ZAMIR-LJ is in Ljubljana at tel: +386 61 126 3281
    Email: support@ZAMIR-LJ.ztn.apc.org
    ZANA-PR is in Pristina at tel: +381 38 31276
    Voice support at tel: +381 38 31031 / 31036
    Email: support@ZANA-PR.ztn.apc.org
    ZAMIR-SA is in Sarajevo at tel: +387 71 444-200
    Voice support at tel: +387 71 444-337
    Email: support@ZAMIR-SA.ztn.apc.org
    ZAMIR-TZ is in Tuzla at tel: +387 75 239-146 (3 lines)
    Voice support at tel: +387 75 239-147
    Email: support@ZAMIR-TZ.ztn.apc.org
    ZAMIR-ZG is in Zagreb at tel: +385 41 423 044
    Voice support at tel: +385 41 426 849.
    Email: support@ZAMIR-ZG.ztn.apc.org

Knooppunt * +
    Snoekstraat 52
    B-9000 Gent Belgium
    Tel: +32 (9) 233 81 55
    Fax: +32 (9) 233 43 73
    Dialup lines: +32 (9) 234 1694, 234 1297, 224 04 54
    E-mail: infor@knooppunt.be
    support@knooppunt.be
    www: http://www.knooppunt.be/

LaNeta * +
    Alberto Zamora 126
    Col. del Carmen
    04000 Coyoacan D.F. Mexico
    Tel. (525) 554 1980
    Fax (525) 554 3159
    E-mail: soporte@laneta.apc.org
    WWW: http://www.laneta.apc.org

Table 12.1. APC Member Networks Address List (August 4, 1995) (cont.).

Nicarao * +
    Apardado 3156 Iglesia Carmen
    1 cuadra al lago
    Managua, Nicaragua
    Tel: +505 (2) 283-188/283-092
    Fax: +505 (2) 281-244
    Email: ayuda@nicarao.apc.org
    www: http://nicarao,apc.org.ni

NordNet * +
    Huvudskaersvaegen 13, nb
    S-12154 Johanneshov, Sweden
    Tel: +46 (8) 600 03 31
    Fax: +46 (8) 600 04 43
    E-mail: support@nn.apc.org
    www: http://nn.apc.org

PeaceNet/EcoNet/ConflictNet/LaborNet/WomensNet * +
Institute for Global Communications (IGC)
    18 De Boom Street
    San Francisco, CA 94107 USA
    Tel: +1 (415) 442-0220
    Fax: +1 (415) 546-1794
    E-mail: igc-info@igc.apc.org
    www: http://www.igc.apc.org

Pegasus Networks * +
    PO Box 3220
    South Brisbane QLD 4101 AUSTRALIA
    Tel: +61 7 3255 0255
    Fax: +61 7 3255 0555
    Email: pegasus@peg.apc.org
    www:http://www.peg.apc.org

PlaNet (NZ) * +
    78 Straven Rd
    Christchurch, Canterbury 8001 New Zealand
    Tel: +64 3 343-2633
    Email: support@planet.apc.org
    WWW: http://vesta.chch.planet.co.nz

SangoNet * Q
    P. O. Box 31
    13th floor Longsbank Building
    187 Bree Street

Table 12.1. APC Member Networks Address List (August 4, 1995) (cont.).

Johannesburg 2000 South Africa
Tel: +27 (11) 838-6944
Fax: +27 (11) 492 1058
E-mail: support@wn.apc.org
www: http://wn.apc.org/sangonet.html

Wamani * +
CCI
Talcahuano 325-3F
1013 Buenos Aires, Argentina
Tel: +54 (1) 382-6842
E-mail: apoyo@wamani.apc.org
www: http://www.wamani.apc.org

Web * +
NirvCentre
401 Richmond Street West, Suite 104
Toronto, Ontario M5V 3A8 Canada
Tel: +1 (416) 596-0212
Fax: +1 (416) 596-1374
E-mail: outreach@web.apc.org
WWW: http://www.web.apc.org

---

machines to outbound fax and telex machines, to commercial hosts such as Dialcom and GeoNet, and to academic networks such as Janet, BitNet, EARN, and Usenet/UUCP. The entire APC system is funnelled onto the Internet in Brazil, Russia, Ukraine, England, Sweden, the United States, Australia, New Zealand, South Africa, and Canada. The price is low by any standard; in the United States, hourly Internet connect charges range as low as $1 to $2 per hour, depending on the number of monthly connect hours. In Ecuador, Ukraine, Slovenja, and Mexico, the APC networks charge a monthly flat fee for unlimited usage.

In addition to e-mail, the APC networks also oversee about 950 electronic "conferences"—basically a collective mailbox open to all users—on subjects from AIDS to Zimbabwe. It is here that people can publicize events, prepare joint proposals, disseminate vital information, and find the latest data. APC conferences carry a number of important alternative news sources, including Inter Press Service (the Third World's largest news agency), Agencia Centroamericana de Noticias, Enfoprensa (Guatemala/Mexico), Noticias de Guatemala (Canada), Radio Havana Cuba, Africa Information Afrique (Zimbabwe), South Pacific Associated News Service (Australia), the United Nations Information Centre news service, Agencia Latinoamericana de

Información (Ecuador, in Spanish), New Liberation News Service (Cambridge, MA), Pacific News Service (San Francisco, CA), *The Nation* and *Mother Jones*, Public Radio News Service (Australia), and Report on the Americas (New York).

The first large-scale influence of these decentralizing technologies on international politics happened in 1989. When the Chinese government massacred its citizens near Tienanmen Square, Chinese students transmitted detailed, vivid reports instantly by fax, telephone, and computer networks to activists throughout the world. They organized protests, meetings, fund-raising events, speaking tours, and political appeals. Their impact was so immense and immediate that the Chinese government tried to cut telephone links to the exterior and started to monitor the Usenet computer conferences, in which much of this was taking place.[2]

Another example was the 1991 Gulf War, in which computer networks such as PeaceNet and its partner networks in the APC exploded with activity. Although mainstream channels of communication were blocked by Pentagon censorship, the APC networks were carrying accurate reports of the effects of the Gulf War on the Third World, Israel, and the Arab countries and news of the worldwide, antiwar movement. For a movement caught off-guard, amazingly smooth coordination took place rapidly across the country and the world. Competing groups agreed on common platforms, set synchronized action dates, and planned large-scale events across vast distances. Computerists seized the technology and made it work (Frederick, 1991a, 1991b, 1992b).

During the attempted coup in the Soviet Union in August 1990, the APC partners used telephone circuits to circumvent official control. Although the usual link with Moscow is over international phone lines, APC technicians also rigged a link over a more tortuous route. Soviet news dispatches gathered in Moscow and Leningrad were sent by local phone calls to the Baltic states, then to NordNet Sweden, and then to London-based GreenNet, which maintained an open link with the rest of the APC (O'Connor, 1991).

In 1992, the APC played a major role in providing communications services for environmentalists, NGOs and citizen activists before, during, and after the 1992 United Nations Conference on Environment at Development (UNCED) in Rio de Janeiro. The largest United Nations conference in history, UNCED was the first global gathering on the environment since 1972. It was also the first global summit to take place fully within the age of the NGO and computer technologies. Connected to the world through AlterNex, APC's Brazilian partner, the main objective was to create an "internationally interconnected electronic information exchange system."[3] APC maintained over 30 electronic conferences on UNCED documents, agendas, reports, discussion, and debate and even distributed Dian Da Zi Bao, or "electronic wall newspapers," from the conference. APC's information sharing allowed the

---

[2]The first notice of this phenomenon was detailed in Quarterman (1990).

[3]"ISP/Rio—a final report," Escrito 6:33 pm Sep 6, 1992 por cafonso em ax:en.unced.general.

Earth Summit process to be accessible to citizens around the world, thus providing broader citizen participation in a heads-of-state summit than was possible before. The Information Chapter of UNCED's Agenda 21, as well as the NGO Forum's Communication, Information, Media and Networking Treaty, demonstrated that networking and communication had become an integral part of environmental politics. The Communication, Information, Media and Networking Treaty began with the words: "The right to communicate freely is a basic human right and a necessity for sustainable development." More than half the signers were members of the APC Networks.[4]

At the United Nations Conference on Human Rights in June 1993, NGOs used computer networking facilities provided by the APC (Schneider, 1993). A laboratory of 40 PCs connected to the Internet allowed hundreds of NGOs to communicate with their home constituencies from Vienna, distribute their press releases and position papers online, and collect information needed for the human rights policy debates at the conference.

In 1995, APC's Women's Networking Support Program provided the Internet connections and electronic information services at the United Nations World Conference on Womens and the NGO Forum on Women in China. APC provided e-mail, electronic conferencing, databases, World Wide Web, information retrieval and dissemination of United Nations and NGO documents and other services free of charge. During the course of the conference, there were more than 100,000 visits to the World Wide Web page from Internet users around the world.

MEXICAN TELECOMMUNICATIONS
AND NGO COMPUTER NETWORKING

In this section I review case studies of how Mexican NGOs have taken the first steps to online organizing and coalition building. Later, I also examine the technological environment confronting them. How has NGO computer networking affected Mexican and North American politics? What practical applications have there been of this democratizing and decentralizing new communication medium? What NGO computing activities in Mexico indicate the validity of this chapter's hypothesis, that computer networks promote the emergence of national and transnational coalition networks?

North American NGOs come from different social, historical, and political traditions. They also face quite different national realities. Mexican NGOs have had difficulty solidifying their bases of support due to overt governmental pressure, a restrictive national political climate, and a lack of history of the nonprofit sector. Mexican NGOs also face tremendous political,

---

[4]"Earth Summit NGO Comm/Info Treaty," written by hfrederick in media.issues 4:22 pm Jul 27, 1992.

bureaucratic, and technological challenges in connecting their activities to the Internet. Worse, Mexican NGOs and other mass organizations have suffered a climate of government repression of their activities and a virtual blockade around their information dissemination activities.

Chiapas

One dynamic case in 1994 that demonstrated the impact of new computer technologies on hemispheric politics has been called "Zapatistas in Cyberspace."[5] In January 1994, the Zapatista National Liberation Army (EZLN) arose in revolt against the Mexican government in the southern state of Chiapas. This revolutionary action by peasants and Mexico's native population roused tremendous attention in the world's press and spurred human rights, indigenous rights, and other activist NGOs, not to mention journalists, to travel to Mexico City and Chiapas to observe the event.

The Zapatista Revolution also demonstrated the rise of the Mexican NGO computer network known as LaNeta (in colloquial Mexican, "the real story"), which originated most of this information. Originating on LaNeta and carried on computers around the world, NGOs linked up with local compatriot organizations to voice their recognition of the EZLN's demands, to press for a ceasefire, and to demand that the Mexican government negotiate with the EZLN and accede to democratic reforms (Martinez & Ronfeldt, 1994). For those who could not travel physically to Mexico, the entire Chiapas struggle was quickly taken into cyberspace. Within a few hours after the takeover of San Cristo'bal de las Casas by the Zapatistas on January 1, computer users around the world were actively reading the news of the uprising. By January 3, the subcomandante Marcos was online.[6] Dozens of official EZLN communiques were issued on the Internet, far easier for journalists to obtain than from any other source. Speculation abounded about exactly how these messages were transmitted: Word had it that the subcomandante Marcos carried a laptop! It is probable that official EZLN communications were written on diskettes, which were then carried down from the jungle camp to a BBS in southern Mexico.

Throughout the Net there were several rapidly updated sources of available information and discussion. These Listservs and Usenet newsgroups are still stored in various places on the Net and can be retrieved, either from archive listings or via a database search, for research and historical purposes. Best known is the Chiapas Gopher. The Applied Anthropology Computer Network established

---

[5]"Zapatistas in Cyberspace," posted by Harry Cleaver, Department of Economics, University of Texas at Austin, Austin, Texas 78712-1173. E-mail: hmcleave@ mundo.eco.utexas.edu in CHIAPAS-L List.

[6]"Zapatistas On-Line: Halleck," written 2:47 PM Oct 4, 1994 by nacla in cdp:nacla.report. Reprinted from NACLA Report on the Americas, Sept/Oct 1994. For subscription information, e-mail to nacla-info@igc.apc.org

ANTHAP Archives, an ftp/gopher site with an archive of "Chiapas-Zapatista News" in its computer at Oakland University, Rochester, MI. This archive contained materials (news stories, discussion, EZLN communiques) cross-posted and compiled from Mexico and throughout the world. The existing archive contains a vast body of material, especially from the January-March 1994 period.[7]

There were many other sites on the Internet that also focused on Chiapas. The Chiapas discussion list known as CHIAPAS-L, created in the wake of the uprising, was an unmoderated discussion in English and Spanish concerning the conflict in Chiapas and was used as an interactive forum by people around the world to discuss the status and implications of the EZLN revolt.[8] There were also two lists emphasizing indigenous peoples' aspects of the struggle: NATIVE-L (Aboriginal Peoples News and Information List) and NATCHAT (Aboriginal Peoples Discussion List), both part of the NATIVENET series of lists. These lists contained information and discussion (respectively) of struggle among a wide variety of indigenous peoples, including Chiapas.[9]

Another well-known list, CENTAM-L, for years the place in cyberspace for discussion and information on Central America, immediately began focusing on Chiapas.[10] MEXICO-L, the Mexico discussion list, covered everything about Mexico. Originating from Mexico, much of the discussion (but not all) is in Spanish.[11] One of the most widely followed lists on the Internet for progressive activists was ACTIV-L, the Activist Mailing List regularly posted news

---

[7]"Chiapas-Zapatista News" can be accessed via gopher to Michigan/Oakland University/Applied Anthropology Computer Network/Chiapas_news. The archive can also be accessed via ftp vela.acs.oakland.edu (anonymous login, then cd pub/anthap/ls). This material can also be accessed through UT-LANIC at gopher lanic.utexas.edu /Latin America/Mexico/Chiapas-Zapatista News.

[8]CHIAPAS-L: Chiapas Discussion. To subscribe send a message to <majordomo@profmexis.dgsca.unam.mx. Post messages to <chiapas- 1@ profmexis.dgsca.unam.mx. Put the word subscribe in the body of the message followed by your complete e-mail address. For more information contact the list owner, Arturo Grunstein , at grunst@profmexis.dgsca.unam.mx, and Nicole Wolf, at wolf@ profmexis.dgsca.unam.mx.[9]The native-l archives are maintained at Texas A&M University (listserv@ tamvm1.tamu.edu). Subscribe by sending the command "subscribe native-l (or natchat) your_name" to listserv@tamvm1.tamu.edu (leave "SUBJECT:" line empty). Parallel Usenet newsgroups are alt.native and <soc.culture.native.

[9]The native-1 archives are maintained at Texas A&M University (listserv@ tamvm1.tamu.edu). Subscribe by sending the command "subscribe native-1 (or natchat) your_name" to listerv@tamvm1.tamu.edu (leave "SUBJECT:" line empty). Parallel Usenet newsgroups are alt.native and <soc.culture.native.

[10]Send e-mail message to listserv@ubvm.cc.buffalo.edu. Post messages to centam-1@ubvm.cc.buffalo.edu.

[11]Subscribe by sending the command "subscribe list-name yourname" to majordomo@udlapvms.pue.udlap.mx (leave "SUBJECT:" line empty).

stories/analyses on the Zapatistas.[12] ACTIV-L's discussion group is also mirrored on the Usenet as the newsgroup misc.activism.progressive.

It is important to note that this kind of support by activist NGOs in response to the upheaval in Chiapas was not the first such instance. Previously, PeaceNet's subnetwork, known as the Central American Resource Network (CARNET), promoted North American support for the Sandinista revolution in Nicaragua. Now defunct, CARNET demonstrated that even in the early years of the computer revolution, solidarity communications could be carried out cheaply and reliably. In these and other cases around the world, NGOs make use of an expanding infrastructure of decentralized and autonomous computerized conferencing systems, electronic mail, fax machines, and telephone systems, as well as traditional face-to-face contacts, to communicate and coordinate among themselves. In the case of Chiapas, NGOs formed transnational, network-style coalitions to wage an impressive information-age "netwar" to constrain the Mexican government and indirectly support the rebels. Martinez and Ronfeldt (1994) argue that NGO computer activism altered the dynamics of the confrontation in Chiapas and helped convert a military confrontation into a political one. This activism also altered the context for decision making in Mexico City and helped propel the government to negotiate with the EZLN.

North American Free Trade Agreement (NAFTA)

Another well-known example of Mexican NGO networking was the debate over the North American Free Trade Agreement (NAFTA). In 1993, the NAFTA reform coalition used a new tool for organizing and influence, one that reinforced all the other strategies—computer networking. In this sense, the trinational coalition united in an electronic web of information sharing and communication. From grassroots groups in border towns to labor union headquarters in national capitals, the anti-NAFTA NGOs shared information, established mutual trust, and developed action strategies to carry out common goals.

NGO computer networking against the US-Canada Free Trade Agreement (FTA) began in 1987. One of the APC's most gifted technicians, Mike Jensen, has the distinction of posting the first public computer message about free trade. He opened a conference called web.freetrade on November 13, 1987 with these words: "This discussion area has been set up to examine the free trade issue. In particular, its impact on the environment and jobs will be important subtopics." Within minutes a Web user responded:

> Should be lots of interest. I'm taking part in an information booth type of thing for the public being staged in . . . St. Catharines. It is set up by the CAW. Getting lots of support from local politicians. John Turner may be there

---

[12]Subscribe by sending the command "subscribe activ-l" to listserv@ mizzou1.missouri.edu (leave "SUBJECT:" line empty). To get only the daily list, send the command "set activ-l index" to the same address.

tomorrow—Saturday. Had Jim Bradley talking about the environment and trade unionists talking about jobs. Jim Hasler.

web.freetrade grew to include megabytes of information focused on the US-Canadian Free Trade Agreement (FTA). Canadian and U.S. NGOs used this conference for sharing ideas and resources, soliciting feedback on position papers, and gaining a sense of community in an adverse atmosphere as they confronted the government and the marketplace.[13] With web.freetrade as an important precedent and model, U.S. and Canadian computerists helped jumpstart the new large-scale NAFTA reform coalition. Most prolific of the new breed of "keyboard warriors" against NAFTA was the Institute for Agriculture and Trade Policy (IATP—iatp@igc.apc.org), the Minneapolis-based NGO dedicated to creating environmentally and economically sustainable communities and regions through sound agriculture and trade policy.

IATP began online publication of gatt.news, which expanded eventually to become trade.news, an often-daily compilation of news and resources on GATT and NAFTA. IATP also published eai.news on the Enterprise of the Americas Initiative (EAI), President Bush's proposal to expand the proposed North American Free Trade Agreement (NAFTA) throughout Central and South America and the Caribbean.[14] IATP also moderated several important electronic conferences: trade.strategy, in which trade issues were discussed, events planned, and actions strategized; and trade.library, a conference repository of major trade-related documents, reports, fact lists, analyses, quote sheets, and reports.

The most significant Mexican NGO in this electronic coalition was the Red Mexicana de Acción Frente al Libre Comercio (RMALC), also known as the Mexican Free Trade Action Network (rmalc@igc.apc.org). RMALC was composed of labor, women, peasants, and environmentalists from Mexico City and northern regions where the maquiladoras operate. RMALC gained immeasurably from the news and information transmitted by IATP and other organizations. Because the Mexican government had virtual control over the media, information to affect the NAFTA had to come from the United States and Canada. Furthermore, RMALC provided the conduit from the Canadian and U.S. NGOs to the Mexican public.

---

[13]The major suppliers of information during the critical 1987-1989 period in the Free Trade Agreement (FTA) were Conservation Council New Brunswick (ccnb@web.apc.org), Canadian Environmental Law Association (cela@web.apc.org), Canadian Environment Network (cen@web.apc.org), Energy Probe (eprobe@web.apc.org), Society of Gaia Principles (gaia@web.apc.org), Ontario Public Interest Research Group (opirgo@web.apc.org, opirgont@web.apc.org, opirgw@web.apc.org) as well as Web Staffers Mike Jensen and Walter Roberson.

[14]eai.news covered CBI (Caribbean Basin Initiative), CARICOM (Antigua & Barbados, Bahamas, Belize, Dominica, Grenada, Guyana, Jamaica, Montserrat, St. Kitts-Nevis, St. Lucia, St. Vincent/Grenadines and Trinidad, and Tobago), MERCOSUR (Brazil, Argentina, Uruguay, and Paraguay), and the ANDEAN PACT (Colombia, Bolivia, Peru, and Ecuador).

Women's groups were very active in the on-line community fighting for reform of NAFTA. Mujer a Mujer [Woman to Woman], or MAM, based in Mexico City (mam@igc.apc.org), organized exchanges, workshops, tours, and retreats to promote strategic connections among grassroots and feminist organizations in North America. MAM discovered that it could not operate without electronic communications. For years MAM women depended on bi-monthly trips to the United States, where they would engage in marathon long-distance calls to organize events and keep in touch with key contacts. Using computer communications, MAM was in daily contact with other key players throughout the region (Waterman, 1992).

Drawing on their years-long experience networking on APC Network EcoNet, environmental organizations were very active online, from Friends of the Earth (foedc@igc.apc.org) and Earth Island Institute (earthisland@igc.apc.org), to the Environmental Defense Fund (edf@igc.apc.org), Environmental Health Coalition (dtakvorian@igc.apc.org), the Environment and Democracy Campaign (jmcalevey@igc.apc.org), the Natural Resources Defense Council (nrdc@igc.apc.org), and the Sierra Club (scdc1@igc.apc.org). One organization making special contributions to the online information base was Arizona Toxics Information (aztoxics@igc.apc.org), a nonprofit environmental advocacy and policy organization based in Bisbee, just north of the Arizona-Mexico border. Another important member of the online environmental coalition working against NAFTA was the Pesticide Action Network North America Regional Center (panna@igc.apc.org), one of a worldwide network of resource centers in over 60 countries organizing against the harmful uses of pesticides and toward safer alternatives.

Especially active during and after the NAFTA debate were unions and labor activists in Mexico and in the United States (Brenner, 1994). NAFTA spawned widespread international labor communication among the United States, Mexico, and Canada. A broad-based debate was generated, which helped create coalitions and alliances out of environmental, consumer, community, religious, and labor groups in the three countries. Burgeoning online communication enabled the exchange and sharing of ideas and strategies around free trade, environmental and worker rights, and possible alternatives. An interesting example of transborder solidarity by computer occurred on May 1, 1991, when an urgent action appeal was sent out through LaborNet (Brenner, 1994). The appeal described the abduction of Braulio Aguilar Reyes, the brother of one of the main leaders of several thousand irregular workers of the government oil company, PEMEX. After the closing of "Refineria 18 de marzo" at Atcapozalco—which had been heavily polluting the environment and had been subject to public pressure—regular and irregular workers were fired. Denied legally required severance pay, the fired irregular workers protested. Braulio's brother, Gustavo Aguilar Reyes, was one of their leaders. The Comisión Mexicana de Defensa y Promoción de los Derechos Humanos believed that Braulio's abduction was a consequence of his brother's political activity and asked receivers of the message to send requests for urgent action to other groups and unions, using PeaceNet, GeoNet, Web, or SoliNet, if accessible.[15]

One U.S. local union distinguished itself in online communication and cross-border solidarity work on free trade. St. Paul Minnesota's UAW Local 879 established the "MEXUSCAN" solidarity committee in their local group. During one of a burgeoning number of trinational labor conferences, auto workers from the United States, Mexico, and Canada planned one of the first trinational worker demonstrations of the NAFTA period. On January 8, 1991, workers in all three countries wore black ribbons bearing the name of Cleto Nigmo, commemorating the murder of the Mexican Ford worker in 1990. Such efforts were seen as helping union members to understand more clearly the connection between disappearing workers' rights and Ford's ability to freely invest money in low-wage areas and "to consider the long-range benefit of solidarity among all Ford workers" (Moody & McGinn, 1992, p. 30).

Of course, we know that despite weeks of intense lobbying, the U.S. House of Representatives voted in November 1993 to approve the North American Free Trade Agreement. The U.S. Senate approved the accord, and the Mexican Senate voted its approval of NAFTA the following week. As Canada had already ratified the agreement, implementation began as scheduled on January 1, 1994.

THE IMMIGRANT RIGHTS MOVEMENT

Spurred on by NAFTA, the Haitian refugee situation, and California's Proposition 187, in 1994 there emerged an active immigration rights network on the APC Networks that was trying to follow the model of the NAFTA reform computer networking movement. This development was especially significant within the context of the Immigration and Naturalization Service's own entrance onto the information superhighway.[16]

The National Network for Immigrant and Refugee Rights in Oakland, CA (nnirr@igc.apc.org) was among the first online organizations to raise issues that were taboo during the NAFTA debate, namely, international migration and labor mobility. In 1993, the online organizing effort was activated by IGC's news desk and National Network for Immigrant and Refugee Rights (NNIRR),

---

[15]jscott carnet.mexnews 10:32 am May 1, 1991.

[16]Using funding authorized by the September 1994 Crime Bill, a contract for more than $100 million for computer hardware was awarded C3 Incorporated/Telos Corporation to provide the computers necessary to modernize INS's operations. Called the Personal Workstation Acquisition Contract (PWAC), it is the single largest hardware contract ever awarded by INS and will provide up-to-date computers for INS offices throughout the world. A $300 million contract was awarded to EDS on August 30 by the Immigration Service to develop software and support services for the entire INS operations. "Crime Bill Accelerates INS onto InfoHighway," "FYI - INS On the Infohighway," Written 3:39 PM Sep 20, 1994 by ggundrey in cdp:pol.immigrate.

who posted its monthly newsletter. During the 1994 election campaign, California's Proposition 187 was the subject of intense Internet discussions. The 187 resist Gopher Server archived all discussion lists and linked users to immigration files at UCLA's LatinoNet and Berkeley's Economic Democracy Information Network (EDIN). It also gave official documents on Prop 187 and breakdowns in voting patterns by county and demographic groups.[17] An Immigrant Rights Urgent Response Network (URN) was organized to catalyze action on the issue. For example, URN mobilized a fax and e-mail protest to Immigration and Naturalization Service Commissioner Doris Meissner to end Operation Blockade, a Border Patrol action began in September 1993 on the El Paso/Ciudad Juarez border area.

One of the hottest topics on the immigrant rights networks was about how environmentalists are reacting to the immigration debate. The Conservation & Resource Studies Program at UC Berkeley (crsucb@igc.apc.org) attacked the Carrying Capacity Network (ccn@igc.apc.org) as a "gang of population bomb theorists . . . who prefer the rhetorical steamroller of population theories." These "Malthusians have decided to join the ranting of racists and nativists in the US, favouring anti-immigration policies."[18] The Ecology Center of Berkeley, CA issued on the Internet its Board statement "viewing with concern the recent trend within the mainstream environmental movement to argue for limitations on immigration into the United States, and particularly into California. . . . To that end, we encourage environmentalists concerned with human rights and justice issues to weigh carefully the complex issues involved in human migration before endorsing simplistic immigration curbs in the name of the environment."[19]

Another important Internet initiative within this effort was an electronic newsletter called Migration News, originating from the Department of Agricultural Economics, University of California, Davis (migrant@primal.ucdavis.edu). Migration News summarized key developments in immigration and integration issues each month. There were three versions: The paper copy is eight pages or about 6,000 words; the e-mail version is 10,000 to 12,000 words; and the gopher version is 12,000 to 15,000 words.[20]

---

[17]To connect to the 187 resist gopher, access it at: gopher garnet.berkeley.edu 1870. Or you can find it listed under California gophers in the "Mother Gopher" list at University of Minnesota.

[18]Topic: environmentalists bash immigrants!! Written 5:57 PM Dec 13, 1994 by crsucb in cdp:pol.immigrate

[19] /** pol.immigrate: 47.0 **/** Topic: Statement: Ecology & Immigration ** ** Written 8:43 AM Jan 20, 1994 by ecologycntr in cdp:pol.immigrate ** January 1994.

[20]Migration News July 1994 Written 6:56 AM Jul 6, 1994 by kmander in igc:trade.library From: migrant@primal.ucdavis.edu (Migrant News PLM) Date: Wed, 29 Jun 94 20:57:48 -0700.

Among the other innovators in the immigrant rights computer networking efforts were the Boston-based National Immigration Project of the National Lawyers Guild (nip@igc.apc.org), San Antonio's Refugee Aid Project (refugee@igc.apc.org), and the Tucson Ecumenical Council Legal Assistance for Central America (tecla@igc.apc.org). Academic interest was also apparent in the University of California, San Diego's Center for U.S.-Mexican Studies (usmexstudies@igc.apc.org), Tucson's Border Links publication (borderlinks@igc.apc.org), the well-known binational Mexico-U.S. Diálogos (dialogos@igc.apc.org), and the Seminario Permanente de Estudios Chicanos y de Fronteras (DEAS-INAH—neip@igc.apc.org). An irregular user of networking was the American Friends Service Committee's Immigration Law Enforcement Monitoring Project (afscilemp@igc.apc.org). These initial contacts and networking efforts will doubtlessly expand into a more cohesive U.S.-Mexican immigration network (immigration being a low priority for Canadian NGOs), especially if the NAFTA reform negotiations under the Clinton Administration include immigration as a major issue.

TELECOMMUNICATIONS AND NETWORKING IN MEXICO

Mexico was a relative latecomer to the networking scene. Lacking basic infrastructure requirements throughout the 1980s, it has only been in the mid-1990s that Mexican civil society institutions have begun to catch up with their partners around the world. Mexican civil society is building channels of political expression within the context of the current regime and the exhaustion of the conventional models of civil organization. Only now are Mexican NGOs connecting to the online universe. In this section I discuss the current networking scene in Mexico.

First, I discuss Mexico as a communicating society. Mexico is one of the few developing countries to have exceeded UNESCO's minimum recommendation for newspaper copies per capita (beating even Spain). It is one of a handful of developing countries operating communications satellites, which now connect 40 private networks, 35 television channels, 120 cable television systems, and 35 radio stations ("Nuevo satellite," 1994). It is perhaps the only developing country broadcasting directly into a First World country. Mexico is a world leader in feature film and television production and imports only a third of television programming from other countries, a low-to-moderate rate. Yet there is a vast gap between the inforich and infopoor in Mexico. Although the literacy rate of 87% is high, millions of citizens have no access to the information revolution. Mexico is near the bottom in international phone calls per capita and international dispatch of letters. Although there are 1.8 million personal computers in Mexico (5.1 million estimated by 1997), basic software is out of reach for minimum-wage workers (Frederick, 1993).

To understand the status and potential of Mexican NGO networking, it is important to understand two starting points: NAFTA and Telmex. NAFTA liberalizes trade in telecommunication equipment and services (Shefrin, 1993). It contains rules on telecommunications investment, intellectual property, licensing and standards. NAFTA's principal telecommunications component guarantees end-users the right to attach and use terminal equipment to public telephone networks, to build and interconnect private leased networks, and, especially important for this study, to use dial-up access as a means of network connection (Bacon, 1992). The immediate effect on Mexico's telecommunications is that U.S.-based firms are investing new resources in value-added data services and are benefiting from the estimated $6 billion Mexican telecommunications market created by NAFTA. Many people expect Mexico to become the new telecommunications hub for the hemisphere. Computer manufacturers view NAFTA as the key to unlocking a large market (Bottoms, 1993; Brotman, 1994).

The privatization of Teléfonos de Mexico (Telmex), the national telephone company, foreshadowed the neoliberal policies of NAFTA. In 1990, the Mexican government sold the state-run telephone monopoly to the Carso group, which operates Telmex jointly with Southwestern Bell and France Telecom. Telmex controls almost the entire telecommunications sector in Mexico and is the biggest telecommunications firm in Latin America and the Caribbean (Hardman, 1992; Molina, 1993). Telmex plans to have 70% of its network digitized by the year 2000 and to achieve a telephone penetration rate of 20 per 100. This is important because the Mexican telephone system is overpriced and inefficient. An 85-kilometer telephone call from Monterrey to Saltillo costs almost as much as a call between the U.S. towns of Houston and Washington, 2,416 kilometers apart. Users in Monterrey pay the same for a one-minute call to Houston as residents in Houston are charged for a seven-minute call to Monterrey. Similarly, tariffs for calls within the same district in Mexico are seven times as high as those in the United States. But the charges are not the only problem. The service is also poor. The firm claims that Telmex is still investing in infrastructure and promises better service in the future. The advances have included a 13,500 kilometer fiber-optic network that links up the country's 54 most important towns, a fax mailbox, teleconference services, and a 40,000-line digital network with 120,000 users (Molina, 1993).

Meanwhile, U.S. telecommunications giants have teamed up with Mexican companies in preparation for the 1997 opening of lucrative long-distance services in Mexico. Smaller firms are laying the groundwork for foreign competition in the local telephone services. In 1994, U.S. companies such as MCI and Bell Atlantic Corp. announced joint-venture plans totaling billions of dollars to enter the Mexican market. Sprint Corporation and Grupo Iusacell SA announced their intent to offer national and international long-distance telecommunications services in Mexico. Furthermore, Telmex, facing challenges from foreign companies, is beginning to get tough, even with little competitors. Telmex cut off Access Telecom Inc's lines in 1994 because Access had bought time from MCI Communications Corp. and was able to offer long-distance rates 22% below Telmex's on calls to the United States. Yet, Telmex's potential for growth is enormous because it knows the market better than any potential competitor (Caroll, 1994a, 1994b; DePalma, 1994; Keller, 1994; LaFranchi, 1994; "Mexico's giant Telmex," 1994; "Sprint, Grupo Iusacell plan,"1994; Torres, 1994a, 1994b).

INTERNET PROVIDERS

As we have seen, Mexico has embraced information technology, and all sorts of information services, including the Internet, are becoming available. The surge of interest in information technology is expected to radically change the political and economic climate in Mexico. Some of the more prominent developments in Mexican communication networks are introduced and described next.

BESTNET

In the earlier period, only Mexican education institutions had access to the Internet or the Bitnet network. Bellman, Tindimubona, and Arias (1993) described the first U.S.-Mexico transnational computer network, called BESTNET—the Binational English and Spanish Telecommunications Network (see also Watkins, 1994). Initially, BESTNET used computer conferencing and electronic mail as an interactive component to bilingual video lectures or telecourses. The BESTNET project now involves over 3,000 students and faculty accounts from over a dozen institutions in the United States and Mexico.

TELEPAC

Mexico's first public data network is known as Telepac and is operated by the government-owned Telecommunicaciones de Mexico, but it has become prohibitively expensive for users in Mexico to access the United States via this method. Connection charges to the United States costs 11 cents per minute; within Mexico the charge is 20 cents per minute! The signal is frequently busy and, worse, can only run at 1200 baud. This vastly increases the cost and inconvenience of all data communication. In fact, it is important to point out that the experience with Telepac is typical of the Mexican networking scene. In the descriptions that follow, it is important to remember that the typical Mexican user must battle many bureaucracies to get online, even to get a telephone installed.

CONACYT

Mexican networking began in the early 1980s, when Mexican academic institutions joined the now-obsolete Bitnet network. Since 1986, CONACYT began coordinating a series of initiatives toward the goal of a single national network and expanding communication channels. The National Council of Science and Technology (Consejo Nacional de Ciencia y Tecnología—CONACYT), equivalent to the U.S. National Science Foundation, has been responsible for coordinating the Mexican Academic Networks (Redes Académicas Mexicanas—RAM) through programs supporting scientific research and technological development. In an era in which Mexican researchers and business had little access to the Internet and to foreign databases, CONACYT established an appropriate solution for online database searching, known as Information Bank Consulting Service (Servicios de Consulta a Bancos de Información—SECOBI). Established in 1976, SECOBI acted as a "super-service," or overall gateway to the major national and international online databases. SECOBI contracted with DIALOG, BRS, and other services, thus lowering the costs for financially strapped universities and businesses and allowing them to pay in pesos rather than dollars (Levison & Iglesias, 1993).

CONACYT helped fill the gap in a period when there was no Mexican "modem culture," when there were only a handful of hobbyist BBSs in the country and almost no computer owners using recreational services such as CompuServe. During this time CONACYT helped develop the networking infrastructure by connecting research centers and establishing connections with the Internet in the United States. It undertook important initiatives such as MEXNET, RedUNAM, and IPN (see later). Beginning in 1992, with the goal of establishing a new networking platform for Mexican national development, CONACYT proceeded to create the National Technological Network (Red Tecnológica Nacional—RTN). Such networks unite the existing Mexican national information infrastructure and connect it with the expanding Global Information Infrastructure (Gore, 1994).

MEXNET

Mexnet is a networking organization that interconnects more than 32 public and private institutions into the legal framework of a cooperative civil association. It uses 64 kbps terrestrial links among its nodes in Monterrey, Nuevo Leon (Instituto Tecnológico de Estudios Superiores de Monterrey—ITESM), Puebla (Universidad de las Americas—UDLA), Mexico City (Instituto Politécnico Nacional—IPN), Guadalajara, Jalisco (Universidad de Guadalajara—UDG, and Instituto Tecnol'ogico y de Estudios Superiores de Occidente—ITESO). Other nodes are connected via lower capacity terrestrial links. Mexnet's 56 kbps international link runs from Monterrey to Houston, Texas.

REDUNAM

RedUnam is the telecommunications network of the National Autonomous University of Mexico (Universidad Nacional Autónoma de México—UNAM) and affiliated institutions. Within the Mexico City area it uses radio modems, leased lines, and microwaves. RedUNAM uses satellite connections for its sites outside the capital, including to Boulder, CO, and Houston, TX.

RUTYC

The University Teleinformatics and Communications Network (Red Universitaria de Teleinformática y Comunicaciones—RUTyC) is a project initiated by the University of Guanajato and financed by the Secretaría de Educación Pública (SEP) to interconnect 35 public universities. This network is not yet online, although the sites have been provided with satellite earth stations and networking equipment.

RED TOTAL CONACYT

This initiative connects the research centers coordinated by SEP-CONACYT through 64 kbps satellite links. Since the end of 1993, it has 2000 kbps terrestrial connections between Mexico City and Fort Worth, TX. It serves as a hub for the RedUNAM, RedUAM, RedIPN, and the RedITESM. It also uses a 64/128 kbps satellite connection to the U.S. NSFNet in Boulder, CO.

RED TECHNOLOGICA NACIONAL (RTN)

The purpose of the Red Tecnológica Nacional (RED) is to unite these networks into a national backbone that optimally interconnects all the initiatives of existing networks and saves them from duplication. The backbone is being built on the wide- and narrow-band infrastructure of the Red Total CONACYT. To date, the RTN integrates the Mexnet institutional nodes of ITESM (Monterrey and Mexico City), the University of Guadalajara, the University of the Americas in Puebla, and the National Polytechnic Institute, plus the Sinoloa Science Center in Culiacán. RTN is working to bring in the RedUNAM, the RedUAM, the Autonomous University of Chihuahua, the Center for Technical and Higher Education in Tijuana (Centro de Enseãnza Técnica Y Superior—CETYS), and the Juarez Autonomous University in Tabasco as regional nodes of the RTN.

There are various ways to connect to the RTN, from telephone line (19,200 baud), private line (28,400 baud), fiber optics (2.048 Mbs), satellite connection (64,000 bps), even microwave (64,000 bps). All these connections utilize fiber optics. The backbone runs from Tijuana/Ensenada in the north all the way to Merida in the south. The entire RTN spills into a 2 mbps terrestrial connection to Fort Worth and a satellite connection to Boulder. Current (as of December 1994) costs range from US$300/year for unlimited dial-up accounts providing Usenet and e-mail and US$1100/year for complete access to telnet, ftp, and SLIP.

LANETA

Although we should consider the Mexican education networks properly as part
of the nongovernmental sector, in practice there are considerable obstacles for
NGOs to connect to them. As a result, a separate Internet-connected network
has emerged to serve the needs of these communities in Mexico. The original
idea of a Mexican NGO network arose at the 1988 Latin American Studies
Association conference, when Joanne Scott, then-head of the Central America
Resource Network (CARNET) at the Institute for Global Communications,
spoke with David Barkin, professor of economics at the Universadad Autónoma
Metropolitana, who had long worked with Mexican community development
organizations. Scott and Barkin felt that Mexico was ripe for NGO networking.
At the time, it had a large community of mass organizations, a X.25 packet-
switching network (Telepac), and a relatively high number of personal
computers for a developing country. Alternatives such as SECOBI, run by the
Mexican Science Foundation (CONACYT), were very expensive and the
Mexican universities' Bitnet and Internet connections were on-again off-again.
Barkin proposed to promote the idea among Mexican NGOs toward the goal of
establishing an APC node in Mexico.[21]

During this period, in anticipation of establishing an independent
Mexican network, Barkin was able to establish a private "joint account" with
Telepac for Mexican NGOs to connect directly to PeaceNet and EcoNet in San
Francisco. Barkin called the system PAXMEX. By 1992, from about 40 to 50
cities in Mexico and without long-distance charges, more than 85 NGOs and
citizens joined the IGC Networks in San Francisco. Using Telepac they
connected to Sprint Net in the United States to address the IGC system. The
advantage of this arrangement was that the Mexican NGOs avoided the fixed
Telepac charges as well as the bureaucratic process of obtaining an account.

In 1991, NGOs gathered to lay the groundwork for a system in Mexico.
Groups represented included: Servicios Informativos Procesados (SIPRO), Centro
de Estudios Ecuménicos, Equipo Pueblo, Mujer a Mujer, Unión de Vecinos y
Damnificados 19 de Septiembre, Casa y Ciudad, Comité del DF, Red Inter-
Institucional, and Comité de Enlace de Convergencia. At that meeting, organized
by Adolfo Dunayevich, who has since become the coordinator of LaNeta, the
decision was made to launch a low-tech "single-user" system until growth
necessitated a more powerful computer and several phone lines. Later, SIPRO
convened an even larger meeting of Mexican NGOs with the purpose of creating
a Mexican NGO computer communications network. Groups attending included:
Unión de Colonos y Solicitantes de Vivienda de Veracruz (CIDIU-UCISVER),
Consejo Regional de Intercambio Ecuménico (CRIE), Centro de Estudios
Ecuménico (CEE), Instituto de Capacitación para la Democracia (ICIDAC),
Mujer a Mujer, APIS a.c., Comisión Mexicana de Promoción y Defensa de los

---

[21]jscott igc.intlcomm 7:31 pm Apr 5, 1988.

Derechos Humanos, Casa y Ciudad, Fronteras Comunes (CECOPE), Centro de Tecnología en Electrónica y Informática (CETEI), Grupo de Estudios Ambientales (GEA), Frente Auténtico del Trabajo (FAT), Centro de Ecodesarrollo (CECODES), Centro de Estudios y Diálogo, and ENLACE.

These groups decided to begin an experimental network for a six-month evaluation period. The node was located first at Equipo Pueblo and then at the Centro de Estudios Ecuménicos (CEE), which had offered the use of a computer and a telephone line.[22] The managing team included SIPRO, Mujer a Mujer, Casa y Ciudad, Centro de Estudios Ecuménico (CEE), and Consejo Regional de Intercambio Ecuménico (CRIE). On April 11, 1991, that experimental system went online as a BBS using WWIV software operating 16 hours per day from 16.00 to 9.00 hours, later expanding to 24 hours when a new telephone line was installed. About 20 NGOs began using the network, including Centro de Estudios Ecuménico (CEE), Consejo Regional de Intercambio Ecuménico CRIE, Equipo Pueblo, Frente Auténtico del Trabajo, Casa y Ciudad, Grupo de Estudios Ambientales (GEA), Centro de Investigación en Derechos Humanos para América Latina (CIDHAL), and Mujer a Mujer y SIPRO.[23]

By April 1992, there was still no formal group promoting the Mexican network, so decision making about the networks' growth was difficult. The groups' legal status was still undefined, although it was loosely affiliated with the Convergencia coalition of some 150 NGOs. Financing was still uncertain, even for paying the local telephone line. The BBS software was incompatible with the APC Networks, making the exchange of information very difficult. Furthermore, technical problems prevented a firm X.25 connection with IGC through Telepac.[24] A small grant from the Fundación de Apoyo a la Comunidad allowed the node to buy a 386 DOS computer, do fundraising and promotion, and, most importantly, to have a daily link to IGC. Dunayevich believes the Mexican Nets needs 150 subscribers paying about $15 monthly to be self-sufficient.[25] The new service, called LaNeta, began in 1993. Currently there are 150 Mexican NGOs and individuals using LaNeta. The largest concentration is, of course, in Mexico City, but there are considerable numbers of users in San Cristóbal de las Casas, Chiapas, and Cuernavaca, Morelia. There is a diverse selection of Mexican NGO from human rights organizations to environmental organizations.

During 1994, LaNeta users posted hundreds of messages to conferences on APC networks, which were subsequently carried around the world on the Internet. The most active concentration of LaNeta postings has appeared in reg.mexico, a general interest conference about Mexico. Topics

---

[22]For about one month this BBS was located in Equipo Pueblo. Afterwards, it moved to a small company dedicated to desktop publishing of a grassroots publication, Texto e Imagen, for a period of about two months. When Texto e Imagen moved in with Casa y Ciudad, the node moved with it.

[23]sipro Fri May 31 11:18 PDT 1991.

[24]agduna apc.mexico 11:12 am Apr 15, 1992.

[25]agduna tech.fido 9:25 am Jul 20, 1992; and agduna Tue Sep 15 17:07:34 1992.

range from family violence and human rights to election politics and labor conflict. Mexican women computerists have also seized this medium to distribute their information, especially in amlat.mujeres (Latin American Women) and dh.mujer (Women's Human Rights). Trade, labor, and syndical activities are also very frequently posted in trade.strategy and sindicatos. Because Guatemala is still totally outside the Internet universe, Guatemalan news agencies are very active in publicizing events on LaNeta and the APC Networks. Even Mexico's HIV community has found a home on the network.

AGRINET

Another network that is serving the needs of Mexican civil society is known as AGRINET. Mexico's small agricultural producers are the backbone of this country. Relying almost entirely on traditional farming methods, they lack the technological advantages of the large agribusinesses with their mechanized production of high-profit crops for export. The small producers themselves, the country's campesino farmers, are aware of the fact that their greatest challenge lies in developing ways to function effectively in this context, and that their greatest need is for access to vital information and for greater ease of communication with other producers and potential buyers of their products.

The Electronic Network for Small Producers, or AGRINET (Red de Información Ejidal), intends to create an information-exchange system designed to meet this need with instantaneous access by computer modem to interactive databases in each state of the Republic, giving small producers access to the information they need in order to compete effectively in domestic and export sales of their produce. The AGRINET project was initiated in 1992 with the support of a planning grant from the Ford Foundation. It has received broad endorsement from national and local campesino organizations. With its Mexico City base at the Universidad Metropolitana Iztapalapa campus, AGRINET has set up a network of cooperating state universities that will provide key logistical support (through the universities' Internet-linked computer network, RUTYC). AGRINET has recently received additional Ford Foundation support that will cover about half the expenses of establishing the network's first phase, which will be in the southern and southeastern regions of Mexico.[26]

INFOTEC

Created in 1975 by CONACYT and the National Financial Council (NAFIN), INFOTEC now services the growing RTN network. It offers Internet consulting, training, and information services to small- and medium-size businesses.[27]

[26]Scott Robinson, ssrobinson Mon Jan 31 11:41:17 1994. Red Ejidal may be reached at gopher tonatiuh.uam.mx.

[27]INFOTEC, Av. San Fernando no? 37, Col. Toriello Guerra, Tlalpan, C. P. 14050 Mexico, D.F. Tels: 606-0011, 606-1620, Fax: 606-0386, E-mail: infotec@ mailer.main.conacyt.mx.

PIXELNET

PixelNet offers e-mail, Usenet news, gopher, World-Wide Web, and other commercial services in Monterrey Nuevo Leon, Guadalajara, and Mexico City.[28] PixelNet was founded in 1989 in Monterrey, Nuevo Leon with support from Compaq Computer Corp. Pixelnet is an authorized Compaq distributor and also a public access point to the Internet. It primarily serves corporate clients.

Other BBSs in Mexico

Of the 59 BBSs listed in Arturo Garza's list, 27 are FidoNet nodes. To date this has been the only way for many computer users to connect to the rest of the world.

COMPUSERVE

Compuserve now offers local access to its online network from Cancun, Guadalajara, Mexico City, and Monterrey (Kutler, 1994, p. 13). Less than 90 days after opening its operations, CompuServe had 500 Mexican users and hoped to double that by the end of 1994. With an initial capacity of about 9,000 users, CompuServe plans to increase to 30,000 Mexican users in the medium term. Formerly available only through the expensive Telepac connection, CompuServe is connected by a direct line to Ohio through a Telmex optical to Dallas, TX and from there to Ohio. Mexico is the 13th country to have direct access. An agreement was signed in November 1993, with 60% of the $500,000 investment coming from InfoAccess and 40% from Infotec. The subscription costs 85 pesos, and the monthly rate is 35 pesos. In addition, users pay 28 pesos per hour connection charge (Aguilar, 1994).

CONCLUSION

Clearly Mexico is undergoing an information revolution that will have significant consequences for the future of its political system. Mexican education networks are consolidating and providing access to global knowledge to the entire country's university system. By providing a low-cost, appropriate solution for NGOs and poor countries, Mexican NGO networks such as LaNeta and Red Ejidal are attempting to civilize and democratize cyberspace and to bridge the gap between the inforich and the infopoor.

Through the NAFTA reform, immigration network and Chiapas experiences, it is increasingly clear that computer networks have helped in the process of self-identification, solidification of ties among NGOs with diverse

---

[28]jpadres@pixelnet.pixel.com.mx, Garza Garcia N.L. Rio Amazonas 331 Ote Col. del Valle Tels (8) 3354924, 3358166, 3356498, 3356348, Fax 3356513.

agendas, exchange of valuable information, planning of joint strategies, and agreement on policy statements. As the immigration, trade, and Mexican revolutions are not closed subjects, this "electronic community" will be heating up the wires connecting three countries.

As we approach the third millennium, communications technologies such as these are transforming international relations. They have greatly accelerated the rise of global civil society and the NGO movements. As Thorup (1991) has rightly prophesied, these networks and the coalitions they engender also lead to the "transnationalization of civil participation, [which] may serve ultimately to ameliorate power asymmetries" (p. 15). Indeed, it is important to conclude by asking how many communicating publics there are in the information age. The nature of borders is changing. A map of NAFTA shows a line running from the Pacific across the continent on the 49th parallel for some 2,500 kilometers, dipping to follow the contours of lakes, rivers, and waterways until it reaches the Atlantic Ocean. Traditionally, message traffic originating in North Dakota tended to flow southward and eastward toward Minnesota and the U.S. side of the Great Lakes, following the transcontinental railway, microwave, and highway networks. Similarly, if we could see every phone call made, every idea passed on, every letter sent, and every journey undertaken, the flow map of the Mexican-U.S. border, messages from Tijuana, Baja California, tended to flow largely southward toward Mexico City. From San Diego, "upper" California, messages flowed northward and eastward.

Our old definition of border was an area in which the settlement densities and traffic densities decline quite sharply. Borders defined a state, which thus comprised a unified economic and communication community. A message from the capital of a country was likely to be disseminated with equal frequency throughout the territory of a country. Trade and economic policies were promulgated throughout the entire territory of a country. This comfortable view of border and sovereignty no longer is compatible with the age of global communication and free trade. The Canadian, U.S., and Mexican peoples are uniting increasingly in terms of their physical proximity. As the new regimes emerge, the North American publics will also increasingly be united in terms of their media consumption.

Take the emergence of "Hispanic United States" as an example. By the end of this decade, the Spanish-speaking audience in the United States will total 37 million. Include their English-speaking relatives and there are now 50 million. This can easily support a fifth authoritative, television system in the US, a Spanish-English network with a new bilingual patois. So we could better speak of peoples and publics. A *people* are groups of individuals united together by a high ability to communicate. They communicate not just on a few topics, but on many different ones. A *people* have a history, shared experiences, and customs. They can predict one another's behavior. What is a public? An attentive *public* are peoples unified by media who are pursuing common social, political, economic, and cultural goals.

Thus we might venture the observation that the development of continent-wide computer networks is encouraging the emergence of the North American Public as a force in international relations. In the past, the very powers that obstruct civil society at the local level—markets and governments—also controlled most of the North America's communication flows. Now a small but not insignificant change has occurred. As the North American Information Infrastructure continues to develop, we can speak of an emerging North American public concerned about trade and the environment, human rights and labor issues, continental democracy, and development. Clearly the advent of new democratizing and decentralizing communication technologies is accelerating this trend.

REFERENCES

Aguilar, G. (1994, August 4). *El imperio del modem: Más de mill b00 empresas han conectado sus computadoras con el primer mundo.* El Financiero, n.p.

Bacon, K. H. (1992, August 11). Mexico agrees to speedy end of some tariffs. *Wall Street Journal,* p. A4.

Bellman, B., Tindimubona, A., & Arias, A., Jr. (1993). Technology transfer in global networking: Capacity building in Africa and Latin America. In L. Harasim & J. Walls (Eds.), *Globalizing networks: Computers and international communication* (pp. 237-254). Cambridge, MA: MIT Press.

Bottoms, D. T. (1993, December 13). Computer, telecom firms win with NAFTA. *Electronics,* p. 4.

Brenner, J. E. (1994, Spring). *Internationalist labor communication by computer network: The United States, Mexico and NAFTA.* Paper prepared for the course "International and comparative communication policy," School of International Service, The American University, Washington, DC.

Brotman, S. N. (1994, March). Markets see opportunity in NAFTA. *National Law Journal,* p. 29.

Carroll, P. B. (1994a, July 5). Mexico to allow unlimited competition for Telmex in long-distance service. *Wall Street journal,* p. A9.

Carroll, P. B. (1994b, June 17). Protexa, Sprint discuss Mexico phone service. *Wall Street journal,* p. A9.

DePalma, A. (1994, July 18). Telmex in competition, so far with just itself. *New York times,* p. D1.

Frederick, H. (1991a, November). The technologies of peace and war. *Impact* (Boston Computer Society), pp. 13-16.

Frederick, H. (1991b). Peacetronics: Computer networking for peace and human rights. *International Peace Research Newsletter, 23*(2), 55-56.

Frederick, H. (1992a). *Electronic democracy. Edges: New Planetary Patterns* (Canadian Institute of Cultural Affairs), 5(1), 12-35.

Frederick, H. (1992b, January). Breaking the global information blockade using the technologies of peace and war. *Impact* (Boston Computer Society), pp. 14-17.

Frederick, H. (1993a). *Global communication and international relations.* Belmont, CA: Wadsworth.

Frederick, H. (1993b). Computer networks and the emergence of global civil society: The case of the Association for Progressive Communications (APC). In L. Harasim & J. Walls (Eds.), *Globalizing networks: Computers and international communication* (pp.). Cambridge, MA: MIT Press.

Gore, Vice President A. (1994, March 12). Speech to the International Telecommunications Union, Buenos Aries, Argentina.

Hardman, A. (1992, September 15). Private lines, public lessons. *Financial World*, pp. 64-65.

Keller, J. J. (1994, January 26). MCI to hook up with Mexico's Banacci in plan to build long-distance network. *Wall Street Journal*, p. A11.

Kutler, J. (1994, July 5). Compu-Serve adds services for Mexico, Pacific Rim. *American Banker*, p. 13.

LaFranchi, H. (1994, October 4). Competition lines up for long distance opening in Mexico. *Christian Science Monitor*, p. 9.

Levison, A., & Iglesias, H. R. (1993, May). The on-line industry in Mexico. *ONLINE Magazine*, pp.116-119.

Martinez, A., & Ronfeldt, D. (1994). *Netwar in Mexico.* Santa Monica, CA: RAND.

Mexico's giant Telmex faces fight in local phone service market. (1994, October 2). *The Journal of Commerce.*

Molina, E. (1993, September 3). Mexico: Telecoms went private but telephones still a mess. *InterPress Service.* telenet://igc.apc.org/conference/ips.english (subscription required).

Moody, K., & McGinn, M. (1992, January). Unions and free trade: Solidarity vs. Competition. *Labor Notes*, p. 30.

Nuevo satelite geoestacionario mejorara comunicaciones. (1994, October 6). *Interpress Service.* telenet://igc.apc.org/conference/ips.english (subscription required).

O'Connor, R. J. (1991, August 25). Computers staged news coup. *San Jose Mercury News,* p. F1.

Quarterman, J. S. (1990). *The matrix: Computer networks and conferencing systems Worldwide.* Bedford, MA: Digital Press.

Schneider, B. (1993, June 17). APC networks run well. *Terra Viva: Independent daily of the World Conference on Human Rights* (Vienna).

Shefrin, I. H. (1993). The North American Free Trade Agreement: Telecommunications in perspective. *Telecommunications Policy*, 17, 14-26.

Sprint, Grupo Iusacell plan joint venture in Mexico. (1994, July 26). *Wall Street Journal*, p. A13.

Thorup, C. (1991, Summer). The politics of free trade and the dynamics of cross-border coalitions in U.S.-Mexican relations. *Columbia Journal of World Business*, p. 15.

Torres, C. (1994a, June 29). Future is on the line for Mexico's telephone company. *Wall Street Journal*, p. B4.

Torres, C. (1994b, August 8). Phone giant in Mexico seeks to crush rivals. *Wall Street Journal*, p. B6.

Waterman, P. (1992). *International labour communication by computer: The fifth international?* The Hague: Institute of Social Studies.

Watkins, B. T. (1994, March 23). Breaking down barriers. *Chronicle of Higher Education*, p. A25.

Chapter 13

The Extended Pulpit: Church-Media Alliance in Kenyan Politics*

Morompi Ole-Ronkei

The political events of 1990 in many countries on the continent of Africa marked a major turning point in the continent's political process. During 1990 alone, citizens took to the streets of capital cities in 14 African countries to express discontent with economic hardship and political repression and to demand democratic reforms (Bratton & Van de Walle, 1992). Prior to 1990, however, much of Sub-Saharan Africa appeared to have been politically docile with a citizenry that appeared apathetic to things political. This impression was shattered and replaced with one of people who were out to shape and define their own political future by reclaiming it from military and autocratic rule.

After three decades of political dormancy, there developed a massive political awakening on the African continent. A number of theories have been advanced to explain the awakening of the African people. For instance, Bratton and Van de Walle (1992) argued that the protest and reforms of 1990 in Sub-Saharan Africa were partly shaped by the crippling effects of a structural economic crisis and precipitated by democratic initiatives in Eastern Europe,

---

*The chapter is part of a doctoral dissertation completed in Spring 1995 at the University of Oregon, School of Journalism and Communication, under the title, "Emerging Communication Strategies and the Press-Church Alliance in Kenyan Politics."

China, and South Africa. They further acknowledge the fact that African governments introduced governance reforms primarily in response to indigenous political demands. Another contributing factor was the end of the Cold War. Following the collapse of the Soviet Union in 1989, many Western countries, led by the United States, "changed their permissive attitude toward autocracy and malfeasance among strategic allies" in the Third World (Bratton & Van de Walle, 1992, p. 29). For instance, in 1990, according to Bratton and Van de Walle (1992), the United States reduced or eliminated military aid to Kenya, Somalia, and Zaire in response to these governments' violations of political rights. The West, confident of the bankruptcy of the Soviet Union and its communist ideology, could now afford to pressure the third-world countries to democratize without them opting to join the rival camp.

In Kenya, 1990 was ushered in with a call for democratic reforms by the Reverend Dr. Timothy Njoya of the Presbyterian Church of East Africa (PCEA). The Rev. Njoya, in his New Year sermon, called on African leaders to reexamine their preference for single-party political systems in light of the recent debacle in Eastern Europe. The outspoken clergyman declared in his sermon that Africa could not convert one-party political systems that they adopted from Eastern Europe into democracies by baptizing them with local names (*Daily Nation,* January 2, 1990, p. 1). The sermon, which received nationwide media coverage, came under heavy government criticism. What seemed to have irked the government most was Dr. Njoya's attempt to draw a parallel between the falling dictatorships in Eastern Europe and the situation in Africa, Kenya in particular, and his assertion that those events in Eastern Europe ought to be instructive to the one-party system in Kenya. Some members of Parliament who condemned Rev. Njoya's criticism of single-party politics called on his church to defrock him and on the government to arrest and detain him.

The exchange between the clergy and the political establishment in Kenya, played out in the local media, is central to this chapter. Of particular interest is the alliance forged between the Church and the media in a bid to disseminate information to the general public during a time period when the traditional institutions of political opposition were either outlawed or muzzled into silence by the government. The sermons delivered from Church pulpits during Sunday services became, by the mid-1980s to early 1990s, the primary source of stories capturing headlines in the local media. The power of the church as an agent of communication and its ability to exert and influence political life and the country's political process became abundantly clear. For those among the clergy who support active participation by the church in the nation's political process, the media coverage of Sunday services was viewed as the extension of their pulpits to cover the entire country. For the government, however, this was a political nuisance it would rather have done without.

My focus in this chapter is on the role of people, specifically within the context of Kenya, in actively shaping and transforming their social and communicative environment. The church's use of the mass media, especially the press, was key to its ability to criticize the country's political system while promoting political awareness among the general public and contributing toward the establishment of democratic institutions in the country. I focus on the joint contribution of the local churches and the media toward the establishment of a democratic society in Kenya. Specifically, I examine the media coverage of the clergy between 1982 and 1992 in two privately owned national papers: a daily newspaper, the *Daily Nation* (DN); and a weekly political magazine, the *Weekly Review* (WR).

GOVERNMENT IN CRISIS: ONE-PARTY STATE IN KENYA

To understand why the church[1] in Kenya became a major player in the political arena, we first need to examine the institution of government and the nation's political system. Such an examination will set the stage for a discussion on the role of the church in secular politics. The church felt that the government had, over a period of time, destroyed the traditional institutions of political opposition and eliminated all legal avenues for legitimate criticism of the government. The government also instituted policies and Constitutional amendments that removed the political checks and balances guaranteed by the Constitution and necessary for a functioning democracy, thus concentrating power in the executive branch.

By early 1982, the political truce that had lasted since President Daniel Arap Moi came to power in October 1987 was rapidly coming to an end. The political honeymoon was over. Clearly, a rift between the rulers and the ruled in the country had become eminent. In May 1982, faced with the emergence of dissenting voices in the country, the President[2] threatened to reinstate "detention without trial" to deal with dissidents, a practice he discontinued shortly after he came to power.

The outburst of political activities in 1982 was triggered by Mr. Oginga Odinga, a former Vice-President under the late President Jomo Kenyatta, while on a lecture tour in Britain. He was reported in a British daily as having said he planned to form an opposition party to challenge the ruling party, the Kenya African National Union (KANU),[3] upon his return to Kenya.

[1]For the purpose of the chapter the term the church is used to refer to all Christian denominations (Catholic and Protestants) that contributed to the political debate in the country. Para-church organizations like the National Council of Churches of Kenya (NCCK) or the Evangelical Fellowship of Kenya (EFK) also fall under this category. The Daily Nation, in an editorial (July 6, 1983), used the term to refer to "all religious bodies" and has since referred to them as such.

[2]In Kenya, only the head of state bears the title President. Any mention of the term the President in this chapter should be taken to mean President Daniel Arap Moi.

[3]Following a constitutional amendment in June 1982, which made Kenya a de jure one-

The reaction from the Kenya government was swift and immediate. Odinga was expelled from KANU (*Daily Nation*, May 21, 1982).[4] At the same time, the KANU Governing Council met and passed a resolution instructing the party's Parliamentary group and the country's Attorney General to pass legislation making Kenya a de jure one-party state (*Weekly Review*, May 28, 1982). The rush to take immediate actions to legalize the one-party system was intended to preempt the possibility of Odinga, or any of his associates dissatisfied with KANU policies, from forming an opposition party.

The Bill to make Kenya a one-party State was gazetted one week after it was first proposed by the KANU Governing Council (*Daily Nation*, June 4, 1982). On June 9, 1982, Kenya became a de jure one-party state. The Constitutional amendment was unanimously passed by a full House of Parliament. The amendment made the Kenya African National Union (KANU) the only legal political party in the country (*Weekly Review*, June 11, 1982). To accomplish this political milestone, several sections of the Constitution were repealed and some new sections substituted. The most significant was the insertion of a new Section, 2A, which says that "there shall be in Kenya only one political party, the Kenya African National Union." Several other sections of the Constitution were changed to reflect the new monolithic political arena. Although no public debate preceded this major Constitutional change, the Minister for Constitutional Affairs pointed out that KANU was only following "the wishes of the people . . . the 99 per cent of Kenyans who want the one-party state," (*Weekly Review*, June 11, 1982). It is noteworthy to point out that at the beginning of the Parliamentary debate to change the Constitution, the Vice President had moved a procedural motion reducing the publication period of the Bill from 14 to 6 days (*Daily Nation*, June 10, 1982). The public was never given a chance to debate the merits and demerits of a single-party state. The government proposed it, made it into law, and the citizenry was stuck with it.

THE RETURN OF DETENTION

On May 27, 1982, a former deputy Director of Intelligence, Mwangi Stephen Muriithi, became the country's first detainee by the Moi government. He was followed shortly by George Anyona, a former legislator. As in all detention cases, the government does not give reasons for detaining a person. The public is

---

party state, the Kenya African National Union (KANU) became the only legal political party in the country. From then on, the terms the ruling party, the Party, and KANU were used as standard terms in the local media to refer to the political party. In this chapter I use the three terms interchangeably.

[4]This chapter is based on materials from two Kenyan papers—a daily newspaper, the Daily Nation (DN) and a weekly political magazine, the Weekly Review (WR)—over an 11-year period, from January 1982 to December 1992.

generally left to speculate as to the crime of the detainee. Muriithi had taken the government to court for alleged "forced" early retirement. He lost the case in the high court and was reportedly preparing to take his case to the Court of Appeal.

On June 3, 1982, the lawyer for Anyona, John Khaminwa, was picked up by police. His office and home were thoroughly searched before he was taken into police custody. Two days later, he too was detained. The wave of detentions and people being picked up by police only heightened an already tense situation, with Kenyans asking themselves, "Who would be next?" The ominous "big brother is watching" syndrome appeared to permeate the nation. Every other person was a probable government informer, and the sight of policemen—the traditional symbol of security and protection—evoked anxiety, trepidation, and plain fear among the general public.

The government crackdown on dissidents shifted to the University, with President Moi condemning what he called "Marxist agitators" on the campus (*Weekly Review*, June 4, 1982). He pointed out that "we shall not allow a few individuals who regard themselves as revolutionaries, promoting foreign ideologies, to disrupt our education and training programs." The crackdown on university "Marxist agitators" started with the arrest of Maina wa Kinyatti (Department of History), who appeared in court on June 7, 1982, charged with being in possession of a seditious publication. The next day, two other lecturers were picked up by police, and three days later another two were picked up and taken into police custody after their offices and homes were thoroughly searched. The Nation, on the same day, quoted the Minister of Higher Education confirming that 11 students from Kenyatta University had been expelled for their role in campus riots (*Daily Nation*, June 11, 1982).

On June 16, 1982, David Mukaru Ng'ang'a became the sixth University lecturer to be picked up by police since the crackdown started. The fate of these lecturers soon manifested itself. Willy Mutunga appeared in court on June 18, 1982 and denied possessing a seditious publication. His bail application was denied. Mazrui and Mukaru Ng'ang'a were detained under the Public Security Regulations (*Daily Nation*, June 25, 1982). While all this was in process, Dr. Edward Oyugi (Department of Psychology), became the seventh lecturer to be picked up by police. On July 15, 1982, Oyugi and Wachira were detained.

The crackdown on the University had a major demoralizing effect on the institution and, in particular, the teaching faculty. The government, however, had accomplished its goal. To start with, those lecturers in police custody were finding it difficult to engage lawyer's services. A relative of one of the lecturers in police custody claimed "he went to more than four legal firms which refused to take up his relative's case" (*Daily Nation*, June 10, 1982). The legal firms, according to the Daily Nation, gave no reason for the refusal, but also declined to comment on the issue to the press. Second, the crackdown spread fear among the other teaching faculty causing them to jointly request an audience with the President "to express their loyalty to him, the government and the ruling party KANU" (Daily Nation, June 28, 1982). The President, who is also the Chancellor of the University, turned down the request. Within a span of less than two months, 32 lecturers were either in detention, in police custody awaiting trial, or in self-imposed exile. The one-time robust institution of higher learning was reduced to a political eunuch.

A government in crisis resorts to detention without trial as a weapon. The then Minister for Constitutional Affairs told Parliament that "detention is Constitutional in Kenya and is not questionable in any court of law" (Daily Nation, 6/10/82). A few days later, the President announced that "detention of anti-government persons would continue until disgruntled elements and unpatriotic people are rooted out of Kenya" (Daily Nation 6/19/82). Clearly, no Kenyan was immune from arrest and detention. "Possession of seditious publication" became the most notorious means for arresting people by police. In June 1982, for example, two "illiterate" men in their 70s were held in police custody charged with possessing a seditious publication (Daily Nation, 6/25/82). A Nairobi journalist, Wangondu Kariuki, charged with possessing a seditious publication, reportedly found in his house (Daily Nation, 7/8/82), was jailed for 4 1/2 years.

The first sign that the political tension in the country was heating up came on July 20, 1982, in the form of a hard-hitting, uncompromising newspaper editorial. The Editor-in-Chief of the *Standard*, in a bold move, published a scathing attack on political detention, calling for the release of all detainees and the repeal or amendment of the *Preventive Detention Act* (*Weekly Review*, July 23, 1982). Although the Editor, George Githii, was summarily fired from the *Standard*, and the paper apologized to the government, he had made his point.

Githii had pointed out in his editorial that "fear and apprehension" had gripped the country "because preventive detention allows the state to arrest people, lock them up and thus deny them their freedom without having to go through the due process of the law, or even to give satisfactory explanation for their arrests." He went on to argue that the detention law was inconsistent with the Bill of Rights incorporated in the Kenya Constitution, and that detention should only be applied during wartime, a condition that did not exist in Kenya. Githii called on the government to take steps to put an end to the prevailing fear and insecurity in the body politic, for, as he put it, a timid, diffident, suspicious, and apathetic nation cannot thrive.

THE COUP AND AFTERSHOCKS

George Githii, in his editorial of July 20, 1982, spoke of the "prevailing fear and insecurity" in the country, and barely 10 days later that fear and insecurity manifested itself in the form of an attempted military coup.

The abortive coup of August 1, 1982 appeared, at least on the surface, to have been the culmination of a series of political events that had taken place in the preceding five months. They ranged from the expulsion of Odinga from KANU, to the changing of the Constitution to make Kenya a single-party state by law, to the spate of detentions and sedition trials that had created undue anxiety among the general public. These events and actions by the government, done in a manner that did not allow for public debate or discussion, only helped to raise the political temperature in the country to a potentially explosive level.

The attempted coup had one immediate dividend to the political process in the country: It helped galvanize support around the President and in the process overshadowed all other political problems the country was facing, ultimately justifying the government's use of tougher measures against those suspected of dissident activities. All throughout the country, "demonstrations of loyalty and support for the President and his government took place" for the larger portion of the first two weeks following the coup attempt (*Weekly Review*, August 13, 1982). The fear and apprehensions caused by detentions and seditious trials before August 1, gave way to justification and acceptance of such extralegal actions by the government. Although the atmosphere of fear had not disappeared, the focus had shifted, and many people now were in support of government actions against perceived dissidents.

Although the government got a needed "shot in the arm," in the form of public support, the ruling party felt it "needed internal self-cleansing." The apparent failure of the court martial trials to implicate politicians who were seen as not "toeing the government line" meant designing other means for political house cleaning.

President Moi, on May 17, 1983, announced that the country would hold elections in September, one year ahead of schedule, in order to give the country time to clean up its house and for a more honest and dedicated government to be formed (*Daily Nation* [Special Edition], May 17, 1983). The September 1983 elections would be the time and place to weed out the undesired political elements. The message to politicians who were perceived as not toeing the government line went out loud and clear. They were either to shape up or they would be eliminated at the "elections." This preelection warning to politicians was significant in that it set the tone for all future elections in the new one-party state.

The election results were not, however, as the authorities would have wanted. Although 60 fresh MPs were elected, some of the "rotten apples" the elections were supposed to have flushed out were returned by the voters. Nonetheless, undesirable Cabinet Ministers from the previous Parliament returned by the voters were not reassigned to ministerial positions.

THE SUPREMACY OF THE PARTY

Since independence, the government of Kenya had been synonymous with the ruling party, the Kenya African National Union (KANU). The Kenyan public, with limited exposure to the practice of multiparty politics, and thus opposition parties and how they function in a democracy, have found it difficult to distinguish between the party and the government. For all practical purposes, the distinction between the two bodies was greatly blurred by the absence of opposition politics.

The question of the supremacy of the party over such institutions as Parliament or the judiciary never arose until a Cabinet Minister, Shariff Nassir, called for the amendment of the Parliamentary Powers and Privileges Acts to reflect the supremacy of the ruling party (*Daily Nation*, November 3, 1986; *Weekly Review*, November 7, 1986). Nassir's line of reasoning was that because KANU was the backbone of the government, it should be supreme to all existing government institutions, and that when conflict arise the supremacy of KANU should prevail. Although the Powers and Privileges Acts was never "officially changed," the MPs remained fully aware that it no longer offered them the Parliamentary protection it was designed to offer. Also, the fact that the Act was not changed on the books did not stop the President from stating very clearly that "the ruling party has supremacy over Parliament . . . and over the High Court" (*Weekly Review*, November 21, 1986).

The ruling party, KANU, was established in 1961 and was seen largely as the party of the five large tribes: the Kikuyu, the Embu, the Meru, the Luo, and the Akamba. The opposition, the Kenya African Democratic Union (KADU), formed in the same year, was made up of the smaller tribes: the Kalenjins, Luhya, Maasai, and the Coastal ethnic groups. These two main parties fought for independence, with KANU forming the first government and KADU the opposition. Within the first year of independence, however, KADU voluntary dissolved itself and joined KANU. By 1966, ideological differences within the party led to the resignation of the Vice President, Oginga Odinga, who defected to form his own party, the Kenya Peoples Union (KPU). In 1969, following a fracas in Kisumu, a PKU stronghold, President Kenyatta proscribed the party and had Odinga and his allies placed in detention.

Without the prospects of political opposition, KANU, as a political party, went into dormancy. Its revitalization as a grassroots political party did not take place until after Daniel Arap Moi came to power in 1978. President Moi embarked on a massive nationwide recruitment drive that was followed by party elections. By 1982, KANU had transformed itself into a strong and visible political force in the country. The rise of KANU as a permeating force throughout all segments of society was soon to become a worrying factor to some sections of Kenyan society. The abortive coup of August 1, 1982, served to further stifle dissent within the party ranks and beyond (*Weekly Review*,

December 9, 1988). The party also went on a major "offensive" to incorporate other organizations into its ranks. It also formed aggressive links with political parties of "friendly countries" around the world and exchanged party delegations.

In March 1982, while preparing to host a one-week workshop on the organization and the efficiency of International Co-operation of Political Parties in Africa—with delegates from Botswana, Nigeria, Senegal, Uganda, Tanzania, Zambia, and Zimbabwe—the Secretary-General of the party (Robert Matano) told a Press conference that "KANU will never entertain attempts to establish an opposition party" in Kenya (*Daily Nation*, March 6, 1982). The workshop, sponsored by the Friedrich Ebert Foundation of West Germany, did not include the opposition—for countries that had opposition parties, like Botswana.

The workshop appeared to have triggered the events that led to the revitalization of KANU as a mass party. A small delegation of KANU officials visited West Germany in May 1982 at the invitation of the Social Democratic Party and funded by the Friedrich Ebert Foundation to study the operations of the West German party. Upon their return, the delegation called for the revitalization of KANU to make it more dynamic and functional at the grassroots level (*Daily Nation*, May 12, 1982). These two events, both sponsored by the Friedrich Ebert Foundation, formed the cornerstone for what was to become a strong and dynamic political party in Kenya. This became the rebirth of a once dormant party.

PARLIAMENT AND KANU

According to the Kenya Constitution, Parliament is the supreme political organ in the country. But when that body is composed entirely of members of one political party, the distinction between Parliament and the Party becomes difficult to separate. When Parliament amended the Constitution and made Kenya a de jure one-party state in 1982, KANU was given supreme power in the land. Without the benefits of a legal political opposition, KANU could steer the country in the political direction it desired. In an interview with the *Weekly Review* in 1987, the Party chairman stated that "at the time of independence, with a multi-party system in the country, supremacy was vested in Parliament, but when the Constitution was amended in 1982, supremacy moved to the Party" (*Weekly Review*, May 8, 1987, p. 6). The chairman's argument was that Parliament, in a one-party state, was simply one of the institutions of the (KANU) government. Examples abound that shows the supremacy of the Party over that of Parliament.

In 1975, President Kenyatta detained legislators Martin Shikuku and Jean Marie Seroney for claiming in Parliament that "KANU was dead." In 1985, Martin Shikuku was sacked from his post as an assistant minister for comments he made in Parliament about the then-powerful Chief Secretary

(*Weekly Review*, November 7, 1986). The MP for Nakuru West, Mr. Njenga Mungai, was suspended from the Party in December 1985, after he tabled a question in Parliament alleging that Nakuru County Councillors had grabbed plots in his constituency. He was pardoned by President Moi nine months later (*Weekly Review*, November 7, 1986). The KANU Governing Council passed a resolution in December 1986 giving the Party the mandate to summon Cabinet Ministers to give an account of the performance of their ministries (*Daily Nation*, December 17, 1986), placing the Party above the Government. In the city of Mombassa, a senior Police Officer was summoned for disciplinary action by the Mombassa KANU branch for contradicting a directive from the branch chairman regarding the flow of traffic on Madaraka Day celebrations (*Daily Nation*, May 27, 1987). Virtually no segment of the Kenyan society remained unaffected by the activities of the party.

The ruling party took its initiatives to unexplored arenas. In April 1986, the Party announced that preliminary elections in which voters queue behind candidates of their choice will precede the 1988 General election (*Daily Nation*, April 10, 1986, p. 1). The new "election" experiment raised a storm of opposition, especially among the clergy, but the President ignored the protest and two weeks later made the announcement that a bill would be moved in Parliament to make the queuing part of the country's electoral law (*Daily Nation*, August 26, 1986). Such a Presidential pronouncement was as good as law. Parliament could not even debate the issue. The role of Parliament at this stage was to go through the protocols and legislate the queuing system, which it did with a unanimous vote.

KANU RECRUITMENT CAMPAIGNS

The party recruitment drive, spearheaded by President Moi, registered more than 5 million people in 1985 (*Weekly Review*, October 14, 1988), 6 million in 1986, and 8 million in 1988. This was a major accomplishment for a party that had only a few thousand registered members when Moi first assumed the Presidency.

To accomplish this, a variety of arm-twisting tactics and plain coercion were used by the administration to get people to register. An incident in the town of Nanyuki, in which civil servants were barred from entering their offices if they did not have KANU cards, was a good example. This incident was only one of many similar cases in various parts of the country.

In September 1984, KANU announced the winners of the membership recruitment drive for the previous year. Nandi district led, having registered 89.58% of its population, and Machakos came in second with 84.7% (*Daily Nation*, September 15, 1984). Machakos also received a shield for having the largest number of members recruited, 399,661, to Nandi's 126,992. Kakamega District was last having recruited only 6.09% of its population.

The pomp and political overtones surrounding the award ceremony provided the bedrock for the zeal with which the districts were to conduct future recruitment. Individual districts set goals for themselves and mapped out strategies for accomplishing those goals. In the stampede to become the next winner of the KANU recruitment award and to capture the highly coveted "Presidential recognition," so as to earn the district a place in the annals of the party records, coercion, blackmail, and other not-so-clean tactics were employed. The final figures were not, therefore, truly reflective of the number of Kenyans who voluntarily joined the party. The figures that might reflect the strength of the party were those of "Life Members," which stood at 14,548 as of May 1985 (*Daily Nation*, May 15, 1985).

In 1985, the Party established a disciplinary committee charged with the task of instilling discipline by taking tough measures against errant party members and politicians (*Weekly Review*, October 14, 1988). The committee was empowered to deal with all disciplinary matters in the Party. But like all unchecked bodies, the committee turned out to be a monster used and manipulated to drive fear into the hearts of Kenyans. The President dissolved the committee arguing that it had transformed itself into an instrument of fear and had arrogated itself too much power (*Weekly Review*, September 18, 1987). In other words, the committee appeared to have been rivaling the President's own powers.

KANU AND OTHER ORGANIZATIONS

In its quest to influence every sector of the Kenyan society, the ruling party instituted a strategy to incorporate other organizations and bodies into its own machinery. One of the first such organizations to be incorporated into KANU was Maendeleo ya Wanawake Organization (MYWO), a nongovernmental nationwide women's organization. Maendeleo has a membership of more than 20,000 women's group throughout the country. The majority of its membership reside in the rural areas. The affiliation in May 1987 turned the organization into KANU-MYWO (KMYWO for short).

The next major organization to be incorporated into KANU was the Central Organization of Trade Unions (COTU). This affiliation was announced by KANU's national chairman (Oloo Aringo) as a move to strengthen the country (*Daily Nation*, April 29, 1989). Although MYWO and COTU appeared to have accepted their affiliation fate to KANU without major struggles, the same was not true for the Law Society of Kenya (LSK). An announcement from the KANU Director for Legal and International Affairs, saying that the Party would soon embark on a campaign to affiliate various organizations to it, including the LSK, "in order to enhance unity and economic development," met with very strong reaction from the LSK. Known for its radical views and uncompromising position with the government, the mention of the LSK by KANU might have been a trial balloon by the government. When it failed, the President reacted by condemning the LSK, saying, "it was absurd, ridiculous and obnoxious to think that the LSK, which has no Kenyan identity, could be affiliated to KANU" (*Daily Nation*, December 13, 1989). The President pointed out that the suggestion by a Party official was "his own personal view" and not a KANU policy position.

These and numerous other changes undertaken by the Kenya government were causing concern among many in the country. The concerns of the church were that in the absence of a legal political opposition, the government was becoming reckless in the running of the country. The systematic silencing of the population, the unwarranted changes of the Constitution, rampant corruption, tribalism, nepotism, high unemployment, and a chaotic academic system among other government-created ills were all destined to bring the country into ruins. Sections of the church, both Catholic and Protestant, felt they had a moral duty to point out the shortfalls of the government in the hope of rescuing the situation before it got any worse.

THE CHURCH

The church in Kenya has, for many years, been politically engaged. Its pro-active stand in politics can best be understood from within the context of liberation theology. The spread and popularity of liberation theology, especially among third-world churches, finds its roots and relevance in the local context in which it operates. Liberation theology is not merely an attempt by the Church to get involved in national politics; rather, it is a quest for solutions to the political and social injustices taking place within the borders of their own nations. Evidently, the clergy in contemporary Kenya have borrowed heavily from the thoughts and practices of liberation theology from around the world.

Gustavo Gutierrez (1973), one of the foremost liberation theologians from Latin America, offered what he calls three different levels of liberation: (a) political liberation—release from economic, social, and political oppression; (b) personal liberation—Christ the Savior liberates man from sin; and (c) historical liberation—man assumes conscious responsibility for his own destiny (p. 176). Liberation theology emerges from the interplay between Christian belief and Christian practice.

In terms of its applicability to society, liberation theology could be understood as a contemporary strategy better able to address and to change social conditions in which "the oppressed come together to understand their situation through a process of conscientization, discover the cause of their oppression, organize themselves into movements and act in coordinated fashions" (Boff & Boff, 1987, p. 5). For the church in Kenya, liberation theology has meant addressing the issues that are foremost to Kenyans and doing so in a manner that would have the greatest impact. It has meant developing strategies to communicate to the nation as a whole—to extend the pulpits of their local churches to cover an area far beyond that of the immediate congregation, to encompass the whole country. It has meant working in alliance with the secular media.

Michael Zweig (1991) identified four themes that he says permeates liberation theology. He observed that: (a) liberation theology calls on each person to be socially active in the process of human history, for it is in "our temporal works" that the work of God is done; (b) that in history, it is correct to side with the poor and the oppressed; (c) that it is necessary to go beyond acts of individual charity and good works to identify and then change the institutions through which poverty is created and the poor are oppressed; and (d) that it is necessary to have a social analysis of poverty and oppression, wherein religion and social science must converse. McGovern (1980) points out that many Christians have not only developed a new awareness of a call to denounce injustice, to be on the side of the poor and the oppressed and to transform the world, but have come to the realization that ways of addressing these concerns in the past have failed. Charity toward the poor, appeals to the rich and the powerful, the promise of technology, reliance on political changes, all these have failed (McGovern, 1980). Many in the third world have come to subscribe to the view that liberation theology is an attempt to make religion relevant to the lives of religious people seeking justice.

THE CONTEXT

Liberation theology is a critical reflection of the socioeconomic and political situation in the world from a Christian perspective. As such, the methodology of liberation theology takes politics seriously, but not merely as an additional aspect of religious life; rather, it places it squarely in the center of theological development itself (Pottenger, 1989). Liberation theologians are interested in assessing the dynamics of society in their search for the cause of social injustice. As a result, argues Pottenger, the theologians utilize studies and theories (including Marxist) that can assist them in this quest. The ultimate target of liberation theology is the existing political system that is seen as being structurally unjust, and it is only through changing it that real change can occur elsewhere within the system.

African theologian, Jean-Marc Ela (1986), has challenged the African Church to awaken the consciousness of the masses, and for the Church itself to become a sign of hope for those who live in hopelessness. Indeed, for Ela, the Church must feel that it is its duty to liberate Africa (p. 77). The church in Kenya has taken up this challenge and has long functioned as the "unofficial" political opposition to the government. Although "personal liberation," as pointed out by Gutierrez, is important, political and historical liberation are equally important.

Ela (1986) has challenged the use of "national unity" by most African governments as an excuse to liquidate all opposition. He contends that once those in power decide national unity (ambiguous as that might be) is a necessary condition for economic and social development, the exercise of basic freedoms is erased from daily life. The tendency, he says, is to make police repression a national institution in the name of unity. The Church, he argues, has to stand up as "the conscience of the nation," stating that in a political system in which all opposition is illegal, and in which torture is used not only to obtain information but also as a method of governing and to stifle opposition, the church cannot remain silent.

The point to be made here is that under such a historical context of abusive power, in which the government controls the means of communication (the entire mass media), in which intellectuals have lost their power of expression and unionism has become a myth—as clearly demonstrated in Kenya—the Church, says Ela (1986), might be the only institution capable of speaking out and saving what is left of freedom in Africa. The Church, under such circumstances, Ela has argued, can no longer afford to be silent. Its silence would be a grave omission, a betrayal of Africa and the gospel. The Church will need to speak up and voice its protestation against the system, doing so in the name of the Creator and Savior. A young breed of theologians from both the Catholic and Protestant churches in the country have taken the challenge from liberation theologians like Ela and vigorously worked at putting it into practice. They have challenged the political process without regard for their own lives.[5]

The pastoral letters issued by the Catholic church and read throughout the country, and followed by small group discussions on the significance of the messages, are clearly reminiscent of the Christian base communities (CBCs) that sprung up throughout most Latin and Central American countries in the 1970s. The progressive and radical clergy who worked through the CBCs implemented innovative techniques developed by Brazilian educator Paulo Freire to overcome illiteracy among the poor. Freire's method of "conscientization" extended beyond simply helping the poor overcome debilitating problems of illiteracy; it included an ideological critique of prevailing socioeconomic conditions to help them become literate about and overcome the oppressive state as well. Through the CBCs, peasants were educated to become aware of the "true nature" of their socially dependent and

---

[5]The Rt. Rev., Alexander Kipsang Muge, Anglican Bishop of Eldoret Diocese, and one of the leading critics of the government, was killed in a mysterious road accident in August 1990. The accident occurred only a few days after a Cabinet Minister had threatened the Bishop that if he (Bishop Muge) set foot in the Minister's District, he would not leave there alive. When that threat came true, the government found itself having to plead its innocence, but to date the Kenyan public hold the government responsible for the death of Bishop Muge. The death of Bishop Muge also came at a time when the government was facing a legitimacy crisis following the murder of the Minister for Foreign Affairs, Dr. Robert Ouko, and the fingers pointed at some powerful government officials

unjust situation. From their new religious perspective, they saw the State as supporting and thus giving legitimacy to that which was illegitimate in the eyes of God (Pottenger, 1989). As the poor came to a new awareness of themselves, they began to critically question their situation and to recognize the possibility of changing it. This new awareness meant looking critically at the overall national social, political, and economic contradictions and taking action against the oppressive elements of reality. For the poor peasants, such awakenings proved to be a major source of empowerment for them and a sore spot for those in political power.

The pastoral letters from the Catholic church in Kenya were not only read from the pulpit during Sunday Mass, but their content was translated into the local vernacular languages to allow for in-depth discussion and personalized analysis by the rural population. The small discussion groups sought ways to understand where they fit within the context of the bigger socioeconomic and political power play of their country. Individuals were encouraged to make suggestions on what they thought they could do to improve their own situation. The translation of pastoral letters and other religious materials dealing with contemporary issues into local vernaculars and contextualizing their discussions, was one of the most disturbing activities of the church to the country's political establishment. The same materials written, produced, and distributed in English appear to pass unnoticed by the authorities. A number of church leaders have confirmed that some materials, once translated to local vernaculars, have caused major friction with the government, and some, as a result, were confiscated.

Liberation theology, in its many forms, is a phenomenon that is here to stay. It is a movement that has shaken the Christian foundation and the political establishment in many third-world nations. It is a movement that will continue to resurface every time social injustices reach an intolerable stage. Liberation theology speaks to those who are suffering and offers them clear and forceful solutions. The clergy, within this political equation, becomes the voice of the voiceless, the voice of the ordinary people.

THE CHURCH-MEDIA ALLIANCE IN KENYA

The alliance forged between the church and the media in Kenya was precipitated by events in the country's political process. The 1982 Constitutional amendment had effectively silenced all legitimate political opposition in the country. The only institution in the country that could still speak out against the de facto government was the church. As the clergy in a number of churches began speaking out from their pulpits on national issues, the media saw an opportunity to tap into the church as a source of political news. The church, which had argued all along that the content of its message had never changed, nevertheless, welcomed the new interest taken by the media on its Sunday sermons and other religious functions. The church saw the media as the ideal channel for extending its message of personal, political, and historical liberation to the entire country. It became a means for the church to critique the country's political system at a time when those who would have done so had been systematically silenced.

For many years, the church and the government in Kenya enjoyed a cordial relationship. The government, which controls broadcasting in the country, allowed the church to have live radio broadcast for Sunday Services. A timetable was worked out for the live broadcast to be done from different churches each Sunday. The government, angered by what it called unwarranted criticism from the clergy, withdrew this "privilege" in the mid-1980s. From then on, all religious radio broadcasts were prerecorded, then screened and portions edited out if found to be undesirable. In the ensuing church-media alliance to disseminate information to the general public, the use of radio broadcast was quickly discarded due to tight government censorship. The gatekeepers would not let anything remotely critical of the administration go through, lest they lose their jobs.

The ensuing war of words between the church and the state, aimed at swaying public opinion on issues of national importance, came to be played out in the press. The government's paper, *Kenya Times*, launched in 1983 to function as the principle government mouthpiece, also joined the private press in posting its reporters to cover a select number of churches. The centrality of the church as a key player in national politics was underscored.

"THE CHURCH BEAT"

By 1986, all the three national daily newspapers—the *Standard*, established in 1902, the *Daily Nation*, established in 1964, and the *Kenya Times*,[6]—were operating a regular "church beat." Each paper had reporters assigned to cover a selected number of churches in Nairobi and around the country. According to the Editor-in-Chief of the *Weekly Review* magazine, Amboka Andere, who had previously held the same position at *Kenya Times*, the church beat tradition began in the early 1970s when the Reverend Dr. Henry Okullu (Anglican) was the Provost of All Saints Cathedral, Nairobi. Dr. Okullu, who later became the Anglican bishop of Maseno South, used to deliver very interesting sermons on Sundays. His sermons were reproduced in the then-Christian publication,

---

[6]The circulation figures for these three papers differ slightly depending on the source. The *Europa World Year Book 1994* shows the *Nation* with 165,000, the *Standard* with 70,000, and *Kenya Times* with 36,000. The *Willings Press Guide* 1993 shows the figures as: *Nation* 201,164; *Standard* 30.537 (City edition) and 27,522 (national edition); and *Kenyan Times*—no figures. A media survey conducted by Research International East Africa limited in March 1989 to determine newspaper readership showed the Nation with circulation figures of 234,600 (*Daily Nation*, August 16, 1989).

Target. One of the things that seasoned Dr. Okullu's sermons was his candid and repeated criticism of the then-powerful Attorney-General, Charles Njonjo. When all other segments of society shied away from criticizing so powerful a political figure, Okullu made a name for himself by doing so. The newspapers decided to join in the act by covering Okullu's Sunday services. This media coverage did not, however, spread to other churches, although coverage of major religious functions did take place.

Dr. Okullu was among a crop of clergymen who, following the banning of the only opposition political party in 1969, came forward as the "voice of the voiceless" and determined to champion the rights of the common people in the absence of opposition politicians. The clergy began discussing from their pulpits what the politicians could no longer discuss in public. Subsequently, the press shifted its "political beat" to reporting from the church. This process of change took time. All throughout the 1970s and the early part of the 1980s, the institution of Parliament remained robust and politically effective. Within the single-party Parliament, the back benchers (non-Cabinet MPs) provided a formidable opposition by criticizing the government and asking searching questions of Cabinet Ministers. In fact, President Kenyatta was not immune from embarrassing questions in Parliament (Hachten, 1971). Furthermore, the Parliamentary proceedings were fully reported in the daily papers, giving the country a sense of true political freedom. But by the early 1980s, the structure within the one-party state had acquired new dimensions. The President, surrounded by a group of thin-skinned politicians, who equated criticism of the government to sedition and treason, began to crackdown on all those thought to be dissidents. The institution of Parliament was reduced to a mere "rubber stamp" for the Executive branch of government. Progressively, power was concentrated in the Executive and away from other branches of government.

Between 1984 and 1992, the church came out and opposed virtually every major decision proposed and taken by the government. In fact, this led to a split within the church as some denominations took issues with others over the level or degree of church involvement in politics. A number of churches, mostly Evangelical churches and those whose origin are indigenous to Kenya and are known to hold moderate views on political issues, opted to side with the government. Some of these churches decided to terminate their membership in the National Council of Churches of Kenya (NCCK), accusing the body of becoming too political. At the height of the Constitutional Amendment debate in November 1986 (to remove the security of tenure of the Office of the Attorney-General), the African Inland Church withdrew its membership from NCCK (*Weekly Review*, December 5, 1986). The African Gospel Church also withdrew its membership from the NCCK, claiming the council had taken "to questioning the powers of the ruling party" (*Weekly Review*, December 12, 1986, p. 11). During this time period, other indigenous churches that were not members of the Protestant umbrella body, the NCCK, came out in support of the government and in condemnation of the NCCK.

The church in Kenya came out with strong opinions on several issues including elections, Constitutional amendments, the supremacy of the ruling party, detention without trial, expulsion of politicians from KANU, the role of the church in politics, corruption in government, tribalism, among others. Although the church repeatedly reminded the political establishment that church and politics were inseparable, the government repeatedly accused the clergy of setting up an unofficial political opposition from the pulpit. The clergy argued that the church cannot be divorced from politics, and church leaders have a right to comment on political events. The Anglican bishop of Mount Kenya East, the Rev. Dr. David Gitari, argued that "politics is too important to be left to professional politicians" (*Daily Nation*, November 7, 1987), especially in the political context of a one-party state.

A close examination of the press coverage of the church, from January 1982 to December 1992, shows that the press took the lead in its effort to report on what was being said by the churches. To determine the working relationship between these two institutions, all the stories on "church and politics" appearing on the *Daily Nations* newspaper were summarized into three main categories: (a) stories originating only from Sunday morning services or sermons, (b) stories originating from all other functions attended or presided over by the clergy, and (c) stories emanating from the clergy through press releases or press conferences. The resulting figures are reported in Table 13.1.

The first category shows the press commitment to venture out and cover what was being said from the church pulpits. This is the category that shows the trend in the establishment of the "church beat" in Kenyan journalism. By 1988, the clergy started to take a clear pro-active approach to the dissemination of information. Instead of relying entirely on the press to come and cover their Sunday sermons or other official church or secular functions,

Table 13.1. Church and Politics Stories in the Kenyan Daily Nation.

Year	Sermons	Other functions	Press release/conference
1982	0	7	0
1983	3	16	6
1984	7	28	5
1985	1	15	3
1986	25	25	8
1987	19	17	8
1988	20	26	13
1989	35	19	33
1990	108	34	58
1991	92	26	31
1992	40	8	38

they called press conferences and issued press releases to state their position on particular pertinent political issues.

What these figures show was that once the press was convinced of the national importance of what the clergy were saying on Sunday mornings, it posted more correspondents to cover more churches than it had done in the past. The result was that the stories from the churches reaching the press increased tremendously.

In many countries around the world, the church has had a strong media, both in print and broadcast. This has not been the tradition in Kenya. Since independence, the broadcast media has been exclusively owned and operated by the government, under a policy that only the government can own and operate broadcast media in the country.

In forging an alliance, the church and the press separately and jointly came up with communication strategies used to keep the de facto government accountable and to nudge it towards democratic ideals. The notion of an "extended pulpit" was one such communication strategy. The press found within the church a large number of clergy who were saying from their church pulpits what the outlawed political opposition would have been saying in Parliament, in political rallies, or on the streets of urban areas. The church saw the free service provided by the press as a service to the country. Their Christian message was communicated nationwide at no cost to them. In other words, the church pulpit was "extended" from its physical location to all corners of the country.

In January 1988, the Catholic Church in Kenya established a Justice and Peace Commission in a bid to respond adequately and in a timely fashion to the country's political problems (*Daily Nation*, January 2, 1988). By the following year, the church was able to issue a pastoral letter, signed by all the bishops, within a couple of weeks. Prior to this, the bishops traditionally issued one or two pastoral letters a year. Other churches like the Anglican or the National Council of Churches of Kenya started using pastoral letters as a communication tool. These letters were also translated into local vernaculars and discussed in detailed in small groups in churches all across the country.

The church, by virtue of being a spiritual place of worship, exempt from many regulations governing other forms of public gatherings, became a communication strategy in its own right. The press could still cover the churches with a relative degree of "immunity" from overt government harassment. The "church beat" for the Kenyan press was, for all practical purposes, the equivalent of covering a political opposition party in a country that has no such opposition. The church answered the call of opposition politics in the absence of such an opposition.

Other strategies used included press releases and press conferences by the clergy, seminars, workshops and conference on specific topics, and the cross-denominational invitation of clergy by other clergy as guest "speakers" in their churches.

The press in Kenya, aware of its limitation within the political environment it must function in, approached the church from the point of view of a "neutral and objective" observer. This was not, however, always the case. The press had its own mission and agenda, and the church became a convenient and worthwhile partner. Although the press did not always set the agenda for the issues discussed, it framed the discussion in such a way as to prolong the debate on certain issues. In the end, both parties appeared pleased with the alliance; it was mutually beneficial.

CONCLUSION

Freedom of the press, the right to fully report and criticize the conduct of government without fear of official recrimination (Hachten, 1971), was a principle shared by both the media and the clergy in Kenya. The church constantly stood behind the press in fighting for press freedom, especially in calling for an end to the harassment of journalists by the authorities. The NCCK, aware of the power of the press, launched its own monthly magazine, *Beyond*, in June 1985, and used it as a forum to discuss most of the issues raised by the clergy. However, although the clergy could speak with the immunities of the "cloth," their communication tool, *Beyond* magazine, could not escape the powers of the government. It was proscribed by the government following its coverage of the 1988 controversial elections.

A partnership for democracy between the church and the press is, by all counts, a unique political phenomenon. Since the emergence of liberation theology, with its emphasis on a praxis, the possibility of the church colluding with other institutions in society for the purposes of pursuing democracy has received serious consideration. What has yet to received similar consideration is an integrated approach that brings together these odd institutions. In other words, the continued exclusion of the church in both political and communication studies reveals the existence of a theoretical blind spot begging for attention. In third-world countries, in which the church is clearly involved in the day-to-day politics of the country and functioning as a leading catalyst for political change, their role needs to be included, not as a separate entity, but in conjunction with the institutions of politics and communication.

The clergy in Kenya hold the view that they are called on, as part of their ministry here on earth, to serve as the "conscience of the nation" by pointing out evil in society; that they have been appointed by God as "watchdogs" over the nation and are responsible for failing to carry out that mandate.

REFERENCES

Boff, L., & Boff, C. (1987). *Introducing liberation theology.* New York: Maryknoll.

Bratton, M., & Van de Walle, N. (1992). Toward governance in Africa: Popular demands and state response. In G. Hyden & M. Bratton (Eds.), *Governance and politics in Africa.* Boulder, CO: Lynne Rienner Publishers.

Daily Nation. (1982, January—1992, December). Nairobi, Kenya.

Ela, J. M. (1986). *Africa cry.* New York: Maryknoll.

Gutierrez, G. (1973). *Theology of liberation.* New York: Maryknoll.

Hachten, W. A. (1971). *Muffled drums: The news in Africa.* Iowa: Iowa University.

McGovern, A. F. (1980). *Marxism: An American Christian perspective.* New York: Maryknoll.

Pottenger, J. R. (1989). *The political theory of liberation theology: Toward a reconvergence of social values and social science.* New York: State University of New York Press.

The Standard. (1982, July 20). Nairobi, Kenya

Weekly Review. (1982, January—1992, December). Nairobi, Kenya

Zweig, M. (Ed.). (1991). *Religion and economic justice.* Philadelphia: Temple University Press.

Section IV

International Institutions: Creating Global Public Spheres or Transnational Markets

Chapter 14

Is There a U.S. Foreign Policy in Telecommunications? Transatlantic Trade Policy as a Case Study*

Andrew Calabrese
Wendy Redal

The principle aims of this chapter are to identify the mechanisms and strategies for U.S. foreign trade in telecommunications and its rationale with respect to the concept of the "public interest" for U.S. citizens. Clearly, much more is at stake on a global level than the interests of U.S. citizens when it comes to US foreign policy in telecommunications. However, it is misguided to assume that all U.S. citizens are the beneficiaries of U.S. foreign policies, particularly with respect to trade, and it is increasingly necessary to understand the relationship between foreign and domestic telecommunications policies. Although it has never been more important to critically assess U.S. foreign trade policies, particularly with

*This chapter was presented at the 19th General Assembly of the International Association for Mass Communication Research, Seoul, Korea, in July 1994, and a shorter version was published in the journal *Telematics and Informatics* in 1995 12(1), pp. 35-56. It is republished here with permission from the publisher, Elsevier Science Ltd. The data on the Uruguay Round of the General Agreement on Tarrifs and Trade, and on U.S. and European policies and investments in telecommunications, have not been updated since July 1994, although our argument remains the same.

respect to peripheral nations, it becomes all too easy to disregard how those trade policies relate to U.S. domestic social policy and issues of domestic peripheralization (Calabrese, 1991). In pursuing opportunity and wealth in other countries, what impacts are telecommunications monopolies having on U.S. citizens? This is not a jingoistic question, but rather one which draws attention to the concept of citizenship in an age of rapidly expanding global telecommunications. How do we define citizenship in an age of relative decline in sovereignty even among the most powerful states? What responsibility do trade negotiators and domestic monopolies with expanding foreign investments have toward citizens in their own countries? These are questions of much broader significance than for U.S. citizens alone. Despite the relative economic decline of the United States in the global economy, U.S.-based capital and trade negotiators continue to have considerable global influence, both by example and through strategic efforts, on the relationship between capital, states, and citizens.

This chapter raises these issues through an analysis of the role of the United States in telecommunications trade in Europe. U.S. firms have tried, somewhat unsuccessfully, to gain greater access to the telecommunications markets of some of the most affluent countries in the world, only to find that the national governments of many of these countries generally are resistant to the idea of allowing exogenous capital to enter and potentially come to dominate their markets. U.S.-Japan and US-EU (European Union) trade in telecommunications both provide useful case studies, although it is the latter that receives attention in the following discussion. This is a choice arising in part due to the current heightened tensions between the United States and the EU over the GATT talks and over the future directions of European economic integration as it relates to trade policy. A particularly interesting implication of U.S.-EU telecommunications trade conflict is that it vividly illustrates a rude awakening for U.S. policymakers to the limits of U.S. global economic and political dominance. It also calls into question the relative degree to which U.S. policymakers have reconciled the interests of U.S. citizens with the interests of the increasingly mobile capital for telecommunications investments.

THE STATE IN THE GEOGRAPHY OF ACCUMULATION

David Harvey (1975) describes how and why the confinement of capital by the nation-state ultimately is a hindrance to the accumulation process. Quoting from Marx's *Grundrisse*, he states:

> The geographical landscape which fixed and immobile capital comprises is both a crowning glory of past capital development and a prison which inhibits the further progress of accumulation because the very building of this landscape is antithetical to the "tearing down of spatial barriers" and ultimately even to the "annihilation of space by time." (p. 13)

Harvey also notes that "the fresh room for accumulation which capitalism must define can exist only in the form of pre-capitalist societies which provide untapped markets to absorb what is a perpetual tendency for the overproduction of commodities under capitalism" (p. 14). This can be illustrated in the case of Central and Eastern Europe, where telecommunications products and services originating from countries where there is a high degree of market saturation—particularly the EU and the U.S.—are now being developed and exported to countries where there is significant potential demand for expansion among the emerging capitalist class and where the lack of endogenous capital makes it relatively attractive for foreign direct investment and dominance (Calabrese, 1995).

As Marx argued in Volume 3 of *Capital*, "If capital is sent abroad, this is not done because it absolutely could not be applied at home, but because it can be employed at a higher rate of profit in a foreign country" (cited in Harvey, 1975, pp. 15-16). If it is possible to invest cheaply abroad and gain rapid and decisive long-term dominance, such opportunities will not be abandoned if access to domestic markets can be held in check. This motivation underlies industrial policies designed to mount barriers to entry into home markets while simultaneously attempting to reduce or eliminate barriers to entry into foreign markets. Although their industrial policies differ, the EU and the U.S. share this motive. Ultimately, U.S.—and EU-based telecommunications firms are both after the same thing, namely, expanded markets and dominance on a sectoral or geographic basis. Neither wants to lose dominance in home markets, and each want to enter the other's markets with fewer obstacles than currently exist. What distinguishes them is that the EU is undergoing a process of internal integration or "harmonization;" a condition already present in the U.S., but also a condition that is in some ways contradictory toward another stated EU objective— liberalization. "Harmonization" as practiced by the EU appears in some senses to be a nationalist (or regionalist) movement. Liberalization, to the extent that it presses for transnational development, potentially works against nationalism. In order to liberalize and thereby promote competition, EU national governments and industries have had to begin to sacrifice some of the tight controls over national industries that historically have characterized the operation of national post and telegraph and telephone systems (PTTs) in Europe.

What motivates this movement towards harmonization and liberalization in the European Union? Clearly, external political and economic pressure, particularly from the United States, has been a critical factor. As numerous observers have noted, the domestic telecommunications market of the US was liberalized unilaterally at a time when market conditions in Europe and Japan were far more restricted, the result being an open invitation for foreign competition (e.g., Arlandis, 1993; Reynolds, 1991). The breakup of AT&T was, as domestic and foreign critics have suggested, probably a mistake because it created a lack of parity between the U.S. and its major trading partners, namely, Europe and Japan, and it did not provoke the immediate desired result of reciprocal liberalization. This apparent error on the part of the U.S. may have seemed in 1982 like a primarily domestic-oriented decision, but it has had far-reaching global resonance not simply by reducing domestic barriers to U.S.-based companies seeking international markets, but also by inviting foreign competition into U.S. markets. As the Office of Technology Assessment (OTA) of the U.S. Congress (1993) noted:

> Deregulation resulted in opening the US telecommunications equipment market to foreign as well as American firms. This had immediate and significant trade consequences. The US balance of trade in telecommunications equipment went from a surplus of $275 million in 1982 to a deficit of $2.6 billion 6 years later, due largely to the lack of reciprocal overseas; markets for customer premises equipment (handsets and other terminal equipment). (p. 136)

Consequently, through various unilateral and multilateral moves, some entities (generally uncoordinated) in U.S. government have had to respond to pressure from U.S.-based telecommunications equipment and service providers by working, sometimes aggressively and ineptly, at trying to force open European and Japanese markets in a manner and at a pace which generally has not been accepted. Nevertheless, official U.S. efforts in telecommunications trade continue to be directed at the aim of liberalizing foreign markets, particularly through what are characterized as "retaliatory measures" in response to what are viewed as nonreciprocal trade relations. This pattern of trade conflict is evident in U.S.-EU telecommunications trade as EU efforts toward internal market harmonization continue apace while liberalization, particularly to the extent that it opens the EU to exogenous competition, moves more slowly. Perhaps a lesson was learned by EU members from the hasty movement towards liberalization in the United States, and EU telecommunications trade and industry leaders do not want to quickly "sell the store" as some suggest the United States has done.

In general, EU integration is a defensive measure designed to consolidate a geographic space through which supranational European capital can compete both within and beyond Europe. As Ernest Mandel (1970) noted, the political geography of accumulation is such that the larger and more harmonized the European market, the greater the profits, and the greater the opportunity to maintain endogenous and resist exogenous control over European economics, politics, and culture, and likewise the greater the opportunity for European-based enterprises to compete favorably in world markets. As he argued in reference to the Common Market,

> Confronted by the inherent conflict between the bourgeois mode of production and the bourgeois nation state, the European bourgeoisie is attempting the best partial and provisional solution available to it for the moment, the creation of a large free trade area. (p. 53)

Individual bourgeois European nation states, according to Mandel, could not survive American competition unless they converged in the direction of "supranational state organs" in which there is "increasing interpenetration of capital" and banks and businesses "cease to belong to this or that national Capital and become the property of capitalists in all member states" (p. 62, emphasis added). The choice for European capital, he concluded, was either a united Europe or a Europe dominated by U.S. capital:

> Ultimately, the alternatives are the following: either a general tendency towards the interpenetration of European capital, with a greater chance of successful competition with America, or the disintegration of the Common Market and a reversion to narrow economic nationalism, leaving the door wide open to increasing US domination of the world capitalist system. (p. 65)

Of course, from Mandel's perspective it is not only U.S. capital that is a threat, but also the U.S. government. The post-cold war US trade strategy and pursuit of a so-called "peace dividend" must be interpreted in light of the economic integration of the European Union, which threatens to hasten the continued decline of U.S. hegemony over Europe. The United State's trade positions, as reflected in the GATT and NAFTA, also should be interpreted to a significant degree in light of European unity. The end of the cold war and European economic unity have led to an opportunity for the national governments of the EU to collectively challenge some of the less desired outcomes of the post-World War II settlement, manifested most notably in the legacy of the U.S. "Marshall Plan." No historian doubts that postwar Europe was in need of U.S. aid, and U.S. firms seized the moment by flooding goods into war-torn countries with minimal productive capacity. But as a recent United Nations Economic Commission for Europe (UNECE) report noted, the Marshall Plan established a pattern of bilateral (contra multilateral) trading relationships with individual European countries, which "restricted the growth of intra-European trade and the development of specialization on the basis of comparative advantage," and assured for a period of time a dependency on U.S. producers (UN Economic Commission for Europe, 1990, p. 10; quoted in Milenkovitch, 1991, p. 161). Despite the fact that exploiting bilateral trading opportunities worked to the advantage of US companies operating in Europe, bilateralism was not unilaterally sought or imposed by the United States. Rather, European leadership efforts towards a postwar recovery did not from the start include a strong vision for a politically united continent and the prevailing political sentiment among European leaders was that market integration should not require significant sacrifices in national sovereignty (Stirk & Willis, 1991). Given the current waning of these former obstacles to European economic unity and the relative decline of U.S. global economic and political hegemony, the EU now has increased ability, incentive and opportunity to rival and exceed U.S. global economic power. As many intellectuals, including Mandel, have concluded, the celebrated and short-lived "American Century" is over, and other economic powers, namely, Japan and a single-market European Union, seriously challenge U.S. economic and political influence.

It may have been simplistic and premature for Mandel to assume that U.S. capital represented the only significant threat to European capital and sovereignty, although the growth and global power of the Japanese economy was not yet much of a concern in 1970. To assume that the present establishment of a single European market was provoked by competitive threats from the United States alone would be simplistic and erroneous. In all likelihood, a revision of Mandel's analysis would acknowledge the global economic ascent of Japan. However, to fail to acknowledge continued U.S. threats would be highly misleading, and European regional economic integration should be interpreted in that light. At the same time, the U.S. push for a North American free trade agreement must be interpreted in large part as a response to the European movement towards regionalization (Weintraub, 1991).

Although there are significant differences between the United States and the EU in terms of the geography of accumulation, there is limited value in deciding whether the United State's or the EU's capitalists are kinder and gentler in a world of increasing transnational mergers and acquisitions, foreign direct investment, capital flight from markets in which labor demands and public policies raise business costs, and other evidence of capital's global mobility and footloose perspective towards particular locales. The evidence and analysis provided in this chapter provides a basis for understanding "public interest" issues in telecommunications with respect to related developments in technological convergence and global economic restructuring, as they are manifested in the relations within and between two core "states," that is, the United States and the EU.

U.S.-EU TRADE IN TELECOMMUNICATIONS

As the following discussion demonstrates, the telecommunications and audiovisual services industries constitute particularly contentious and complex arenas in trade relations between the United States and the European Union. As in other parts of the world, U.S. influence on telecommunications in the EU is manifest in several ways, including directly through U.S. influence on EU policies and through business partnerships between U.S. and EU firms. Indirect means of influence include examples set by U.S. domestic policies such as the Federal Communications Commission (FCC) "open network architecture" policy and the distinction made in the United States between "basic" and "enhanced" services. What follows is an overview of these forms of influence and related tensions.

UNILATERAL U.S. TELECOMMUNICATIONS TRADE INSTRUMENTS AND POLICIES: SECTION 310(B) OF THE COMMUNICATIONS ACT

The primary U.S. restrictions on foreign ownership of U.S. broadcasting and common carrier facilities can be found in Section 310(b) of the Communications Act of 1934. In that provision, the U.S. Congress prohibited ownership of such facilities by foreign citizens or by corporations organized under foreign laws. Furthermore, no more than 20% of the capital stock of a U.S. broadcasting station or a common carrier can be "owned of record or voted by aliens or their representatives or by a foreign government or representative thereof or by any corporation organized under the laws of a foreign country" (47 U.S.C.310(B)(3)). Finally, unless the FCC decides that "the public interest will be served," it is illegal for a broadcasting station or common carrier to be "directly or indirectly controlled" by a corporation THAT has an officer who is not a U.S. citizen or which has a board of directors constituted by 25% or more non-U.S. citizens, or THAT has more than 25% of its capital stock "owned of record or voted by aliens, their representatives, or by a foreign government or representative thereof, or by any corporation organized under the laws of a foreign country" (47 U.S.C.310(B)(4)).

The precursors to these laws were enacted in 1912 and 1927. In 1927, a primary concern was that national security could be breached during wartime, a concern THAT arose because during World War I U.S. radio facilities had been used to send warnings to German ships. Another motivating concern, according to the National Telecommunications and Information Administration (NTIA), was the fear that foreigners who owned radio stations (television did not exist yet) might "spread propaganda" during wartime (U.S. Department of Commerce, NTIA, 1993b). As the NTIA has concluded, these fears no longer have much validity, if they ever did. Yet, the rules exist and continue to serve as a lever for preventing foreign entry into U.S. broadcasting and common carrier markets. Whether their motives stem from security concerns or not, many countries in the world, including Japan, most EU countries, India, Canada, and Mexico have similar or more restrictive barriers to foreign ownership.

THE MODIFIED FINAL JUDGMENT AND THE CABLE ACT OF 1984

Domestic telecommunications policy in the United States ostensibly has focused on promoting increased competition since the 1982 decision to break up the Bell system. Among the notable outcomes of that decision has been the accelerating rate of technological innovation and the rapid increase in the number of domestic and foreign competitors in equipment and value-added services.[1] Other outcomes of that decision have been the prohibition of the

---

[1] According to the U.S. Department of Commerce (1994), "value-added network

seven regional Bell holding companies (RHCs), the owners of most of the U.S. local telephone monopolies, from manufacturing telecommunications equipment or from providing interstate long-distance service. Furthermore, the Cable Communications Act of 1984 prevents local telephone companies from owning or operating cable television services in their own telephone service areas. Jill Hills (1993) argues that if U.S. telecommunications carriers currently expanding abroad, such as the RHCs, AT&T, GTE, and MCI, were to have restrictions lifted from certain domestic markets their interests in foreign expansion would subside. Although it is impossible to know for sure what the strategies, for instance, of the RHCs and GTE, would be if existing domestic prohibitions were lifted, these companies reportedly would not lose their interest in pursuing global rather than simply national markets. As one telecommunications consultant argues, "They [the RHCs and GTE] absolutely have enough money to play on both sides of the pond. In fact, when the remaining restrictions on the RHCs are lifted, you're going to see money spread around like you can't even imagine, as they buy their way into whatever they're interested in" (Paul Kirvin, quoted in Watson, 1993, p. 22). Hills assumes that there would necessarily have to be checks on the flow of revenue from monopoly services to competitive ventures, which would, of course, be in the public interest, but there appears to be a no-holds-barred view on future expansion emanating from the industry and its cheerleaders.

At the same time, it seems unlikely that foreign competition, most likely European and Japanese companies, would be capable of moving swiftly into these currently restricted markets, given the leverage possessed by Congress and the FCC to limit foreign investment in U.S. telecommunications. Foreign investments in domestic services may increase, but what may mitigate against it is the prospect of barriers to foreign entry, which can help slow down competition while a stable American cartel works at further expanding U.S. telecommunications dominance abroad, as in the case in the United Kingdom, Central and Eastern Europe, and other parts of the world. The lobbying power of the RHCs, GTE, and the domestic long-distance carriers in the United States should not be underestimated as a means for preventing significant competition to encroach heavily on the significant market opportunities that will arise once the bans mentioned inevitably are lifted. As in the case of the EU, the relatively affluent internal market of the United States is not likely to be traded away easily to foreign investors.

The MFJ's significance to global telecommunications cannot be underestimated. It may very well have been the primary trigger in stimulating liberalization and privatization in telecommunications around the world.

---

services" (VANs), include packet transmission and protocol conversion, information services such as online databases and electronic directories, messaging and conferencing services (e.g., voice mail, electronic mail, specialized fax services, and audio conferencing), and specialized data services, including frame relay, transaction processing, and new ISDN services.

Furthermore, it has created more liberal conditions for entry into U.S. domestic markets by foreign competitors. By many assessments, the liberalization of telecommunications in the United States, particularly through the MFJ, was a foolish unilateral move in terms of creating an unfavorable balance of trade in telecommunications equipment (e.g., Reynolds, 1991; U.S. Congress, OTA, 1993). Today, a considerable amount of public and private effort in U.S. telecommunications trade is aimed at rectifying that perceived imbalance as far as liberalization is concerned. In particular, attention is being given to opening up equipment markets in Europe:

> US equipment manufacturers believe the way to gain access to European telecommunications equipment markets is to break the link between PTOs and their national preferred monopoly suppliers. One way would be to liberalize service markets, which would engender competing service providers, and, in turn, result in more competitive equipment markets, since each national competitor would try to develop its own sources of supplies. (U.S. Congress, OTA, 1993, p. 138)

THE FCC'S "DOMINANT CARRIER" REGULATION

Prior to November 1992, the FCC classified all foreign-owned carriers with 15% or more stock owned by a foreign telecommunications entity as "dominant," regardless of size or the route being served. Since that time, the FCC regulates as "dominant" only routes served by foreign-owned carriers whose foreign affiliates have the ability to discriminate against unaffiliated U.S. international carriers through controls over access to bottleneck services and facilities in the foreign market (Commission of the European Communities, 1993; U.S. Congress, OTA, 1993).

SPECIAL 301 OF THE *1988 OMNIBUS TRADE AND COMPETITIVENESS ACT*

Telecommunications is the only industry-specific part of the 1988 Omnibus Trade and Competitiveness Act, which established the U.S. Trade Representative (USTR) with "the leading role in multilateral telecommunications trade negotiations" (U.S. Congress, OTA, 1993, p. 155). The Telecommunications Trade Act, as this portion of the omnibus act is titled, seeks to rectify the trade imbalance that is the result of the U.S. market being more accessible to foreign suppliers than foreign markets are to the United States. The Act cites barriers in many nations that prevent U.S. competition: government equipment procurement policies, "buy national" industrial policies, and a variety of tariff and nontariff barriers. The Act requires that the USTR make investigations into existing foreign trade situations that inhibit "fully competitive market opportunities" for the United States and establish negotiating objectives for each country identified. If the USTR determines that an "act, policy, or practice of a foreign country" is not in compliance with a trade agreement with the United States, the USTR is authorized to terminate, withdraw, or suspend the agreement in order to "offset fully such act, policy, or practice" or to "restore the balance of concessions in telecommunications products and services trade between the United States and such foreign country" (Section 206(d-e)).

The Telecommunications Trade Act calls for the identification of "priority countries" that deny U.S. telecommunications interests mutually advantageous access to their markets. Foremost among those identified since the passage of the Act have been Korea and the EU. Negotiations with the EU have continued since the Act's passage, recognizing that changes are occurring with the gradual integration of the telecommunications market in Europe. Under the Clinton Administration and current representative Mickey Kantor, trade talks have taken on a more adversarial line, as the United States pushes harder for bilateral negotiations with European countries during the slow-moving GATT talks, sparking a European action challenging the legality of such moves when the goal was a multilateral policy, and no new policies or retaliatory moves were to be made while telecommunications talks were still in progress.

In essence, the USTR has come to be perceived by European negotiators for a belligerent, retaliatory and uncompromising approach:

> The Community cannot accept that the US unilaterally determines what constitutes a barrier or when "mutually advantageous market opportunities" in telecommunications have been obtained. Nor can the Community accept US efforts to negotiate under threat of unilateral retaliation, which can only hinder the multilateral negotiations. In addition, such reciprocity is inconsistent with the principles of the multilateral trading system. (Commission of the European Communities, 1993, p. 15)

Not only has the USTR been criticized by Europeans for bad diplomacy, but as one U.S. critic has noted, aggressive U.S. telecommunications trade measures have had limited overall success, "despite considerable heat and effort," due to a lack of overall trade strategy and a lack of regard for the impact of domestic regulatory policies on international trade (Reynolds, 1991, p. 588). As discussed in a later section, there is more at stake than success in trade, namely, the neglected subject of public interest standards in the relationship between U.S. domestic and telecommunications talks of the GATT, in which the USTR played an important and controversial role.

UNILATERALISM VERSUS MULTILATERALISM

What follows highlights some of the critical tensions and outcomes in multilateral trade talks on telecommunications in the Uruguay Round of the General Agreement on Tariffs and Trade (GATT) talks. These highlights demonstrate the uneasy connection between U.S. and EU negotiators, and they illustrate the motivations underlying nonparticipation in specific GATT agreements. Essentially, nonparticipation reduces to a choice to not engage in multilateralism, but rather to retain the prerogative to act unilaterally or bilaterally.

Governmental Procurement Code

> I am today announcing the initial actions by the United States in response to certain discriminatory procurement practices maintained by the European Community. These discriminatory procurement practices prevent some of our most competitive companies from selling products such as telecommunications and power generating equipment to government owned utilities. . . . I therefore announce the following steps: First . . . the United States will prohibit the procurement of EC sourced products not covered by the GATT procurement code. . . . Second, that the USTR will immediately solicit public comments concerning the impact of other possible actions restricting imports of telecommunications and power generating equipment from the EC. Third, that the US Government will begin an immediate study of the desirability and feasibility of withdrawing from the GATT government procurement Code. (Kantor, 1993, p. 291)

This statement by U.S. Trade Representative Mickey Kantor indicates that US policy has tended toward favoring trade sanctions and retaliatory measures in bilateral talks in cases in which it has been unable to achieve multilateral agreements to its satisfaction. A choice to withdraw from a particular GATT code keeps open the prerogative of using such unilateral trade weapons, while agreement with the code prohibits such measures. The USTR desires a code in which U.S. companies have an EU equipment market that is as liberalized as that which exists in the United States. As noted earlier, however, it was a unilateral move on the part of the United States to liberalize its equipment market, and now the consequences are being felt in terms of an unfavorable balance of trade in telecommunications equipment. Government procurement was not included in the final agreement on the Uruguay Round of the GATT talks, signed on December 15, 1993. Negotiations over government procurement of services is scheduled to take place two years from the actual establishment of the World Trade Organization under the Uruguay Round GATT agreement.

The conflict over government procurement can be summarized as follows. In the EU, government-owned utilities can purchase from government-owned equipment suppliers at subsidized rates, thereby underselling competing domestic and foreign suppliers. In the United States, privately owned utilities can purchase from foreign suppliers that may be government-owned or subsidized, possibly to the disadvantage of privately owned U.S. suppliers. Clearly, the difference places U.S. suppliers at a competitive disadvantage. According to Scott Pearson (1993), director of the USTR office of Europe and the Mediterranean, state-owned PTTs in many EU countries "purchase equipment such as central office switches almost exclusively from national champions at many times the world-wide price" (p. 108). However, the USTR has argued against including U.S. carriers (e.g., the Regional Bell Operating Companies [RBOCs], GTE, and AT&T) under such rules. "Our firms are all 100 percent private and as profit maximizing entities, they have no incentive to favour American products over foreign products" (Pearson, 1993, p. 108). This statement is only half true. U.S. firms have no incentive to "buy American," but they are not 100% private. We cannot categorize as "private" firms that operate as protected local monopolies, as do the RBOCs and GTE. Their revenues and profitability are secured through government manipulation by public utility regulators, not by a competitive market.

Until there is competition in the provision of local telephone service, which some U.S. federal legislators are pursuing, then there is no reason to exclude U.S. telephone monopolies from similar requirements as the USTR has demanded of EU participants. If U.S. public utility regulators wish to impose "buy American" incentives, then that would be their prerogative under the existing nonagreement over procurement. In fact, according to the Commission of European Communities (1993), legislation in at least 40 states have "buy American" procurement restrictions.

Most Favored Nation Treatment

According to the December 15, 1993 GATT agreement, signatories must provide treatment "no less favourable than it accords to like services and service suppliers of any other country," or "most favored nation treatment."[2] The Office of Technology (OTA) Assessment of the U.S. Congress has noted that such treatment is a core principle of GATT, and that it is a general principle of fairness designed to extend or withdraw specific trading privileges on a multilateral rather than a bilateral basis. However, as the OTA has noted, "most favored nation" (MFN) can hurt a country that has already liberalized its markets because such a country would be agreeing to allow the terms of bilateral agreements to become the basis for access by all signatories. As the OTA notes, AT&T (successfully) opposed MFN treatment for basic

[2]Final Act Embodying the Results of the Uruguay Round of Multilateral Trade Negotiations. Part II, Annex 1B; General Agreement on Trade in Services. Part II, General Obligations and Disciplines, Article II: Most Favored Nation Treatment, 15 December 1993.

telecommunications services because of the "market asymmetry" between the United States and many other GATT participants in terms of the degree of market liberalization in domestic telecommunications.

By contrast, U.S. domestic large telecommunications users welcomed subjecting basic telecommunications services to the GATT agreement because if foreign carriers could operate freely in the United States there would be greater price and service competition. However, as the OTA notes, this would also reduce the influence by the FCC over foreign carriers (U.S. Congress, OTA, 1993). The FCC is authorized to regulate foreign carriers under the Federal Communications Act of 1934 in order to protect U.S.-based carriers from unfair competition by foreign carriers who can cross-subsidize their competitive, U.S.-based operations from their domestic monopoly service revenue. Currently, legislation is being proposed in the U.S. Congress to permit domestic local telephone monopolies to compete in the domestic long-distance market. If that happens, the issue of cross-subsidization will apply to U.S. carriers as well as perhaps at that stage foreign long-distance service providers will be permitted to compete in U.S. markets (pending bilateral or multilateral agreements).

Market Access and Open Network Provisions

The Telecommunications Annex of the General Agreement on Trade in Services (GATS) specifically adopts a distinction that was made in U.S. regulatory policy between "basic" and "enhanced" or value-added services. The motivations for this distinction are complex, but they arose from the desire the FCC had to enable telephone monopolies to diversify into competitive markets while continuing to provide "basic" monopoly voice and data transmission services. By distinguishing between "basic" monopoly service and "enhanced" competitive services, the FCC sought to prevent telephone monopolists from transferring costs for providing services in competitive markets (enhanced services) to the cost structures for providing "basic" services. Initially, the FCC sought to distinguish between basic and enhanced services through structural separations by requiring telephone companies to establish separate subsidiaries to provide enhanced services. Later, in response to complaints by telephone companies about the costly duplication of facilities, the FCC permitted "nonstructural" accounting safeguards. Today, the basic-enhanced distinction receives much criticism as more and more of what had been classified as "basic" monopoly service is subject to increased competition (e.g., Shefrin, 1993; U.S. Congress, OTA, 1993).

With the possibility that there will be competition in the provision of local telephone service, the distinction could disappear altogether. As the Office of Technology Assessment (1993) has noted, "there is no agreement among economists about the extent to which modern telecommunications are inherently monopolistic" (p. 151). However, the fact remains that the question of what is "basic" versus "enhanced" is not simply a matter of whether in theory a service is inherently monopolistic but rather of whether in practice the service is treated as such. At present, voice and data telecommunications transport networks in both the local and long-distance markets in the United States are treated as "basic" services that are subject to monopoly regulations.

For better or worse, the logic of that treatment has been extended to the GATT. Under this agreement, "basic" services are not open to competition and negotiations, and competition in this area will be on a voluntary basis. Under the terms of the GATT "negotiations on Basic Telecommunications," voluntary negotiations for liberalizing "trade in telecommunications transport networks and services" (basic services) are scheduled to conclude by April 30, 1996. Resistance to opening basic services to liberalization came mainly from the EU, which has agreed in principle to begin opening competition by 1998. Key U.S. interests served by liberalization in basic services would be the RHCs, GTE, AT&T, MCI, Sprint, and other carriers that initially would be interested in competing in basic long-distance service in EU countries, but perhaps also in local markets as the local basic service market in the United States becomes competitive.

So-called "enhanced services," on the other hand, are open to competition under the GATT, and basic telecommunications carriers are obligated to provide network access to enhanced service providers. Again, borrowing from U.S. regulatory principles, the concept of an "open network architecture" underlies both EU and GATT harmonization and liberalization principles in the area of telecommunications. In its Third Computer Inquiry in 1986, the U.S. FCC introduced this concept as a principle to stimulate the growth of enhanced services. The idea of "harmonization" underlying open network provision in the United States , the EU, and now under the GATT are to minimize the technical and economic barriers to the use of basic telecommunications by a wide variety of competing service providers.

National Treatment

Under the GATT, signatories are required to accord the same treatment to foreign firms as to nationally based private firms. If a country does not permit a nationally based private firm to compete with the national (state-owned) telecommunications carrier, then foreign carriers cannot compete either under the terms of "national treatment."[3] National treatment differs from "most favored nation" treatment in that unconditional access to a market is not required. In other words, if a national government does not allow domestic firms to compete with a national monopoly, then it has no obligation to allow foreign firms to compete either (U.S. Congress, OTA, 1993). Because they are

---

[3]General Agreement on Trade in Services. Part III, Specific Commitments, Article XVII: National Treatment, 15 December 1993.

not "national carriers" in their own countries, U.S.-based firms are at a disadvantage under the national treatment code because governments of countries with "national carriers" can exclude U.S. carriers from market entry, whereas the national treatment code does not protect U.S. carriers (which are not state-owned) from foreign competition. Of course, the U.S. government is able to offset this asymmetry through FCC "dominant carrier" regulations and through Sections 214 (regulating the construction of telecommunications lines) and 310(b) (regulating foreign ownership) of the Communications Act. However, the EU clearly has the upper hand because it can be argued that as no U.S. carrier is a national carrier—and therefore exempted from competition under the national treatment code of the GATT—then any use of domestic policy instruments to restrict or limit competition is in violation of the principle of multilateralism that underlies the GATT. This problem stems not only from the fact that liberalization occurred earlier in the United States, but also that with the exception of a very brief period of state ownership of AT&T during World War I, common carriers have always been quasi-private.

Audiovisual Services

Although the focus of this chapter is on telecommunications services, which are treated separately from audiovisual services under the GATT, it would be foolish to disregard the relationship between telecommunications and audiovisual services, particularly given the rhetoric and realities of technological and industrial convergence. Audiovisual services, in fact, were not included in the GATT services agreement (GATS), due mainly to the inability of the United States to resolve its differences with the EU over broadcast quotas. In particular, the government of France argued for special GATT treatment of audiovisual services as a "cultural exception," thereby continuing to subsidize these industries. The result, however, was nonagreement and the exclusion of audiovisual services from the GATS ("Cultural defense," 1994).

This nonagreement reflects distinct philosophies in the United States and the EU about cultural industries. In its "Directive on Broadcasting," the EU agreed on October 3, 1989 that "broadcasters reserve for European works . . . a majority proportion of their transmission time . . . having regard to the broadcaster's informational, educational, cultural and entertainment responsibilities to its viewing public." Rather than commit to an agreement which allows quotas, the United States chose not to do so and instead reserved the prerogative of taking unilateral, retaliatory actions, a position that of course, has been encouraged by the Motion Picture Association of America (MPAA, 1994). According to the MPAA, nearly 55% of the Motion Picture Export Association of America (MPEAA) member companies' earnings come from the EU, so it is understandable that MPEAA members would want to secure or further widen access to EU film and TV markets. Recently, the EU adopted a draft "Green Paper" on audiovisual matters designed to tighten enforcement of European quotas and to create a Europewide subsidy system for the film and TV industries (Mahoney, 1994a, 1994b). According to the GATS agreement, subsidies "may have distortive effects on trade in services," and multilateral disciplines should be designed to avoid them.[4] Given nonagreement on audiovisual services, not only is the EU free to launch a unionwide subsidy program, but the USTR is free to pursue retaliatory measures on behalf of MPEAA members, which Mickey Kantor has threatened to do ("Cultural defense," 1994).

Despite the laudable EU aim of preserving distinctively national and European cultural identities through quotas and subsidies, it seems that such forms of intervention are likely to have minimal or no effect on limiting access to EU markets by U.S. film, television, and music exporters. In the increasingly multichannel, audiovisual environment of the EU, the converging telecommunications and audiovisual interests of the United States are likely to increase the presence of U.S. cultural exports to European markets in absolute if not relative terms, with or without the "help" of belligerent trade representation. This is not to imply that such an increase is a good thing, but rather to simply acknowledge the coalescence of significant amounts of telecommunications and audiovisual industry capital with designs on a market in which demand is higher than cultural ministers, particularly in France, wish to tolerate.

US-EUROPEAN TELECOMMUNICATIONS INVESTMENTS

Provided next is a sketch of the rapidly evolving U.S. telecommunications investments and trade relations in Europe and, on a less detailed basis, some comparable data about the EU. These data provide the basis both for a comparison of the two and for understanding the nature of the interaction between them, which has far-reaching implications. Although deals and consortia in the European telecommunications market involving American investors are happening very rapidly, there are nevertheless four main patterns that have evolved in terms of U.S. firms' investments in Europe:

1. There is a great deal of activity in the United Kingdom because regulatory barriers are least prohibitive here, and U.S. phone companies are allowed to operate combined cable and telephone systems, something they cannot do at home.
2. Central and Eastern Europe are the second site of intense investment activity, largely because the opportunities here, despite the risks, are so vast. These countries are in desperate need of Western capital and technology to upgrade their totally inadequate telecommunications infrastructures, and alliances with such firms are eagerly sought (Calabrese, 1995).

---

[4]General Agreement on Trade in Services. Part II, General Obligations and Disciplines, Article XV: Subsidies, 15 December 1993.

3. Most of the investments made by American firms are joint ventures, in which they are partnered with one or more private and/or public European telecommunications companies.
4. Overseas investments by the regional Bell holding companies (RHCs) have tended to take three primary forms: (a) the construction and/or operation of cellular networks, especially in Europe; (b) experimentation with other infrastructures, especially cable television; and (c) investments in the privatization of state telephone companies (so far, mostly outside Europe, although increasingly so in Central and Eastern Europe).

According to the Office of Technology Assessment (1993), the number of U.S. firms entering the European telecommunications market is expected to continue to expand over the next several years. Although only 15% of the market is currently open to U.S. competition, that number should increase significantly over the next 5 to 10 years. Thus far, the European market has been open primarily to cellular communications, cable television, and some enhanced services, although opportunities have been greater in other sectors in Central and Eastern Europe. OTA projects that the European markets for "enhanced" or value-added products and services—those that go beyond voice and data transmission (i.e., enhanced phone service and multimedia systems)—will grow at a much faster pace than will U.S. markets. Comparatively speaking, U.S. markets are largely saturated and more competitive. The report also states that "the most important criterion for foreign ventures and investments is the ability to earn high returns." Second in importance is "the experience and political leverage that the RHCs can bring back to the United States" because the companies are able to experiment with services and businesses that they are barred from participating in the United States. Appendix A provides an overview of these relationships and experiments.

Although U.S. telecommunications companies are forging alliances with public telecommunications operators to serve European markets, it is also true that the openness of the U.S. equipment and network markets have enticed extensive investments from European telecommunications companies. As noted earlier, numerous U.S. trade advocates and policymakers argue that a major reason for the growing U.S. trade imbalance in telecommunications is due to the influx of foreign equipment providers, whose presence was enhanced by the breakup of AT&T. Illustrative of these trends is the fact that the shares of 19 foreign-based telecommunications firms are traded on U.S. stock exchanges, including Alcatel of France and Finland's Nokia, the second largest mobile phone maker in the world.

Another recent arrangement illustrating these trends occurred in June 1994, when the state-owned telecommunications companies of France and Germany agreed to invest $4.2 billion in order to jointly acquire 20% of Sprint, the third largest U.S.-based long-distance carrier. The proposed deal has drawn criticism from AT&T, which claimed that "there's something very wrong when telephone companies like France Telecom and Deutsche Telekom monopolies can buy into the US telecommunications market while keeping their home markets closed tighter than a drum" (quoted in Redburn, 1994, p. C3). AT&T is negotiating an alliance with Unisource, a joint venture between the state telecommunications operators of Sweden, Switzerland, and the Netherlands that would provide "one-stop" telecommunications services to transnationals (Adonis, 1994, p. 32; "AT&T reportedly to announce linkup," 1994). Likewise, British Telecom (BT), which has recently had a proposed alliance with MCI approved by the U.S. Department of Justice, also criticized the Sprint deal. Britain has one of the most liberalized telecommunications markets in the world, whereas France and Germany, the two largest telecommunications markets in Europe, are more closed to competition.[5] As BT has argued, the BT-MCI deal is riskier because BT faces greater competition in its domestic market than France Telecom and Deutsche Telekom (Schrage, 1994, p. F3). In sum, the opposition from AT&T and BT-MCI comes as a result of arguably asymmetrical competition. Due to these objections, it is expected that the Sprint deal will undergo more stringent scrutiny by both the Justice Department (regarding possible antitrust violations) and the FCC (regarding compliance with Section 310(b) of the Communications Act, discussed earlier). (For further examples of the increased involvement of the European PTOs in the United States, see Appendix B.)

The Sprint deal raises some interesting issues that are not adequately addressed by the objections of BT and AT&T. Certainly the question of state ownership is significant in terms of competition, but it is hardly the pivotal distinction among these various acquisitions. BT and AT&T are still dominant in their domestic markets and their ability to invest in international ventures depends on their passing along costs to their domestic subscribers. Furthermore, BT was only recently privatized, and AT&T, until 1984, enjoyed a degree of federal protection that it may as well have been a state-owned monopoly. What the objections of BT and AT&T amount to is a familiar and self-serving rhetoric among telecommunications companies to limit competition or, at the least, stall for time while they gain significant portions of the market share before new major competitors in the "harmonized" global telecommunications playing field are up and running. If one closely analyzes the patterns of deregulation in telecommunications and broadcasting in the United States over the past 20 years, one becomes aware that "competition" is usually presented by the party seeking deregulation as a public good, but it usually means "Let me enter new markets (i.e., compete), but keep my competition out." This has been the case in

---

[5]Both France Telecom and Deutsche Telekom are fully state-owned but, according to the Office of Technology Assessment, Deutsche Telekom was planning in 1993 to privatize 49% of its stock in order to finance the expansion and upgrade of telecommunications facilities and services in eastern Germany (U.S. Congress, OTA, 1993).

relationships between the newspaper and telephone industries, and now between so-called "private" and "public" telecommunications monopolies. Yet, there remain other ways of addressing questions of "fairness" outside the narrow frameworks constructed by global telecommunications giants trying to hamstring one another in their quest for competitive advantage.

WHOSE PUBLIC INTEREST? CITIZENSHIP AND GLOBAL TELECOMMUNICATIONS

Neoclassical economic theory provides a useful vocabulary to justify deregulation, particularly in claiming that it is in the public interest in terms of price and quality to have competition. However, such reasoning overlooks the fact that the emergence of global competition in telecommunications trade was made possible only after the garnering of investment capital from the citizens of the home countries of these firms. The fact that France Telecom and Deutsche Telekom are moving in the same direction, albeit more deliberately, is just an indication that the dominant trend in global telecommunications is to serve global private interests at the expense of national or local public interests.[6] The key issue is the loss of state control over telecommunications capital. At best, the governments of even the most powerful states seem only committed to stalling the continued concentration of telecommunications capital. Of necessity, "the national interest" is equated with corporate interests. Under these terms, in telecommunications policy, as in other political-economic spheres, the concepts of "citizenship" and "the public," to the extent that they have any force or meaning, remain tied to localities that are rapidly losing ground to increasingly mobile capital.

What is the social contract between states and citizens to justify the push for a global telecommunications trade regime? Is what is good for AT&T and the RHCs also what is good for the citizens of the United States ? How do we reconcile this logic with the fact that AT&T plans to have 50% of its revenues from international markets by the year 2000 (U.S. Congress, OTA, 1993)? Will AT&T be repatriating profits? Into whose hands? Will there be any assured connection between foreign profits and domestic public interest standards? On the issue of monitoring the foreign investments of U.S. carriers, the following candid observation was made by the Office of Technology Assessment (1993):

---

[6]Deutsche Telekom reportedly intended in 1993 to privatize up to 49% to enable it to expand and upgrade facilities and services in eastern Germany (U.S. Congress, OTA, 1993, p. 51), although no recent indications of the success of these efforts were found at the time of the writing of this chapter. As noted earlier, the EU has stated its commitment to begin full liberalization in telecommunications by 1998.

Eight major carriers told the Office of Technology Assessment that they strongly object to the concept of monitoring as an additional paperwork burden. Although any well-run corporation has such information for internal decision making, it is jealously guarded so that it will not fall into the hands of competitors and critics. (p. 22)

How is it possible that the U.S. government is unable to impose monitoring requirements on carriers? These issues are relevant not only to U.S. citizens. Substitute the name of the company and the country and it is possible to see that the same conditions giving rise to these questions are being or will soon be asked throughout the world. The threat of "domestic disinvestment" looms over any country with a large enough domestic telecommunications subscriber base from which revenues can be siphoned for foreign ventures. Public telephone operators (PTOs) are, according to one source, "the privatization plums." Along with the privatization discussed earlier, other countries that have recently privatized or are now moving quickly to do so are Italy, Portugal, Turkey, Pakistan, Venezuela, Thailand, and Brazil ("Investment banking," 1994).

As in other areas of foreign policy, the Clinton Administration has been criticized for its lack of vision in international telecommunications (Reynolds, 1991). However, this is an unfair criticism because the Administration's vision is quite clear and adamant about realizing, through domestic and foreign policy instruments and strategies, the global trade aims of some of the wealthiest, most powerful companies in the world. Yet, this Administration also claims an interest in realizing a broader set of aims for global telecommunications. In a speech to the International Telecommunications Union (ITU) earlier this year in Buenos Aires, Vice President Al Gore (1994) stated that "an essential prerequisite to sustainable development for all members of the human family" is to "build and operate a Global Information Infrastructure":

This GII will circle the globe with information superhighways on which all people can travel. These highways—or, more accurately, networks of distributed intelligence—will allow us to share information, to connect, and to communicate as a global community. From these connections we will derive robust and sustainable economic progress, strong democracies, better solutions to global and local environmental challenges, improved health care, and— ultimately—a greater sense of shared stewardship of our small planet.

The trouble with this vision is that, when coupled with the "trade vision," it carries no weight. The formation of a global regime in telecommunications policy is about trade and commerce, not democracy. The rhetoric of the Clinton Administration is supportive of democratic communication, universal access, and the idea of a harmonious "global community," but the action of the same Administration, reflected in time and money invested, political strategy, and deal making in foreign telecommunications, points toward trade and responds to the concerns of a narrow set of constituents. Again, the question is what is the social contract between states and citizens to justify the push for a global telecommunications trade regime? It would severely and inaccurately underestimate the political awareness of this Administration to conclude that Gore's rhetoric is borne of naiveté. The White House, which plays a powerful leadership role in shaping U.S. foreign policy in telecommunications, is made well aware of the serious misgivings by analysts in the executive and the legislative branches about the public interest shortcomings of its efforts in this arena (U.S. Department of Commerce, NTIA, 1993a; U.S. Congress, OTA, 1993). Unfortunately, the Administration also lacks the leverage and the political will to do much to change the tide. Instead, as the OTA has noted, the Administration has confined itself to a narrow emphasis, via the efforts of the U.S. Trade Representative, to securing access to foreign markets for U.S. companies, at the expense of other public policy goals. This is reflected in how the USTR formulates foreign policy in telecommunications:

> State regulators, the Consumer Federation of America, and the Communications Workers of America (a labor union) also are consulted in developing USTR negotiating positions. However, some of their representatives complain that their participation in the process is usually invited well after the critical elements in the negotiating position have been worked out between USTR, carriers, and large users. (U.S. Congress, OTA, 1993, p. 170)

With the rise of regionalism and multilateralism in telecommunications trade policy, there is a lack of a parallel discourse and structure for social policy. NAFTA and GATT address trade, not citizenship; markets, not publics. At the global level, the concept of "the public interest" has no meaning. Trade is the global concern. In sum, there are no mechanisms nor obvious political advantages at this time for political leaders to redefine public interest standards transnationally, and evidence points clearly in the direction of weakened ability to sustain such standards at the national and subnational levels.

CONCLUSION

At its core, U.S.-EU trade conflict is little more than a complex mating dance. The President of the United States and the U.S. Trade Representative would have to be politically suicidal to seek an all-out trade war with Europe over telecommunications, and the vested interests of U.S.- and EU-based telecommunications companies will assure that this does not happen. To date, it can be fairly concluded that there is a stronger public interest ethos underlying the relatively slower pace of trade liberalization on the continent versus Britain or the United States. However, it would be simplistic to lay public-interest-based criticisms of EU liberalization at the feet of aggressive U.S. trade negotiators, despite the reality that many of the neoliberal concepts underlying the emergence of a global trade regime in telecommunications were made in the United States. Hopefully, EU liberalization plans in 1998 will yield a stronger vision and commitment toward establishing and enforcing public interest standards that are more responsive at subnational, national, and transnational levels to the needs of citizens than can be found elsewhere in the world at this time. Although at present the emergence of such a vision does not seem immanent, if one were to emerge it could become a very valuable European export.

In conclusion, the U.S. government does have a foreign policy in telecommunications, but it would be difficult to make a convincing argument that the existing policy is in the best interest of U.S. citizens, or citizens elsewhere for that matter. It has not been the aim of this chapter to aid in making that argument, but instead we have attempted to provide an adequate understanding and critical assessment of the nature of that policy. The message of this chapter can be reduced to a simple statement: The emergence of a multilateral regime for telecommunications policy is morally bankrupt to the extent that the stakes and stakeholders remain as narrowly defined as they are today. If current trends in transnational telecommunications development are to serve interests beyond those of mobile capital, then it is imperative that intellectuals, activists, and political leaders (not mutually exclusive categories) focus their attention on the possibilities and limitations of those developments for citizens in their own and other countries.

APPENDIX A: DATA ON U.S. INVESTMENTS IN EUROPE

AT&T

- Overall, AT&T expects the amount of its revenues earned internationally to increase to 50% in the next 10 years or so.
- European strategy will involve extending its presence in service provision as the European market is deregulated by 1998, in addition to strengthening current status as equipment provider. Europe's $160 billion telecom service is four times larger than the market for equipment, and profit margins in services are higher, too.
- CEO Robert E. Allen announced this spring that AT&T's international sales would be boosted from 25% to 40% of the company's overall income. Dan Hesse, president of AT&T's Network Systems Intel., based in the Netherlands, announced that the company's goal is to have roughly a 20% market share in equipment in Europe in less than 10 years. Alcatel and Siemens are currently tied for the lead in Europe, followed by Sweden's Ericsson and AT&T.

- AT&T has switching contracts with many leading European telecommunications organizations (beating out European suppliers), including Telia of Sweden, PTT Telecom Netherlands, BT, and Telefonica of Spain.
- Involved with Britain's Mercury Communications in offering a gateway between the AT&T Accunet switch 384 digital service in the United States and Mercury's ISDN service in the United Kingdom will allow AT&T customers to access ISDN lines in the United Kingdom, and vice-versa. Plans are eventually to extend Mercury's Switchband service from the United Kingdom across Europe.
- Entering into a partnership in Spring 1994 with Mannesmann Mobilfunk, the operator of Germany's D2 cellular network, to offer D2 subscribers the facility to make cut-price international calls via AT&T's international calling-card service instead of direct-dial through Deutsche Telekom's international networks.
- AT&T has been involved in a major joint project (worth $11 million) since last June with Russia's Sevtelekom, a network operator based in Murmansk, to modernize the region's infrastructure and increase subscriber lines through a digital fiber-optic network. AT&T has been involved in the former Soviet Union since 1991, establishing positions in Armenia, Russia, Kazakhstan, and Ukraine. In the Ukraine, it is allied with Netherlands PTT Telecom to build and operate a modern telecommunications network (AT&T holds 39%, Netherlands PTT 10%, and the Ukraine State Committee 51%).
- Purchased 80% of Telfa, S.A. in November 1992, the first of three Polish equipment divisions to be sold. Paid $28 million; plans to invest $45 million more over six years.
- Purchased NCR (National Cash Register) in 1991 to solidify its European presence: not only does the acquisition strengthen AT&T's position in the computer business, it greatly expands its employment base in Europe—about half of NCR's 54,000 employees are overseas.
- AT&T has strategic alliance with the Italian local carrier ItalTel, involving equipment sales and consulting to develop Italy's infrastructure. It also has an equipment manufacturing facility in Spain and is involved in a strategic relationship with Telefonica.
- Currently in final negotiations with Unisource, a European consortium of Swedish, Swiss, and Dutch partners, with the goal of bidding on a private, cross-border telecom network for a group of Europe's biggest companies, including among its 30 members Xerox, DuPont, ICI Philips, and 3M. The group would have combined annual phone billings of $2 billion. Major competitor in the bidding is British Telecom.
- Has been in talks during Spring 1994 with Energis, a British company seeking to launch a third national long-distance network in the United Kingdom in April, about taking a one-third stake in the new operator.

MCI

- Anxious to form global partnerships, MCI spearheaded the formation of the Financial Network Association, a group that includes 11 European carriers targeting communications services for international financial firms. It is also part of a loose partnership with 23 other operators, including European companies, in Global Communications Services, which intends to provide "global one-stop shopping" or a full range of services to multinationals.
- In June 1993, MCI reached an agreement with British Telecom for the latter to acquire 20% of MCI for $4.3 billion and in the creation of a joint venture firm to offer global voice and data services to multinational users. BT will name three directors to MCI's board, whereas MCI's chairman will join BT's board. The deal was recently approved (in June 1994) by the U.S. Justice Department, which concluded that the British market was sufficiently open to competition, including the participation of foreign (i.e., U.S.) companies, to justify allowing BT entree to U.S. markets via their alliance with MCI.

Sprint

- Has also experienced explosive growth in its share of international telephone traffic, doubling between 1990 and 1991. Currently involved with a project called Hermes to build a pan-European network for voice and data. Sprint International accounts for approximately $2 billion in revenues compared with $8.8 billion for the parent company.
- Has applied for a license from the Department of Trade and Industry to offer long-distance and international service in the United Kingdom. If approved, Sprint will team with British Waterways to build a fiber-optic backbone network.
- In February 1993, joined with Alcatel NV, the French equipment manufacturer, to form Alcatel Data Networks. Sprint will own 49%. Company plans to develop and market products based on ATM technology for the data networking needs of large international business customers.
- Forged a deal in June 1994 for partial acquisition by France Telecom and Deutsche Telekom in order to expand international (and especially European) presence; intentions are for Sprint to be in a position to acquire shares in both European firms once they are made available in the privatization process later in the decade. The deal requires approval by the U.S. Department of Justice and the FCC.

Bell South

- Main European emphasis is on cellular communications: owns 29% of a consortium to build and operate a cellular network in Denmark; was awarded a license for Germany's third cellular network (to compete against Deutsche Telekom and Mannesmann, of which PacTel is a partner).
- Holds shares in several diverse operations in France, including a small stake in Societe Francaise du Radiotelephone, which holds a license for GSM; and a partnership with France Telecom to offer cable television.

Bell Atlantic

- Expects 10% of company revenues to come from international operations by end of 1994, although European ventures have been limited until very recently.
- Agreed in April 1994 to develop interactive multimedia television service for the Italian market with Stet, Italy's state-controlled telecommunications utility. By early 1996, the companies hope to be able to offer feature films on demand, followed by video shopping, banking, and do-it-yourself instruction, as well as commercial applications such as video conferencing and training. The subsidiary of Stet formed by the new joint venture will be called "Stream," and Bell Atlantic will hold a 49% stake. They are looking toward a commercial launch in 1996.
- Par of Italian Omnitel consortium (16.6%), which has joined forces with former rival Pronto Italia, to make joint bid for Italy's second cellular license.
- Involved in a joint venture since September 1991 with US West and the state phone company to supply cellular phone service in the former Czechoslovakia. The single state company has since split into separate Czech and Slovak companies. Both US West and Bell Atlantic each own a 24.5% stake in the nation's EUROTEL SYSTEM.
- Has indicated interest in acquiring part of Czech Telecom—the state firm has announced its intent to find a strategic foreign investor in 1994 to take 27% of its holdings.
- Involved in partnership talks with Spain's national telephone operator, Telefonica, which plans to sell a 24% stake in Telefonica International, its overseas subsidiary.

US West

- The company expects that as much as 20% of its revenues may come from international operations by 2000.
- A joint venture announced between US West and Time Warner in May 1994 will expand cable development in Spain—a $5 billion plan to cable at least 6 million Spanish homes over the next 10 years. Plans are to operate a broadband network of 25-50 channels, expandable to 150. The corporate duo will work in tandem with Spanish cable operator Multimedia Cable to form the corporation Cable and Television of Europe S.A. US West and Time Warner will retain 49%, whereas Multimedia Cable will hold 51%.
- US West is also negotiating similar cable partnerships with the new Basque cable company Euskalnet and with potential partners in Andalusia. Much recent market research by US West has identified Spain as a particularly ripe market for cable expansion.
- US West is one half of Tele-West Communications Group Ltd., a joint venture with TCI, in the United Kingdom, where it is a major provider of cable and telephone service. The company is able to provide telephone service for 20% less than that offered by BT. Will soon be providing video-on-demand in the United Kingdom, after trials in the Denver area showed that people's video use increased 12 times over their use without the service. Tele-West has 225,000 subscribers in London, Windsor, Birmingham, and the West of England, with a potential customer base of 3 million households. The company held 16 franchises as of 1993.
- US West also owns cable businesses in France, Hungary, Norway, and Sweden.
- Merged operations to develop personal communication networks in the United Kingdom with Cable and Wireless in March 1992.
- Extensively involved in Central and Eastern Europe, including the former Soviet Union, US West recently announced a partnership with France Telcom and Deutsche Bundespost Telekom in a domestic long-distance upgrading project known as "50-50" after the 50 switching centers and 50,000 km of long-distance lines involved. US West has secured $40 million from its own institutional investors, as well as loan guarantees for $125 million from the Overseas Private Investment Corp. (U.S. government agency that helps finance private deals in emerging markets), to go into a newly formed entity called the Russian Telecommunications Development Corporation, to be managed by US West. All told, the venture should have $400 to 500 million to invest in a variety of telecommunications projects in Russia.
- Involved in Westel, a GSM mobile telecommunications company comprised by a joint venture between US West and the Hungarian

national telecommunications company, MATAV. Westel inaugurated Central Europe's first digital cellular mobile phone service in Hungary in March. Analog cellular service has been offered since 1990, and the company now serves more than 35,000 customers. In 1993, revenues reached $68.4 million.

- US West also operates GSM systems in Moscow and St. Petersburg. It won tenders midway through 1993 to build digital mobile networks in another eight Russian cities.
- Involved in a joint venture since 1991 with Bell Atlantic and the state phone company to supply cellular phone service in the former Czechoslovakia. The single state company has since split into separate Czech and Slovak companies. Both US West and Bell Atlantic each own a 24.5% stake in the nation's Eurotel system.
- Overall, US West has invested $450 million in Eastern Europe from 1988 through 1993.
- Headed the Unitel partnership, which included Thorn EMI, Northern Telecom, and Deutsche Bundespost Telekom, which was awarded a license in 1989 to build a PCN system. US West Int'l. has joined with BMW and GTE to bid on a German PCN license.

Nynex

- Nynex Network Systems Company, responsible for overseas communications networks and services, has regional headquarters in Brussels, as well as Hong Kong, with officers throughout Europe.
- Announced it will spend $3 billion on multimedia projects in Britain over the next four years. Currently has the largest cable/phone subscriber base of any firm in the United Kingdom (2.7 million households), with an investment of approximately $2 billion. Holds 14 cable TV-telephony licenses in the United Kingdom with an investment of approximately $2 billion.
- Owns 50% of Gibraltar Tel; helping the government to modernize the system there. Also publishes Yellow Pages directories in Gibraltar, Prague, and the Czech Republic.
- Has indicated interest in acquiring part of Czech Telecom—the state firm has announced its intent to find a strategic foreign investor in 1994 to take 27% of its holdings.

Ameritech

- In a joint venture with Deutsche Bundespost Telekom, Ameritech was awarded its bid to acquire 30% of the Hungarian state telephone system, MATAV, in December 1993. The two firms spent $437.5 million for the acquisition, the first such telephone privatization in eastern Europe.

- Is part of a $120 million joint venture with France Telecom and Poland's state telephone company, Telecomunikacja Polska S.A. (TPSA), to form Centertel, Poland's first cellular phone network. TPSA owns 51%; the two foreign firms hold 24.5% each. After starting one year ago (June 1993), Centertel has 15,000 customers.
- Service was inaugurated by Ameritech in September 1993 on the first privately supplied cellular system in Norway, along with partners in the Norwegian firm NetCom GSM. A Scandinavian consortium holds 51.1% of NetCom, whereas the other 49.9% is held by Ameritech and its partner, Singapore Telecom.
- Is building a cellular system in Hungary.
- Announced plans in June 1994 to participate in telecommunications privatization in up to four European countries, including Belgium, the Czech Republic, Portugal, and Poland. The operations could involve investments of $500 million to $1 billion, according to Ameritech Int'l. president Andres Bande.

Southwest Bell

- Partnered with Cox Cable in the United Kingdom, the company owns 75% of one of Britain's largest cable systems, controlling eight franchises covering over a million households.

Pacific Telesis

- Flagship European venture is a 26% stake in Mannesmann Mobilfunk, a consortium that builds and operates a digital cellular network in Germany. This second national cellular franchise competes with the first, operated by DBT.
- Extensively involved in additional provision of cellular service throughout Europe, including a 23% interest in a consortium in Portugal since 1991 (9 million subscribers, or 90% of country's total population); a 51% interest in Sweden's NordicTel, with 800,000 subscribers (70% of population); a 25% interest along with Belgacom in a new Belgian mobile phone system; and interests in France and Spain.
- Holds major share in Pronto Italia of 34%; Pronto Italia currently engaged in bid with former rival Omnitel for Italy's second cellular phone license.
- Involved in partnership talks with Spain's national telephone operator, Telefonica, which plans to sell a 24% stake in Telefonica International, its overseas subsidiary.
- The company also plans to bid for additional licenses this year in the Netherlands, Spain, and France.

- Was formerly involved quite extensively in offering cable TV service in the United Kingdom, but since 1992 has sold its interests to various companies including Nynex.

APPENDIX B: DATA ON EUROPEAN INVESTMENTS IN THE U.S.

British Telecom

- England in a joint venture with MCI; BT purchased 20% of MCI for $4.3 billion, whereas MCI purchased BT North America for $125 million. BT is the world's fourth largest telecom company; hopes to go head to head with AT&T in the provision of long-distance service as a result of this merger. The BT investment marked the largest foreign investment ever in a U.S. telecommunications business. The deal was recently approved (in June 1994) by the U.S. Justice Department, which concluded that the British market was sufficiently open to competition, including the participation of foreign (i.e., U.S.) companies, to justify allowing BT entree to U.S. markets via their alliance with MCI.
- Other attempts by BT to gain access to the U.S. market include its acquisition of the data network firm Tymnet from McDonnell Douglas, in 1989; and its location of Syncordia, its consortium (joint venture with MCI), offering global network services, in Atlanta.

France Telecom and Deutshe Telekom

- Attempting to keep up with its bigger rivals AT&T and MCI, Sprint has been engaged in talks for several months with France Telecom, Deutsche Telekom, and Nippon Telegraph and Telephone to form an alliance to extend its global reach. As of June 7, 1994, the French and German companies have announced plans to invest in a minority stake in Sprint that is similar, but not identical, to BT's alliance last year with MCI. The French and Germans would invest about $4.2 billion for a 20% stake in Sprint.
- France Telecom has also expressed an interest in acquiring Westinghouse Communications, which offers a variety of switched, virtual, and private-line voice and data services to more than 100 companies, including its parent company, Westinghouse Electric.

Cable and Wireless

- Operates a small interexchange carrier in the United States with approximately 1% share of the total international market.

Telefonica

• Spain's national operator is attempting to purchase 80% of Puerto Rico's long-distance carrier, according to the September 1993 OTA Report.

REFERENCES

Adonis, A. (1994, June 15). France-German pact defies skeptics. *Financial Times*, p. 32.

AT&T reportedly to announce linkup with unisource. (1994, June 23). *AFX news*.

Calabrese, A. (1991). The periphery in the center: The information age and the 'good life' in rural America. *Gazette, 48*, 105-128

Calabrese, A. (1995). Local versus global in the modernization of Central and Eastern European telecommunications: A case study of US corporate investments. In F. Corcoran & P. Preston (Eds.), *Communication and democracy in the new Europe* (pp. 233-256). Cresskill, NJ: Hampton Press.

Commission of the European Communities. (1993). *Report on United States trade and investment barriers: Problems of doing business with the US*. Brussels: Commission Services.

Cultural defense. (1994, May). *Media International, 21*(5), 36.

Gore, Vice President A. (1994, March 21). Speech to the International Telecommunications Union, Buenos Aires, Argentina.

Hills, J. (1993). US hegemony and the GATT: The liberalisation of telecommunications. *Media Development, 2*, 8-12.

Investment banking: Please call again later. (1994, March). *The Banker, 144*(817), 26-27.

Kantor, M. (1993). Title VII action with respect to the EC. Statement by Ambassador Michael Kantor, United States Trade Representative, February 1, 1993. In C. Johnson & S. Bruno (Eds.), *The telecom regatta: EC '92 and beyond* (pp. 291-292). Washington, DC: Center for Strategic and International Studies.

Mahoney, W. (1994a, April 11). Draft raises eyebrows. *Multichannel News*, p. 34.

Mahoney, W. (1994b, April 11). Stronger quotas and subsidies ahead in Europe? *Multichannel news*, p. 34.

Motion Picture Association of America (MPAA). (1994). *Trade barriers to exports of US filmed entertainment*. Washington, DC: Author.

Pearson, S. (1993). The winds of trade: GATT and beyond." In C. Johnson & S. Bruno (Eds.), *The telecom regatta: EC '92 and beyond* (pp. 107-109). Washington, DC: Center for Strategic and International Studies.

Redburn, T. (1994, June 15). Sprint forms European alliance. *New York Times*, p. C3.

Reynolds, G. H. (1991). United States telecommunications trade policy: Critique and suggestions. *Tennessee Law Review, 58*, 573-601.

Schrage, M. (1994, June 17). German-French deal with Sprint is a regulatory wrong number. *Washington Post*, p. F3.

Shefrin, I. H. (1993, January/February). The North American Free Trade Agreement: Telecommunications in perspective. *Telecommunications Policy*, pp. 14-26.

U.S. Congress, Office of Technology Assessment. (1993). *US telecommunications services in European markets* (OTA-TCT-548). Washington, DC: U.S. Government Printing Office.

U.S. Department of Commerce, National Telecommunications and Information Administration. (1993a). *Comprehensive examination of US regulation of international telecommunications services.* 58 Fed. Reg. 4846.

U.S. Department of Commerce, National Telecommunications and Information Administration. (1993b). *Globalization of the mass media* (NTIA 93-290). Washington, DC: US Government Printing Office.

U.S. Department of Commerce. (1994). Telecommunications services. In *1994 U.S. Industrial Outlook*, pp. 29-1-29-20. Washington, DC: U.S. Government Printing Office.

Watson, S. (1993, December). US carriers go overseas in search of telecom's "holy grail." *Telephony*, pp. 19-28.

Chapter 15

The Shifting Contexts of International Communication: Possibilities for a New World Information and Communication Order*

Dwayne Winseck

This chapter introduces the historical and emerging contexts of international communication with an emphasis on the movement for a New World Information and Communication Order (NWICO) and the General Agreement on Tariffs and Trade (GATT). An argument is presented that a primary consideration of NWICO and scholarship about international communication has been the democratization of communication. The first section of the chapter provides an overview of the processes necessary to democracy and discusses the technical and communicative dimensions of democracy. Key aspects of communication and information are discussed that provide a foundation for thinking about the historically close link between communication and

*This chapter was originally commissioned for a reader being prepared for the Center for Mass Communication Research, Leicester University. The author thanks Dr. Marlene Cuthbert and Dr. Mashoed Bailie for their helpful comments and critique of the original chapter.

democracy and possibilities for expanding the realm of communication freedoms at the national and international level.

The chapter then considers how historical and contemporary definitions of communication freedom stressing legal restrictions against government intervention in, and control of, the communication process (negative freedoms) are necessary but partial attributes of democratic communication. I suggest that although the concept of "negative freedom" preventing state intervention in the communication process is necessary, and has underwritten the legal status of freedom of communication in many countries and the "free flow of information" doctrine in international communication law, it is an insufficient basis for a fuller concept of democracy. I suggest that it is this insufficiency that has driven NWICO-related critiques of the inequitable organization of international communication. I then indicate how the recent integration of telecommunications and information into the GATT incorporates all of the ambiguities of the concept of negative freedom, as it privileges expanded legal protections for the transnational free flow of information and secures market-based approaches to communication. My argument is that these arrangements fail to emphasize the historical linkages between communication and democracy, obscure the unique qualities of information and communication, and limit the ability of citizens to participate in the communication policy processes shaping the organization, uses, and goals served by the new technologies.

In contrast, throughout the chapter are suggestions for how a more adequate concept of a "right to communicate" and various public policy initiatives could expand the realm of democratic communication commensurate with the potentials of the new technologies and the requirements of citizenship in the so-called information age.

DEMOCRATIC COMMUNICATION AND THE PRINCIPLE OF INCLUSIVENESS

It is difficult to provide an adequate account of the democratization of societies and communication. However, it is possible to show some of the key principles central to this process and to a strong definition of democracy. In this section, several key principles are discussed with an eye to how they inform the underlying issues addressed by NWICO. This is done by considering the technical and communicative dimensions of democracy, the characteristics of information/communication that align them with ideas of the public good and the role of the state in forming communication policies.

Democracy can be characterized as the historical process of eliminating totalizing systems of authority. These give way to institutional and functional separations among the major actors of society—state, civil society, economy. It also includes the division of such functional institutions into public and private spheres (Weber, 1946) and the reintegration of personal life with public authority through communication, access to information and public opinion rather than fear, coercion, and violence (Habermas, 1989). Other crucial features of democratic societies include the adoption of a political and legal framework based on "general rules . . . equally applicable to all citizens" (Hayek, 1986, p. 24) and processes that allow the procedures and normative goals of society to be opened to citizen participation through public spheres of communication. According to these characteristics, democracy requires more than just functionally based, institutional separations and laws equally applicable to all (the technical prerequisite of democracy). More importantly, to live in a democracy means that the adoption of rules, and the ends toward which they will be directed, are shaped through spheres of public communication that are open to all, directed toward the discovery of public rather than private interests, and driven by the force of argumentation, not power (the communicative dimension of democracy; Habermas, 1989). Although many societies meet the first condition, few, if any, have satisfied the second, communicative dimension.

According to communication theorist, Jurgen Habermas, the crucial feature accompanying expanded public spheres of democratic communication is the principle of nonexcludability. Through the process of democratization, Habermas suggests that communication relations have become more inclusive as the requirements—property and gender—for entering public spheres of communication are minimized and the range of public discourse expanded. Yet he recognizes that the potential of communication to become more inclusive over time has not been fully realized. A similar recognition underpins the history of NWICO and continues to animate the concerns of its proponents. By discussing how all media systems have only partially realized the potentials for democratic communication, NWICO addresses a set of universal issues. Underlying all the studies showing one-way information flows, inequalities in access to basic communication resources, and the control over knowledge by the few to the detriment of the many that propelled much of the NWICO efforts is the assumption that the majority of the world's people are excluded from a basic resource of human existence and democracy: communication. That is why it has been such a powerful force driving research, analysis and discussion throughout the world and across the divides separating the world's people into north and south, east and west, rich and poor.

The principle that communication should be as inclusive as possible coincides with the basic qualities of information. Perhaps one of the most unique features distinguishing information from other commodities is that it is not depleted through use. In fact, its use tends to multiply, allowing communication, knowledge, and information to proliferate under normal conditions. The declining costs of information production and the ease with which information can be reproduced and distributed by the new technologies creates a condition in which information tends to spread and become more easily accessible to all. Generally speaking, the costs of communication are rapidly driven toward zero because it is not used up during consumption and because costs to reproduce another copy of a film, videocassette, or book, or to attach someone to the public telecommunications network, quickly diminish with each additional copy or subscriber (Babe, 1994). Information, thus, tends to spread and include, although legal and economic mechanisms such as copyrights, patents, access charges, closed-user group contracts, attempt to curtail these properties as they are used to secure the economic value of information.

These "public good" attributes of information point to the contradictions in Western legal frameworks. For instance, although prohibitions against state intervention in the flows of communication are consistent with the inherent properties of information, the role of the State in sanctioning and enforcing legal mechanisms for the private appropriation of value—copyright and patents—point to the tension between private property and democratic communication in capitalist democracies. Proponents of NWICO comment that the use of such mechanisms work against the free flow of information and knowledge to those most in need of these resources for economic and cultural development (Hamelink, 1993). Even staunch critics of NWICO, such as Ithiel de Sola Pool (1990), acknowledge this point, when they identify copyrights and patents as impediments to the free flow of information and advise governments in the LDCs to ignore such legal regimes.

These contradictions help to explain the historically shifting balance between the use of communication policy as a means of social policy during one era, whereas concerns with realizing the economic value of communication predominate in another. The question is not whether the state will be involved, as is so often stressed by the opponents of NWICO, but "what goals will intervention seek to achieve and who is to benefit from inevitable government intervention?" (Mosco, 1989, p. 9). Essentially, such questions turn on the balance of political power prevailing at any given point in time, conditions within the larger economic environment, the way we think about communication and the state's ability to draw on compelling reasons for its actions either way—not on an underlying system of Constitutional principles that prohibit state intervention in communication matters. The larger overriding question is whether state institutions involved in communication policy are committed to the value of private property or the "nonexclusive" qualities imminent in information and the history of the democratization of society. The one position excludes, whereas the other embraces: That is the crux of democratic communication, and one of the animating concerns of NWICO.

The Concept of Negative Freedoms and the Partial Democratization of Communication

The ambivalent status of these concerns has been fully integrated into the concept of negative freedoms defining communication rights in the media systems of

Western countries and internationally throughout modern history. Taken up within the context of Western societies, constitutional, legal, and regulatory concepts have been formulated to curtail the coercive measures wielded by the state—taxes, licensing, and prior restraint measures—that interfere with the rights of citizens to communicate and by provisions that guarantee open channels of communication among people within civil society and between civil society and the state (Keane, 1991). Such a concept of democratic communication finds its classic expression in the First Amendment of the U.S. Constitution, with its clear provisions against any government restraints on freedom of speech, the press, and assembly. This partial concept of democratic communication prohibits state actions restricting the right to communication among citizens, but does not specify measures to ensure that the possibilities for communication are equitably distributed. Because of this, one often finds critics arguing that Western democracies inadequately ensure access to a basic human right, and second that they only guarantee channels of communication between the state and civil society, with no similar guarantees for communicative relations between civil society and capital (Galtung, 1994; Schiller, 1989).

Such limited forms of access to communication also means that media systems are organized by the logic of representational, rather than more participatory forms of, democracy. This system of communication freedoms confirms the contours of representative democracy, as citizens are situated as consumers rather than producers of information, satisfy their needs through market transactions, and engage politics through the periodic vote, appointed representatives, and by privately giving or withholding their acclaim of elite governing bodies and technocratic experts (Habermas, 1975; Held, 1987). A more encompassing notion of freedom of communication would include the right to receive a diverse range of ideas and "provide access for those who wish to reach their fellow citizens" (Bagdikian, 1989, p. 812). Similarly, C. W. Mills (1956) has suggested an alternative and powerful framework for the critical analysis of existing communication systems and for thinking about what kind of systems could be created in the future. According to Mills, democratic communication systems should allow:

> (1) Virtually as many people [to] express opinions as receive them. (2) Public communications are so organized that there is a chance to immediately and effectively answer back any opinion expressed in public. Opinion formed by such discussion (3) readily finds an outlet in effective action, even gains—if necessary—the prevailing system of authority. And (4) authoritative institutions do not penetrate the public, which is thus more or less autonomous in its operation. (p. 392)

The power of this particular framework resides in the fact that it is universal in its reach (1), enhances the possibilities for people to actively shape the societies in which they live (2, 3), and goes beyond, but does not abandon, negative freedoms (4). Although discussions introduced later indicate that existing communication systems hardly approximate such criteria, it is nonetheless instructive to use these tools to address the history, contemporary conditions, and prospects of NWICO—the task of the following sections.

THE GLOBAL EXTENSION OF PARTIAL
SYSTEMS OF DEMOCRATIC COMMUNICATION

The negative concept of freedom provides the theoretical foundation of the free flow of information doctrine at the international level. The United States and a few other Western governments have been staunch advocates of the "free flow of information" doctrine, and have been generally successful in getting such a right recognized in international law (Fortner, 1994).

Convinced of the power of centralized media systems to mobilize public opinion for the purposes of war, after World War II the United States sought to curtail the role of the state in German and Japanese media systems. Efforts were undertaken in Germany to reduce the control of the federal government over the broadcasting system in favor of the decentralized control of the Lander governments. In Japan these efforts included inserting U.S. style "free press" provisions into the new Constitution constructed under the oversight of American supervisors and compelling the country's newspaper association to adopt a code of ethics modeled on that of the American Society of Newspaper Editors (Ito & Hattori, 1989).

The United States also sought to influence the media systems of Europe by enhancing the status of its own companies there. One such measure adopted toward this end was the encouragement given to the Hollywood majors to form a legal cartel under the provisions of the Webb-Pomerene Act. In doing so, it was felt that the combined power of the U.S. film industry would enhance their position within the European media industry, augment the activities of the USIA and VOA, and provide a stronger defense against any attempts to restrict the free flow of U.S. media products into Europe (Guback, 1969).

Finally, the media systems of the LDCs were shaped by U.S. media interests and the assistance offered by France and England to their former colonies. Through these relationships an extensive network of control over the communication systems of most of the LDCs took shape. Such networks incorporated countries from every region of the world, including Brazil, Mexico, Venezuela, Jamaica, the Philippines, Thailand, Hong Kong, Japan, Australia, New Zealand, Kenya, the Sudan, Ethiopia, among others (Fortner, 1993; Schiller, 1969). Through such arrangements the media systems of the LDCs were wedded to the programming flows of a few industrialized countries and the free flow doctrine. Yet rather than this partially democratic concept creating access for citizens of the LDCs to the emerging communication networks, it more often secured the rights of private owners, who lined up against any attempts to achieve a balance between private and public ownership, place limits on advertising, or expand the range of media content available or proposals to establish any kind of formal regulatory regime. Such resistances were formed through alliances among national private broadcasters, foreign-owned communication system operators, and U.S.-based media groups and legitimated on the familiar grounds of guarantees of a free press (White, 1993).

Furthermore, the expansion of media systems from mainly the United States and a few other countries into the LDCs were legitimated and given an extensive gloss by theories of modernization. According to the modernization theorists, a lack of "psychic mobility" among the citizens of the LDCs tied them to dysfunctional behavioral patterns, systems of belief, and ways of life that were incommensurate with modernization. Whereas earlier attempts to aid the LDCs were grounded in economic assumptions, the new approach sought to shape people's ambitions, personality profiles, and political culture through the introduction of new "frames of reference" via the mass media (Pool, 1990; Pye, 1966). Thus, the extensive spread of technological and legal systems from the west was accompanied by an intensive process of psychological and political reorganization, carried out, in large part, through mass communication.

As such, the extension of communication systems were occurring within the context of transformations of whole ways of life. Furthermore, the end goals of such transformations were not left open to negotiation, but modeled explicitly on highly idealized visions of the United States[1] Such a vision involved the functional separation of institutions into distinct spheres of competency, centralized systems of mass communication to harmonize social agendas around particular models of life and development goals, and a political system of representational democracy (Pye, 1966). Yet, although all the institutional features of democracy were included, modernization theory excluded the very people whose lives were being transformed through processes of social engineering and the public spheres of communication through which the procedures and normative goals of society could be opened to citizen participation and legitimation. As such, these plans tended to be more technocratic than democratic, exclusive not inclusive.

If one function of power is to narrow the range of options that are validated and made available to people in the everyday conduct of "getting through life," then the theories of modernization functioned as systems of power, validating particular visions of the future and specific ways of organizing the networks of communication. Yet, this is not surprising given the even larger context of the Cold War surrounding such initiatives. What is surprising is that the idealized model of representative democracy envisioned by

---

[1]Recognizing that this particular model might be resisted in favor of different forms of social, political, and economic organization, Pye (1966), among others, did not hesitate to include chapters in his book or write entire manuals instructing governments on topics such as "Insurgency and the Suppression of Rebellions."

the modernization theorists was maintained at all because it was increasingly under criticism in the industrialized countries. Responding to the outbreak of countercultural movements, protests, and an upsurge in radical thought, some criticized representative democracy for creating excess levels of political participation that were incompatible with the needs of governance and economic growth (Brittan, 1975). Others of a more critical bent suggested that the problem with representative democracies was that they limited citizenship to the periodic vote and technocratic forms of economic and political management that no longer reconciled themselves with the body politic through open systems of public communication. From this perspective, communication systems had been turned over to the production of consumption and consent, rather than legitimacy (Habermas, 1975; Held, 1987).

It is within this context that a convergence between critics of representative democracy and modernization theories took place across national lines, polarizations of the Cold War, and the North-South divide. The critique of modernization theory's tendency to push the cultural practices of people in the LDCs behind efforts of social engineering converged with critical thought in the West that saw the political and economic administrative systems of these societies as increasingly severed from any form of communicatively generated norms (Habermas, 1975). Out of this convergence emerged critiques of dependency and cultural imperialism that, coupled with the material conditions increasingly present in the LDCs, generated the basis for attempts to achieve greater autonomy for national media systems and efforts toward a NWICO. To be sure, however, just as there had been a coalescence between forces for more democratic changes, others linked causes against the "excesses of democracy." These forces, too, would also shape future developments and try to subordinate the human interest in communication to more instrumental goals of economic accumulation or outright repression.

CHALLENGES TO PARTIAL SYSTEMS OF DEMOCRATIC COMMUNICATION OR NEW SYSTEMS OF CONTROL?

After decolonization many new nations entered the UN system, altering the relations of power within these agencies and significantly shifting their mandates. One early example that things were changing was the 1948 UN *Universal Declaration of Human Rights*. The Declaration promoted a positive system of civil, political, and socioeconomic rights that, as C. B. MacPherson (1985) notes, strove to guarantee rights protected from state interference, such as freedom of speech and the press, rights for citizens to actively engage the state in acts of political participation and, finally, efforts by the State to bring about adequate material conditions to support the civil and political rights of all citizens. Identifying the centrality of communication as a human right[2] Article

---

[2]This is a point worth bearing in mind because later discussion in the chapter traces the

19 of the UN's 1948 *Universal Declaration of Human Rights* stated: "Everyone has the right to freedom of opinion and expression; this right includes freedom to hold opinions without interference and to seek, receive and impart information and ideas through any media regardless of frontiers" (pp. 1959-1960; emphasis added).

Although the declaration acknowledged the importance of constitutional principles prohibiting state interference with freedom of speech, it is obvious from debates that ensued that the right to "seek, receive and impart information" was also a right not to be excluded from the communication process, saw citizens as active producers of communication, and held open the possibility that steps might be needed to secure such rights in practice. Furthermore, the phrase "regardless of frontiers" also aimed to ameliorate technical and economic barriers to expression, rather than just to circumscribe government attempts to impede transnational communications—although this was an important goal as well (Fortner, 1994; U.S. NTIA, 1983; U.S. Subcommittee on Communications, 1988).

During the 1960s, these issues were primarily pursued within the framework of the New International Economic Order (NIEO). However, as the issues involved became more refined, the relationship between communication and economic development more salient, and the imbalances in access to the basic resources of communication and information flows between countries better understood, the distinctions between the NIEO and the NWICO began to fade. Representative of this trend, a 1979 resolution by the UN General Assembly encouraged UN members to

> establish . . . a new world information order, which will be conducive to greater reciprocity in the exchange of information and correct the quantitative inequality in the flow of information to and from developing countries and between them, would contribute to the strengthening of international peace and security and the realization of the aim of establishing the new international economic order. (cited in McPhail & McPhail, 1987, p. 302)

Yet NWICO was not just the preserve of the LDCs. Indeed, efforts toward a NWICO also generated the interest of many in the industrialized countries. NWICO type concerns were high on the agenda of countries such as Canada, France, Finland, among others. For instance, Canada, with one of the most sophisticated communication infrastructures in the world, has discovered that these networks serve primarily as retransmission conduits for U.S. cultural products. In general, 72% of programs broadcast across the Canadian media system are foreign, whereas in certain genres of English-language television programming, for example, drama, imported content is about 90% (Ferguson, 1992; Roach, 1990). In the 1980s, France addressed similar concerns by

---

increasing tendency to think about freedom of communication not only as a human right, but as a corporate one as well.

building its entire communication technology and cultural policies framework around the goals of retaining control over its technological infrastructure, thwarting the dominance of IBM over its domestic computer industries, and decentralizing cultural production and distribution within the country (Mattelart & Stourdze, 1985). Similar efforts continue to animate the European Union's 1989 television directive as it tries to maintain a balance among local, regional, and international cultural products. It is also true that one of the more colorful critiques of the "free flow" doctrine was leveled in the early 1970s by the Finnish president, Kekkonen. According to Kekkonen:

> The traditional Western concept of freedom . . . has meant that society has allowed freedom of speech to be realized with the means at the disposal of each individual. In this way freedom of speech has in practice become the freedom of the well-to-do. . . . Globally the flow of information between states . . . is to a very great extent a one-way, unbalanced traffic, and in no way possesses the depth and range which the principles of freedom of speech require. . . . In a different judicial system . . . the State would be obliged to arrange for its citizens the practical possibility towards the realization of their rights. (cited in Gerbner, Mowlana, & Nordenstreng, 1993, pp. x-xi)

Based on the breadth of concerns about the inadequacy of the free-flow doctrine, in 1978 it was scrapped. Through the consensus of UNESCO members, the "free flow and a *wider and better balanced dissemination* of information" principle was adopted (UNESCO, 1978, Article I; emphasis added). However, the formula was accepted to the chagrin of the United States, United Kingdom, and others comfortable with the narrowly tailored free-flow doctrine, secured as it was on the familiar constitutional principles of negative freedoms and presumptions in favor of private, commercial control of communication. Although the United States voted in favor of the new principle, it would later cite it as one of the reasons behind its 1984 withdrawal from UNESCO. The United Kingdom and Singapore withdrew from the agency a year later, ostensibly for the same reason. Later efforts to woo the return of these important actors in international communication and the appointment of a new Secretary-General would see a change in the institution once again through the resurrection of the free-flow doctrine (MacBride & Roach, 1993; Roach, 1990).

In the meantime, however, the efforts toward a NWICO and a larger definition of freedom of communication were propelling changes in the ITU. One of the first key achievements in the ITU was the elimination of the colonial system of voting in 1973 that had carried the day since its inception in 1865. Prior to this, nations voted according to the number of colonies they administered. This system sublimated conflicts between the industrialized countries and LDCs to imperial rule, allowing Western nations to dominate the ITU and to reach agreements through consensus (Codding & Rutkowski, 1982). After the influx of new members and the elimination of colonial voting, the ITU became much more attuned to the needs and issues of the third world. In this process, the limitation of communication issues to technical and economic considerations was forsaken in favor of a broader set of social, political, historical, and development criteria.

Reflecting these developments, in 1982, the ITU's mandate was altered to direct the agency to address the "special needs of the developing countries." One response to this new mandate was to make the level of financial contributions commensurate with the amount of participation in ITU activities. The effect was to transfer more financial responsibility to the industrialized countries (Codding & Rutkowski, 1982). Later plenipotentiary conferences extended the ITU's mandate toward developing countries by increasing the agency's emphasis on technology assistance programs and enhanced budgetary allocations to these ends; recognizing claims of the developing countries regarding the limited nature of the radio spectrum and geosynchronous orbit and the need to ensure, on a limited basis, a scheme of guaranteed access to these resources; expanding the Administrative Council to more accurately reflect the composition of the forum; revising to the election procedures for membership to the board of directors of the consultative committees; adopting accounting rates favorable to the telecom systems of the LDCs; and changing the agency's Convention to indicate the expanded approach of the ITU vis-à-vis developing country concerns (Codding & Rutkowski, 1982; Trotti, 1993).

However, alterations to fundamental issues, such as the "first-come first-serve" regulatory procedures have been very limited, and efforts to expand the development initiatives have been underfunded and marginalized in relation to other issues important to the countries with more developed telecom infrastructures. Yet, even given these minimalist responses, the United States still pushed to eliminate references to NWICO, worked to internationalize regulatory liberalization through the agency, and even threatened to leave the organization (Hills, 1993; Solomon, 1983).

Communication Policies: Democracy, Repression, Ambiguity

In addition to pursuing NWICO related goals through UNESCO and the ITU, many countries began to construct national communication policies. Up until this time many LDCs lacked formal communication policies. In others, especially the African and Caribbean countries, communication infrastructures and policies bore the stamp of colonialism. In Africa, for instance, this meant that information flows followed patterns of communication laid down by the railways and telegraphs of the 19th century, as almost all (94%) of inter-African telecommunications traffic transits through metropolitan centers outside the continent, such as London or Paris (Turan, 1989). In the Caribbean it meant, at least until the mid-1980s, that the telecom infrastructures and policy frameworks followed the model of Cable and Wireless (United Kingdom) or the paternalist model of broadcasting constructed by local, postcolonial authorities under the tutelage of BBC officials (Brown, this volume). Although administrations changed, communication infrastructures stayed relatively unaffected.

Beginning mainly in the 1970s, many in the LDCs began to realize that the lack of a national communication policy supported the continued colonial organization of communication, abiding underdevelopment of communication infrastructures or the prolongation of imbalanced international communication flows. In the 1970s, many began to accept that national communication policies could play a key role in directing the process of socioeconomic development and strengthening national sovereignty. The importance of national communication policy is not unique to the third world, but rather has been of key importance to all countries. As articulated in UNESCO (1976) documents, national communication policies are a "set of principles to govern the functioning and use of the communications and information media in the service of objectives democratically chosen by national communities in accordance with criteria specific to each country" (p. 7).

Efforts to achieve a relative degree of autonomy though national communication policies were initiated by several countries. For example, in 1962, Brazil adopted the Telecommunications Law and, after 1972 amalgamated the various, mainly foreign-owned, networks into the national telecom authority, Embratel (Sa, 1994). During the 1980s, Brazil also endeavored to develop a domestic computer industry and strove to assure national control over the domestic telecom system by reforming its Constitution to prevent privatization or foreign control of the national telecom network. As well, between 1963 and 1973, Mexico nationalized the foreign controlled telecom systems of Ericsson (Sweden) and ITT (United States; DEA, 1990). Mexico also established the Morelos satellite system a few years later. Similar efforts with respect to domestic control over telecom networks, media outlets, computers, and satellite systems were undertaken during this period by India, the People's Republic of China, Venezuela, and Peru (White, 1993). Additionally, regional consortiums were undertaken in Latin America, Africa, Southeast Asia, and the Middle East to establish telecom facilities. Whereas this is not an exhaustive account, nor applicable to all developing countries, the examples indicated a tendency, inspired by formal independence and the NWICO movement, toward autonomy in the global communication system, greater national control over domestic communication facilities, and more extensive co-operative ventures among the LDCs.

In contrast to those who stressed NWICO-related concerns primarily in terms of the quantity and quality of information flows, national communication policies took a much broader, structural view of the issues. The focus of some cultural imperialism theorists and modernization theorists on media content was displaced by a much broader approach that saw communication problems operating at the level of content, across the entire technological, legal, institutional and normative infrastructure of media systems (Boyd-Barrett,

1977) and within the macro-context of the global political economy. These were the ingredients of a structural and institutionalist theoretical and analytical framework that increasingly displaced the stress on content and crude behaviorist assumptions about media effects, apparently held in common by the opposed modernization and cultural imperialism schools of thought. This changed the focus of policymakers and researchers away from stressing the relationship between adopting Western forms of media organization, and the use of media content as a means of fostering the psychological conditions of modernization, toward initiatives seeking to adopt alternative models of media organization and the use of media to extend and amplify local cultural resources. Ultimately, communication systems came to be seen as part and parcel of the more general effort to strengthen the position of LDCs in the international political economy and further objectives of decolonization and cultural autonomy.

One of the successes of these communication policies is that many LDCs now have formal communication policies. Another is the increased autonomy gained by several countries and regional groupings who share in the construction, operation, and management of news pool services (e.g., Caribbean News Agency), satellite systems (e.g., Rascom in Africa), and broadcasting associations, such as the Asian Broadcasting Union. A third and more measurable index of such successes are alterations in the patterns of information flows, especially in terms of intraregional exchanges of news and television programming (Mowlana, 1985; Straubhaar, 1991; Varis, 1986).

This latter point appears to confirm the earlier thesis of "cultural diffusion" originated by Karl Deutsch in the 1950s and extended by Ithiel de Sola Pool, one of NWICO's sternest critics, in the 1970s and 1980s. According to Pool (1990), cultural interaction goes through natural phases of initial dependence, followed by the growth of independent financial and technical capital, and finally by complementarity as the local cultural production base matures. Although the evidence introduced earlier, and additional indications by Straubhaar, point toward the confirmation of this thesis, two qualifications are necessary. First, although certain countries have become regional production centers and others have increased the percentage of local content in their media systems, such as Bolivia and the Dominican Republic, other studies by Brown (this volume) for the Caribbean region, Ferguson (1992) regarding Canada, Pendakur and Kapur (this volume) for India, and recent information on the European Union (Fraser, 1993) suggest that dependence on foreign content is increasing, and that the dominant source remains the United States. Second, the growth in national media systems that Straubhaar points to, namely, Brazil, have not been based on any unique production values, but an integrated finance/industrial/media complex content with reproducing imported formats (Straubhaar, 1991). Anecdotal observations of the media systems in Turkey and Cyprus by the author suggest a similar pattern. This question is taken up later.

The experience of national communication policies in the LDCs point to three fundamental tensions. The first is the tension between those seeking such policies and others opposed to these efforts. As many have noted, efforts to construct national communication policies in the LDCs have encountered strong opposition from entrenched national and transnational interests. As Armand Mattelart (1994) and Rafael Roncagliolo (1993) have shown, efforts to broaden the participation of Latin American citizens in the media process through pluralistic media councils that would include church groups, civil rights organizations, labor unions, and academics (instead of the traditional alliance of the State, military and private sector), and efforts to secure access for local cultural producers to the channels of distribution, have been steadfastly opposed by the private sector and/or not carried out by national governments lacking the political will.

The second factor behind the failure to democratize the communication systems of the LDCs is the convergence of the state and private interests around the goal of economic accumulation. This condition applies equally to capitalist LDCs, such as Brazil, Singapore, South Korea, and so on, and their socialist counterparts, such as the People's Republic of China. Whereas earlier efforts taken up in the name of NWICO eschewed narrow economistic thinking about communication, the recent media policies of some countries in Latin America, the Near East, the former Soviet Union, and Asia suggest that policymakers now subscribe to the "excesses of democracy" thesis described earlier. The problem is that the repressive actions of states are increasingly legitimated through recourse to the promise of better material living standards, as all sites of public experience are turned into economic values through privatization, regulatory liberalization, and international free-trade agreements. One result is that the goals of creating strong national media sectors capable of competing regionally or even internationally outpace efforts to create legal systems capable of controlling concentrated ownership or market power. Consequently, regional conglomerates such as TV Globo (Brazil), Star TV (Southeast Asia), or Show TV in Turkey are based on underlying systems of vertical integration and diversified holdings that would not be permissible even according to the weak standards adopted by the U.S. Federal Communication Commission (FCC) to regulate ownership and control (Pendakur & Kapur, this volume; Straubhaar, 1991).

The third principle incongruity between NWICO initiatives to democratize communication and actuality is the continuation of state repression in capitalist and noncapitalist countries alike. In Kenya, for instance, as Morumpi Ole Ronkei (this volume) indicates, the state continuously expanded its coercive influence over all areas of society during the 1980s. In other countries, such as the People's Republic of China, media systems have been opened up to limited forms of public participation through call-in programs, people-on-the-street interviews, readers' letters, and so on. However, such openings are not based on an interest in democratic communication, per se, but serve as a mechanism for mobilizing society around centrally determined economic objectives and permitted so long as participation is constrained to reformism rather than challenges to the larger political and economic context within which such participation occurs (Hong, this volume). Similar conditions abound throughout the industrialized countries and many other LDCs (Herman & Chomsky, 1988).

The United State's opposition to NWICO was grounded almost exclusively in a critique of this third incongruity. As such, the criticism was mainly correct. Yet the partiality of this criticism lies in its recourse to a partial standard of democratic communication—the concept of negative freedom, and that the United States actively cultivated resistance to well-intentioned communication policies or remained unconcerned with the subordination of social policy objectives to the imperatives of economic accumulation. Nonetheless, for proponents of NWICO-related objectives, it also seems wise to take heed of the legitimacy of the U.S.-based criticism by turning greater attention toward the tensions existing within nation-states around communication policies. Traditionally, those laying out the conceptual framework for NWICO have directed their critique primarily at the actual threat of economic and foreign domination of domestic media systems instead of toward the potential of censorial activity by the newly emerging states (Schiller, 1969). This is no longer adequate. As recent studies suggest, it is important to focus on the practices of national church groups, educators, human rights proponents, and labor unions taken to further goals central to NWICO initiatives. Such efforts have already been taken up in Kenya (Morumpi, this volume), Mexico, Latin America (Frederick, this volume), and the new nations of the former Eastern bloc (Kleinwaechter, this volume). This readily coincides with similar activities undertaken by a wide range of groups in the industrialized countries, as the recent spate of efforts to expand our understanding of the concept of democratic communication indicates (Bailie & Winseck, 1995; Keane, 1991; Splichal & Wasko, 1993).

PARTIAL CONCEPTS OF INFORMATION AND DEMOCRACY IN AN AGE OF ABUNDANCE

The ambiguous accomplishments of communication policies in the LDCs are inseparable from larger shifts in the global political economy. This final section traces three such shifts and considers their implications for the future of NWICO. The first shift is the reorganization of the world political economy away from the bipolar opposition of North and South and the Cold War toward the organization of the world into a triad of political economic power connecting North America, Western Europe, and Japan. The first shift also brings with it the emergence of a transnational economy divided among the triad, the semiperipheral Newly Industrialized Countries (NICs), and the continued peripheralization of the rest of the world. The second concern connects the increased economic importance of national and transnational communication systems to the integration of policymakers from the industrialized countries, the NICs, and peripheral countries around the hegemonic notion of the "information economy." The third relates to the restructuring of legal systems—nationally, regionally, and internationally— designed to increase the economic value of information. This latter development involves the externalization of the regulatory policies of a few core countries, the usurpation of the international communication policy regime by GATT, and the expansion of the free flow of information doctrine.

A Tale of Two Worlds: Paradoxes of the Global Information Economy

During the 1960s and 1970s, the economic conditions in most LDCs were improving. This increased economic strength and the ability of the LDCs to play the superpowers off one another created space for initiatives directed at increasing the autonomy and status of the LDCs in the world political economy. In addition to the development of national communication policies, efforts to increase literacy were in full swing; agreements regulating the prices of primary commodities—the largest source of income for LDCs—were initiated to increase the share of LDCs in the volume of world trade; and real per capita income rates were rising twice as fast as those in OECD countries (Cardoso & Faletto, 1979; Gill & Law, 1988).

Similar conditions failed to hold during the 1980s. By 1992, the LDCs' share of global trade remained the same as it had in 1960—29%—although shifts took place among the LDCs themselves in light of the emerging division between the NICs and the peripheral economies (Noyelle, 1994). In addition, between 1980 and 1990, the value of primary commodities declined by 30%, and the rate of indebtedness almost doubled (from 32% of the GDP to 61%). Under such conditions, the earlier tendency for economic growth in the developing countries to surpass that of the industrialized countries by a factor of two reversed. Although economic growth in the core triad of around 3% was considered unacceptable by economists, in Africa, Asia, the Middle East, Caribbean, and Latin America it was between .25% and 1.25%, whereas the NICs of Southeast Asia achieved the highest growth rates of 7.4% (United Nations, 1992). Throughout the world, income disparities between the rich and poor intensified (Galbraith, 1992). From a social perspective, the situation appears similar. Investments in education remained extraordinarily low in most of the LDCs, ranging between .9% (e.g., Nigeria, Indonesia) and 2.5% (e.g., Sri Lanka and Pakistan) of the GNP, in comparison to between 5% and 7% of GNP in most of the NICs and core countries. Illiteracy rates also continued to map out the boundaries among the various regions of the world and between men and women (United Nations, 1992).

In contrast to this rather pessimistic situation, an almost pristine state of affairs emerged in the economics of global communication. Indicative of the contrasting worlds of people and communication was the enormous expansion in the economic value of the communications industries, the increased availability of basic and sophisticated technologies of communication, and an explosion in the volume of international information flows. A recent survey of global telecoms by the ITU found that the total value of equipment and services offered through public telecom networks in 1992 was US $535 billion (ITU, 1994a), about one-third of the transnational communications economy estimated at US $1,420 billion in 1995.[3]

Similar conditions held for the broadcasting, cable, and film industries. During the 1980s, U.S. film industry revenues from all media quadrupled to US $10 billion (Murphy, 1990, pp. 7-10). Several years later, the Motion Picture Export Association of America reported revenues of $18 billion (USD) (Wasko, 1994). Whereas the U.S. film industry had experienced a drop in European revenues during the early part of the 1980s due to cultural policies adopted there, the entrenchment of privatization, regulatory liberalization, and commercialization of public service media occurring later in the decade resulted in revenues climbing tremendously.

These same combinations also benefited the major broadcasting conglomerates as well. The 1980s saw vast expansions in the international networks of CNN, BBC, CBC, Capital Cities/ABC, Time-Warner, News Corporation, Hatchette SA, Bertelsmann, and so on, as well as TV Globo (Brazil) and Star TV (Southeast Asia; Bagdikian, 1989; Pendakur & Kapur, this volume; Straubhaar, 1991). Paradoxically, the international expansion of the news arms of these transnational corporations occurred at the same time that the budgets for public service media—the BBC and CBC—were being slashed and the news divisions of the private ones, except CNN, severely curtailed (Winseck, 1992). Yet rather than these developments shrinking the scope of media operations, an imperative emerged for public service and private media to shore up their faltering budgets with international revenues and the search for new channels through which their programs were circulated. Such changes also created openings for the emergence or expansion of a number of television news-based services on a global and regional basis, such as CNN, Visnews, Euronews, Reuters Financial Network, and proposals by the Japanese for their own regional network.

The Global Information Economy: Hegemony, Absorption, and Struggle

The effervescent glow of the economics of the transnational communication industries that stand in such opposition to the sociological realities of everyday

---

[3]The estimation is based on the figure of U.S. $900 billion cited in U.S. Congressional hearings and an annual growth rate of 8%—a rate indicated by the studies of national governments and the ITU (Canada, 1992; ITU, 1994a; U.S. Subcommittee on Communications, 1988).

life in the information economy has also captured the attention of the world's communication policymakers. In stark contrast to earlier efforts to seek a balance between the public interest and industrial imperatives, the majority of policymakers appear to have fully embraced the thesis of the information economy. Although evidence introduced later indicates that the economic dividends of the emerging communications environment outstrip the social dividends associated with increased access to basic communication resources by a factor ranging from 2:1 to 5:1,[4] policymakers from the core, semiperipheral, and peripheral countries have increasingly lined up behind the thesis that the information economy will produce social benefits for all. Why?

The main reason for the seismic shift in the position of policymakers is related to the academic work of economists in the United States who, during the 1960s and 1970s, showed the increasing importance of information related economic activities to the economy as a whole (Babe, 1994). According to such studies, information-related activities are continuously displacing agriculture, manufacturing, and natural resources as sources of economic value and growth. As one of the leading proponents of the information economy, Marc Porat showed that the size of the workforce employed in information related activities grew from only 10% in 1900 to 27% in 1960 and were in excess of 50% in the latter part of the 1970s (cited in Pool, 1990). Such findings have been given significant support by a host of academic, industry, and governmental studies. For instance, the OECD and ITU have consistently demonstrated that communication/information activities continue to grow and outpace other areas of the economy. An example from Canada indicates that in contrast to a 3% rate of growth for the rest of the economy, the telecom industry currently grows at 8.6% per year (Communications Canada, 1992). In the United States it has been consistently argued that the "rapidly changing world economy. . . involves the collection, analysis, and dissemination, as well as the transport of information. Telecom . . . has played, and continues to play, a critical role in our nation's economic development" (U.S. Subcommittee on Communications, 1988, p. 5). The list of such studies is long, but similar.

Given the ubiquity of such thinking about the information economy in most of the industrialized countries, it is not surprising that a similar emphasis has proliferated in countries outside the core triad as well. Thus, in a recent issue of the trade magazine Communications, policymakers from Tanzania, the Philippines, Chile, Brazil, Ghana, and the newly independent Ukraine all stress the importance of telecoms to their economic development (Gatica, 1994; Kiula, 1994; Prozhivalsky, 1994). In these countries, communication technologies and services are increasingly integrated into policies aimed at overcoming

---

[4]Although the methodology is somewhat crude, I arrived at these conclusions by comparing the rate of economic growth with the rate of increases in people's access to the basic technologies of television, newspapers, and telephones. A fuller presentation of these data is introduced in Table 15.1.

imbalances in the distribution of the world's communication resources and toward attaining the status of a newly industrialized country by the year 2000.

Yet, despite the hegemonic power of the information economy thesis in much of the policy community, the thesis side-steps several critical issues. First, it reduces the concepts of information/communication solely to their economic dimensions (Babe, 1994). As a result, the unique qualities of information and the history of democracy are eliminated. The result is an ideological construction of the world that severs information/communication from their unique qualities and history to suit policies that are partially legitimated by their appeal to people's desire for real improvements in their economic condition.

Second, the treatment of information as a commodity averts equity issues arising from the inclusive properties of information. As Table 15.1 indicates, although there have been quite impressive increases in the distribution of basic communication resources throughout the world, the patterns of distribution are uneven, the rate of access is growing at about 20% to 50% as fast as the rate of economic growth achieved in the information/communication sectors (see note 4), and enormous gaps among and within regions persist at unacceptable levels.

The claim that the significant improvements noted in Table 15.1 remain unacceptable can be substantiated by reference to recent ITU-sponsored studies and initiatives. For instance, earlier policy recommendations made during the 1980s called for efforts to increase the number of telephones available to at least 1 per every 100 inhabitants in all countries. However, in the present context, 24 countries of the OECD have one telephone for every two citizens, whereas 50 countries fall behind even the minimal rate of access recommended by the ITU. Another recent ITU report notes that the OECD countries contain only 15% of the world's population, but account for more than 71% of the telephone lines, whereas the other 85% of the population share access to the remaining 29% (ITU, 1994a; Tarjanne, 1994a).

Although gaps between the industrialized countries and LDCs persist, closer inspection reveals that there have been fundamental changes in the global distribution of access to basic communication resources that mirror more general shifts in the emerging world system. Table 15.1 indicates that, once we distinguish between the NICs and LDCs, imbalances occur regionally as well as across the North-South divide. This pattern is not unique to Asia, but also prevails in the Middle East, South and Central America, and other regions. Within this world system of communication the gaps among, for example, Myanmar, Vietnam, and Indonesia (each with less than .5 of the population having access to basic telephone service) and South Korea and Singapore (29.6 and 45.6 access lines per100, respectively) are often as great as that suggested by figures demonstrating the bifurcation of the world into rich and poor across the North-South divide. The global distribution of communication resources is no longer based on distinctions between the North and South, but according to

Table 15.1. Global Distribution of Basic Communication Resources.

Region	Press 1979	1988	% +/-	TV 1980	1988	% +/-	Phone 1980	1989	% +/-
Africa	18.1	14.7	-22%	25.1	26.5	+.5%	1.1	1.4	+30%
S. Asia	42.4	63.16	+49%	50.6	65.8	+30%	1.5	2.2	+50%
S. Korea & Sing.	246	289	+18%	238	281	+18%	19	37.6	+98%
S. Amer.	70.3	58.2	-17%	100	123.5	+24%	6.1	7.6	+25%
C Amer.& Car.	56.4	74.9	+33%	135.3	146.8	+24%	7.9	5.7	+39%
M. East	32.4	54.8	+69%	130	195	+50%	10.5	15.9	+51%
EE/SU!	242	277.4	+14%	257.5	325.5	+26%	21.3	14.3	+49%
OECD	341.2	376.3	+10%	360	400.2	+11%	46.4	56.8	+22%

aFigures are based on number of newspaper copies and television receivers available per 1000 inhabitants.
bFigures are based on lines per 100 inhabitants.
cFor demonstration purposes two countries with the largest communication systems in Asia—Singapore and South Korea—were treated separately from the rest of the Asian countries, as a way of illustrating the quite dramatic differences between the LDCs and the NICs regionally.
dEE/SU stands for Eastern European countries formerly part of the Soviet Union and present-day Russia.
From *Statistical Yearbook* (37th Issue, pp. 192-208, 746-752), by the United Nations, 1992, New York: Author.

the trifold division of the world economy into the categories of core, semiperiphery, and periphery.

Similar patterns are also borne out by the shape of world information flows. Three characteristics visible in the geography of transnational information flows merit mention. First, the volume of international telecom traffic has increased dramatically over the last several years. The average telephone subscriber now makes over 70 minutes of international calls per year (Tarjanne, 1994b). Thus, there is an increasing flow of information outside the channels of unidirectional mass media systems. The implications of this observation are not lost on those such as Jill Hills (1993) who recognize that:

> telecoms . . . can play a part in facilitating the interchange of information between citizens. It is no coincidence that where civil and political rights have been denied, although . . . centralized broadcasting system[s] used for propaganda have been well developed, . . . telecoms . . . have remained undeveloped. . . . [Telecoms enable] citizens within a democracy to receive information on which to determine their . . . political interests and the right to communicate and join with others to further their interests. (pp. 21-23)

The second notable feature of these communication flows is the increased contribution of those residing outside the traditional core countries. For example, the largest users of international telecom services are sub-Saharan African subscribers fortunate enough to have access to the sparse networks within the continent. Although in most of the African countries there is fewer than 1 telephone line per 100 people, and often less than 1 per 500 people, those with access use international telephone services on an average of 200 minutes per year, or approximately three times the global average (Tarjanne, 1994b, 1994c). However, despite these decentralizing tendencies in the geography of transnational communication flows, it is also true that slightly less than 60% of world telecom traffic flows among networks linking the core regions of North America, Japan, and Western Europe (Cowhey, 1990). Thus, not unlike the history of all communication technologies, the emerging communications infrastructure simultaneously include and exclude along the lines of commerce and power.

The Reshuffling of Transnational Space: Integration, Separation, and the Extraterritorial Application of Core Communication Laws

That the transnational networks of communication are shaped by existing lines of commerce and geopolitical power is illustrated by spectacular and more mundane efforts to harmonize and police transnational networks of communication. This occurs simultaneously through the repressive control over the transnational media system, subtle shifts in the patterns of community and communication, and the almost mundane extension of the technical rules governing communication from the national contexts of a few core countries to the global level through the remote institutions of the ITU and GATT.

The Spectacular. Perhaps one of the more vivid examples of the spectacular occurred with the extraterritorial application of the repressive arm of U.S. media law during the Gulf War of 1991. During the Gulf War restrictions formulated in the interregnum of the Cold War—the McCarran-Walter Act and Defense Department rules governing the press during the time of war—were extended to the transnational plane to control the foundations of public knowledge internationally about the war. Although the world's people with access to television were encouraged by the commentary, subtitles, and illusions of "live" video to form the impression of unhindered coverage of the war, in fact, all information coming from the "zones of operation" were filtered through carefully selected representatives of the transnational media system and U.S. military censors before being presented to the public (United States District Court, 1991). Moreover, most of the media organizations capable of mustering the resources to cover this transnational media spectacle capitulated to the massive control over the foundations of international public knowledge about the war, although Agence France Press, a few nonmainstream members of the U.S. media system, and some independent journalists did mount an unsuccessful legal challenge to CENTCOM's press pool restriction on First Amendment Grounds. Although the U.S. District Court responsible for adjudicating the challenge did acknowledge that significant freedom of the media questions were raised, the ending of the war caused it to dismiss these questions as moot (Winseck, 1992).

The Subtle. Although this reference to the control over international public space during the time of war is a somewhat spectacular example of the continued availability of repressive measures of media control, the Gulf War, along with the examples of Tiananmen Square, the collapse of the Soviet Union, and the continuing conflagration in the former Yugoslavia, point to the fact that media events have been transnationalized and made available to the increasing number of people with access to basic communication technologies throughout the world. Coupled with the rise of sizeable pockets of high-income elites in the NICs and LDCs, widening income gaps within countries, broadened access to the means of initiating and receiving communication, and "technologies without boundaries" (Pool, 1990)—computer networks, satellites, and so on—there is an unmistakable emergence of transnational, communicative associations.

Yet, rather than this being an all-inclusive community, the boundaries of transnational space are mapped by differences between those using the available technologies to produce and receive the transnational flows of communication and the rest of the populations cut off from such means and thus tied to more local forms of culture. These reconfigurations of transnational space harmonize a portion of the world's people around the patterns of commerce and communication, whereas increasing fragmentation within the periphery resuscitates local forms of cultural expression and sends citizens in search of other mechanisms of social integration to overcome the feelings of alienation and inefficacy created by the larger political, economic, and communication contexts shaping their lifeworlds. Thus, in the transnational communication system there is simultaneously an homogenization of the core and heterogeneity of cultural experience at the dispersed peripheries. Whether the latter will be a source of liberating practices or narrow parochialism remains to be seen. However, the surge of fundamentalism, racism and ethnic strife are not auspicious (Comor, 1994; Mattelart, 1994; Straubhaar, 1991; Tehranian, 1994). One thing is certain, though, increases in the global circulation of information does not equal knowledge and/or peace.

The Mundane. Behind these economic, technological, and communication mechanisms of transnational integration are alterations in the rules governing communication systems. Although there have been periodic setbacks and anomalous conditions persist, there is a clear tendency among national governments and the ITU to adopt regulatory systems originated in the United States and subsequently diffused to the United Kingdom, Japan, and ever-wider circles thereafter. The general results of regulatory diffusion brought about by the extraterritorial application of core communications law are that in many countries the use of public policies to guide the development of new technologies and services has been curtailed, cost-based accounting procedures applied to nonregulated services, and concepts of a positive right to communication have been eliminated (e.g., FCC, 1988; U.S. Subcommittee Communications, 1988).

These processes create similar structural conditions throughout the communication systems of the LDC, NIC, and core countries. For example, as we saw earlier, in the NICs and LDCs policies designed to create companies capable of competing regionally and internationally are inseparable from the effect they have on limiting citizens' opportunities to participate in the media process. The priority of economic goals means that most policies interfering with efforts to realize the full economic value of communication—ownership limitations, advertising restrictions, local production requirements, public ownership, cultural objectives, and so on—are removed through regulatory liberalization. When this legal/normative order prevails, communication networks serve mainly to integrate markets rather than civil society, as in many of the former Eastern-bloc countries (Kleinwaechter, this volume; Prozhivalsky, 1994). Or, as the earlier references to TV Globo (Brazil), Show TV (Turkey), and Star TV (Southeast Asia) indicated, regulatory frameworks allow media systems to become fully integrated into financial and industrial spheres, and any measures designed to monitor the extent of ownership concentration and control in the communication industries are weak or nonexistent. The overall result is that any attempts to democratize communication systems can only be limited to representative, not more participatory, forms of democracy and must occur within the contours of ownership and control prevailing in any given country.[5]

---

[5]The power of this particular interpretation is that it allows us to recognize the seeming

Similar conditions are shared by citizens in the industrialized countries, as the State and private sector unite around projects creating conditions for national companies' conquest of global markets and increased rates of technological innovation. In the United States this process has supported the merger of Time Warner, the acquisition of broadcasting companies by the telecom operators, the purchase of some of the Hollywood majors by Japanese hardware producers, and increased efforts to bring about alliances between the telecom and cable industries (U.S. Department of Commerce, 1993). In other countries, for example, Canada, the result has been the elimination of the common-carrier model of regulation that separated control over the channels of communication from control over the contents of communication. Such shifts accommodate the industrial imperative of technological innovation and, for example, the merger between the cable and telecom giant Rogers/UNITEL and the publishing conglomerate Maclean Hunter. It also paves the way for further consolidation in the communication industries, as other telecom operators and broadcasters merge, acquire, and/or form partnerships with publishers and other software producers.

Accompanying the expansion of communication companies across space, the media, and the economy as a whole are transformations in the legal constructions of communication rights. In practice, this has meant the extension of the right to free speech to corporations in general, cable and broadcasting companies in particular (Schiller, 1989) and, most recently, to the telecom operators. Thus, in 1994, the U.S. Courts declared that policies designed to decentralize communication and prevent corporate control simultaneously over the channels and contents of communication were "a limitation depriv[ing] telephone companies of the editorial judgment, control and discretion that are the essence of their First Amendment rights" (U.S. Court of Appeals, 1993, p. 12; emphasis added). Wedded to partial concepts of democratic communication, and immersed in the nascent power relations of the information economy, the Court was unable (or unwilling?) to distinguish between the legal fiction of the corporate person and citizens. As such, it was able to draw equivalencies between the rights of AT&T, GTE, and BellSouth, among the largest telecom corporations in the world with revenues between US \$12 to 40 billion, and citizens, although no such equivalencies exist in their respective ability to shape the communications environment. That this is a unique interpretation coincident with the power relations of the information economy and the drive toward the construction of new technological environment, is revealed by the inconsistency

---

abundance of information created by the new private sector media taking hold in the Middle East, Asia, Latin America, Africa, and the Caribbean, while also drawing our attention to how these new systems are integrated into the broader political economy of these regions. As a result, questions of democratic communication turn on issues of (a) access to the means of information production and reception, and (b) the nature of ownership and control within any given country, rather than a simple, but oft-used, equation that more information equals more democracy.

between this decision and another 25 years earlier. In that decision, the judge recognized the tension between the values of private property and democratic communication and declared the rights of citizens to freedom of expression paramount to the competing rights of communication corporations.[6]

THE DETERRITORIALIZATION OF ELECTRONIC SPACE: GATT AS INTERNATIONAL COMMUNICATIONS POLICY

The emerging communication order taking hold in various national settings is also being generalized to the international level. This is being accomplished as telecom operators press for voting rights in the ITU, advertisers push the European Union to recognize a U.S.-style right to freedom of "commercial" speech, the free flow of information doctrine is expanded through NAFTA and GATT, and the Secretary-General of the ITU advises countries to dismantle structural regulations preventing cross-ownership among broadcasters, cable operators, and the telecom companies (Tarjanne, 1994d). The most important recent development mapping out the successes and boundaries of the emerging communication order is the GATT agreement adopted by over 130 countries— the first international agreement ever to treat communication issues as a "trade in services" issue.

Exemplifying the trend for U.S. communication policy to first embrace regionally and then be asserted at the international level is the origins of the agreement in the Canada-United States Free Trade Agreement (1989), followed by the Canada-United States-Mexico NAFTA (1992), and ultimately by the GATT (1993). In fact, GATT's Telecom Annex is a carbon copy of the NAFTA agreement on telecoms, with minor changes in syntax and the addition of two additional clauses dealing with developing countries and international organizations, such as the ITU. Although many realized that the earlier free-trade agreements would provide a model for GATT, few realized that NAFTA would be the model subsequently adopted (Canada, 1992; TNC, 1993).

One of the defining features of the GATT agreement is the distinction drawn between different areas of the communication field. Mainly because of the strenuous opposition of Canada, some European countries, and a large number of the developing countries, GATT's provisions only explicitly apply to telecom and computer-generated information services, not broadcasting, film, and cable. Because countries opposing the extension of the agreement to these

---

[6]The problem with the Red Lion decision being referred to here is that the judge tied democratic communication to the particular technological infrastructure of broadcasting, rather than properties inherent in the history of democracy or information. As such, once the conditions "scarcity" associated with broadcasting were transformed by the conditions of abundance made possible by the new technologies of communication, citizens' hard-fought battle for a more expansive concept of democratic communication was curtailed (see Streeter, 1990).

latter areas refused to accept the definition of culture as an industry, and disagreements among France, some other European countries, and the United States over the type of copyright measures that would apply to the film industries, the final agreement was unable to include provisions relating to the cultural sector (Fraser, 1993). The only provisions dealing specifically with film and television reaffirm the application of previous international copyright agreements and extend these to cover genetic/biological information and electronic databases.

The most important area of the agreement is the Telecommunications Annex. The Annex lays out several provisions that have not yet been accepted within the ITU, but have been extended to many countries through bilateral negotiations and the extraterritorial application of U.S. communications and trade law. One of the most important provisions is the requirement that countries allow foreign direct investment in the construction of private networks, and that these networks be allowed to connect with, and provide enhanced services over public networks (TNC, 1993, Article 5). This clause expands the "free flow of information" doctrine so that it now covers the contents of communication and the infrastructures through which such messages flow. In the past, private networks have usually not been permitted by many countries and by most of the NICs and LDCs because of concerns that such networks would siphon traffic and revenues away from public networks. However, GATT side-steps these concerns in favor of private networks that serve the specialized needs of professional and corporate users unwilling to wait or contribute to building more inclusive public networks (McDowell, 1994).

By allowing direct foreign investment in the construction of private communication networks and encouraging LDCs to rely on private network operators to meet the specialized needs of sophisticated users (TNC, 1993, Article 6(4)), GATT parallels the recent trends toward privatization in the LDCs and NICs. Indicative of this trend is the observation that between the early 1980s and 1994 the number of private telecom systems among the world's 40 largest operators increased from less than a handful to about 18 (Bellchambers, 1994). In contrast to ideas embodied in the NIEO and NWICO, privatization has extended the operations of Western telecom TNEs, like SouthWest Bell, Ameritech, Bell Atlantic, and France Telecom, and has been used by U.S. financial institutions as a means to recover debt. For example, 60% of the value of the Argentina telecom operator was exchanged for the assumption of the government's debt by U.S. commercial banks (Hills, 1993).

GATT also expands the "free flow of information" doctrine by shielding the new information technologies and services from public intervention and communication policies. In contrast to NWICO, UNESCO, and even recent ITU efforts, the Telecom Annex fixes the range of basic communication services and prevents communication policy initiatives from defining an expanded range of publicly regulated services commensurate with the emerging technologies and requirements of citizenship in the "information age" (TNC, 1993, Articles 3 & 5). As a consequence, it is unlikely that basic public communication services could be expanded to encompass certain Internet features, electronic databases containing government or public information, or a plethora of other Value-Added Network Services (VANS).

Although the Telecom Annex presumes that its efforts to draw boundaries around the reach of public communication policies are based on transparent technical criteria and economic practices, many policy analysts suggest that these distinctions rest on the balance of power among the constituents shaping the regulatory framework rather than properties inherent in the technologies or services involved (Connell, 1993; Bouwman & Latzer, 1993; Mosco, 1990). What is most striking is that by preventing countries from extending communication policies to the new technologies and VANS providers, GATT denies citizens the opportunity to shape the emerging communications environment and enshrines in international law that same model of corporate freedom of expression adopted in the United States (TNC, 1993, Article 5(4)(6)). This will have enormous implications for the ongoing shifts in the patterns of ownership, legal frameworks, and technologies that are bringing about a convergence of telecoms, broadcasting, cable television, electronic databases, and computers around some form of integrated broadband networks (IBNs; Bouwman & Latzer, 1994; Connell, 1994).

In contrast to the "freedom without responsibility" perspective adopted by GATT, public policies in this area could be directed at, for instance, requiring VANS providers and video distribution networks to provide access to all users under similar terms, to reserve portions of the network for noncommercial and nongovernmental organizations, and to refrain these network and service providers from interfering with the contents of communications. Without such provisions, it is likely that there will be a lack of balance between public and commercial services, and that those who control the technologies will control the contents. This is the same situation that has affected the broadcasting and cable industries for decades and been recently extended to the telecom operators. This flies in the face of decentralizing tendencies present in the emerging technologies and the promises of the "information age" to democratize society and open up the channels of communication to all "those who wish to reach their fellow citizens" (Bagdikian, 1989, p. 812). The ongoing practices of U.S.-based CompuServe to exercise editorial control over the contents flowing through its commercially available network, and the recent experience of labor unions in the United States denied access to Dun and Bradstreet's commercially available electronic database containing corporate information vital to the union's negotiating efforts, are not auspicious signs for the embryonic transnational, electronic "free press." However, according to the concept of negative freedoms, such actions are permissible and within the realm of democratic communication. As a recent U.S. Supreme Court decision noted, the First Amendment prevents government from making any law abridging the freedom of expression, but contains no similar restrictions against the actions of private telecom operators that have the same effect (cited in Gregg, 1989). Thus, it appears that as economic and ideological filters shape the communications of the traditional media (Herman & Chomsky, 1988), so too will they in the emerging media.

As a means of curtailing the usurpation of communication rights by those controlling the means of communication, perhaps structural regulations could be maintained and extended that separate ownership of communication networks from the services offered. Such policies, as indicated by the French Minitel project during the 1980s and the earlier common carrier model adopted in many countries, expand the range of telecom services made universally available, and open up opportunities for citizens to become media producers rather than just consumers by decentralizing information and cultural production (Mattelart & Stourdze, 1985). In the absence of such efforts it is likely that GATT will increase the fragmentation of communication networks according to the needs of different classes of users and, as proponents of trade agreements note, force regulatory systems "closer to the American position" (Globerman & Booth, 1989, p. 325). As was indicated earlier, the American position is moving toward the eradication of the common-carrier model and the bestowing of "free speech" rights onto corporate behemoths.

One more reason for the development of communication policies for the new technologies might be to prevent patterns of concentrated ownership and control apparent in the telecom, broadcasting, cable, and film industries from occurring in the emerging array of telecom services. As one of the fastest growing areas in communications, VANS are drawing large investments from existing media interests and traditional telecom operators searching for new sites of growth. As such, there are already trends toward concentration in these services, as recent studies in Canada, Europe, and the United States show. As one study indicates, control over VANS and electronic databases in Europe is already concentrated among a small number of firms, most of whom are American and/or telecom operators (Bouwman & Latzer, 1994).

In essence, GATT does for the new technologies and information services internationally what the First Amendment did for the press and subsequently all forms of media in the United States—transfers communication rights from citizens at large to those who own the means of communication. This is not surprising given the move in many countries, of which Canada, the United States, and the United Kingdom are paramount examples, away from the common-carrier and broadcasting models of regulation as they remove technically based, legal distinctions to facilitate the birth of IBNs, the information economy, and globally competitive media industries. What is surprising is that GATT built a regulatory framework around such a partial concept of democratic communication and a set of technical distinctions that are withering in the face of legal transformations, mergers and acquisitions, and the imperatives of transnationalization sweeping across national regulatory contexts. Although GATT allows the broadcasting, film, and cable industries to be exempted, it is unlikely that the technical and economic basis for such an exclusion will last as single companies, such as the Rogers/UNITEL/Maclean Hunter conglomerate, Time-Warner, and US West, offer computer, telecom, enhanced, and video programming services over the same technological infrastructure.

The GATT regulatory framework is based on distinctions that will not withstand the seismic shifts in the technoeconomic and legal infrastructure of the emerging communications environment. The prospects of this happening are almost certain. This is especially so in light of the already heavily contested nature of the boundaries that GATT draws between conceptions of communication as commodity and communication as culture. As the entire debate between the United States and many other countries over the suitability of including the "cultural industries" in GATT show, there is already enormous political pressures to remove these distinctions. Although these forces of monumental change will take time to work themselves out, the United States, United Kingdom and other supporters of free trade in cultural commodities are already exerting pressure through bilateral negotiations and domestic trade laws to remove the remaining barriers to the "information economy."

CONCLUSION: WITHER NWICO? THE PROSPECTS FOR DEMOCRATIC COMMUNICATION IN A TRANSNATIONAL WORLD

By creating a body of research showing how communication systems are shaped by political and economic power within and between nations, NWICO defined the context of international communication issues for about two decades and spawned national and international policies designed to create more inclusive systems of communication. As a result, countries now have communication policies where before there were none; cooperative ventures provide more balance between regional flows of information among the developing countries and the still mainly one-way flow of information from the few to the many; and expanded mandates adopted by UNESCO and the ITU simultaneously constructed more equitable communication policies and sowed the seeds of regulatory liberalization, privatization, and international trade agreements that transcend the efforts of NWICO.

In contrast, the emerging context typified by GATT eschews attempts to link communication issues with those of power, responsibility, and measures aiming to ensure that the possibilities for communication are more equitably distributed. Whereas the earlier formula of communication rights adopted by the UN, and even the United States, realized that there are contradictions between communication as a human right and communication as a corporate right, the new legal frameworks obliterate such tensions. Immersed in the power relations of the transnational information economy, new legal frameworks formally extend the system of corporate rights in relation to the new technologies, national communication policies, and the international communication policy agencies, whereas the prospects of democratic communication for citizens turns on the informal possibilities present in the new technologies and decisions to consume or not consume.

As a result, the emerging institutional, legal, and technological environment is designed less to serve the goals of democratic communication than, as the ITU notes, to extract "an increasing share of the work, leisure time and . . . disposable income of . . . consumers . . . , and to deepen the market by trying to persuade consumers to spend more time using telecommunications-based applications" (Tarjanne, 1994d, p. 4). Although such a focus may meet the technical requirements of economic growth and assist the recovery of a lethargic global economy, it has little to do with the technical and communicative dimensions of democracy introduced in earlier sections of this chapter.

REFERENCES

Babe, R. (1994). *Information and communication in economics*. Boston: Kluwer.

Bagdikian, B. (1989, July). The lords of the global village. *The Nation*, pp. 885-820.

Bellchambers, W.H. (1994). New world-new mind-new ITU. *ITU Newsletter, 2*, 9-14.

Bouwman, H., & Latzer, M. (1994). Telecommunication network based services in Europe. In C. Steinfield, J.M. Bauer, & L. Caby (Eds.), *Telecommunications in transition: Policies, services and technologies in the European community* (pp. 161-181). Newbury Park, CA: Sage.

Boyd-Barrett, O. (1977). Media imperialism: Towards an international framework for the analysis of media systems. In J. Curran, M. Gurevitch, J. Woolacott, & T. Bennett (Eds.), *Mass communication and society* (pp. 116-135). London: Edward Arnold.

Brittan, S. (1975). The economic contradictions of democracy. *British Journal of Political Science, 5*(1), 129-159.

Canada. (1992). *Canada, U.S. and Mexico North American Free Trade Agreement*. Boulder, CO: Westlaw.

Cardoso, F.H., & Faletto, E. (1979). *Dependency and development in Latin America*. Berkley: University of California Press.

Codding, G., & Rutkowski, A. (1982). *The International Telecommunication Union in a changing world*. Boston: Artech House.

Communications Canada. (1992). *Telecommunications in Canada: An overview of the carriage industry*. Ottawa: Communications Canada.

Comor, E.A. (1994). Communication technology and international capitalism: The case of DBS and US foreign policy. In E.A. Comor (Ed.), *The global political economy of communication* (pp. 83-102). New York: St. Martin's Press.

Connell, S. (1994). Broadband services in Europe. In C. Steinfield, J.M. Bauer, & L. Caby (Eds.), *Telecommunications in transition: Policies, services and technologies in the European community* (pp. 236-34). Newbury Park, CA: Sage.

Cowhey, P. (1990). The international telecommunications regime: The political roots of regimes for high technology. *International Organization, 44*(2), 169-199.

Department of External Affairs (DEA). (1990). *Market study on telecommunication equipment and systems in Mexico.* Ottawa: Latin American Affairs Division, Department of External Affairs.

Federal Communications Commission (FCC). (1988). *Telecommunications policies of foreign governments (Decision 88-71).* Washington, DC: Pike and Fischer Inc.

Ferguson, M. (1992). The mythology about globalization. *European Journal of Communication, 7,* 69-93.

Fortner, R. (1994). *International communication.* Belmont, CA: Wadsworth.

Fraser, M. (1993). A question of culture: The Canadian solution resolves a GATT stand-off. *Macleans, 106*(52), 50-51.

Galbraith, J. (1992). *The culture of contentment.* New York: Oxford University Press.

Galtung, J. (1994, January). *State, capital and civil society: A problem of communication.* Paper presented at the 6th Annual MacBride Round Table at the University of Hawaii—Honolulu.

Gatica, L. (1994). Liberalization and tariff legislation in Chile. *IEEE Communications Magazine,* pp. 34-5.

Gerbner, G., Mowlana, H., & Nordenstreng, K. (Eds.). (1993). *The global media debate: Its rise, fall and renewal.* Norwood, NJ: Ablex.

Gill, S., & Law, D. (1988). *The global political economy.* London, UK: Harvester, Wheatsheaf.

Globerman, S., & Booth, P. (1989). The Canada-US Free Trade Agreement and the telecommunications industry. *Telecommunication Policy, 13*(4), 319-328.

Gregg, R. (1989). A political economic analysis of Dial-A-Porn. *Studies in Communication and Culture, 1*(4), 74-83.

Guback, T. (1969). *The international film industry.* Bloomington: Indiana University Press.

Habermas, J. (1975). *Legitimation crisis.* Boston: Beacon Press.

Habermas, J. (1989). *On society and politics: A reader.* Boston: Beacon Press.

Hamelink, C.J. (1993). The right to knowledge—a balancing act. *Media Development, 2,* 3-7.

Hayek, F. (1986). Economic freedom and representative government. In J. Donald & S. Hall (Eds.), *Politics and ideology* (pp. 23-6). Great Britain: St. Edmunds.

Held, D. (1987). *Models of democracy.* Cambridge, UK: Polity Press

Herman, E., & Chomsky, N. (1988). *Manufacturing consent: The political economy of the mass media.* New York: Pantheon.

Hills, J. (1993). Telecommunications and democracy: The international experience. *Telecommunications Journal, 60*(1), 21-29.

International Telecommunications Union (ITU)(1994). Report on the state of world telecommunications. *ITU Newsletter, 1*, 9-12.

Ito, Y., & Hattori, T. (1989). Mass media ethics in Japan. In T.W. Cooper, C.W. Christians, & R.W. White (Eds.), *Communication ethics and global change* (pp. 168-80). White Plains, NY: Longman.

Keane, J. (1991). *The media and democracy.* Cambridge, UK: Polity Press.

Kiula, N. (1994). Telecommunications development in Tanzania. *IEEE Communications Magazine*, 36-37.

MacBride, S., & Roach, C. (1993). The new international economic order. In G. Gerbner, H. Mowlana, & K. Nordenstreng (Eds.), *The global media debate: Its rise, fall and renewal* (pp. 3-12). Norwood, NJ: Ablex.

MacPherson, C.B. (1985). *The rise and fall of economic justice and other essays.* New York: Oxford University Press.

Mattelart, A. (1994). *Mapping world communication.* Minneapolis: University of Minnesota.

Mattelart, A., & Stourdze, Y. (1985). *Technology, culture and communication: A report to the French Minister of Research and Industry.* New York: North-Holland.

McDowell, S.D. (1994). International services liberalisation and Indian telecommunications. In E.A. Comor (Ed.), *The global political economy of communication* (pp. 103-124). New York: St. Martin's Press.

McPhail, T., & McPhail, B. (1987). The international politics of telecommunication: Resolving the north-south dilemma. *International Journal. 42*(2), 289-318.

Mills, C.W. (1956). *The power elite.* New York: Oxford University Press.

Mosco, V. (1989). *The pay-per society.* Norwood, NJ: Ablex.

Mosco, V. (1990). Toward a transnational world information order: The Canada-U.S. Free Trade Agreement. *Canadian Journal of Communication, 15*(2), 46-63.

Mowlana, H. (1985). *The international flow of information: A global report and analysis* (UNESCO reports and papers on mass communications, No. 99). Paris: Communications Sector, UNESCO.

Murphy, A.D. (1990). Globe gobbling up US pix in record doses. *Variety, 339*(11), 10.

Noyelle, T. (1994). Revamping world trade: What's in it for the South? *Choices: The Human Development Magazine, 3*(2), 27-31.

Pool, I. (1990). *Technologies without boundaries.* Cambridge, MA: Harvard University Press.

Prozhivalsky, O.P. (1994). Development of telecommunications in Ukraine. *IEEE Communications Magazine*, pp. 42-43.

Pye, L. (1966). *Aspects of political development.* Boston: Little, Brown.

Roach, C. (1990). The movement for a New World Information and Communication Order: A second wave? *Media, Culture and Society, 12*, 283-307.

Roncagliolo, R. (1993). Toward the year 2000: A Latin American view. In G. Gerbner, H. Mowlana, & K. Nordenstreng (Eds.), *The global media debate: Its rise, fall and renewal* (pp. 167-172). Norwood, NJ: Ablex.

Sa, R. (1994). Telecommunications in Brazil: The role of the private sector. *IEEE Communications Magazine*, pp. 44-45.

Schiller, H. (1969). *Mass media and American Empire*. Boston: Beacon.

Schiller, H. (1989). *Culture Inc.: The corporate take-over of public expression*. New York: Oxford University Press.

Splichal, S., & Wasko, J. (Eds.). (1993). *Communication and democracy*. Norwood, NJ: Ablex.

Solomon, J. (1983). Rejoinder: The politics of relevance and the ITU. *Telecommunications Policy, 7*(3), 243-248.

Staubhaar, J.D. (1991). Beyond media imperialism: Assymetrical interdependence and cultural proximity. *Critical Studies in Mass Communication, 8*, 39-59.

Streeter, T. (1990). Beyond freedom of speech and the public interest: The relevance of critical legal studies to communications policy. *Journal of Communication, 40*(2), 43-63.

Tarjanne, P. (Secretary-General, ITU). (1994a, January). *The missing link: Still missing?* Paper presented at the 16th Annual Pacific Telecommunications Conference, Manoa, HI.

Tarjanne, P. (Secretary-General, ITU). (1994b). *The implications of global telecommunications systems for the ITU*. Internet: International Organizations Server.

Tarjanne, P. (Secretary-General, ITU). (1994c). *Opening presentation for Africa Telecom `94 Forum*. Internet: International Organizations Server.

Tarjanne, P. (Secretary-General, ITU). (1994d). *Regulating the international information infrastructure*. Internet: International Organizations Server.

Tehranian, M. (1994, January). *Where is the new world order: At the end of history or the clash of civilizations*. Paper presented at the 6th Annual MacBride Round Table at the University of Hawaii-Honolulu.

Trade Negotiations Committee (TNC). (1993). *Final Act embodying the results of the Uruguay Round (General Agreement on Trade in Services—Annex on Telecommunications)*. Geneva: GATT Secretariat.

Trotti, M. R. (1993). Charging and accounting in the international telephone service: A developing country's point of view. *Telecommunications Journal, 60*(11), 421-427.

Turan, O. (1989). Reflections on the methods to be used for establishing tariffs between countries in Africa. *Telecommunications Journal, 56*(1), 48-50.

UNESCO. (1978). *Declaration of fundamental principles concerning the contribution of the mass media to strengthening peace and international understanding, to the promotion of human rights and to countering racialism, apartheid and incitement to war*. Paris: Author.

UNESCO. (1976). *Conference working paper, Intergovernmental Conference on Communication Policies in Latin America and the Caribbean.* Paris: Author.

United Nations. (1948). *Universal Declaration of Human Rights.* Geneva: Author.

United Nations. (1992). *Statistical yearbook* (37th issue). New York: United Nations.

United States District Court. (1991). Lexis/Nexis 4853.

U.S. Court of Appeals (4th Circuit). (1993). *The Chesapeake and Potomac Telephone Company of Virginia, et al. v. United States of America and National Cable Television Association* (Nos. 93-2340, 93-2341). Internet: Bell Atlantic Gopher Server.

U.S. Subcommittee on Communications of the Committee on Commerce, Science, and Transportation. (1988). *International telecommunication issues* (100th. Congress, 2nd Sess.). Washington, DC: U.S. Government Printing Office.

U.S. Department of Commerce, NTIA. (1983). *Long-range goals in international telecommunication and information: An outline for United States' policy.* Washington, DC: U.S. Government Printing Office.

U.S. Department of Commerce. (1993). *Globalization of the media.* Washington, DC: U.S. Government Printing Office.

Varis, T. (1986). Patterns of television program flow in international relations. In J. Becker, G. Hedebro, & L. Paldan (Eds.), *Communication and domination: Essays to honour Herbert Schiller* (pp. 55-65). Norwood, NJ: Ablex.

Wasko, J. (1994). Jurassic Park and GATT: Hollywood and Europe—and update. In F. Corcoran & P. Preston (Eds.), *Democracy and communication in the new Europe* (pp. 157-171). Cresskill, NJ: Hampton Press.

Weber, M. (1946). *From Max Weber: Essays in sociology* (H.H. Gerth & C.W. Mills Eds.). New York: Oxford University Press.

White, R. (1993). The new order and the Third World. In G. Gerbner, H. Mowlana, & K. Nordenstreng (Eds.), *The global media debate: Its rise, fall, and renewal* (pp. 21-34). Norwood, NJ: Ablex.

Winseck, D. (1992). CNN, the Gulf War and democracy in the global village. In J. Wasko & V. Mosco (Eds.), *Democratic communication in the information age* (pp. 60-74). Norwood, NJ: Ablex.

Chapter 16

The New World Information and Communication Order (NWICO) in the Context of the Information Superhighway

Richard C. Vincent

If a free society cannot help the many who are poor, it cannot save the few who are rich.

—John F. Kennedy (Inaugural Address, 1961)

The less developed countries of the world require large injections of information in the form of technology transfer if they are to have economic growth and development. However the means of acquiring it are largely beyond their reach.

—Ithiel de Sola Pool (1979, p. 150)

Our analysis of the problems and the recommendations we have made show that there is no single remedy. A range of actions over a wide front and at different levels is required. Progress will be made only in stages. But, if the effort is sustained, the situation world-wide could be transformed in twenty years. All mankind could be brought within easy reach of a telephone by the early part of the next century and our objective achieved.

—Sir Donald Maitland (1984, p. 69)

- The entire developing world has a mere 4% of the world's computers.
- European countries average 1,400 libraries, African countries have 18.
- Thirty-four countries of the world have no television sets.
- Africa has less than 3 newspapers per country, whereas the United States has 1,687 and Japan 125 dailies.
- There are more telephones in Tokyo than on the entire African continent.
- Fewer than half the world's population has ever made a telephone call; more than two thirds of the households have no phone.
- Twenty-four countries of the Organization for Economic Co-operation and Development (OECD) account for 70% of the world's telephone mainlines and 90% of mobile phone subscribers, yet have only 16% of the globe's population.
- The developing world has access to only some 10% of the electromagnetic spectrum.
- Less than 2% of World Bank lending goes to telecommunications projects; regional development banks give less than 3%.

These are harsh figures on the state of world communication. They describe acerbic conditions indeed. Questions arise, then, about: What to do? What can be done? What can people of the developing world do to help themselves? The New World Information and Communication Order (NWICO) attempted to provide answers to these questions and, more specifically, how communications inequities could be resolved. However, as the dialogue came under pressure from a variety of forces, NWICO efforts became defensive and its attempts to resolve long-standing problems in global communication put on hold. Today the terrain of international communication policy has radically shifted from the earlier information flow concerns to the present agenda on trade, with the dialogue, if it can be called that, being monopolized by the West, particularly the United States. This chapter charts these changes and examines the implications of recent communication and information policy shifts on the developing world.

COMMUNICATION ACCESS AS JUSTICE
AND THE GOODS OF EQUITY

According to the principles of humanist liberalism, basic rights and liberties are inalienable. When basic rights are not guaranteed, says Johnson (1994, pp. 175-77), people "lack a means that is essential for them to be effective agents in their societies, and participants in the processes of political deliberation and decision making." Of course, what we define as basic rights is a difficult and arduous task. Yet, be that as it may, many social theorists and philosophers have presented ideas on what a package of basic rights might include. For example, Mill (1967) contends that property should be included within any definition of basic human rights and concludes that a lack of property can be just as tyrannical as a lack of constitutional rights. As he states, while people are usually

> no longer enslaved or made dependent by force of law, the great majority are so by force of poverty; they are still chained to a place, to an occupation, and to conformity with the will of an employer, and debarred by the accident of birth both from the enjoyments, and from the mental and moral advantages, which others inherit without exertion and independently of desert. That this is an evil equal to almost any of those against which mankind have hitherto struggled, the poor are not wrong to believe. (p. 710)

Another contributor to the effort to conceptualize the nature of basic human rights and justice is Rawls. In a relatively recent work, Rawls (1993) argues for equal opportunities and a social contract conceptually more general than that found in the earlier treatises of Locke, Rousseau, and Kant. Rawls argues that there are two principles central to understanding rights and justice:

> a. Each person has an equal right to a fully adequate scheme of equal basic liberties which is compatible with a similar scheme of liberties for all.
>
> b. Social and economic inequalities are to satisfy two conditions. First, they must be attached to offices and positions open to all under conditions of fair equality of opportunity; and second, they must be to the greatest benefit of the least advantaged members of society. (p. 291)

Another method for determining how basic rights can be defined and distributed so that people can be effective agents in their communities is offered by Johnson (1994). In order to achieve this task, Johnson distinguishes between value-independent and value-dependent goods. Within this framework, value-dependent goods are not necessarily needed, whereas the other type of goods are. Johnson offers an indication of how his framework for thinking about rights and justice might be applied to electronic media and, more generally, concerns raised by international communication policy and relations, when he stated:

> In a society with no written language, literacy is not among the powers that constitute an adequate share. In a society with no electronic media, access to a radio or other electronic source of information is not one of the material goods that constitute an adequate share. In a society in which the information is transmitted mainly through the written word and electronic media, both of these things should be included in the bundle of means that constitute an adequate share. It will also vary in part for reasons that may be culturally specific. The ability to understand, read, speak, and write in the language or languages in which public affairs are discussed in one's society is a part of the bundle of means that constitute an adequate share. (p. 175)

Given the centrality of electronic media to effective participation in modern societies and international relations, they can be defined as a necessary aspect of basic human rights and fundamental to determinations of what is just and unjust. Applied to international communication, this framework allows us to claim as unjust a situation in which the developing countries have control over only 10% of the electromagnetic spectrum and less than half the population is unable to make even one telephone call in the course of their lives. For the people of Kikwit, Zaire, to be without any radio or television deprives them of basic access to an adequate share of communication resources and thus negatively affects their ability to participate in society and, more broadly, international relations. Thus, when we start to think about communication within the framework of basic rights and justice, it immediately becomes apparent that communication equity becomes a prerequisite of modern society.

Although these ways of thinking about international communication may appear to be novel, this is really not the case. Such efforts have been at the core of U.S. international communication policy for at least 70 years and a central element affecting the way in which international institutions—from the League of Nations to the present day UNESCO—have historically thought about the relationships among communication, technology, and society. For the United States, the historical link among human rights, justice, and communication was forged through a commitment to the "free flow of information" doctrine that was underpinned by a broader philosophy of libertarianism. For international institutions, the historical link between communication and ethics has been forged on different grounds. Within such institutions there has been more emphasis on communication imbalances in the world, and how such inequities might cause universal harm. These concerns can be traced back to late 19th-century efforts to seek agreement about the responsibilities and practices of journalists. The concern with unfairly distributed opportunities for access to and the use of communication media were also prime topics within the League of Nations during the 1920s and 1930s (UNESCO, 1977). Although this is only a brief historical survey of the issues at hand, the examples nonetheless indicate that concerns over journalistic practices, the distribution of communication technology, and international communication are long-standing topics preceding the formation of the United Nations (UN).

However, it is within the UN and its subagencies that more recent attempts to deal with communication issues have taken place. This recent history can be traced back to the formation of the UN in 1948 and its early efforts to situate communication as a fundamental aspect of universal human rights. As Article 19 of the UN's 1948 Universal Declaration of Human Rights put the issue:

> Every individual has the right to freedom of opinion and of expression, which entails the right to be free from harassment for his opinions and the right to seek out, to receive and to communicate, regardless of frontiers and ideas, by whatever means of expression he may choose. (pp. 1959-1960)

The UN and the United Nations Educational, Scientific and Cultural Organization (UNESCO) have been involved in freedom of expression and freedom of information issues since their inception. For UNESCO, such involvement took place through the development and adoption of the Beirut and Fiorenzo Accords, and then through some of the early studies on one-way information flows between developed and developing nations (Kayser, 1953). Resolutions were adopted on these issues as early as 1954 (e.g.,, Res. 522C(XVII); UNESCO, 1954), and the results of studies conducted on international communication shared among members and nonmembers (Eek, 1979).

As these issues became more central to the organization during the 1950s and 1960s, UNESCO (1970a) sponsored a number of meetings on factors impeding the free flow of ideas. However, the expansion of activities and research within UNESCO began to produce findings and conclusions that were not always welcomed by all the organization's members. In particular, three broad conclusions coming out of UNESCO-supported research located the center of future debates about international communication and ultimately led to efforts to severely curtail UNESCO's role in international information and communication issues. The first conclusion was that individuals were becoming prisoners of foreign concepts and these were incessantly and systematically being forced upon them. Another was that information media were treated as a privilege of the ruling elite—a power that is out of the influential sphere of the public. The ultimate conclusion stemming from these observations was that it might be necessary to find new ways to protect the concepts of independence and freedom of information (UNESCO & IAMCR, 1968).

These results were important for two reasons. On the one hand, they marked the beginning of a loosely organized decolonization discourse that linked communication issues to issues of international political and economic power. On the other hand, they raised the claims that UNESCO had far overstepped its mandate and become politicized.

Although nothing immediate ever came out of these early observations, the seeds for a NWICO had been sown, and the rhetoric over problems in international communication became louder and stronger. Indicative of the changing circumstances, during the Sixteenth Session of the UNESCO General Conference in 1970, a delegation led by India presented its concerns on inequitable information flows. The group "asserted that [UNESCO] must continue to emphasize the rights of less privileged nations to preserve their own culture" and assist in the formulation of mass communication policies (UNESCO, 1970b, p. 109). UNESCO (1971) responded to these calls by mapping out a research agenda on news flow and holding several meetings in which the idea of "cultural neo-colonialism" was formed and identified as a consequence of the rapid, but imbalanced, expansion of communication technology (UNESCO, 1972). The continuation of these activities into the 1970s contributed to the formation of a broad-based movement for a NWICO.

WHAT IS NWICO?

Although NWICO obviously involves concerns with journalism and particular communication technologies, it can be more properly thought of as an effort to locate communication and issues of equity, human rights, and justice within the context of global history and political economy. It espouses structural modifications, not challenging capitalism per se, but improving the ability of developing countries to define and determine their position and future within the world system (Galtung & Vincent, 1992). It is an effort to engage in a dialogue, on an international level, concerning the role of communication and the possibilities of organizing and using the means of communication to better reflect the needs and aspirations of all the world's people.

For technological determinists, the emphasis of NWICO challenges their assumptions about the link between technology and human progress, the role of the market, and the determinacy of politics, economics, and history over the innovation, deployment, and uses of communications technology. Yet more than just an intellectual challenge, NWICO raises questions about the communication development strategies adopted by the United States, the European Union (EU), the G7, the ITU, and many other policymaking bodies of the 1990s. This is an especially important challenge to the international status quo and power at a time when the United States is positioned as the only remaining superpower, but has also lost its hegemonic role in the organization of the world system.

Given the importance of communication to the international political economy, and the way that people understand one another and their position in the world, it is not surprising that efforts to fundamentally change the international communication system along the lines promoted by NWICO have met with either a nonchalant reaffirmation of the status quo or outright misrepresentation and suppression. After all, what better way to insure continued domination when those promoting alternative visions are prevented from being equal participants in the construction of the future or, better yet, not allowed to participate at all? By maintaining a communication order more or less as it has been in recent time, the Western monopoly on power and resources continues.

THE CHALLENGE TO POWER: AUTONOMY, CRITIQUE, AND ALTERNATIVE PROPOSALS FOR THE FUTURE

Historically, as part of the efforts to redefine the terms of participation in the world system, developing countries have established formal alliances to lobby for their mutual interests in the world community and to avoid slavish alignments with either of the superpowers. The most important of such alliances has been the Non-Aligned Movement (NAM, also known as the Group of 77), formed in Bandung, Indonesia in 1955. Although many meetings of NAM occurred in between, perhaps one of the most important meetings influencing contemporary international relations between developed and developing countries was held in Algiers in 1973. During this conference the members of NAM put forth their concerns about information flows and cultural imperialism. Some have suggested that later resolutions by UNESCO on the New International Economic Order (NIEO) were also a consequence of this meeting (Smith, 1980; Van Dinh, 1977).

The Algiers meeting of the NAM also introduced the idea of a third-world; news agency, a notion that was taken up later by, UNESCO-sanctioned symposia held in Lima, Tunis, and Mexico City. After much discussion the proposal was turned into reality by the Ministerial Conference of NAM during a meeting in Delhi, India in 1976 (Non-Aligned Countries, 1976). As a result, a self-financing news pool was created, with none of the participants having a dominant role. Operational guidelines were later approved at the Fifth summit Meeting of Heads of State or Government of Non-Aligned Countries. With the organization of the news pool, developing nations had finally created a mechanism they hoped would effectively compete against the major Western agencies and provide a vehicle for a more balanced international news flow.

While this was occurring, efforts were also taking place to create a set of nonbinding principles to guide the operations of the international media and journalists. Such efforts later came to be known as the Mass Media Declaration, a document whose first draft was presented in 1974. While reiterating the ideas of freedom of speech and the press laid out in the 1948 Universal Declaration of Human Rights, drafts of the new Declaration also called for media responsibility in disseminating information and opinion (UNESCO, 1974). The Declaration attempted to stretch the conceptual boundaries of freedom of expression beyond merely the rights of those who owned and controlled the international media to insure that the public had an effective "right to seek, receive and transmit information" (UNESCO, 1974, Articles II & III). However, this attempt to formally expand the boundaries of the public's participation in the systems of international communication immediately raised resistance in the West.

Two years later, at the Nineteenth Session of UNESCO's General Conference in Nairobi, efforts to push the concept of NWICO forward were made by the Secretary-General, M'Bow. M'Bow's comments were two-pronged, as he acknowledged "the efforts of non-aligned countries to institute regional co-operation in the field of communication and information," but also noted that "the distribution of communication media and the immense potential they represent reflects the uneven international distribution of economic power" (UNESCO, 1976, p. 22). During the same conference the Soviet Union also floated proposals for strong government control of the mass media (Legum &

Cornwell, 1978). Although this proposal was never adopted and met the resistance of many first- and third-world journalists who strongly supported the concept of a free press, the critiques being leveled against Western media and the Soviet proposal brought forth a backlash from Western countries, especially the United States, from which UNESCO has never fully recovered.

The United States threatened to withdraw from UNESCO should the organization continue to deal with NWICO-related concerns in an unsatisfactory manner. Recognizing the severity of the U.S. threat for any work that UNESCO might pursuit, M'Bow organized a "negotiating group as a face-saving format for those backing the Soviet resolution" (Sussman, 1977). As a result, the matter was momentarily abandoned. The General Conference did, however, adopt a resolution underscoring the important role communication plays in the global environment (UNESCO, 1976, Resolution 100, para 22 & 23) and another resolution calling for UNESCO to construct communication systems that would help to free developing countries from a state of dependence (UNESCO, 1976). Part of this latter resolution was a decision to establish an International Commission for the Study of Communication Problems (later known as the MacBride Commission) that would study world communication, specifically the principle of a free and balanced flow of information, "within the perspective of a new international economic order" (UNESCO, 1977, p. 3). The final report was presented to the next General Conference in 1980.

THE MACBRIDE COMMISSION

The newly formed Commission was headed up by the Irish Ambassador, who was also the Director of Amnesty International and a Nobel Peace laureate, Sean MacBride. MacBride's task, along with the other 16 members appointed to the Commission by M'Bow, was to study the existing state of affairs in international communication and to make recommendations that might form the basis of a new communication order.

In 1978, the Commission submitted an intensely debated interim report to the 20th General Assembly. The interim report focused on the nature and organization of the Western press, especially the transnational wire services. Key proposals concerning communication policies and the protection of journalists, an idea that was personally promoted by MacBride, were received very poorly by Western media organizations and governments (McPhail, 1987). Nonetheless, there was enough common ground in the report that a compromise declaration could be issued by the Conference participants.

Two years later the Commission's final report was presented to the 21st General Conference in Belgrade. Mixed within the report was a tempering of the original anti-Western rhetoric and a series of recommendations for action that could contribute to the accomplishment of a NWICO. Areas that had been moderated included sections dealing with the terms of technological exchange between countries and alterations in the call for a "free and balanced flow" to the goal of a "free flow and a wider and better balanced dissemination of information." On the other hand, nestled within the report were 82 recommendations, including proposals related to telecommunications tariffs, administration procedures, technological implementation, and uses, training, and research in the media. It also resolved to deal with professional integrity and standards, although it eliminated suggestions about the licensing of journalists (UNESCO, 1980). The elimination of this proposal is worth noting for it resurfaced later as a major rationale for the United States's decision to withdraw from UNESCO and underpinned much of the anti-UNESCO campaign conducted in the Western media.

Despite the conciliatory approach adopted in the final report, the document was still criticized widely. Many faulted it with being too philosophical and for trying to seek consensus on issues in which the divisions were simply too deep to be overcome. Others were bothered by its generalities and lack of a solid implementation program. It also failed to adequately address issues of telecommunications infrastructures and the sociocultural effects of technology, existing tariff structures and the distribution of the spectrum resources (Hamelink, 1985; Jussawalla, 1979, 1980, 1981). Although many of the recommendations were, in fact, not all that philosophically removed from practical concerns or that difficult to implement, they were left unenacted by the Belgrade General Conference.

Nonetheless, one significant outcome of the Belgrade Conference was the creation of the International Program for Development Communication (IPDC), which was designed to implement many of the objectives of the NWICO in a practical manner. Major funding for the IPDC was promised by many Western countries in order to assist, coordinate, and finance the development of communication infrastructures in developing countries and to help promote self-reliance. However, once the definition of what was practical became the subject of competing definitions, opposition among many of the Western backers arose. Due to the flexible nature of the funding system that allowed donors to choose the programs they wished to fund, programs caught in the middle of struggles over what should be done simply went unselected and, thus, unfunded.

The Belgrade Conference also saw the adoption of the so-called Venezuelan resolution, which called for a study of elements to be included in a NWICO, attempted to create a universal definition of "responsible" journalism, and sought assistance for the Palestine Liberation Organization (PLO). This further raised the ire of the United States, who saw in such resolutions the continuance of MacBride Commission-style rhetoric ("Split decision," 1980).

Following Belgrade, the anti-UNESCO sentiments continued to rise. Amazingly, it was the NWICO debate that was receiving most of the attention, not its correlate program the NIEO, with its far more ambitious attempts to change the world. Contributing to this rather odd state of affairs, the World Press Freedom Committee sponsored a conference in Tallories, France, where delegates gathered to build a defense for the practices of Western journalism (Declaration of Tallories, 1986). The conference couched its stance as a reaffirmation of UNESCO's original intent and the 1948 Universal Declaration of Human Rights. It then urged UNESCO to seek practical solutions to global communication problems, not regulation.

Throughout the NWICO debates, perhaps the most defensive position regarding alterations to international communication has been held by the United States. Not only has it assumed an uncompromising position in UNESCO, but it has also extended this posture to other international institutions involved in communication matters, such as the ITU and its World Administrative Radio Conferences (WARC). For instance, during the two-part Space WARC Conference held in 1985 and 1988, developing countries sought a regulatory regime that would secure them "practical, guaranteed access to the geo-stationary orbit and radio spectrum." Despite the possibility of the developing countries' actual use of the resources being, for most, in the distant future, and the consistency of these proposals with international law, the United States only offered to relinquish a much smaller range of expansion bands (Winseck & Cuthbert, 1991). Although most countries were dissatisfied with the outcome of the conference, the U.S. delegation was able to leave Geneva in a very positive mood. As the U.S. Ambassador to the ITU noted, "We feel very good about . . . [the satellite situation]. An allotment plan will not place a cloud over our operational bands. . . . Considering our vital interests, we came out very well" ("Space WARC," 1985a, p. 41; see also "WARC 1985," 1985b).

THE U.S. WITHDRAWAL FROM UNESCO

Despite the ability of the United States to secure its "vital interests" in international forums dealing with communication issues, there was nevertheless a surprising amount of discontent in some circles over the international communication debates and calls for the radical reformation of UNESCO and the ITU, or even outright withdrawal from these UN organizations. Much of this discontent was circulated in the American press during the height of the NWICO debates, and among a relatively small group of fairly conservative editors. Although much of this early activity amounted to little, especially after the development of a compromise plan to guide the approach taken by UNESCO with respect to NWICO in 1983, serious hints about the possibility of a U.S. withdrawal from UNESCO began to be floated in the early 1980s ("Editorial,", 1983; "UNESCO approves," 1983; "U.S. weighs," 1983). Then, in late December 1983, Secretary of State George Schultz sent a letter to UNESCO Director-General M'Bow, informing him of the U.S. intent to withdraw its membership at the end of 1984. In the letter, Schultz cited matters of "policy, ideological emphasis, budget and management of UNESCO" that were "detracting from the Organization's effectiveness." Schultz further charged that UNESCO had drifted from "the original principles of its Constitution," leading to a situation that now "served the political purposes of member states" (Tehranian, 1984, p. 141; see also Schultz, 1983).

There is strong evidence that the withdrawal itself was something less than a well-reasoned move by the Reagan Administration. In order to make sense of the ultimate decision to depart from NWICO, it is necessary to look at two other factors that help account for the decision. One factor that stands out is the fact that many American conservatives were fierce critics of UNESCO long before the communication debates began. The effect of the NWICO debates was to solidify their opposition, whereas the debates themselves, with their discussions regarding the concentration of media ownership and control, the right to communicate, the responsibility of journalists, and so on, served to broaden the base of the conservative forces to include the influential US media (Sussman, 1984). As Leonard Sussman (1989), a critic of NWICO, as well as of the U.S. decision to withdraw from UNESCO, noted, "the case against UNESCO was won not in 1984 or 1985, but in the years from 1976 to 1983 when UNESCO programs critical of news flows were vilified regularly and made to appear to be the only program of the multi-faceted organization" (p. xiv).

In addition to these powerful influences on international communication policy, calls for withdrawal gained force with the U.S. State Department, although the agency had only a short time earlier recommended against leaving UNESCO. McPhail (1989) notes that in contrast to the earlier State Department position, some in the agency began to build a campaign based on "selective misrepresentations" directed at mobilizing support for the "withdrawal" position. Those promoting this campaign worked to align the State Department with the long-standing conservative opponents of UNESCO, especially the Heritage Foundation, and undertook to shape the public discourse and knowledge about UNESCO and NWICO through a series of op-ed pieces and letters to elite newspapers in the United States ("Editorial pressure," 1984; Giffard, 1989; "Government wages," 1984).

The consequence of the U.S. departure for UNESCO was an immediate loss of $43 million from its general budget. The subsequent withdrawal of the United Kingdom and Singapore in 1985 reduced the agency's budget even further. In the end, UNESCO was left operating with two thirds of its original budget and without the participation of key actors in the field of international communication.

THE FUTURE OF NWICO

The New World Information and Communication order debate has been heavily criticized for its inability to sharply delineate the problem, failure to effectively merge the NWICO with a major examination of economic concerns, and an inability to find an equitable solution to gross imbalances in information flows and exchange. As Eli Abel (1982) has observed, that nobody knows what it would mean. The new world order means different things to different people. "It is more slogan than plan of action" (p. 5). It is this situation of uncertainty, with no real alternative, that has lent to the quandary.

UNESCO (1989) efforts are now directed toward emphasizing the development of infrastructures and capacities, personnel training, and media education. Although these initiatives are designed to help ensure "a balance in regard to the flow of information" (p. 102) and includes the study of media and new communication technologies, it is a more moderate stance toward communication issues necessitated by the costly lessons of the 1980s.

Although UNESCO has become less central to NWICO, debate is certainly far from finished. Other parties are providing leadership and proving to be effective hosts for the continuing dialogue. Examples of the alternative channels for this dialogue have been the National Lawyers Guild, the World Association for Christian Communication (WACC), the Institute for Latin America (IPAL), and the Union for Democratic Communication (UDC). Another group carrying on the NWICO concept that embodies the ideas communicated by Sean MacBride, shortly before his death, to Kaarle Nordenstreng, is the MacBride Round Table. From the beginning the group dedicated itself to building on the belief, expressed in the *MacBride Report*, that communication is a basic human right, an individual need, and a social requirement ("The Harare statement," 1990). The group first met in Harare, Zimbabwe to evaluate world communication 10 years after the *MacBride Report* had been first published. Sponsors of the inaugural meeting were the Federation of Southern African Journalists, along with the International Organization of Journalists (IOJ), and the Media Foundation of the Non-Aligned (NAMEDIA). The MacBride Round Table has met six times since that first meeting. The last two meetings, held in Honolulu and Tunis, respectively, brought together an international group of scholars, activists, journalists, and other communication experts devoted to the monitoring of world communication rights and balances. The conclusions of these meetings were reported to community groups, UN agencies, nongovernmental organizations (NGOs), and the news media. In addition to these activities that continue to promote the concept of an NWICO, various NGOs have taken up the crusade for communication equity (see Frederick, this volume).

These efforts seem to have contributed to the brightened prospects for the future of UNESCO and continuing discussions concerning international communication issues. For instance, in 1989 a panel chaired by former U.S. Senator Robert T. Stafford recommended that the United States reinstate its membership with UNESCO. In the recommendation it was noted that UNESCO performs a vital role in the promotion of free speech and unimpeded international dialogue. Four years later, in April 1993, the Washington Post called for reentry

("Why UNESCO?", 1993). In that year the same recommendation was issued by a United Nations Association Panel and by a task force headed by U.S. Assistant Secretary of State, Douglas Bennett. The latter recommended a return by October 1995, the requested delay being due to budgetary concerns in the early days of the Clinton White House (Meisler, 1993).

Even with these endorsements pointing to a more conciliatory approach toward UNESCO, there remains a certain skepticism in the United States—as reflected in one New York Times editorial ("Don't rush back," 1994). According to the editorial, the country should not "rush back into UNESCO," even if Secretary General Frederico Meyer has "cut the payroll and generally returned UNESCO to its original mission as a promoter of literacy, a protector of cultural movements and a champion of a freer flow of information" (p. A18). In a somewhat ironic shift in topic, the Times, suggested that one of the primary roles of UNESCO should be "to represent the world's cultural conscience by speaking out against the deliberate targeting of cherished monuments—and then to restore as best it can what wars tear apart" (p. A18). This lack of an understanding of the issues, and a likely desire to keep UNESCO in an apolitical posture when it comes to promoting "cultural consciousness", has long been a problem with the Western, and in particular the U.S., press. With this, the continuing move toward political conservatism and isolationism in the U.S. government, the growing anti-UN and anti-UNESCO rhetoric heard every day at all levels of the Congressional leadership, the future of UNESCO, and even the UN as effective agents for the promotion of mutual understanding and dialogue is not at all promising (Harris, 1995). In fact, with the current wave of budget cutting since the start of 1995, it appears highly unlikely that the United States will rejoin UNESCO at any time in the foreseeable future.

VISIONS OF AN INFORMATION SUPERHIGHWAY AND GLOBAL INFORMATION INFRASTRUCTURE (GII)

Although the previous section suggests that the prospects of UNESCO as a formal arena for the discussion of international communication are uncertain, new arenas are opening that offer a far different vision about how to think about global communication and the possible solutions to the problems therein. Much of the contemporary discussion is being driven by the ideas of Information Superhighways and the Global Information Infrastructure (GII), topics that are fundamentally shifting the policy contexts away from the analysis of the underlying historical, political, and economic factors that have created inequities in global communication toward a view that such problems can best be dealt with through the application of new technologies.

From a technological perspective, the information superhighway and GII involve the possibility of the world being linked together through a web of digital telecommunications technology, fiber optic cables, and high-capacity satellite systems capable of high speed and superior quality voice and data transmission. This convergence of wire, wireless, broadcast, cable, and satellite communication technologies into a global information network is at the heart of the information superhighway project. Yet, the information superhighway is not only a technological project, but also an initiative that links governments and major communication corporations at the highest levels. Perhaps one of the strongest indications of this unification of state and corporate power is the seeming almost single-handed ability of U.S. Vice President Gore to capture the imagination of those thinking about new communication technologies and to map out the possibilities for the new technologies at home and abroad.

In remarks to the ITU on March 21, 1994, Gore called for seizing the "technological breakthroughs and economic means" to help unite the world. Gore was referring specifically to "highways" that would serve as "networks of distributed intelligence," enabling all to "share information, to connect, and to communicate as a global community." According to Gore, these highways would lead to "robust and sustainable economic progress, strong democracies, better solutions to global and local environmental challenges, improved health care, and—ultimately—a greater sense of shared stewardship of our small planet." He further claimed that:

> The Global Information Infrastructure will help educate our children and allow us to exchange ideas within a community and among nations. It will be a means by which families and friends will transcend the barriers of time and distance. It will make possible a global information marketplace, where consumers can buy or sell products. (Gore, 1994)

Gore insisted that Americans have already found that "the integration of computing and information networks into the economy makes U.S. companies more productive, more competitive, and more adaptive to changing conditions" and proposed that "it will do the same for the economies of other nations." Addressing the very real economic problems facing many of the world's people, Gore went on to invest the new technologies with the ability to alleviate economic hardship as they add "hundreds of billions of dollars . . . to world growth."

The program for the new GII suggested by Gore, and subsequently taken up by the Group of 7 countries and the ITU, is to be based on private investment, competition, open access, flexibility, and universal service. Key aspects of this program, as the Group of 7 countries noted, is the adoption of an agenda to liberalize regulations for information technology and a series of technology projects designed to promote the objectives of the information superhighway and to garner support for the initiative by eliminating public skepticism and ambivalence towards the new information machines.

Also crucial to the overall GII project is privatization, the process of opening up new areas for private investment and profits by eliminating the public sector media. Again, Gore (1994) has taken the lead on these initiatives as he argues for privatization and competition:

> In recent years, many countries, particularly . . . in Latin America, have opted to privatize their state- owned telephone companies in order to obtain the benefits and incentives that drive competitive private enterprises, including innovation, increased investment, efficiency and responsiveness to market needs. Adopting policies that allow increased private-sector participation in the telecommunications sector has provided an enormous spur to telecommunications development in Argentina, Venezuela, Chile and Mexico. . . . But privatization is not enough. Competition is needed as well. . . . Today there are many more technology options than in the past and it is not only possible, but desirable, to have different companies running competing—but interconnected—networks.

The hoped for results of such initiatives are increased accessibility to information and data for a larger portion of the world's population, a faster and more efficient worldwide communication network, and lower costs for communication technology. Although these are indeed laudable goals that could meet some of the issues raised by NWICO, and it is true that the concepts of information superhighways and a GII have sparked the imagination of many, there are some who continue to raise questions about the ability of the new technologies to address basic communication needs, such as universal service. Whereas the means to achieving such goals remain ambiguous, at best, there has generally been a denial that the information superhighway will further exacerbate the inequalities between richer and poorer countries and people. Although the directions offered in this respect by the U.S. Administration, the G7, and the ITU have been far more ambiguous than other aspects outlined, and tend to suggest that technologies will overcome historical realities, the issues have not gone totally unaddressed. Once again, Gore (1994) has staked out the dominant perspective on the issue by linking the development of telecommunications infrastructures to economic development, a process that should in turn allow for the realization of social policy objectives. Although such potentials may very well be part and parcel of the emerging technological framework, it is also just important to consider the larger contexts shaping the design, implementation, uses, and goals to be served by the new communication technologies. It is to this task that we now turn.

BACKGROUND FOR UNDERSTANDING THE NEW TECHNOLOGIES AND EMERGING INTERNATIONAL COMMUNICATION POLICY

In an excellent study on U.S. communication policy, Hollifield and Samarajiva (1994) trace the movement away from the traditional libertarianism found in the

U.S. position on international communication policy, especially in terms of the "free flow of information" doctrine. According to Hollifield and Samarajiva, the policy rationale that had prevailed in U.S. international communication policy for almost 70 years is now being dominated by economic rationality and blatant self-interest. This view became most salient after 1978, as Congressional concerns focused on information and communication issues almost exclusively in terms of how they impact U.S. industry and commerce. In 1980, business leaders began testifying before Congress that communication policy should be taken out of the "free-flow" context and situated within a trade framework. In particular, there was pressure to help protect the international leadership of U.S. industry over telecommunication goods and services by "advocat[ing] and adopt[ing] international communications policies which foster competition and move toward increasing reliance on market forces, while accounting for differing national policies" (FCC, 1984, para 41).

Under the Clinton Administration, the discourse continued and can best be seen in Gore's "Global Information Infrastructure" speech noted earlier. Other actions by the Clinton Administration included the appointment of Joan Spero, a strong trade policy advocate, as undersecretary for economic affairs in the Department of State, and moving the Co-ordinator for International Communication and Information Policy in the State Department to the Bureau of Economic and Business Affairs, an action recommended by business leaders as early as 1980 (Hollifield & Samarajiva, 1994).

Although the transformation of the conceptual context for U.S. international communication policy can be traced back to the early deregulation initiatives of the Carter Administration, it is more accurate to locate the thrust and intensity of the changes with the new economic and ideological agenda of the Reagan Administration in the United States and the Thatcher government in the United Kingdom. The new policy framework for communications became a part of a broader program aimed at instituting "supply-side" economics, a program critical of Keynesian-style government intervention in the economy and full employment doctrines, but supportive of policies directed at removing taxes, stimulating investment and promoting a more intense work ethic among the general population. Also part of this program are efforts to pare down government regulations over business, decreased concerns with income inequalities, and the reduced use of government measures to stabilize interest rates and currency values (Adam's, 1993). In addition to these ideas, the British added the concept of privatization as a means of opening up more space for the private sector and reducing the role of the government in the economy. Subsequently, many aspects of the U.S. - British programs for political and economic restructuring have been adopted by most of the Organization for Economic Co-operation and Development (OECD) countries, although they have been resisted somewhat by Japan, Switzerland, and the former West Germany.

Economic restructuring in the North has also had consequences in the developing countries of the South. One of the most noticeable consequences has been the huge increase in developing countries' external debt. For non-OPEC countries this meant an almost fivefold increase between 1973 (US$ 130 billion) to 1982 (US$ 612 billion), and a further doubling for all developing countries between 1980 and 1990 . At the same time, economic growth rates fell from being twice that of the OECD countries during the 1960s and 1970s to less than half the OECD rate of economic growth during the 1980s (de Vries, 1985; Winseck, this volume). Most influential were the costs of oil and the effects of an industrial world-spurred recession. Such factors were met with a loss of export revenues and the inability to pay back loans—mainly to U.S. banks—that had been made during an earlier period of steep interest rates and an overvalued U.S. currency (Adam's, 1993).

The International Monetary Fund (IMF), with fewer resources than it once had and now a player in the efforts to internationalize U.S.-UK political and economic restructuring, further contributed to the problems of the developing countries. Development loans and debt-rescheduling packages offered by the IMF and the World Bank exacerbated the problems of the developing countries by imposing the conditions that markets be fully liberalized, exports be increased despite drastic drops in the value of basic commodities on the world market, and subsidies for food, health, education, and social welfare programs be severely curtailed.

The results were twofold. On the one hand, debts to mainly U.S. creditors were partially recovered, whereas, on the other hand, economic growth was reversed, massive unemployment ensued, incomes dropped, and shortages of basic goods, including medicine, prevailed (Adam's, 1993; Brown, 1993). Such factors led to the conclusion that the IMF has not followed its original purpose of bringing about adjustments with minimal economic disruption, but rather served to promote Western stability, economic growth, and visions of how the political and economic systems of countries everywhere should be organized. Nurske (1993) concludes that the most fundamental outcome of this restructuring of the international political economy has been an incredible "income transfer from poor to rich countries" (p. 244). These trends have resulted in the 1980s being described as the "lost decade" for the developing countries.

The tight financial strangulation and the heavy political pressures brought on the developing countries by the restructuring of the global political economy have left them with little room to maneuver. There now also appears to be substantial evidence that the ability and energy of the developing countries to promote programs like the NIEO, NWICO, and the restructuring of international organizations, such as the ITU and UNESCO, has become a spent force since the late 1980s. Evidence for such a view began to surface as early as 1981 during the Cancun Summit organized by West German Chancellor Willy Brandt to consider the viability of NIEO-type goals at that time. Doubts about the ability of developing countries to alter the conditions of the international economy also surfaced a few years later at a meeting of the United Nations Committee for Trade and Development (UNCTAD). During this meeting, a

U.S.-controlled panel was successful in scaling back the number and scope of future UNCTAD meetings. The United States was also able to redefine the future of UNCTAD as primarily an arena that allowed "member states to discuss their concerns and share their views with others, reach common understandings on the nature of concerns, and only then to seek agreement on issues or parts of issues where action was possible or likely" (UNCTAD, 1984, p. 26; emphasis added). The pacification of structurally based conflict was also obvious in the final meeting of the ITU's 1992 WARC in Terremolinos, Spain. Here, for the first time since the evolution of NWICO, "no extraneous political issues were raised . . . [and] there was no serious North-South cleavage," according to an account by the U.S. representative to the ITU, Gerald B. Helman (1992, p. 41).

It is within this context that the discourse of NWICO has given way to the discourse of the information superhighway. The West is now firmly in control of bodies responsible for the articulation of international communication policy and can largely set the agenda for any discussion. With these trends in mind, it comes as little surprise that contemporary approaches to communication information policy have taken the course they have. Nonetheless, pertinent questions remain about the effects of these new paths on the prospects of the third world and international communication. To address these prospects, the remainder of the chapter considers four questions: (a) What will result in the development of an information superhighway? (b) How is the concept being sold to the developing world? (c) Who really benefits in the information age? and (d) What courses of action can be taken to shape the future?

WHAT WILL RESULT IN THE DEVELOPMENT OF AN INFORMATION SUPERHIGHWAY?

At the Pacific-Telecommunications Council (PTC) meeting in Honolulu in 1994, the author of the 1984 *Maitland Report* noted that wide disparities in access to basic telecommunication facilities were still widespread, and that the "global picture is not uniformly encouraging." Maitland went on to discuss the link between these disparities in access to basic communication resources and levels of economic development. As he observed (1994), "Almost all countries with a per capita GDP of US$ 7,000 or more have a teledensity of more than 30 lines per 100 inhabitants, but most countries with a per capita GDP of US$ 2,000 have a teledensity of less than five lines per 100" (p. 18). Given this relationship between economics and telecommunications, how is it possible to secure universal access to the information superhighway, let alone basic telephone service, in a world where the vast majority of people do not live in countries with high GDPs and, thus, developed telecommunication infrastructures?

To illustrate the gravity of the situation, we can draw on an estimate by Klaus Grewlich (1992) about the costs involved in bringing 60 million telephones to some 200,000 towns in the former Soviet Union. A program on this scale that would result in a teledensity rate of about 27 to 30 telephone lines per 100 citizens, a level similar to that of South Korea and other OECD countries, for example, would require an investment of US$100 billion. How will such a massive upgrading of the telecommunications infrastructures in these communities be financed? And, if we are really serious about a universal global information infrastructure, what would be the additional costs of providing this?

Obviously, the costs involved are staggering and become even more so when we consider that the previous example, if the proponents of global universal service are serious, would need to be multiplied several times over to include the developing world. Although the task does indeed appear to be daunting, the questions about financing are not totally without something resembling an answer. The currently existing framework for financing such massive telecommunications projects include private and government financing, proposals made by the *Maitland Report* in 1984, lending support for telecommunications projects from the World Bank, and the possibilities suggested by earlier international aid programs.

Thus far the most appealing route for many countries wishing to develop their domestic telecommunication systems, and given the deterioration in developing countries' economies and the severity of the debt crisis, has been privatization. Privatization has been carried out in Mexico, Argentina, Chile, Venezuela, Thailand, Pakistan, many of the new countries of the former Soviet Union, and is being proposed in Turkey, among other countries. As noted previously Vice President Gore has strongly promoted privatization, arguing that it is an integral component of the broader project of creating the information superhighway, economic growth, and, perhaps most importantly, "stronger democracies." Yet there are some indications that privatization may not contribute to such goals, especially the latter. For instance, Petrazzini (1993) observes that it is "countries with a highly autonomous state and strong concentration of power in the executive branch that are more capable of privatizing the SOEs and liberalizing the telecom market than those nations in which these patterns are absent" (p. 33). Essentially, a system of authoritarian power is necessary to circumvent the opposition to privatization raised by telecommunications workers, civil servants, and some members of the general public. Finally, whereas privatization may raise capital in the short term, it has to be noted that telecom operators have almost always contributed to the public purse, not drained them, and there are enormous difficulties in getting private corporations to serve publicly-determined social policy objectives (Winseck, this volume).

Other options include the use of World Bank loans. Yet, given the alignment of the World Bank with the political and economic restructuring programs initiated by the United States and UK noted earlier, loans for telecommunication projects are now usually granted on the condition that half of the financing for such projects should come from private sector investments. Thus, this route tends to extend privatization, rather than offer an alternative.

Furthermore, the money available from the World Bank and other regional development banks is not sufficient for the task. Only 2% of World Bank and 3% of regional development bank funding is earmarked for the development of telecommunications infrastructures (Winsbury, 1994). Realizing the paucity of available funds, and the problems associated with the efforts of the earlier discussed International Program for Development Communications (IPDC), in 1984, the Maitland Report suggested that "Member States of the ITU . . . set[] aside a small proportion of revenues from calls between industrialized countries . . . to finance pre-investment costs of telecommunications projects" in the Third World" (ITU, 1984). Despite the feasibility of such a proposal, the increasingly hard-nosed economic rationality displayed in international communication policy has left the recommendations lying fallow.

A final approach to the financing of the development of telecommunications infrastructures might come from general international aid programs offered by many of the industrialized countries. We can recall that in the post World War II period, massive aid programs were initiated for Western Europe and Japan and others for reconstruction and development purposes. Yet, it also needs to be recognized that aid programs are underpinned by ideological considerations that extend far beyond their stated mandate. For instance, the Marshall Aid program for Western Europe and Japan provided over $4 billion a year between 1949 and 1951, but U.S. economic aid to all developing countries was only between $2 billion and $2.5 billion per year throughout the 1950s. Looking at it from a slightly different perspective, The Colombo Plan (1953-1959) for economic assistance to Southeast Asia (600 million population) meant slightly more than US$1 per person per year, whereas in Europe (300 million population) there was US$ 3 per person during the same period (Brown, 1993). Current international aid programs are far more modest in their scope and have been curtailed quite substantially in recent years. For instance, the United States presently only devotes about .7% of its annual budget to international aid programs, compared to about 1.2% among other G7 countries. At this point in history, we are left wondering if the same ideological props supporting these levels of international aid financing and the patterns of funding distribution will differ just because there is a new technoeconomic environment taking shape that has been euphemistically termed the *Global Information Infrastructure.*

So what is likely to occur as the proposed information superhighway develops? As is promised, it will certainly help to strengthen the infrastructure and ultimate effectiveness of the Western-dominated business community. And other countries, particularly those who already successfully managed to reconstruct their economies two, three, and four decades ago, will be included. However, what is to happen to those people for whom it is not profitable for the large communications corporations to serve? Although it is still profitable to serve some areas in sub-Saharan Africa, in which dense pockets of elites have "the highest level of outgoing international [telephone] traffic per subscriber (more than 200 minutes a year)" (Winsbury, 1994, p. 24), this is decidedly not the case for most citizens of Africa and the 70% of the total Asia-Pacific population cut off from the means of communication.

The concept of an information superhighway accessible to all is certainly an admirable goal. But the notion as currently offered is still ill defined and closely aligned with ideological assumptions that conflate the interests of communication corporations with the interests of citizens. When social policy objectives are merged with economic policy, any hope for a more equitable world communication system is dashed. As a result, we are no closer to the objectives espoused by NWICO, and most likely even further from them than we ever were in the 1960s and 1970s.

HOW IS THE INFORMATION SUPERHIGHWAY BEING SOLD IN THE DEVELOPING WORLD?

The possibilities of the information superhighway are real, and many nations, particularly those in the Occident, stand to prosper under this commitment to a technologically sophisticated communication system. Although there are promises of a utopia for everyone—better education, stronger democracies, improved social services, global business opportunities—the evidence to support such claims is by no means clear or solid. For those who see technologies as symbols of human progress, the new communication technologies will resolve problems in the third world and "provide two-way links that enable people in backward regions of a country to participate and share in the process of economic development" (Jussawalla, 1979, p. ID-7; see also Hudson, 1990; Pool, 1983). Others such as Sussman and Lent (1991), suggest that such views tend to envision technologies as agents of social change and obscure the role of people and power in making the future.

The competing views on how we think about the new technologies are also played out in the uses and abuses of statistics as a measure of value and well-being. What we often find is an abundant supply of appropriately organized data supporting and promoting the new technologies and the recently constructed framework for international communication policy. Thus, as the World Bank notes, the past decade has seen an average growth rate in telecommunications lines of 55% in middle-income countries and 25% in low-income countries (Dougan, 1994). Although this paints an optimistic picture and serves to inspire confidence in the technologies and policy measures being adopted, when we take the data and interpret it in a slightly different way, a much less sanguine view emerges. For instance, when we look at Africa, the continent most in need, an unacceptably low level of development is occurring, and there is often less than one telephone line per 100, even 500, people. Furthermore, many of the telecommunications systems in the third world are poorly maintained and inoperative. One ITU study reported that at any one time, some 40% of the telephone lines installed in some African cities are out of order (Mutambirwa, 1992).

More generally, recent studies by UNCTAD (1990) on the overall effects of political and economic restructuring on 12 of the Least Developed Countries during the period from 1980 to 1987, indicate that just 3 had higher than average growth rates and that the rest were experiencing deteriorating social services and living standards, particularly among the poorest of the population, that could be directly attributable to such programs (Brown, 1993). It is even questionable how beneficial these reform policies are for larger and relatively more prosperous countries such as Brazil that underwent liberalization at a time when the government was plagued with other political problems that reform served to aggravate (Cammack, 1993). Within this context, it is very difficult to gauge the desirability of the more general process of political and economic restructuring in which proposals for the information superhighway and GII are couched.

WHO REALLY BENEFITS IN THE INFORMATION AGE?

As has already been indicated, many anticipate that the benefits of the "communications revolution" will be equally shared by all. Those who support such a view point to the recent role played by television and other forms of electronic media in the collapse of the Soviet Union and in political movements in China, Thailand, Mexico, and elsewhere. From this perspective, the new media, especially the private sector communications networks, have made these momentous political changes possible by linking people together across space and in real time. Thus, it was the ability of television to spread the news of the Moscow political turmoil to the neighboring republics that allowed formerly disparate pockets of resistance and political action to coordinate their actions into unstoppable nationwide acts of civil disobedience and political transformation. The decentralized technologies of the telephone, fax, and computer networking allowed news and reports to be spread to the outside world, even once the official media had been closed down or brought under control (Jones, 1994; Wilhelm, 1994). Furthermore, alternative print, broadcast, performing, and computer media are credited with allowing those with oppositional viewpoints in the developing world, from Southern Asia and the Philippines to the Caribbean and Africa, to link with others across time and space into coordinated networks of political action and social change.

Although the potentials of the new communication technologies have no doubt facilitated coordinated political action and quite radical social changes, it is crucial to think about some of the following points. First, it is primarily people that initially hold the ideas and capacities for action that can bring about massive changes in repressive systems of power. People everywhere, including the Soviet Union and the developing world, no doubt held ideas and committed actions that challenged the status quo long before, and even without, the new means of communication. The new means of communication, perhaps, can be best seen as amplifying, extending, and coordinating these already nascent potentials for change. Second, although these examples of the potential of communication technology for social change are illustrative, it is important to recall that in most countries people are still barred from participating in the public communication process by a lack of formalized communication rights. It is also important to think about how NWICO efforts to expand the envelope of citizens' right to communicate were vehemently opposed by many interests, including those in the Parliamentary democracies of the West. Finally, recent history has demonstrated that the repression that many seek to overcome in the developing world through the use of new communication technologies is often underpinned not only by domestic power elites, but also through external ties to Western powers. When we think about the many years of support the United States gave to the Shah of Iran, Hussein, Marcos, Duarte, Noriega, among many others, it should become obvious that all of the communications technology in the world, although potentially helpful, are insufficient for changing the real conditions standing between people and democracy.

Although the benefits of the new communications media for democracy and political change appear ambiguous, the benefits of the international move toward market and regulatory liberalization for the U.S. economy are clear. With respect to the information superhighway, John Sculley, President of Apple Computer, Inc., estimates that the development of a system of integrated networks could create a US\$ 3.5trillion market ("Route being paved," 1993). Coupled with the dominant position the United States already enjoys in the international distribution of news, television programming, and films, and in the telecommunications and emerging network services market, it is understandable why Washington politicians and numerous business leaders are singing the praises of the information superhighway and market liberalization.

Presently, of the top 15 international telecommunication network operators, 9 are U.S. based. Similarly, in the telecommunications equipment market, 3 of the top 10 firms are from North America (AT&T, Northern Telecom and GTE), 5 are from Europe (Alcatel (France), Siemens (Germany), Ericsson (Sweden), Bosch (Netherlands), and Philips (Netherlands), and 2 are from Japan (NEC and Fujitsu; ITU, 1994). When it comes to computers, most developing countries are heavily dependent on imports. During the mid-1980s, for example, some 70% of the computer market in Chile was in the hands of five transnationals: IBM, Digital, NCR, Burroughs, and Wang. Even when communication technology, such as radio and video equipment is manufactured in the developing countries, it is usually produced by affiliates of the transnational firms such as Sony, Sanyo, Philips, ITT, GTE, Hitachi, Toshiba, Cable and Wireless, and so on. Transnational firms also dominate much of the communications software and programming markets.

Of the global computer hardware market worth US\$114 billion in 1992, 5 of the top ten firms were from the United States (IBM, Apple, Compaq, Dell, and Hewlett-Packard), 3 from Japan (NEC, Fujitsu, and Matsushita), and 2 from Europe (Olivetti and Groupe Bull). Within the workstation segment of the market, 80% of the sector is controlled by the U.S. firms IBM, Sun Microsystems, Hewlett-Packard, DEC, Silicon Graphics, and Intergraph. Of the global mainframe market, 64% or total sales are controlled by the U.S. firms IBM, DEC, Unisys, and Hewlett-Packard. Five U.S. firms—Cray Research, IBM, Convex, Thinking Machines, and Intel—hold 69% of the revenues in the US$2 billion supercomputer market ("Global competitiveness," 1994). Hence, from all indicators, the United States and other G7 countries dominate the international communications markets and would like to further consolidate their control. That is the main objective of the new international communications policy environment, not the attainment of the goals of NWICO or the democratization of communication.

　　We should not be surprised by these circumstances. Brown (1993) reminds us that markets are always supported by the actions of the state, and that regulatory mechanisms serve the maintenance of power or the structural principles of international capitalism, that is, the creation and protection of wealth. At best, regulatory mechanisms provide only a moderate means for achieving justice and the redistribution of power. As Adam's (1993) observes, as the United States was losing ground in the traditional industries of international trade, it sought to bring about new regulatory arrangements that would open up new markets, including those in communications and new network services. Part and parcel of these efforts to open up new areas for trade were the liberalization programs designed by the IMF and World Bank to overcome trade barriers still sanctioned by GATT, whereas the U.S. and EC countries simultaneously used restrictive trade measures such as voluntary export restraints. These voluntary export restraints curtailed the flow of trade from developing to industrialized countries in many economic sectors— agriculture, steel, footwear, and electronic products—and were applied to countries such as Argentina, Brazil, Korea, Taiwan, the People's Republic of China, Thailand, Uruguay, Trinidad & Tobago, and Yugoslavia, among others (Adam's, 1993). Consequently, many countries were asked to open their markets at the same time that they "voluntarily" restricted their opportunities in the markets of the developed countries.

　　This framework for international trade stands in stark contrast to the conditions that prevailed from the 1950s to the 1970s, which contributed to the emergence of the newly industrialized economies of Korea, Taiwan, Hong Kong, Thailand, Singapore, and Japan. All these countries were allowed to exercise measures to protect "infant industries," while at the same time obtaining relatively unrestrained access to the more developed markets of the Western countries (Kraemer, 1994). This is no longer the case as the United States and a few other Western countries seek new arrangements to shore up their faltering dominance in the multilateral system of the global political economy. It appears that one of the greatest victims of this process is the loss of any interest in the goals of achieving justice in the global community.

CONCLUSION: PROSPECTS FOR THE FUTURE

As the discussion in this chapter has pointed out, the possible links among communication, technology, and democracy on a global scale cannot be considered outside the more general political and economic context in which they are situated. The previous sections describing contemporary developments affecting the relations between developed and developing countries, and the increased tendency to locate communication policy within the context of trade policy, suggests that programs such as the information superhighway and the Global Information Infrastructure will serve little more than narrowly defined instrumental interests rather than the much larger and more encompassing goals of NWICO. Yet, despite this rather bleak picture, there are at least three sources of hope that suggest that the efforts of those wishing to push forward with a reconceptualized notion of a New World and Information and Communication Order are not in vain.

First, as is true of all political economic regimes, the currently emerging world order will be transitory and, thus, replaced in the future by some not yet known convergence of social, political, economic, and technological forces. Although the regime now being ushered into the annals of history has been in existence since at least the end of the World War II, indicators are already on the horizon to suggest that it is a yet-to-be-defined successor who will not be able to generate the political, economic, and moral prerequisites necessary for its survival. Key institutions of the "new world order" such as the World Trade Organization are already experiencing a "legitimation crisis" as many critique the usurpation of national sovereignty by an unaccountable international institution and the developing countries express strong reservations toward Western plans for global economic reform (Dale, 1995).

Although the transformations of history are no doubt relentless, it is possible that the narrow instrumental rationality at the core of the "new world order" will be succeeded by other social formations capable of resuscitating and superseding some of the moral categories generated in the past. Although such historical "moral categories" will no doubt not be entirely appropriate for the future, it is nonetheless instructive to briefly consider some of their ingredients as a foundation for determining where we might go from here. Instructive on this matter are the words spoken over 75 years ago by US President Woodrow Wilson (1918), as he offered his "Fourteen Points" program:

> What we demand . . . is nothing peculiar to ourselves. It is that the world be made fit and safe to live in; and particularly that it be made safe for every peace-loving nation which, like our own, wishes to live its own life, determine its own institutions, be assured of justice and fair dealing by the other peoples of the world. . . . All the peoples of the world are in effect partners in this interest, and for our own part we see very clearly that unless justice be done to others it will not be done to us.

The possibility that such moral categories might be viable foundations for future thinking is made all the more plausible by the contradictory responses and seemingly ambivalent adherence to the "new world order" by existing institutions central to the organization and implementation of the emerging international communication order, such as UNESCO and the ITU. UNESCO still invokes the moral categories of libertarian philosophy as it reinstates its commitments to the "free flow of information" doctrine. Although the narrowly tailored free flow of information doctrine is incommensurate with much NWICO effort to secure a more encompassing understanding of democratic communication, it still surpasses the moral bankruptcy of a trade paradigm for international communication policy. In addition, other agencies such as the ITU have demonstrated a contested and ambivalent relationship to the emerging framework for international communication over the last several years. Although the current Secretary-General of the ITU, Pekka Tarjanne, has sometimes whole-heartedly embraced the "new model of telecommunication development . . . [built on] . . . entrepreneurship, competition and private-sector participation", at other times he has stated that the ITU needs to expand its "universal mission . . . to promote the development of telecommunication and to ensure that its benefits are available on an equitable basis" (Tarjanne, 1994, p. 17; see also Tarjanne, 1992). Furthermore, Tarjanne (1992) has recommended that "the Universal Declaration of Human Rights be amended to recognize the right to communicate as a fundamental right" (p. 42). Thus, although the link between communication and justice has no doubt been truncated and the moral categories of communication policy obscured by current developments, it is nonetheless true that such links and categories remain not too far from the surface awaiting the breath of new life.

For the present, perhaps the most promising possibility for the future lies with the efforts of the many private agencies and NGOs that have stepped in to serve the interests of fairness and justice. Such agencies dealing specifically with communication issues, as noted earlier, include the World Association for Christian Communication, the MacBride Round Table, the Union for Democratic Communication, and the National Lawyers Guild. Yet, even more broad-based associations have been addressing the communication and economic needs of those disenfranchised in the global community. These far-ranging organizations include Christian Aid (London), the World Development Movement (London), Alter Trade Japan (Tokyo), Co-op America (Washington), the International Federation for Alternative Trade (Netherlands), North & South Exchange AB (Sweden), Traideirann (Ireland), and Women's World Banking (New York)—all from the industrialized countries—as well as Alter Trade Corporation (Philippines), Coor, Nac'l de Organizaciones (Mexico), Community Development Society (India), Last Hope International (Nigeria), New World Trading (Chile), and Nyumba Ya Sanaa (Trade not Aid) (Tanzania)—from the developing world (Brown, 1993).

To conclude, perhaps the relentless processes of historical and social change, the ambivalent commitment of international agencies to the "new world order," and the erstwhile efforts of private sector, nongovernmental organizations can be conjoined to construct alternative structural possibilities and moral categories sufficient for a more encompassing and humane context for the development, organization, and uses of the new means of communication. Although such a task is no doubt daunting and extremely idealistic, so too are the technologically driven visions of a universally accessible GII being sold to the world's people by government officials, industry, and the majority of communication scholars. The difference between the two is that the first effort foregrounds the interests and role of people in democratizing communication, whereas the latter obscures such interests behind the veils of technological determinism and corporate philanthropy.

REFERENCES

Abel, E. (1982). What is the new world information order? In *Third World news in American media* (pp. 5-8). New York: Columbia University Graduate School of Journalism, Monograph.

Adams, N.A. (1993). *Worlds apart: The North-South divide and the international system*. London: Zed Books.

Brown, M.B. (1993). *Fair trade: Reform and realities in the international trading system*. London: Zed Books.

Cammack, P., Pool, D., & Tordoff, W. (1993). *Third world politics: A comparative introduction*. London: Macmillan Press.

Dale, R. (1995, June 27). When "free trade" is not so free. *International Herald Tribune*, p. 13.

de Vries, R. (1985). International debt: A play in three acts. *Journal of development Planning. 16*, 186.

Declaration of Tallories. (1986). *Voices of Freedom*. Paris: Author. (Reprinted in UNESCO (1987). A documentary history of a New World Information and Communication Order seen as an evolving and continuing process: 1975-86 (Report no. 19).

Don't rush back to UNESCO. (1994, February 23). *New York Times*, p.A18.

Dougan, D.L. (1994, September/October). The Global Information Infrastructure Commission. *Transborder Data and Communications Report*, pp. 11-14.

Editorial. (1983, September 30). *New York Times*.

Editorial: Pressure by the State Department. (1984, February 4). *Editor & Publisher*, p. 4.

Eek, H. (1979). Principles governing the use of the mass media ad defined by the United Nations and UNESCO. In K. Nordenstreng & H. Schiller (Eds.). *National sovereignty and international communication* (pp. 173-194). Norwood, NJ: Ablex.

Federal Communications Commission (FCC). (1984).

Galtung, J., & Vincent, R. (1992). *Global glasnost: Toward a new world information and communication order?* Cresskill, NJ: Hampton Press.

Giffard, A. (1989). *UNESCO and the media.* New York: Longman.

Global competitiveness of US computer industry. (1994, May/June). *Transnational Data and Communications Report*, pp. 44-47.

Gore, A. (1994, March 21). Speech to the International Telecommunications Union, Buenos Aires, Argentina.

Government wages UNESCO campaign. (1984, February 4). *Editor & Publisher*, p. 7.

Grewlich, K.W. (1992, May/June). Telecom—Key element in economic partnerships. *Transnational Data and Communications Report*, pp. 43-45.

Hamelink, C. (1985). *The new international economic order and the new international information order* (Publication no. 34). Paris: UNESCO, International Commission for the Study of Communications Problems.

Harris, J.F. (1995, April 29-30). White House opens fire on "backdoor isolationism." *International Herald Tribune*, p. 3.

Helman, G. B. (1992, May/June). After WARC. *Transnational Data and Communications Reports*, pp. 41-42.

Hollifield, A., & Samarajiva, R. (1994). Changing discourse in U.S. international information-communication policy. *Gazette, 54,* 121-143.

Hudson, H. (1990). *Communication satellites: Their development and impact.* New York: Free Press.

ITU. (1984). *The Maitland Report: The missing link.* Geneva: Author.

ITU. (1994). *World telecommunications development report.* Geneva: Author.

Johnson, D. (1994). *The idea of liberal theory.* Princeton, NJ: Princeton University PRESS.

Jones, A. (1994). Wired world: Communications technology, governance and the democratic uprising. In E.A. Comor (Ed.), *The global political economy of communication* (pp. 145-164). New York: St. Martin's Press.

Jussawalla, M. (1980, May). *Economic and information orders: Emerging issues for international communication.* Paper presented at the World Communications Conference, Decisions for the Eighties, Annenberg School of Communications, Philadelphia.

Jussawalla, M. (1979). The economic of telecoms for development. In D. Wedemeyer (Ed.), *Pacific telecommunications conference proceedings* (pp. 1D/1-1D/9). Honolulu: Pacific Telecommunications Council.

Jussawalla, M. (1981). *Bridging global barriers: Two new international orders: NIEO & NWIO* [pamphlet]. Honolulu: East-West Center.

Kayser, J. (1953). *One week in the world.* Paris: UNESCO.

Kraemer, K. L. (1994, March/April). IT investment payoffs in the Asia Pacific. *Transnational Data and Communications Report*, pp. 33-39.

Legum, C., & Cornwell, J. (1978). *A free and balanced flow: Report of the Twentieth-Century Trust Fund on the international flow of news:*

Background paper. MA: Lexington Books.

Maitland, D. (1984). *The missing link: Report of the independent commission for world-wide telecommunications development.* Geneva: ITU.

Maitland, D. (1994, March/April). Forging new links for telecom development. *Transnational Data and Communications Report,* pp. 17-20.

McPhail, T. (1987). *Electronic colonialism* (2nd ed.). Newbury Park, CA: Sage.

Meisler, S. (1993, August 31). US should rejoin controversial UN agency, Task Force says. *Los Angeles Times,* p. A3.

Mill, J. S. (1967). *Collected works* (Vol. 5). Toronto: University of Toronto Press.

Mutambirwa, R. (1992, March/April). Telecommunications and African development. *Transnational Data and Communications Report,* pp. 31-34.

Non-Aligned Countries. (1976). *Report on the Ministerial Meeting of the Coordinating Bureau.* New Delhi: Author.

Nurske, R. (1993). Trade theory and development policy. In H. Elliot & H. C. Wallich (Eds.), *Economic development for Latin America* (Chapter 9). London: Macmillan.

Petrazzini, B. A. (1993, May/June). Politics of telecom reform in developing countries. *Transnational Data and Communications Report,* pp. 27-34.

Pool, I.S. (1979). The influence of international communication on development. *Media Asia, 6*(3), 149-156.

Pool, I. S. (1983). *Technologies of freedom.* Cambridge, MA: Belknap.

Rawls, J. (1993). *Political liberalism.* New York: Columbia University Press.

Route being paved for US Information Super Highways. (1993, May/June). *Transnational Data and Communications Reports,* pp. 5-6.

Schultz, G. P. (1983, December 28). Letter, Secretary of State, United States of America, Washington, DC, to the Honorable Amadou-Mahtar M'Bow, Director-General of the United Nations Educational, Scientific and Cultural Organization, Paris.(Reprinted in *Journal of Communication. 34*(3), 82.)

Smith, A. (1980). *The geo-politics of information.* New York: Oxford University Press.

Space WARC reaches consensus. (1985, September 16). *Broadcasting,* p. 41.

Split decision over UNESCO. (1980, November 3). *Broadcasting,* p. 28.

Sussman, L. R. (1977). *Mass media and the Third World challenge.* Beverly Hills, CA: Sage.

Sussman, L. R. (1984). World forum: The US decision to withdraw from UNESCO. *Journal of Communication, 34*(3), 159.

Sussman, L. R. (1989). Who did in UNESCO? In to C. A. Giffard (Ed.), *UNESCO and the media* (p. xiii). New York: Longman.

Tarjanne, P. (1992, March/April). The missing link: Still missing? *Transnational Data and Communications Report,* pp. 10-17.

Tarjanne, P. (1994, March 18). Africa and the Information Super Highway. Address to the Seminar on *L'autoroute de la communication* organized by the Association Tunissienee de Communication (AUTUCOM), The Seventh MacBride Round Table, Tunis.

Tehranian, M. (1984). World forum: The US decision to withdraw from UNESCO. *Journal of Communication, 34*(3), 141.

The Harare statement of the MacBride Round Table on Communication. (1990). *Media development, 1,* 13.

UNCTAD. (1984). *Official records: Annex V* (29th Session, September 27-30). New York: Author.

UNCTAD. (1990). *Export restraints and the developing countries* (prepared by T. Murray). New York: Author.

UNESCO, & International Association for Mass Communication Research (IAMCR). (1968). *Symposium on mass media and international understanding.* Paris: Author.

UNESCO approves a compromise on world communications plan. (1983, December 15). *New York Times,* p. A6.

UNESCO. (1954). *Resolution 522* (XVII). Paris: Author.

UNESCO. (1970a). *Mass media and society* (Reports and Papers in Mass Communication, no. 59). Paris: Author.

UNESCO. (1970b). *Records of the 16th General Conference.* Paris: Author.

UNESCO. (1971). *Final report from the Meeting of International Group of Specialists in Communication Research.* Paris: Author.

UNESCO. (1972). *Final report (COM/MD/24) from the Meeting of Experts on Communication Policy and Planning.* Paris: Author.

UNESCO. (1974). *Document 18C/35 Presented to the 18th Session of the General Conference.* Paris: Author.

UNESCO. (1976). *Report on the 19th General-Conference.* Nairobi. Paris: Author.

UNESCO. (1977). *Origins and mandate* (Paper no. 2). Paris: Author.

UNESCO. (1980). *Many voices, One World.* Paris: Author.

UNESCO. (1989). *Third medium-term plan* (Resolution 25 c/4/104). Paris: Author.

United Nations. (1948). *Universal Declaration of Human Rights.* Geneva: Author.

US weighs UNESCO pullout over budget and policy fight. (1983, December 15). *New York Times,* p. 1

Van Dinh, T. (1977). Non-aligned and cultural imperialism. In A. W. Singham (Ed.), *The non-aligned movement in world politics* (pp. 73-85). Westport, CT: Lawrence Hill.

WARC 1985: The politics of space. (1985, September 23). *Broadcasting,* p. 56.

Why UNESCO? (1993, April 19). *Washington Post,* p. A22.

Wilhelm, D. (1994). *The politics of global information.* New York: Longman.

Winsbury, R. (1994). Who will pay for the Global Village? Funding the Buenos Aires decision. *Intermedia, 22*(3), 23-31.

Winseck, D., & Cuthbert, C. (1991). Space WARC: Toward global communication equity in satellite communications? *Gazette, 47,* 195-203.

Chapter 17

World Communication:
Business as Usual?

Cees J. Hamelink

ATHENS AND ALGIERS

A key theme in contemporary debates on the democratization of communication is the emerging Global Information Infrastructure project (GII). According to the sponsors of this project, we are definitely moving towards a new democratic communication order in the world. The GII:

> will circle the globe with information superhighways on which all people can travel. . . . These highways—or more accurately, networks of distributed intelligence—will allow us to share information, to connect, and to communicate as a global community. From these connections we will derive robust and sustainable economic progress, strong democracies, better solutions to global problems and—ultimately—a greater sense of shared stewardship of our small planet. The Global Information Infrastructure will help educate our children and allow us to exchange ideas within a community and among nations. (Gore, 1994)

The essential aspiration of the GII-project has been stated eloquently by Al Gore, Vice President of the United States: "The development of the GII . . . must be a democratic effort . . . In a sense, the GII will be a metaphor for democracy itself . . . I see a new Athenian Age of democracy forged in the fora the GII will create" (Gore, 1994).

In many respects this discourse resonates an earlier debate that also put the creation of a new global communication order on the public agenda. This order would be democratic, support economic development, enhance the international exchange of ideas, share knowledge among all the people of the world, and improve the quality of life. The early debate emerged in the late 1960s and became public in the early 1970s through a meeting of nonaligned heads of state in 1973 at Algiers. That meeting signaled the beginning of a series of political and intellectual activities that were aimed at the creation of a New International Information Order (NIIO). The key item on the agenda was the democratic redistribution of one of the world's most important resources: information.

The similarity in political rhetoric between the information debates of the 1970s and the 1990s produced the leading question for this chapter. If we assume that the main aspiration of both projects is to democratize world communication, can the GII project succeed where the NIIO project failed?

THE NIIO PROJECT

The NIIO project started with the recognition that despite the formal liberation from military occupation and political administration, most developing countries were, in the early 1970s, still economically and culturally colonized. The former was in most cases abundantly manifest, the latter tended to be far less clear. This was due to a number of factors.

There was the prevailing acceptance of such concepts as the free international flow of information, the largely unrecognized hidden agenda of most cultural traffic, and the identification of cultural imports as indicators of development. In 1973, the powerful cultural legitimation of the Metropolis-Satellite structure was exposed, publicly debated, and proposals for counteraction offered. From this point the debate moved toward the recognition that the need to reorder cultural/informational relations in the world was intrinsically linked to the need to restructure the international economy.

In the 1970s, the Non-Aligned countries recognized that almost two decades of international technical assistance had not altered their dependency status, that the North-South communications gap persisted, and that in fact their cultural sovereignty was increasingly threatened. They therefore opened the debate on the need of normative standard setting regarding the mass media. The key agenda issue for this debate was the demand for a new international information order. This demand expressed the third-world concern about disparity in the communication capacity along three lines.

First, there was the concern about the impact of the inequitable information relations between North and South on the cultural development of third-world nations. Actually, the first Non-Aligned summit in Bandung, Indonesia in 1955 already referred to the impact of colonialism on culture in stating: "The existence of colonialism in many parts of Asia and Africa, in whatever form it may be, not only prevents cultural co-operation but also powers have denied their dependent peoples basic rights in the sphere of education and culture" (Bandung, 1955). The 1973, Non-Aligned summit at Algiers expressed a strong concern about cultural colonialism which it perceived as the effective successor to the earlier territorial modes of colonialism.

Second, there was the concern about the largely one-sided exports of information from the North to the countries of the third world and the distorted or nonexistent reports in Northern media about developments in the South. The Algiers summit called for the reorganization of existing communication channels, which are a legacy of the colonial past and which have hampered the free and equal exchange of information between the North and the South. The control over this exchange by a few Western transnational companies was criticized by the Non-Aligned movement as an instrument of cultural colonialism.

A third concern addressed the transfer of media technology. It was concluded that preciously little technology had been transferred by the early 1970s. Mainly technical end-products had been exported from the industrial nations. This was often done under such disadvantageous conditions that in the end the technical and financial dependence of the receiving countries had increased.

At the Algiers summit in 1973, the Non-Aligned movement formulated a position of strong support for the emancipation and development of information media in the developing nations. Following Algiers, the pace of the debate stepped up. More actors became involved. Controversies heated up. Resolutions, counterproposals, and conference reports followed on each other with remarkable speed. Information colonialism had attained international visibility. By 1976, the international debate culminated in the demand for a New International Information Order (NIIO). A Non-Aligned information symposium at Tunis stated in March 1976: "Since information in the world shows a disequilibrium favouring some and ignoring others, it is the duty of the non-aligned countries and other developing countries to change this situation and obtain the decolonization of information and initiate a new international order of information" (Hamelink, 1977, p. 177). This was followed by the New Delhi Declaration on the Decolonization of Information which claimed that the establishment of a NIIO was as necessary as the New International Economic Order (NIEO). Herewith a clear linkage was established between information/communication issues and the proposal for a fundamental restructuring of the international economy that had been put forward in 1974.

Although the precise meaning of the NIIO was not defined, it was evident that its key notions were national sovereignty and cultural autonomy. The NIIO reflected the Non-Aligned aspiration to an international information exchange in which states that develop their cultural system in an autonomous way and with complete sovereign control of resources fully and effectively participate as independent members of the international community. A crucial concept in the NIIO debate was the democratization of world communication.

From 1976, the Western news media began to take a critical attitude toward the demand for a NIIO. The majority of international mass media expressed their opposition to the Non-Aligned initiative. In various commentaries the following points were recurrently made. There is no relationship between the demand for a new economic order and a new information order. The core of the problem of disequilibrium lies in the third world itself and is caused by paucity of technical and financial resources. The NIIO proposal is authoritarian by nature and under the pretext of aiding the third world it attempts to undermine Western liberties. Proposals for reformation coming from third-world countries are necessarily influenced by governments and therefore unacceptable. The NIIO is basically inspired by Soviet interests.

By 1978, most members of the international community admitted that something was wrong in international information relations. The 20th General Conference of UNESCO, in 1978, in Paris asked the International Commission for the Study of Communication Problems (the so-called MacBride Commission) to propose measures that could lead to "the establishment of a more just and effective world information order." The hostile opposition toward the idea of a new order was softened. It was unanimously accepted that third-world countries had justifiable complaints, and that concessions had to be made by the industrialized states. With complete consensus the UNESCO member states articulated the need for a new order in the field of international information, albeit in rather ambivalent semantics. The original concept (NIIO), which was coined by the Non-Aligned movement, was replaced by the proposal for a "new, more just and effective world information and communication order" (NWICO). According to the interpretation of U.S. Ambassador John Reinhardt at the 1978 UNESCO General Conference this new order required:

> a more effective program of action, both public and private, to suitable identified centers of professional education and training in broadcasting and journalism in the developing world . . . [and] . . . a major effort to apply the benefits of advanced communications technology . . . to economic and social needs in the rural areas of developing nations. (Hamelink, 1983, p. 69)

The new order (NWICO) that was now acceptable to all UNESCO member states was mainly interpreted as a program for the transfer of knowledge, finances, and technical equipment. The problem of the international information structure was being reduced to mere technical proportions. In response to this, an intergovernmental program for support to the development of communication was launched as a Western initiative in 1980. The international community embraced a new order, but darkness prevailed for those inquiring 'whose order' this was supposed to be.

What actually happened during the UNESCO General Conferences of 1976, 1978, and 1980 was that the Western minority managed to achieve most of its policy objectives against the expressed preference of the majority of member states. In the end the debate did not yield the results demanded by the developing countries. Their criticism of the past failures of technical assistance programs was answered by the creation of yet another such program—the International Program for the Development of Communication (IPDC). This program was seen by many third-world delegates as a suitable instrument to implement the standards of the NWICO.

The UNESCO General Conference of 1980 stated (Res. 4. 19) that among these standards were the elimination of the imbalances and inequalities that characterize the present situation, the capacity of the developing countries to achieve improvement of their own situation, notably by providing infrastructure and by making their information and communication means suitable to their needs and aspirations, and the sincere will of developed countries to help them. The IPDC, however, was not going to meet these expectations. Apart from the inherent difficulty of approaching world communication problems in a manner that had not worked to the benefit of third-world nations in the past, the IPDC also suffered a chronic lack of resources.

Moreover, in 1981, there were clear indications that the opponents of the third-world demand for a new information order had not yet been satisfied. They continued to see dangers to the liberties of the Western mass media. At Talloires, in France (May 15-17, 1981), a Voices of Freedom Conference of Independent New Media was held. The conference was attended mostly by representatives of publishers' interests (from 21 countries). There were no representatives of the international journalists' federation. The conference participants adopted the Magna Charta of the Free Press, which stated:

> We believe the time has come within Unesco and other intergovernmental bodies to abandon attempts to regulate news content and formulate rules for the press. Efforts should be directed instead to finding practical solutions to the problems before us, such as improving technological progress, increasing professional interchanges and equipment transfers, reducing communication tariffs, producing cheaper newsprint and eliminating other barriers to the development of news media capabilities. (Nordenstreng, 1984, p. 400)

In 1981, the first indications for the withdrawal of the United States from UNESCO (realized in 1984) also became visible. President Reagan said in a letter to the House of Representatives (September 17, 1981):

> We strongly support—and commend to the attention of all nations—the declaration issued by independent media leaders of twenty-one nations at the Voices of Freedom Conference, which met at Tallories, France, in May of this year. We do not feel we can continue to support a Unesco that turns its back on the high purposes this organization was originally intended to serve. (Servaes, 1987, p. 237)

The US withdrawal was subsequently officially announced on December 29, 1983 in a letter by Secretary of State George Schultz. According to the letter: "UNESCO has extraneously politicized virtually every subject it deals with, has exhibited hostility towards the basic institutions of a free society, especially the free market and the free press, and has demonstrated unrestrained budgetary expansion" (Frederick, 1993, p. 185).

In the effort to maintain a fragile international consensus the UNESCO General Conference began to erode the original aspirations of the NIIO proponents and shifted from the need to establish a regulatory structure supportive of the new order to ambiguous statements about "an evolving and continuous process" (Paris, General Conference, 1982, res. 3.3). In September 1983, UNESCO convened a round table on a New World Information and Communication Order at Igls, Austria. The meeting focused strongly on assistance to developing countries for the development of their communication infrastructures. A second, and last, round table on the NWICO took place in 1986 (April) in Copenhagen, Denmark.

Although the concept of a new order remained central for some years to come, nothing was done in regard to its implementation. Gradually, UNESCO withdrew support from all research, documentation, or conference activities intended to contribute to the establishment of a new information order. Instead, it moved toward a "new strategy" (for the Medium-Term plan 1990-1995) with an emphasis on the free flow of information, the freedom and independence of the media, the priority to operational activities, and the importance of information technology. Whereas the Non-Aligned summit in Belgrade in September 1989 reiterated its support for NWICO, the UNESCO General Conference strove hard to reach consensus on formulations that represented conventional ideas about freedom of the press, pluralism of the media, freedom of expression, and free flow of information. According to a statement by the UNESCO Director General in 1989, plans for a new information order no longer existed in UNESCO.

THE GII PROJECT

The first strong stimulus for the GII project came from the U.S. Clinton Administration when it recognized the importance of the information society in its 1993 Agenda for a National Information Infrastructure (NII). Among the main principles of this Agenda were the promotion of private sector investment and the development of new universal service concepts, ensuring information security and network reliability, promoting intellectual property rights, and providing access to government information. In January 1994, the government announced the establishment of the U.S. Advisory Council on the National Information Infrastructure (NIIAC). The Council has initiated a series of projects that focus on such applications as education, health care, electronic commerce, and public safety; on issues related to privacy and security; and on the problem of providing access at affordable prices. The Clinton/Gore NII initiative received strong industry support from the beginning.

Following the U.S. lead, reports on the information society were also produced in Japan and Western Europe. In Japan, the Telecommunications Council of the Ministry of Posts and Telecommunications presented its report Reforms Towards the Intellectually Creative Society: Program for the Establishment of a High-Performance Info-communications Infrastructure in May 1994. The report projected that the emerging information society leads to improved care for the elderly, reform of the economy, a more comfortable lifestyle, a more open society, better understanding with other countries, and more adequate ways of addressing environmental problems.

In France a report was published in October 1994, entitled, Les autoroutes de l' information. The report (written by Gérard Théry) argued that the information society leads to new electronic publishing forms, new audiovisual activities, video games, improved care for the elderly, public service in education, medicine, libraries and museums, and video phone applications.

The European Union (EU) appointed a High-Level Group on the Information Society with the EU Commissioner for industrial affairs, telecommunications, and information technologies Martin Bangemann as chair. The Bangemann report (Europe and the Global Information Society) recommended to the EU Heads of State at the European Council at Corfu, June 1994, that applications of the new information infrastructure should include teleworking, distance learning, telematic services for small and medium enterprises, university networking, road traffic management, air traffic control, health care networks, and city information highways (creation of digital cities). The report recommended the EU "to put its faith in market mechanisms as the motive power to carry us into the Information Age." The Corfu summit requested an action plan in connection with the information society.

This was presented in a communication from the European Commission (EC) to the Council and the European Parliament as *Europe's way to the Information Society: An action plan* (July 1994). Strong support for the GII project from the world's top political leadership and the top management from the private sector became abundantly clear during the Summit of the G-7 countries (United States, Japan, United Kingdom, France, Germany, Italy, and Canada) in February 1995 at Brussels. This meeting on the information superhighway was prepared by the Naples G-7 meeting of July 9, 1994, which had agreed to hold a discussion on the development of "open, competitive and integrated world-wide information infrastructures."

The Brussels summit concentrated on the regulatory framework and competition policy, the implementation of information infrastructures and their accessibility for the public, and the social and cultural aspects of the information society. The political top agreed to close cooperation in the development of a global information society. There was, however, some disagreement about the speed at which this would be established. The United States pleaded for fast liberalization of markets and open competition. Japan and Europe were more cautious and preferred a slower pace. The U.S. position was shared by the private sector, which also met in Brussels in the Round Table conference with the captains of industry from such companies as AT&T, Philips, Siemens, Alcatel, Mitsubishi, and British Telecom. The corporate leadership agreed that open markets are the best guarantee for balanced technological progress.

The G-7 Final Declaration stated that key elements are dynamic competition and private investment. Although the information society is expected to enrich people worldwide, there are serious concerns about the disparity between the information-rich and the information-poor, about scope and quality of employment, and the possibilities of abuse and infringement of privacy and copyrights. The G-7 governments committed themselves to "promoting universal service to ensure opportunities for all to participate" and to "encouraging dialogue on world-wide co-operation," such that industrialized countries will work toward the participation of developing countries in the Global Information Society.

The GII project promises a boom scenario in which the Information Society creates new jobs, enhances social solidarity, promotes linguistic and cultural diversity, strengthens democratic participation, improves the quality of health and education systems, enhances the overall quality of life, and brings new leisure and entertainment opportunities. As Bill Gates (Microsoft president) believes, "The networks will protect us from the worst while giving us the best: greater possibilities for communication, training, and health care" (IPA, 1995, p. 6).

Despite the promising tones of GII rhetoric, there are complex problems that need to be resolved. Among these concerns is the question of universal access to the information superhighway. The G-7 partners were determined to ensure that the information society addresses the needs of citizens. They committed themselves to "promote universal service to ensure opportunities for all to participate." A major concern raised during the summit pertains to the protection of intellectual property rights. As Gore (1995) phrased it, "Let's develop and enforce effective intellectual property rights for the GII. If our content providers are not protected, there will not be content to fill the networks and give value to the services." According to Bill Gates, this concern is not too difficult to handle. In his view:

> Inventors have nothing to fear from these new technologies that will protect artists better than the traditional technologies do. It is easier to protect one's rights on an information superhighway than anywhere else. . . . In a world

where physical copies of the works exist you can copy them by millions without anybody seeing you. . . . On the network, however, if a person transmits a song, that is to say a great quantity of information to thousands of unknown people to whom he has never sent information before, this will seem suspicious. Because the network observes everything that is happening, you cannot say that you do not know how you obtained that music—Today you are under observation 80% of the time: when you make a phone call, write out a cheque or use your credit card. (IPA, 1995, p. 6)

This may be good news for holders of intellectual property rights, but it is very disturbing for those who hoped to have a little privacy left. The protection of privacy is certainly another important concern for the GII promoters. The G-7 partners expressed the will to increase efforts to find solutions to "protect privacy and personal data" and to "increase information security." The deployment of smart machines and methods of electronic surveillance raises concerns about volumes of employment and quality of the working environment. The G-7 summit announced that impact of the information society on jobs has to be studied.

There is some concern that the information society may cause social isolation, and that if people limit themselves only to the information they care about, the disintegration of communities may be the end result. The creation of virtual communities could leave people at the end of the day "lone riders" moving from Net to Net as consumers, observers, and Peeping Toms: zapping and window shopping, but not conversing.

A recurrent concern addresses the need to deregulate. The U.S. government proposed during the G-7 summit to open telecommunications markets around the world. However, in Europe, the telecom giants are still in control and not yet ready to give up their monopolies:

While Europe marches toward a 1998 deadline for opening its telecom markets completely, monopoly phone companies are working overtime to block competition in the businesses that have already been liberalized, such as mobile services and private corporate networks. (Edmondson, 1995, p. 20)

Among the anti-competitive 'tricks' the companies deploy are the refusal to grant lines to newcomers, the use of monopoly profits to subsidize price-cutting in liberalized areas such as data packet switching, and charging exorbitant fees for leased lines.

WHY DID THE NIIO PROJECT FAIL IN ITS ATTEMPT TO DEMOCRATIZE COMMUNICATION?

The NIIO project did not produce a significant contribution to the democratization of communication, neither locally nor globally. The world communication order that emerged in the 1980s (following the international debate) was not the one the original protagonists had in mind. The new world order of the 1980s was primarily intended to meet the needs and purposes of the global transnational industrial and financial networks. The NIIO failure can be analyzed in terms of questions about control, access, quality, and people's participation.

Control

The NIIO argument was that in a democratic order information flows should not be the proprietary domain of commercial providers. Information was considered more than a commercial commodity to be bought and sold on a market. It was rather seen as a service provided in the public domain. Because most of the world's information flows are controlled by a handful of corporate gatekeepers, the proposed new order had to diversify and de-monopolize ownership. This remained wishful thinking. The key actors simply refused to play along. Most importantly, they refused public accountability for their operations and by implication rejected a democratic order. The information Trans National Corporations (TNCs), supported by Western diplomacy, had no intention to accept rules on their conduct. Although they publicly professed a dedication to free, open, and competitive markets, their actual conduct preferred concentration, consolidation, and conglomeration. United Nations negotiations (which began in 1975) to formulate and implement a code of conduct on transnational corporations never got beyond the agreement to disagree.

Access

An important obstacle to the aspired democratization was the stark disparity in access to information infrastructures. It was evident that the existing North-South communication gap had to be resolved before the notion of democratic communication would acquire even a minimal meaning. The disparity was eventually recognized by the North, which offered "Marshall Plan"-type aid for communication development in the South to settle the dispute. As key instruments for the implementation of this plan, UNESCO established the IPDC and the International Telecommunication Union (ITU) established the Bureau for Telecommunication Development. Both institutions turned out to be underfunded, understaffed, and powerless to change the North-South disparity. One can only conclude that the North never seriously intended to provide the kind of support that would have enabled developing countries to control their own communication environment. This was very obvious in the persistent refusal of the technology-producing countries to share on an equitable basis the progress in science and technology with the third world. In the context of the international transfer of technology, the United Nations Conference on Trade and Development (UNCTAD) initiated in 1975 negotiations to formulate a Code of Conduct on Transfer of Technology. Throughout the 1980s the negotiations proceeded without success.

Quality

A crucial concern for the NIIO project was the provision of information that projected an inadequate, incomplete, distorted image of the realities of developing countries across the world. Part of the democratization effort was the desire to provide a more balanced information diet based on the notion that democratic societies need well-informed citizens. Proposals for the enhancement of information quality were constructed by the leading information providers as threats to fundamental freedoms such as free speech and tantamount to censorship. The debate on this issue was not helped by the fact that quite a few political elites in the South were rather actively committed to censoring both their own citizens and foreign journalists and had little qualms about the occasional killing of those who exercised free speech claims. This was further aggravated by the fact that pleas for free and balanced information flows received political support from the Soviet leadership. This did not help to make the NIIO a worthy cause to defend.

As a matter of fact, although ignorance poses serious obstacles to social development, many third-world governments preferred their citizens to be ignorant and had little inclination to promote such initiatives as rural telephony that would provide "a voice to the voiceless." The large majority of undemocratic regimes in the world was never particularly keen on broadcasting the needs and aspirations of the voiceless. In most developing countries the sole information provider was the state. Most information state institutions provided was politically biased and of poor quality and not in anyway more helpful for the development process than the commercial provision of "spot" news about incidental, dramatic, and immediate events.

People's Participation

The 1970s effort to democratize communication was never a very democratic process. This probably was the worst flaw in the NIIO project. The debate was mainly an exchange among state and commercial actors. Ordinary people were not on the playing field. The whole project was engineered by political and intellectual elites. There was little or no thinking about people's interests, even less about the need to involve ordinary people in the debate.

The 1970s debate on a new international information order was firmly rooted in the realist paradigm of international relations. This conceives the world as a state-centric system and fails to take serious account of the numerous nonstate actors that have become essential forces in world politics. As a result, the NIIO debate never explicitly promoted the notion that the effective protection of democratic rights could not be guaranteed under the conventional nation-state system. A critical problem is that the realist paradigm tends to gloss over the internal dimension of state sovereignty while focusing on external factors. As a result, the nation-state is seen as protecting the liberties of its citizenry against external claims made by other states. However, the outwardly sovereign state also tends to appropriate sovereign control over its citizens in the process. This is the Hobbesian vision in which only the absolute sovereignty of the state (the Leviathan) can control eternal civil strife.

This position ignores that state sovereignty represents more than the emancipation from the powers of emperors, popes and nobility. The development of legitimate sovereign states went together with the development of egalitarianism in which subjects became citizens. The French Revolution and the American Revolution gave birth to both independent nation-states as well as to citizens with basic civil rights. As a matter of fact, the French Revolution recognized the primacy of the people's sovereignty. This recognition was not taken up in the NIIO project. It was not a people's movement. Insofar as it aspired toward a democratic order, it was a "democratization from above."

CAN THE GII PROJECT SUCCEED WHERE THE NIIO PROJECT FAILED?

To render the comparison fair, the GII project should be assessed in light of the same criteria: control, access, quality, and people's participation.

Control

For the GII project to be democratic on the matter of control, there would have to be a deconcentration of ownership in both infrastructures and content provision, there could not be a oligopoly of gatekeepers, and there should be a level of public accountability for service providers. The chances that this might be achieved are rather slim.

There is in the mid-1990s a consolidation of control over the provision of information that only grows stronger. Powerful gatekeepers dominate the world market and control hardware infrastructures or software provision and often both. The early 1990s have already been christened the Age of Consolidation. "Everywhere you look these days, arch rivals are falling into each other's embrace" (Business Week, 1991, p. 40). Mega mergers in both manufacturing and services sectors are emerging. Consolidation basically means that companies are buying their competitors and thus concentrating market control in the hands of fewer companies. This is what is happening in the world communication market. The major players are actively striving to gain control over the production of messages (ranging from digital libraries to TV entertainment), the operation of distribution systems (ranging from satellites to digital switches), and the manufacture of the equipment for reception and processing of information (ranging from HDTV sets to telephones). Some examples illustrate the degree of control in sectors of the world communication market.

In 1993, the top 12 AV companies controlled over 40% of the world market for AV products, as shown in Table 17.1.

In 1994, the market shares of major Hollywood companies are as shown in Table 17.2.

Table 17.1. The 12 Top AV Companies in 1993 (AV Revenues in Millions US$).

Company	Country	AV Revenues
Sony	Japan	7.320
Time Warner Entertainment	USA	5.755
ARD	Germany	5.581
NHK	Japan	5.254
Capital Cities/ABC	USA	4.663
Matsushita	Japan	4.352
Fujisankei	Japan	4.155
Tele-Communications	USA	4.153
Philips [Polygram]	Netherlands	3.993
Walt Disney	USA	3.673
CBS	USA	3.510
Time Warner	USA	3.334

Table 17.2. Market Shares of Major Hollywood Companies.

Studio	Owner	Market Share
Buena Vista	Disney	19%
Paramount	Viacom	15%
Warner Bros	TIme Warner	14%
Universal	Matsushita	13%
Twentieth Century Fox	News Corp (Murdoch)	11%
News Line	Turner Broadcasting	6%
Tristar	Sony	5%
Columbia	Sony	5%
TOTAL	88%	

The world telecommunications market generated US$535 billion in 1992. The top 10 companies had a 45% share. Market analysts expect that by the year 2000 only five telecommunications megacompanies will control global networks: AT&T, Cable & Wireless, MCI, United Telecom, and British Telecom. The world market for computer hardware yielded, in 1992, US$114 billion. The 20 biggest companies represented an 80% share of the market. On the world market for computer software, Microsoft controlled, in 1994, almost 35%.

There are no indications that the process of consolidation is slowing down. As a matter of fact, the largest service providers are investing billions in the new digital networks, and they are obviously intent on monopolizing access to consumer markets. Time-Warner, for example, plans to be a key supplier of contents and a controller of major delivery systems and has decided to invest US$5 billion for its superhighway ambitions. The Hollywood majors are also preparing themselves to retain their dominant positions (in filmed entertainment) and extend their control to the superhighway as the main content providers. Hardware companies are also interested in the contents, and U.S. telephone companies Bell Atlantic, NYNEX, and Pacific Telesis have put down $100 million to enter the entertainment and information business.

There is no indication that the gatekeepers are more willing to be held accountable than they were in the 1970s. Yet, with the increasing importance of information processing across social domains, the question of information liability, that is, the responsibility for false and misleading information, can no longer be evaded. The decision makers are increasingly private parties that are neither elected nor held accountable. As a matter of fact, the worldwide drive toward deregulation of social domains tends to delegate important areas of social life to private rather than to public control and accountability. Increasingly large volumes of social activity are withdrawn from public accountability, democratic control, and the participation of citizens in decision making. The global corporations that control ever more facets of people's daily lives have become less accountable to public authorities everywhere in the world: "Most corporate leaders, while proudly exercising their constitutionally protected right to influence elections and legislation, deny that they are making public policy merely by doing business. They do not accept responsibility for the social consequences of what they make or how they make it" (Barnet & Cavanagh, 1994, p. 422).

Access

Access is a major concern the G-7 summit acknowledged. The final declaration states that the G-7 countries are committed to "promote universal service to ensure opportunities for all to participate." The EC paper for the summit proposed, "Access to information is a basic right of every citizen. . . . The benefits of the information society should not be limited to business but should be available to society as a whole." In this context it has been repeatedly stated that the GII project should not increase the existing gap between information-rich and information-poor. However, as José Rossi (French minister of industry) said at the summit's final press conference, "While all participants acknowledge universal service is a major concern, it remains an open question."

There are different schools of thought on the question. One approach restricts the notion of "universal service" to "availability," that is, all citizens should have access to basic communications services at affordable prices. Another approach proposes that people should also be able to "use" communication services at affordable prices. It is also contested that services should be categorized as universal: only basic telephony services, or a host of value-added services?

The problem is made more difficult because governments, although recognizing the universal service obligation, want the private sector to pay for the GII. This raises the question of whether the matter of service provision can be left to the market? Will actors driven by commercial interests recognize the obligation? Moreover, in the wider context of world politics, the question is what kind of infrastructures will be available for the developing countries. Can third-world countries "leapfrog" into the Information Society? It can be observed that many third-world countries are presently committed to the leapfrog option as they expect that advanced communications will promote economic development. In several third-world countries a considerable expansion of available telephone lines is planned for the near future.

The expansion of telephone lines in some countries by % in the year 2000 is shown in Table 17.3.

However, the realities of current inequalities are very stark indeed. When we take technical infrastructures, we observe that Europe and the United States have almost 70% ownership of radio/TV sets. The African region has 1.3% of the world share of TV ownership. For radio ownership this is 3.7%. Low-income countries have less than 5% of the world share of telephone lines and 55% of the world population. High-income countries have 50 telephone lines per 100 inhabitants; 49 countries have less than 1 telephone line per 100.

Table 17.3. Expansion of Telephone Lines.

Country	Phone Lines in Millions Needed	% Increase	Investment In $ Billions
China	35.5	19.3	53.3
India	9.1	11.2	13.7
Thailand	4.3	16.7	6.6
Malaysia	3.1	11.9	4.6
Indonesia	2.6	13.6	3.9

Data compiled by the International Telecommunication Union.

The G-7 summit recognized the need to integrate the developing countries into the global information infrastructure. The question is who will pay the bill? The World Bank spends less than 2% of all loans for telecommunications, the African Development Bank even less than 1%. In 1990, UNDP provided US$27 million for 197 telecom development projects. In 1995, this was down to US$2.2 million for 19 projects. Obviously, then, the technology transfer issue has still not been resolved to the advantage of the poorer countries. On the contrary, recent developments in the protection of intellectual property make it more difficult for technology-dependent countries to develop their own technologies and to independently develop their knowledge bases.

There are also problems within countries. If countries reinvest some 50% of telecom revenues in the development of infrastructures, they can significantly decrease the communications gap. However, in many countries reinvestment is under 25%. In many developing countries governments have only a limited interest in the improvement of information infrastructures. There is also the danger that when an interest exists, this may lead to the rapid development of digital capital cities that become part of a global network, leaving the rural populations once again behind.

The GII project is driven by the belief in the market as the ultimate regulator of all social interactions. It remains to be seen how this neoliberal "fundamentalism" addresses the basic realities of our world. The promotional language suggests that a free global market represents people's best interests. The promise that global trading in a deregulated global market leads to unprecedented prosperity to all does not explain why in the real world the development of prosperity is highly uneven, why in fact poverty and inequality are worsening, why of the 5.6 billion people in the world at the end of 1994 over 1 billion try to survive on less than US$370 per year, why 1 billion adults are illiterate, why for over 500 million children there are no schools, or why of the 2.8 billion labor force over 30% is unemployed. A significant characteristic of the new world order is that "far from producing a solution to the gap between the world's 'haves' and 'have-nots', the changing structures of international business and investment may exacerbate them" (Kennedy, 1993, p. 47). It may well be that Al Gore's vision of a new age of Athenian democracy will indeed be implemented. This could mean that just like Athens excluded women and slaves, the GII excludes large numbers of second-rate citizens.

Quality

In a series of judgments the European Court of Human Rights has concluded that the essence of Article 10 of the European Convention on Human Rights and Fundamental Freedoms constructs a right to receive information and ideas and not just to broadcast signals. As the Court stated, "Everyone has the right to freedom of expression. This right shall include freedom to hold opinions and to receive and impart information and ideas without interference by public authority and regardless of frontiers." As such, the decision imposes on broadcasters the duty to accommodate this receivers' right. According to the jurisprudence of the European Court, the European citizen has the right to be properly informed. In several opinions the Court has stated that not only do the mass media have a right to impart information, they have the task "to impart information and ideas on matters of public interest," and the public has a right to receive such information and ideas.

The European Court has ruled that the media are purveyors of information and public watchdogs. This matches with a classical opinion of the U.S. Supreme Court in the *Red Lion Broadcasting versus the FCC* case in 1969, that "the right of the viewers and listeners, not the right of broadcasters is paramount." The right of the public to be properly informed means the right to receive a full, impartial, accurate, and independent account of events. Will the GII deliver this quality information? Or will the information superhighway mainly provide opportunities for teleshopping, video games, soft porno, and similar contents that lend themselves to a one-way street consumptive approach. Will the GII properly inform the citizens of this world? The prospect is not very bright. If services are left to the market with little or no space for a public domain, it is very likely that private actors that spend enormous amounts of capital intend to recoup most of this with profitable "killer" applications.

The closest the world gets to the projected global information superhighway today is the Internet. This is a public meeting place in which some 30 million computer users in some 150 countries exchange information, search databases, play games, and interact. The Internet is beginning to attract the attention of the international business community. Business Week, in its cover story of November 14, 1994, suggested that the Internet is emerging as "one of the most exciting places for doing business" (Verity, 1994, p. 38). The Internet has been guided by the rule of sharing information for free and has now been discovered as a major vehicle for commercial advertising. *Business Week* quotes Bill Washburn (former executive director of Commercial Internet Exchange) saying, "With the Internet, the whole globe is one marketplace" (Verity, 1994, p. 39). This could mean that the Internet turns into a global electronic shopping mall.

People's Participation

Just like the NIIO project, the GII project is steered by the interests and stakes of governments and corporations. It is the bilateral playing field of "princes" and "merchants," and ordinary people are occasionally addressed as citizens or consumers, but they play no essential role.

A concern for the GII elite is actually that people may not be as excited about the digital future as they are. It may be that ordinary men and women are not eagerly waiting to believe that virtual reality can resolve the problems of their daily lives. Therefore, the various official reports on the information society usually stress the need to promote awareness among consumers. A key concern of the constructors of the information superhighway is that consumers may be hesitant about adding new digital services to the present supply, certainly if they have to pay for it. The GII project therefore needs to persuade people that the information society will bring them great improvements in lifestyle, comfort, and general well-being. This certainly makes people important targets for marketing and propaganda. It does not make them serious partners in the project. There is no serious involvement of people's movements in the making of the GII. There are no trilateral negotiations among governments, industrialists, and social movements to decide on a future that we all may want. Like the project of the 1970s, the GII project is guided by a "democratization-from-above" and doomed to fail in making world communication more democratic.

PERSPECTIVE?

The conclusion leaves us questioning whether we could chart a different future? The brief answer to this is: Not as long as we leave the direction of "our common future" to the interests of transnational business and political elites.

The only forces that can shape a future in which "people matter" are those representing the interests of ordinary people. These forces have begun to take an active part in local and world politics in such domains as the environment, human rights, peace and security. The critical issue is whether we can mobilize a similar ethos with regard to the provision of information.

If the world of the 21st century is shaped in the image of a global Disney theme park, this might indeed reflect the deepest aspirations of the human species. If, however, people have ideals that go beyond consumerism, entertain ideas about a just world order, want real communities, protection against interferences that threaten human dignity and integrity, then they cannot sit back on the TV couch and hope that they will not be "McDonaldized."

A "democratization-from-below" is essential to guarantee people's participation in the construction of the digital highways of the third millennium. Until such a process is mobilized, world communication will remain—into the third millennium—"business as usual".

REFERENCES

Bandung (1955). Final declaration of the non aligned head of states' summit.
Barnet, R., & Cavanagh, J. (1994). *Global dreams: Imperial corporations and the New World Order*. New York: Simon & Schuster.
Business Week. (1991, October, 14).

Edmondson, G. (1995, April 24). Telecom giants still have the lines tied up. *Business Week*, pp. 20-21.

Frederick, H.H. (1993). *Global communication & international relations*. Belmont, CA: Wadsworth.

Gore, A. (1994, March 21). Speech to the International Telecommunication Union conference in Buenos Aires, Argentina.

Gore, A. (1995, February 25-26). Speech to the G-7 Information Society Summit, Brussels, Belgium.

Hamelink, C.J. (1977). *The corporate village*. Rome: IDOC.

Hamelink, C.J. (1983). *Cultural autonomy in global communications*. New York: Longman.

IPA Bulletin. (1995).

Kennedy, P. (1993). *Preparing for the twenty-first century*. New York: Vintage Books.

Nordenstreng, K. (1984). *The mass media declaration of UNESCO*. Norwood, NJ: Ablex.

Red Lion Broadcasting Co. v. Federal Communications Commission. (1969). 395 U.S. 367.89 S. Ct. 1794, 23 L. Ed. 2d 371.

Servaes, J. (1987). *Media aid*. Leuven, ACCO.

Verity, J.W. (1994, November 14). The Internet. *Business Week*, pp. 38-44.

Author Index

Subject Index